Heston Blumenthal at home

Heston Blumenthal at home

Photography by Angela Moore
Art direction and design by Graphic Thought Facility

BLOOMSBURY
LONDON · NEW DELHI · NEW YORK · SYDNEY

Welcome to a strand of my cooking that you may not be familiar with. I'm probably best known for the dishes I serve at the Fat Duck, like hot and iced tea, nitro-poached vodka and lime sour, and jelly of quail with crayfish cream, all of which are extremely labour-intensive. I love the technical challenge of such dishes and the thrill of taking an idea and turning it into something that is wonderful to eat, but I'm not into complexity for its own sake. I'm a self-taught chef, and I know just how frustrating and perplexing cooking can be. So I've always been keen to demystify the process. For some time I've wanted to write a book that has both exciting recipes and all the background information that explains how they actually work. A book that makes people feel really at home in the kitchen.

This is that book. There are plenty of classics like onion soup, roast chicken, prawn cocktail, Scotch eggs, pork scratchings, shepherd's pie, lemon tart and, of course, my triple-cooked chips. There are simplified versions of Fat Duck dishes like red cabbage gazpacho, scallop tartare with white chocolate, and bacon and egg ice-cream. And there are dishes that will, I hope, surprise and delight, like a salad that looks like a garden, complete with vegetables growing in edible soil, and a cinnamon and vanilla ice-cream that can switch from one flavour to the other. Most of the recipes are no longer than a page, and most of them require no complex technology. (Though I couldn't resist slipping in some stuff for the cook who wants to push the boat out, like whisky ice-cream made with dry ice, and a chapter on the sous-vide method of cooking, which I'm convinced is the way we'll all be cooking in the near future – you heard it here first.)

I was bitten by the food bug at sixteen, when my parents took me to a three-star French restaurant, and I learned to cook from books, preparing versions of the French classics over and over again. What drove me nuts was that even with a basic thing like chicken stock, there'd be major variations from one recipe to the next. Why did one chef make it by roasting chicken wings, then simmering them in water with flavourings for four hours, while another covered raw carcasses and giblets with water, added flavourings and then simmered for only an hour and a half? With a vanilla ice-cream base, why did different recipes choose to use whipping cream, double cream, crème fraiche or powdered milk? Once you know the answers to such questions, you're no longer simply a slave to a recipe, you can play around with it, or take its principles and apply them to a different dish – in short, you can really experiment and begin to let rip in the kitchen.

The habit of questioning everything that I picked up while teaching myself to cook became the normal way of doing things at the Fat Duck. Constantly challenging the orthodoxy has led to many surprising discoveries that have helped shape the way I cook – like the fact that searing meat doesn't hold in its juices, or that cooking asparagus in water loses a lot of the flavour, or that unrefined sugar caramelizes quicker than refined, so you can brown it on the top of a crème brûlée without overcooking the custard beneath. This know-how underpins the recipes in this book. Try carving meat against the grain to make it more tender, or searing a steak by flipping it regularly and frequently, or adding salt to counteract bitterness, or browning onions with star anise to boost the meaty notes. I guarantee you'll be amazed by the results and make them part of your kitchen repertoire. And, when you read about the difference between taste and flavour, it'll change the way you think about cooking.

Some of the techniques I've developed depend on modern technology. Often people find this daunting, or think that using probes and digital scales and water-baths somehow takes the romance out of cooking. But, like a sharp knife, liquidizer or fridge, these are just tools to make the cooking easier and more accurate, or to create flavours and textures that would otherwise be difficult. A pressure cooker will make a stock with exceptional depth of flavour. A water-bath will cook fish to exactly the right temperature. Dry ice will make ice-cream that's unbelievably smooth. Technology is a part of cuisine that should be embraced rather than shunned.

I've kept the specialist kit to a minimum, but there are a few things that will make a huge difference to your cooking. A digital probe, for example, might seem a bit space-age, but using one removes the doubt about whether food is cooked or not. Probe a piece of meat or fish and, if the readout shows the required temperature, it's done. This kind of accuracy is, it seems to me, far more helpful to the home cook than vague, subjective comments about the right colour or texture. At the Fat Duck, we use technology to help ensure that we consistently produce dishes that are perfectly cooked. If you want to cook these dishes the way I do, precise measuring and careful probing will help you achieve that goal.

However, I don't want talk of technology to obscure the fact that, in the end, cooking is about intuition and emotion, about going into the kitchen and following your instincts, trying things out, having fun. Much of the pleasure of eating comes from the flavours, textures and aromas you coax out of the ingredients – and the pages in this book will help you with that – but a lot comes from the memories and associations and nostalgia that food evokes. Great and memorable meals come from somehow tapping into these feelings and capturing them in the food you put on the table. The key to cooking is thinking about what excites you and working with that. These recipes are the ones that excite me. I hope that they inspire you to go into the kitchen and create something extraordinary.

The essence of flavour

What is the difference between taste and flavour? We all eat every day, and many of us cook every day too, so you would think the answer to the question would be easy, but it's not. How we eat and appreciate food is a fascinating and complex subject. Because it's an essential part of everyday life, we tend not to pay the mechanics of it much attention.

This is perhaps why, until recently, food wasn't generally considered a suitable subject for serious scientific research. However, because eating involves all of the senses simultaneously, it's one of the most complicated acts that the human body performs. Now scientists seem to be making up for lost time and researching every possible aspect of the eating and cooking processes. Gaining a greater understanding of what actually goes on in our mouths (and, as you'll see, in our noses and our brains) makes cooking and eating even more exciting and enjoyable. And it'll help you get the best out of your cooking and the ingredients you're using.

Try this experiment. Choose a biscuit, pinch your nose, take a bite and chew, keeping the nose pinched. You'll notice a salty or sweet taste, but little else. Now release your nose. Suddenly you'll get a rush of flavours. It's a wonderful experience for kids, which is why I suggested a biscuit, but it can be done with many ingredients. Tomato ketchup works really well because you'll be able to taste a range of different things, both before and after you release your nose. Apples are good too and, if you're at a dinner party, you could use red wine instead.

The test is a bit of fun, but it's also a telling demonstration of two of the most important facts about eating. First, that a lot of our enjoyment comes not from the mouth but from the nose. Because we put food into our bodies through the mouth, we are fooled into thinking that that's where all our appreciation of flavour is happening. A kind of sleight of mind takes place. Second, that the nose and the mouth detect very separate and distinct qualities in food. The mouth detects tastes. The nose detects aromas. It's the combination of taste and aroma that makes up flavour.

Tastes and aromas

Although we often use the terms 'taste' and 'flavour' interchangeably, they actually refer to very different things. There are just five tastes: salty, sweet, sour, bitter and the lesser-known umami (which is a savoury taste), and these are detected by receptors within the tastebuds. You might recall school science textbooks that showed a diagram of the tongue and assigned specific parts of it to each taste: the receptors for sweetness at the tip; those for bitterness at the back, etc. This is now out of date. Recent research by scientists has established that receptors are not confined to a specific area. Receptors for each taste are everywhere in the mouth, though unevenly distributed.

Nor do we all have the same number of receptors: some people – so-called 'supertasters' – have a much greater density of some receptors and are much more sensitive to the bitter taste in particular. The term 'supertaster' sounds like something from a comic book and is a little misleading, but the fact that supertasters exist shows that even at a mechanical level we don't all taste food in the same way.

While there may only be five tastes, there are thousands of aromas. Food is made of molecules: microscopic particles composed of a combination of elements such as oxygen, hydrogen, nitrogen, carbon, etc. (A single drop of water, for instance, will contain millions of molecules, each made up of two atoms of hydrogen and one of oxygen.) As we chew, light, volatile aroma molecules leave our food and float up the nasal cavity to be detected by the olfactory epithelium, a small layer of tissue behind the nose. It contains millions of receptors that detect and analyse smells and send the information to the olfactory bulb and orbitofrontal cortex in the brain for processing.

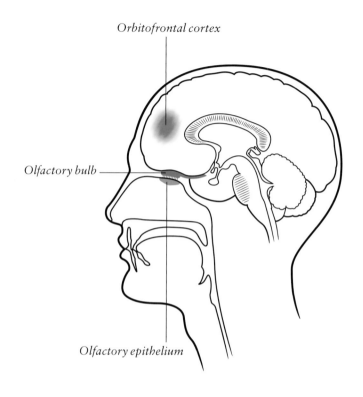

Orbitofrontal cortex

Olfactory bulb

Olfactory epithelium

The system is sensitive enough that we can distinguish between, say, lemon, lemongrass and lemon thyme. (It's said that the average human can recognize about 10,000 separate odours.) This olfactory sensitivity means that a huge part of our appreciation of flavour comes from our sense of smell. (That's why wine tasters spend as much time sniffing wine as they do sipping and spitting it out.) And so if we pinch our nose, preventing the circulation of air that carries aroma molecules to the olfactory epithelium, all we can taste are the five tastes. Nothing else. That's also why, when we have a cold, food seems suddenly flavourless.

I've found that this small piece of information can transform how people think about cuisine. Knowing what's going on in the mouth and nose makes you more aware of food as you eat it, more alert to the broad brushstrokes of taste in each mouthful, and to all the nuances of flavour, as they develop and diminish, to be succeeded by other flavours. The food comes alive, and you become more curious than ever before about the tastes and smells of the food you're cooking. This is, of course, a gift to the cook, because tasting is probably the single most important skill in the kitchen. Once you understand what's actually physically taking place as you smell and taste, you're better equipped to analyse how a dish is coming together and judge what's still needed to make it delicious.

The nose is hugely important to our appreciation of food and can summon all kinds of emotions – think of how the smell of popcorn is bound up in the excitement of going to the cinema, or of the pleasure and anticipation you get from the smell of roast meat when you return from a Sunday walk. The commercial world has long taken advantage of this: some coffee shops pump out the smell of fresh coffee to encourage purchase; estate agents suggest that the smell of bread baking in the oven while a property is viewed increases the chances of a sale. I've heard there's even a Belgian train station that pumps out the smell of waffles so that disembarking passengers really feel as though they've arrived in Belgium. Our smell-memories are powerful triggers, and you can enhance dishes by intensifying their aromas.

One easy technique is putting a flavoured liquid into an atomizer and spritzing it into the air as the food is served. I've done this with Kirsch to accompany Black Forest gâteau and with pickled onion juice to go with fish and chips. They both drew out the flavours to an amazing degree. For some dishes at the Fat Duck I've worked with a perfumier to develop a complementary scent that is released as the food is eaten. The hot whisky sorbet, for example, is served in a bowl in which dry ice is hidden. A waiter pours a scent of woodsmoke, wood panelling and old leather on to the dry ice, which turns to vapour and gusts out across the table, carrying the scent with it. Dry ice is a wonderful vehicle for aroma – and it makes the most amazing ice-cream (pp.277–9) – but if that's a step too far, you can achieve something similar using a fan. I did this for a charity event in Las Vegas, smearing fan blades with a maritime scent I'd had developed to accentuate the seafood flavours of a dish.

However, the fact that there are far fewer tastes than flavours shouldn't blind us to their significance. After all, we have developed a sensitive network of receptors specifically to detect the five tastes. Evolution has determined that these are of particular importance to us: the presence of some of them signals a source of energy or other substance vital to life; the presence of others warns of substances likely to end life. So, the tastes in a dish will have a powerful effect on the eater, and understanding how to work with saltiness, sweetness, sourness, bitterness and umami can make a big difference to your cooking. Good seasoning can take a dish to the next level.

Saltiness

Salt is undoubtedly the single most important ingredient in the kitchen. Not only does it make food taste better, it can draw out or redistribute moisture, alter textures and break down or protect food structures. It plays a vital role in brining, curing, preserving and sausage-making, as well as any number of common culinary techniques, like cooking pasta or making dough. You must, of course, be careful about your intake – given that eating a lot of salt can cause high blood pressure, you shouldn't be cavalier in your use of it. But there's no doubt that, in one form or another, salt is an essential component of most dishes. And let's not forget it's essential for our bodies too. Salt helps maintain the fluid in our blood cells, and it's the means of transmitting information in the nerves and muscles. We need salt to live.

Salt's most obvious culinary contribution is as seasoning, intensifying the characteristics of the various ingredients in a dish. The biggest difference between chefs and home cooks is that professionals will use more salt in their cooking. The professional will taste throughout the cooking process, adjusting the seasoning where necessary. Most home cooks will add salt only in the last minute or so before serving. A surprising number forget to add any seasoning whatsoever.

Good seasoning is a skill that can be acquired – usually through trial and error. You can learn about how much salt is needed to season a dish using a cup of soup. Much of the seasoning of soup is done at the end because, if you

salt it early, it may end up too salty by the time the liquid has reduced. So, once you've puréed your soup but before you reheat and season it, remove a cupful. Add a pinch of salt to the cup, stir, sip and register how salty it is. Continue adding a pinch, stirring and sipping (keeping a note of exactly how many pinches have gone in the soup) until you add the pinch that makes it seem too salty. The right level of salting is exactly one pinch back from that. Try it – I bet it takes more pinches than you expected.

Salting during cooking isn't so far removed from this test. You need constantly to taste, acquiring the habit of continually asking yourself whether the flavours are coming through. If they aren't, salt is often what's needed. It should bring out the flavours of a dish without bringing attention to itself – if you can actually taste the salt in a dish, then you've added too much. The more you experiment with it, the more you'll acquire an instinct for exactly how much is needed.

Although salt is generally seen as a seasoning for savoury recipes, it can have an equally dramatic transformative effect on sweet dishes. During the preparation and cooking of a savoury dish, cooks of all levels of sophistication will add seasoning, as a matter of course; the same should apply to desserts. A pinch of salt sprinkled on a treacle tart does wonders for its flavour, as does the addition of a little salt to crumble, shortbread and other pastry mixes.

Salt is the key ingredient in several practical techniques, such as curing (p.76) and brining (pp.135 and 170). But there's one lesser-known general-purpose property of salt that's immensely valuable to the cook: it can counteract bitterness. I know that this sounds counter-intuitive. If you're making, say, a stock and it turns out a little bitter, the natural inclination would be to reach for the sugar bowl. However, salt will solve the problem more effectively. Perhaps surprisingly, scientists are still not clear about how salt manages to do this, but you can easily test the truth of it. Take a couple of squares of dark, bitter chocolate, add a few flakes of salt to one of them and see what a difference it makes. Alternatively, pour 250ml tonic water into a glass and taste it. You'll find it's extremely bitter. Now add some salt to the tonic water

a pinch at a time, tasting after each addition to monitor the effects. The bitterness will gradually reduce. (It should take about half a teaspoon to do it. Go much beyond that, and you'll find that you're just drinking salty water.)

Sweetness

We are born with a sweet tooth. The body is designed to seek out sweetness, probably because sugars are essential to the body as a source of energy. Our physical alertness to this taste may explain why its presence often seems to enhance flavours – sometimes to startling effect. It can, for example, make you believe a flavour is present even when it's not there. I was the guinea pig for a demonstration of this at the University of Nottingham, where my friend Professor Andy Taylor has developed an extraordinary machine that can actually measure the aromas we experience as we eat. Andy put two tubes into my mouth, one of which contained a banana-flavoured liquid while the other contained a sweetener, and began feeding me various combinations of the two.

As you might have guessed, the banana flavour seemed strongest when I was drinking both banana and sweetener. However, I was amazed to find that when Andy switched off the banana, so that all I was drinking was sweetener, I could still taste banana – even after a good thirty seconds. I was experiencing a flavour that wasn't there! It seems as though sweetness is so important to us that, when it's present, the brain tends to focus on it, and to see whatever other flavours and aromas are present as somehow associated with it. Crudely speaking, in this experiment, once the brain had made a connection between sweetness and banana, it simply assumed banana was present whenever it detected the sweetener.

This works both ways. Just as the presence of sweetness can boost flavours that have become associated with it, so the absence of sweetness can diminish flavour. During my session with Andy's machine, he also asked me to chew gum until the mint and menthol had, in my opinion, gone. Which I did, but when I looked at the readout on the screen it showed that the flavours were still present in the gum. Once more, the association that my brain had made between sweetness and the attendant flavours had fooled my perception. Only the sweetness had disappeared – as the gum's sugar dissolved in my mouth – but the brain assumed that the mint and menthol aromas must have gone as well.

When we think of sugar we picture the white granular stuff, but in fact the term covers a number of substances from the group known as carbohydrates (which are molecules produced by plants and animals for use as energy stores). Sugars are the simplest of the carbohydrates, and the most commonly used in cuisine are sucrose (the one we stir into tea; it's extracted from sugar beet and sugar cane), lactose (which is found in milk), and glucose and fructose (which are found in fruits and honey). But it's a big family with plenty of lesser-known members, like galactose, which is present in sugar beet and various gums, and raffinose, which is found in brassicas and some whole grains.

There are good reasons why sucrose is the best known: it dissolves easily; it's the second sweetest sugar after fructose; and, unlike other sugars, it tastes good even at high concentrations. But that shouldn't blind the cook to the benefits of other sugars. For preparations involving fruit I often use fructose, because it intensifies its 'fruitiness'. (I've done lots of side-by-side tastings, comparing the effects on fruit of these two sugars, and fructose has always come out on top.) It dissolves better than sucrose, too, making it the best candidate for macerating fruits (softening them by tossing them with sugar and letting them stand for a while) and for delicate dishes where you want the sugar to dissolve without heating it. Glucose can be a valuable sweetener for ice-cream. Since it's only 80 per cent as sweet as sucrose, it can be used in place of some of the sucrose to reduce the overall sweetness (though glucose can also mask flavour, so there's a trade-off involved).

Sourness

The sour taste is provided by acids, which are highly underestimated as a seasoning. My chefs are so accustomed to my enthusiasm for acid that when I taste a dish we're developing and say, 'There's just one thing missing…' they're likely to finish my sentence for me: '…a bit of acidity!' A squeeze of lemon juice will really enhance a fish dish or a soup, but there are plenty of other ways to bring acidity to a dish. Vinegar, in particular, can bring real balance without you realizing it's there. White wine vinegar is probably the best all-purpose one for seasoning because it'll go with most ingredients, but others, such as a good sherry vinegar, can introduce extra complexity of flavour. At the Fat Duck I use a variety of other acids, such as tartaric acid in jellies, or lactic acid to introduce a milky note, or malic acid (found in apples, it's particularly noticeable in Granny Smiths) to boost the fresh green-apple notes of a dish.

The rinse of acidity on the tongue also gets the saliva going. In cooking, 'mouthwatering' is a highly desirable attribute, and few things cause the mouth to water as much as acidic ingredients. For me, even thinking of sucking a lemon brings it on. Sourness gives food a wonderful impression of juiciness. Acid also cuts through richness and sweetness, tempering them and making them less cloying.

The ability to offset richness and sweetness in a dish is probably acid's most valuable property in terms of seasoning. You may be familiar with this idea when it comes to desserts, adding lemon juice to a sorbet or treacle tart. But acid can perform the same function in savoury dishes – like a spoonful of tamarind to cut the sweetness of coconut milk. Or gooseberry sauce with mackerel. Or the mustard and vinegar in a mayonnaise. Or some drops of lemon juice on a prawn cocktail.

Wine can be used in much the same way – a glass of red wine added to a meaty stew, for example. This works because the tannins in the wine have an astringent effect, and scientists consider sourness and astringency to be related. However, substances that are especially astringent, like cranberries, black tea and red wine, tend to linger in the mouth far longer than acidic ingredients. If you don't use them carefully, and in small amounts, they can overpower a dish.

Bitterness

In nature, bitterness often signifies danger. Although bitter substances aren't always poisonous, and poisons aren't necessarily bitter, there's a strong enough correlation between the two that the body tends to double-take when it encounters such a taste. Scientists have recently discovered that the arrangement of the receptors for detecting the taste is particularly complex: it appears that we have evolved a high-security defence system to deal with bitterness. Some of the things that we grow to appreciate as adults (children have a marked aversion to bitterness) seem to vindicate this evolutionary caution. Tea, coffee and alcohol can all have damaging effects on the body.

But, like sour ingredients, bitter ones offer a great way for the cook to temper the sweetness and richness of a dish. Thus bitterness has long had a place in dessert recipes – a touch of coffee to balance cream, for example, in a tiramisù. Chocolate is a useful source of bitterness. When we're kids we usually eat milk chocolate, which is relatively sweet, and even as adults we tend to associate chocolate with sweet things, but dark chocolate can be very bitter indeed. (Try some that has 85 per cent cocoa in it and you'll see what I mean.) Chocolate makes such a frequent appearance in gooey, creamy cakes and pastries because the bitterness takes the edge off the cloying sweetness of the other ingredients.

Bitterness can perform the same role in savoury dishes, cutting sweetness and richness. A bit of grapefruit zest works well in a crab salad; endive leaves can provide the perfect counterpoint to cubes of blue cheese. At the Fat Duck the luxurious richness of my cauliflower risotto is counterbalanced by a chocolate jelly disc that is laid over the rice, and the five chocolate jelly cubes that are placed on top.

We often introduce a bitter note to a savoury recipe by seasoning it with pepper. Strictly speaking, pepper is pungent rather than bitter: like ginger, chilli, horseradish, mustard and wasabi, it causes a slight burning sensation. But, like bitter ingredients, pungent ones will bring liveliness and a bit of a kick to a dish. Black, white and green peppercorns are all the fruit of the *Piper nigrum* vine. Black are unripe green berries that have been fermented and dried; they have pungency and spicy, woody, lemony notes. The white are the seeds of the ripe berry, from which all the outer layer of fruit has been removed by soaking in water. They still have the pungency of black pepper but less aroma and are mainly used where specks of black pepper would look unattractive, such as fish dishes. The green are harvested just before they begin to ripen and have a nice fresh green-leaf characteristic in addition to that bit of zing.

Chinese Szechuan peppercorns are the dried fruit rinds of a couple of trees in the citrus family. Although their pungent compounds – the sanshools – are from the same family as piperine (the substance that gives black pepper its heat), their effect is different, producing a tingling, numbing sensation. Pink peppercorns are also the fruit of a separate tree, the Brazilian pepper tree. They have less astringency and a fruity, floral aspect which means they're used in a different way from other types of peppercorn – more in the manner of whole spices rather than as a seasoning.

Pepper is so often mentioned together with salt in western recipes that we think of them as twins, but in fact they're not at all alike. Salt can penetrate and dissolve into food. Pepper, on the other hand, just coats the surface. (That's why it's best to season meat or fish with pepper only after it has been seared, otherwise the pepper is scorched.) Ground peppercorns have a delicate aroma that soon disappears, so they must always be ground just before use. Bear in mind, too, that pepper is not the only source of pungency. Depending on the dish, ginger, chilli, horseradish, mustard or wasabi might well be a suitable alternative.

Umami

Until the early twentieth century, scientists thought there were only four tastes. Then Professor Kikunae Ikeda at the University of Tokyo started investigating the properties of konbu, the giant kelp that is used to flavour Japanese cuisine, particularly the stock called dashi. In 1908 he discovered that its savoury taste came from the glutamic acid it contained, and decided to call the taste 'umami', which translates as 'delicious'.

Over the next fifty years scientists examined meat, fish and vegetables and found several other substances that provided the umami taste. At first there was scepticism, particularly in the West, as to whether it was a separate and distinct taste – but in 2000 scientists found a specific receptor for umami. So the number of tastes has officially increased to five. (And things might not stop there. A number of scientists have been investigating whether we also have receptors for fat and CO_2.)

Professor Ikeda went on to develop a commercial version of glutamic acid, which he called monosodium glutamate (MSG). MSG has had a bad press, fingered as the culprit of so-called 'Chinese Restaurant Syndrome', the symptoms of which are said to be headaches, chest pains and a burning sensation on the skin. But this is largely based on one less-than-rigorous scientific study. Many properly controlled tests have found no evidence of MSG causing such effects. Moreover, plenty of western dishes are high in umami – Parmesan and tomatoes are both full of the stuff – yet there's no such thing as 'Italian Pizzeria Syndrome'. But the bad reputation lingers, nonetheless.

This is a shame because the umami taste can really enliven a dish and give it depth. It's a good alternative to fat for introducing richness and fullness, which is how ingredients like konbu are often used in Japan, where fat is much less common in cooking. And it's present in lots of familiar foods – the aforementioned tomato and Parmesan (the white crystals you can see in a good aged Parmesan are pure MSG), as well as mushrooms, olives, tuna, squid, anchovies, soy sauce and fish sauce (nam pla),

Marmite, meat stock, green tea, ketchup – giving the cook plenty of opportunities for creativity.

Umami-rich ingredients have another property that's of value to the cook: when they're added together, the taste becomes greatly magnified. Serve konbu-cured halibut (p.89) with a ponzu sauce (p.266) and you'll see what I mean. Combining umami-rich ingredients is an easy but effective way of bringing real depth to a dish. Squirt ketchup on your burger and it'll enhance the savoury taste of the meat. The same goes for Parmesan sprinkled on pasta with a tomato sauce, or mushrooms on a pizza. Putting konbu or dried shiitake mushrooms in a meat stock adds a new flavour dimension.

Enhancing flavour

Working with the tastes can be a complex business – and there are only five of them. The thousands of different aromas mean enhancing flavour is a subject with infinite possibilities, and it's difficult to make general comments that have good practical use. In a sense, recipes are the best education in enhancing flavour, and in the chapters that follow I've tried to explain exactly why and how a particular process has an effect on ingredients. There are, however, a few general approaches to enhancing flavour that can easily be pursued at home, among them flavour pairing and flavour encapsulation.

Flavour pairing is putting together ingredients that complement one another to such an extent that the whole is somehow more than the sum of the parts. This process is often invested with a lot of mystique, as though it were a conjuring trick that only the most skilled could pull off. It's true that sometimes a chef does come up with a combination so startling it seems like black magic. When I first put white chocolate and caviar together, I encountered a fair bit of scepticism. But although some people initially considered the dish strange, it actually came from a logical train of thought. A sprinkle of salt enhances chocolate (as it does many sweet things, see p.17), so I began to explore whether other salty ingredients might have the same effect on chocolate.

There were a number of salty dead-ends – cured duck ham, anchovies – before I got lucky with caviar. (Flavour pairing depends, almost literally, on a suck-it-and-see approach.) The combination was remarkable – the rich smoothness of the chocolate melded deliciously with the buttery brininess of the caviar. I was so bowled over that I visited my friend the flavourist François Benzi to see if I could find out why these two ingredients worked so well together. François has access to a computer database called VCF (Volatile Compounds in Food) that shows the chemical constituents of foodstuffs. He can enter the name of an ingredient and the screen will list the compounds it contains. He can then click on any of these compounds to find out which other ingredients contain it. Both white chocolate and caviar had high levels of a group of proteins called amines. This seemed like a clear explanation for the affinity of caviar and chocolate.

On the back of this, I became very excited by the idea that the database could take the guesswork out of flavour pairing. (Looking back, this seems incredibly naive of me, but naivety can be a spur to creativity. Some of my culinary ideas only got off the ground because I blithely ignored how impractical they were.) I developed a number of dishes with very interesting flavour combinations – asparagus with liquorice; mandarin with thyme, banana and parsley – using the database as my starting point. But in the end, I came to realize that two ingredients having a compound in common is no guarantee they'll work together well. Most ingredients contain lots of compounds, any of which might get in the way of a successful pairing. Although tools like VCF are useful and sometimes revelatory, they're never going to replace a chef's instincts.

So flavour pairing still comes down to thinking about food in a slightly obsessive way – trying to pin down all nuances of flavour in an ingredient as you eat or drink it; feeling out connections between different foods; stockpiling flavour memories that might somehow be of use. (Professional wine tasters do this. When we say a taster has a great palate, we really mean they have a great memory. They have built up and can access a vast mental library of flavours and aromas.) Often I'll be eating a particular food and notice little undertones

of some other flavour, like the faint tarragon or parsley note in a banana. Are these two worth putting together? The first step is to take a slice of the fruit, sprinkle on a little of the finely chopped herb and see what you think. If the combination works at this basic level, then it's probably worth exploring further, trying it out with different techniques and in different formats, to see if you can create something exciting. This experimentation is the starting point for many of my dishes. Mango and green peppercorn (p.333), and crab and grapefruit (p.126) – both pairings came from dabbling with the surprising affinity of certain ingredients. It's fun to do, and can produce results that are all the more thrilling for being unexpected.

Of course, it doesn't always work – it's probably best not to serve up the more experimental stages to your guests – and there'll be dead ends as well as breakthroughs. But it's rare that any of this kind of culinary exploration is wasted. At some point, somewhere down the line, you'll find a use for it. Red cabbage gazpacho (p.63) grew out of work I'd done years before on a series of vegetable petits-fours. Red cabbage hadn't worked in that dish but I'd stored a memory of the distinctive fresh, peppery note in the juice, hoping that one day I'd be able to find a dish that would suit it. Later I read that mustard oil gives cabbage its peppery character, tried them together (by the highly scientific method of spooning some Dijon out of a pot and eating it with a couple of cabbage leaves) and began investigating. I had a hazy memory of eating a gazpacho that used mustard as a thickener or garnish or somesuch, so that's the direction in which my recipe development took me.

Flavour pairing is often like this – following a trail of clues, using your gut instincts, flavour memories and experience in the kitchen, not entirely sure where it's all going but hoping it'll lead to an amazing dish. My own work in food pairing has even sparked off a movement and a website – foodpairing.be – where you can explore the molecular make-up of different foodstuffs to see whether they'll work together. Such forums are great – anything that inspires people to experiment more with food has got to be a good thing.

As well as pairing flavours, you can also utilize contrasting, concentrated flavours. When we eat, one of the things we appreciate is the rate of change of flavour. The palate likes to encounter plenty of contrast – of flavour, of texture, of temperature – so that the qualities of the different ingredients are set in sharp relief. A bowl of plain boiled rice would hardly make for an enticing or enjoyable meal, but if you add in a few flavour contrasts – a little chopped softened onion and garlic, and some peas, prawns, coriander seeds, chilli and chopped fresh coriander – you have something very appealing. Those little bursts of flavour create a more stimulating and rewarding eating experience.

This is something that commercial companies have long been adept at exploiting. Some manufacturers of frozen garlic bread, for example, add granules that look like sugar crystals to the butter. When the water in the butter heats up, these melt, creating little pockets of fresh garlic flavour. However, you don't need the high-tech resources of a processed food manufacturer to introduce concentrated bursts of flavour to a dish. There are other ways to achieve the same end. One of the simplest, and most effective, is what I call flavour encapsulation.

Flavour encapsulation is the use of ingredients – or particular forms of ingredients – that deliver intense, concentrated hits of flavour. Often it involves the teeth crushing or breaking into a food where the flavour is tightly packed, ready for release. Take a coffee bean, for example. If you grind a single bean and make coffee with it, you'll end up with a thin, insipid drink because the flavour is dispersed in the water. If, on the other hand, you crunch on the bean and then drink a cup of water you'll have a stronger, longer-lasting impression of coffee because the bean's flavour floods the mouth in a single, swift explosion as the bean shatters against the teeth.

The idea of flavour encapsulation came from an unlikely source. Several years ago I was working on ways of making ice-cream taste less eggy. Traditionally, the mix for ice-creams is cooked to 85°C. However, egg yolks coagulate at around 72°C so in a standard ice-cream base, although the eggs haven't scrambled, they have already begun to form into little clumps of egg flavour. To counter this, I began to lower the temperature at which I cooked the base (as you'll see in the recipes for ice-cream on pp.285–90). It worked: keeping the cooking temperature down produced a much cleaner-tasting ice-cream.

But it also made me curious about what would happen if I took the base to the other extreme and overcooked it. After all, creativity often comes from pushing something as far as it will go. I cooked the egg mixture until it scrambled, and when it was churned, it produced an ice-cream with an egg flavour that came through in encapsulated bursts. It was amazingly powerful, and I wondered how I might use encapsulation in other dishes.

Conveniently, nature offers ingredients that already come in a perfectly encapsulated form. Seeds can provide a hit of flavour and a lovely crunch – a double whammy of contrasts. That slight citrus note in coriander seeds makes them an excellent way to garnish a salmon fillet, finish a soup or even just sprinkle on strawberries. Many spices and other seasonings work well, such as caraway, green and pink peppercorns, sesame seeds and fennel seeds.

The individual cells of citrus fruits are tiny plump sacs of flavour that explode in the mouth. Separated out and dotted on a plate alongside a fish (as they are in the liquorice poached salmon on p.187), they both look wonderful and provide a brisk texture and flavour contrast. And, if you think this is one over-fiddly step too far, you can always simply cut the fruit into small bite-sized pieces. Sometimes, in any case, the refined approach doesn't lead to the best flavour release. Chefs love to make food delicate and wafer-thin, which looks great on the plate but is sometimes too airy and insubstantial to give a powerful burst of flavour. Sometimes thicker is better, providing contrast and forcing the teeth to break into the ingredient, causing it to release flavour. I've tested out 2g of grated truffle compared to a 2g piece of truffle. The grated truffle formed a mound that looked big and flavoursome, but since it was mainly air it had a muted flavour. Chewing the truffle piece provided a more powerful flavour.

I also like to use jelly for flavour encapsulation, either as a layer in a recipe or in the form of little cubes used as a garnish. Jelly's unique texture adds interest to a dish, and it has just the right amount of give, releasing a perfect hit of flavour as it melts in the mouth. We tend to think of jelly as a dessert because that's how we had it as kids, but it can work really well in savoury dishes, too, where it has the added benefit of being unexpected, which helps keep the palate interested.

The substance used to set a jelly will vary depending on whether the dish is served hot or cold. (The usual setting agent, gelatine, melts at about 40°C, so a heat-resistant setting agent like agar-agar may have to be used instead, such as in the liquorice jelly for the salmon on p.187.) But you can flavour a jelly with almost any ingredient, which gives you the freedom to explore flavour encapsulation in whatever dish takes your fancy.

Infusing for flavour

Infusing – putting an ingredient into a liquid so that the flavours spread through it – is an easy and versatile technique for enhancing the flavour of all sorts of liquids: stocks, brines, the cooking liquor for a risotto. And the technique is used as much for sweet dishes as savoury ones. You can use infusion to add interesting flavours to a brûlée (p.326), for example, or a panna cotta (p.328).

Usually the decision about what liquid to use is made by the dish itself: milk or cream for ice-cream and panna cotta, water for sorbets and brines, oil for flavoured oils. Fats and alcohol are, in fact, better at extracting aroma molecules than water: that's why chocolate and cream are often used for infusions, and why several of the drinks in the book, such as the spiced and cucumber gin and tonics on p.382, take advantage of infusing to add complexity. Fat is particularly useful for tea infusions because tannin is not oil-soluble, so tea's bitter notes won't enter the infusion. However, water is still valuable for infusion because there are plenty of dishes in which you want little or no fat or alcohol. You wouldn't make a stock by infusing meat and vegetables in a pot full of fat!

But there are other considerations that are more variable. The first question is whether to do a hot or cold infusion. A cold infusion captures the fresh, natural flavours of an ingredient. That's why it's used in the palate cleanser (p.82), which needs the vibrancy of the raw lime peel and a fragrant tea flavour without the bitter tannins that are released by heat. However, cold infusion works very gradually, and it's too delicate a method of extraction to get much out of ingredients that don't readily give up their flavours. For these a hot infusion works better – the heat speeds up and strengthens the extraction process. There are some drawbacks to this approach: heat also cooks the ingredient, so it loses some of its freshness, and with something such as tea, the hotter the extraction, the more likely it is that less pleasant flavours are extracted. With a hot infusion, you also need to factor in that delicate herbs take on a cooked characteristic surprisingly quickly, so they are often best added towards the end and infused only briefly. You may need to increase the amount you add in order to compensate for this.

The beauty of infusing is that it's a very controllable process: put the ingredient in liquid (be it hot or cold), leave it a while, then taste to see if it's where you want it to be. If it's not, leave it for longer. Whatever you choose to infuse, it's essential that it's as fresh and high-quality as possible. A dull, exhausted ingredient won't have the liveliness and depth of flavour to do the job.

Flavour, sight, sound and touch

We value the taste and smell of food so much that it's easy to forget that the pleasure of eating doesn't come just from these two senses. As I've said, it's one of the few activities we do that involves all the senses simultaneously, so when you're cooking it's worth exploring whether there are ways of making the dish appeal to some or all of the other senses. Sight, sound and touch can also have a huge influence on our enjoyment.

The fact that sight plays a part in eating is, I suppose, obvious. We talk about 'eating with our eyes' and, if we can't finish our food, we say that our eyes were bigger than our belly. If food looks beautiful, it predisposes us to like it, increases our anticipation, and turns a meal into a spectacle. If it looks like a dog's dinner, then no matter what it tastes like, we'll probably be disappointed. But sight's influence extends further than you might imagine. What we see can actually determine what we taste – or at least what we believe we are tasting. At the University of Bordeaux they conducted an experiment in which fifty-four skilled wine students were asked to taste a red and a white wine and note the aromas. They described the white as 'honeyed' with 'hints of apricot', and the red as having the 'scent of red fruits' and 'intense blackcurrant' flavours. In fact, the red wine wasn't red at all – it was the white with some flavourless colouring added to it – yet the tasters experienced the characteristics of red wine.

The fact that the sense of touch influences our enjoyment of food may be less obvious because we tend to think of touch mainly in terms of the fingers and, apart from a big sticky plate of spare ribs, we don't often eat with our fingers. Yet the mouth, tongue and teeth are also incredibly sensitive to nuances of texture. If a steak is tough or mash is lumpy it spoils the pleasure of eating. It only takes a few tiny specks of grit to make a salad or a fish stock completely inedible. These are familiar examples, but the influence of texture extends into other, more unexpected areas. Carving meat in such a way that it's easier to chew, for example, actually makes it seem more tender. Similarly the crisp browned crust on the outside of a rib of beef will make it more chewy, which generates saliva and therefore makes the meat seem juicier, especially if it gives way to a meltingly soft interior.

So where part of a dish's character comes from a particular texture, I like to look for ways to accentuate that texture – not just in the mouth but also on the fingers as you handle the food and whatever it's served in. At the Fat Duck, the first course of my 'Beef Royal' dish (fried sweetbreads and oysters garnished with crispy chervil) is presented in an especially brittle packaging: a cone that feels crunchy to the touch and emphasizes the crunchiness of the ingredients. The inspiration for this idea came from my friend the physicist Peter Barham, who once told me he had worked for a crisp manufacturer on the creation of a crunchy-sounding packet. (Commercial food companies are often ahead of the game as far as scientific developments in food go. There's a massive fund of technical expertise there, even though it's perhaps not always put to the most worthwhile of culinary objectives. They've been using sensory triggers to enhance food for years.) I remembered this when I was working with an ice-cream company that marketed a choc ice wrapped in plastic packaging which somehow boosted the delightful brittleness of the chocolate in the mouth. I cadged a roll of the plastic from them and used it to fashion the cone for the sweetbreads in the Beef Royal.

This is a specialized example, but what I'm getting at is that the feel of food and the tactile qualities of the eating experience can have an influence on our enjoyment. Often the sensations on the fingertips as we handle a food are inextricably linked to our pleasure in eating it – think of the gritty sprinkling of sugar on a seaside doughnut and licking the last granules off your fingers once you've scoffed it. Or the lovely, silky cocoa powderiness on the outside of a chocolate truffle. As a cook it's worth registering these kinds of sensations and seeing if there are ways you can emphasize them when you cook your own versions of foods you like. We all love the crunchiness of the batter on fried fish, for example, and it's a great idea to drizzle extra batter on the fish while it's in the fryer so you get an especially encrusted exterior. Putting together contrasting textures of a particular ingredient can really draw attention to its various textural characteristics – some grated raw apple sprinkled on a tarte tatin before serving, for example, or diced pickled butternut squash as a garnish for butternut squash soup, or even just a little grated raw butternut squash.

Hearing is probably the most undervalued sense in terms of food, yet we all know how strong a grip sound has on our emotions. A favourite song that we haven't heard for a while comes on the radio and we're instantly transported to a time, a place, a feeling. Sound can have a powerful effect on the eating experience, too. I once conducted a test with the head of Oxford University's Department of Experimental Psychology, Professor Charles Spence, in which test-subjects ate ice-cream while listening to a particular soundtrack. The ones to whom we played the sound of chickens clucking thought the ice-cream had an egg flavour, while the ones who listened to bacon sizzling thought it had a bacon flavour. In fact they had all eaten exactly the same thing – my bacon and egg ice-cream – but the sounds had influenced their perception of flavour.

It was experiments like these that formed the foundation for my dish 'Sound of the Sea', in which edible 'sand', shellfish and pickled seaweed are used to create what looks like the shore's edge. It's served with a conch shell that houses an iPod. Put on the headphones and, as you eat, you hear the sound of waves lapping and the faint occasional noise of seagulls. The experience often transports people to a favourite beach, be it Blackpool or Bondi, and triggers strong emotions. Some people have been reduced to tears because the memories that well up are so intense.

As far as introducing sound to dining goes, the home cook has the edge over the professional chef. In a restaurant, where people are not eating the same food at the same time, it's hard to introduce a sonic component. But at home the cook is free to use ambient sound to enhance a meal – the crackle of a roaring fire, perhaps, to accompany Christmassy dishes; the sound of cicadas (CDs of such things exist) to enhance a barbecue. It seems kitsch, I know, but think how strongly that insect chirrup summons up memories of cooking outdoors on holidays abroad. Anything that powerful will surely add something to the eating experience. The only limit is your imagination – and perhaps the recording archives.

Food and the brain

The more you can create food that makes a concerted appeal to all of the senses – sound, sight, touch, taste and smell – the more intense, immediate and satisfying the eating experience will be. The senses, though, are in effect only messengers – it's what the brain makes of these messages that determines our enjoyment of a particular food. We like to think of our food preferences as individual – an extension of our personality – but in fact a lot of our food preferences are learned.

This education begins before we're even born. An eleven-week-old foetus has already developed to the point where it can detect aromas by breathing in flavour molecules from the amniotic fluid that surrounds it. By the time it emerges, it has formed preferences for some of those flavours, and breastfeeding can further encourage a liking for specific flavours. In addition to this, a lot of our likes and dislikes are down to the associations a food has. These can come from personal experiences and events, or simply from social norms.

The stark contrasts between the culinary preferences of nations show how capricious and subjective our food preferences are. The Japanese diet is not dairy-based, so while they will happily eat live soft-shelled crab, they find rice pudding repulsive. In many parts of the world creepy crawlies are devoured that in the West we consider disgusting (witchetty grubs in Australia, fried locusts in Korea, ant larvae in the Philippines, agave worms in Mexico), yet we have no problem with prawns, in spite of the eyestalks, segmented shell and wriggly legs. It goes to show that there is almost no food that is intrinsically disgusting. If it's edible, someone somewhere is eating it.

Moreover our aversions are less deep-rooted than we think. Scientists have established that it takes as few as twenty-one tastings to overcome a food dislike. I've seen this in action at the Fat Duck, where I once had a commis chef who couldn't stand parsnips. Since this kind of dislike disadvantages a chef (because tasting is an essential part of cooking any dish), he was assigned to preparing parsnip purée for the restaurant on a daily basis. Within a short space of time he was choosing to eat parsnips for Christmas lunch!

It has also been observed that Alzheimer's patients are often prepared to eat foods that they previously shunned, showing just how central memory is to our appreciation of food. If we're stripped of our memories, we no longer know if we like something or not. This is a startling reminder that what ultimately enables us to appreciate food is the brain. Without that, eating food would be, at the very least, a far less pleasurable experience.

This is why, when people single out their most memorable meals, they usually talk not just about the deliciousness of the food but about the sense of occasion, the company, the ambience, etc. These can all play their part in our appreciation of food, as can associations and memories triggered by the food put in front of us. The brain processes all these stimuli together: the food is just one aspect of a complete sensory experience. I think that's why bottles of wine sometimes don't 'travel well'. I've drunk Muscadet that tasted delicious on the banks of the Loire. Back home, however, it just didn't taste the same. The wine hadn't changed, but the context had. I was drinking the wine without the sounds, smells, sights and feel (my feet dipped in the water by the bank) of the Loire – and as a result it tasted thinner, less exciting.

So much of the eating experience, and the pleasure we derive from it, is down to perception. We can talk all day long about the importance of good-quality ingredients and skilful technique – and of course this is a hugely important part of cooking – but in the end, it's how food is perceived by the brain that counts. The best meals you cook will be those that are not just well executed but also trigger memories and emotions in you and your guests. I find this idea incredibly exciting. Understanding the importance to cooking of the brain and the senses should encourage you to explore and experiment even more. Certainly, when I first discovered how taste and flavour work, and how central the brain is to our appreciation of food, it really inspired me to look at food in a different way. The kitchen became an even more fascinating and enjoyable place.

Stocks

A stock is the foundation not just of soups and consommés but of all sorts of dishes and parts of dishes. Stocks range from a light broth for risottos, consommés and fish sauces, down to the most concentrated, complex essence of meat juices, known in classic cuisine as demi-glace. Classic sauces, gravies, risottos and savoury gels (such as the lamb jelly on p.98 and the mushroom jelly on p.105) all depend on a good stock.

Broadly speaking, stocks are made from meat, fish or shellfish and vegetables. At its most basic, a stock can be as simple as putting the chicken carcass and any leftover bits of chicken from the Sunday roast in a pot with some aromatic vegetables, covering them with water and simmering for a while. This will have a different character from a stock made with fresh meat – more of a roasted, reheated flavour – but it'll produce something tasty, serviceable and economical.

But there will also be times when you're cooking a dish that needs a stock with real power and character to do it justice. Taking stock-making to that level requires a judicious choice of ingredients, and involves several culinary techniques. It is, I think, one of the most exciting and worthwhile challenges in the kitchen.

Meat in stocks

Meat stocks fall into two categories: brown stocks and white stocks. In the former, a lot of the colour and flavour comes from browning the bones and perhaps some or all of the vegetables. In white stocks the meat isn't browned and the vegetables are often sweated only just enough to develop flavour and sweetness. However, in some white stocks all the ingredients are simply put in water together and simmered for a while. In general a brown stock will be used to make a richer sauce, such as a red wine sauce. For lighter sauces and soups, you're more likely to use a white stock. But you can also use a mix of the two types to get the depth and balance you're looking for.

A stock of quality can't rely on a cooked carcass and leftovers for its flavour. It'll need the strength of *raw* meat, the choice of which will vary according to the type of stock being made. For a strong, dark stock I'd choose beef shin, shoulder or oxtail, because they have plenty of flavour; these tougher cuts need a longer cooking time. Cuts of lamb and pork have very particular and dominant flavours and are best used only in lamb and pork dishes. For a lighter chicken stock, wings are a great source of flavour.

The advantage of all these cuts is that they produce gelatine, which is the key ingredient for many meat stocks. When meat is cooked slowly, the collagen fibres in the connective tissue break down into gelatine. Molecules of gelatine tend to arrange themselves into a tangled network that traps liquid in the interstices, making the liquid thicker and more viscous since it can't move around as freely. (As gelatine cools, it forms such an intricate meshwork that the water molecules can no longer flow and it becomes a fragile solid – jelly.)

As an ingredient for thickening a stock and giving it body, gelatine has some advantages over the other traditional thickening agent, cornflour, which masks flavour. So if a thick, rich consistency is what you're looking for, it's wise to include plenty of cuts of meat with a lot of connective tissue. You want the bits of the animal that have done a lot of work – shoulders, tails, legs. Chicken wings and skin-on thighs are an inexpensive and convenient source of gelatine. You can use a supermarket packet of them to add body to almost any meat stock. If you're making a chicken stock with the carcass of Sunday's roast, for example, or a beef stock from a rib of roasted beef, you won't have as much as gelatine as you would from fresh meat. This can be compensated for by roasting some chicken wings and adding them to the stockpot. (If you've got a heavy knife or cleaver, chop them up before putting them in the roasting tray. Otherwise just open up the meat a bit with a knife.)

Bones are another key ingredient for a brown stock because they're an economical way of adding depth and complexity of flavour. Cookery writers are forever encouraging you to cultivate the local butcher and fishmonger, and here's one instance where it's definitely a good idea. Butchers in particular are the best source for the bones needed for a stock, and only they will have the equipment to chop them up into pieces that'll fit in your pan. You could roast these too before using them to make a brown stock.

Fish in stocks

Making a fish stock is generally more straightforward than making a meat stock. There's no connective tissue to be broken down, and although the bones in the stock on p.42 are very lightly fried, you don't generally brown bones for a fish stock because it might end up overpowering the other flavours in a dish. With a fish stock you're looking to capture the aromatic, sweet characteristics of the vegetables and the flavour from the bones – and sometimes the head – of the fish. Unless you want something very intense, it's best to use the bones of white fish with a mild flavour, and to clean them well.

Fish heads, bones and skin may be the building blocks of most fish stocks, adding body and richness, but you can also include shellfish. Crustacean shells contain lots of fragrant flavour that will reinforce the delicate aromas of shellfish stocks. (Be sure, though, to thoroughly rinse uncooked raw shells to remove all traces of grit and sand.)

You can make a basic fish stock by putting fish trimmings, vegetables and aromatics in a pan, adding water to cover, bringing the pan to the boil and then simmering gently for no more than half an hour. (Any longer and you'll end up with a rather stewed-tasting result.) But there are a few things you can do to produce a stock with more flavour. Softening the vegetables first will make them sweeter, which is very welcome in a fish stock. And, as with any stock, limiting the amount of water you add will result in something more concentrated and flavoursome. It's best to be generous with the trimmings and other flavourings and only just cover them with liquid.

Vegetables in stocks

A good vegetable stock will bring out all of the flavours of the different ingredients, rather than just a composite, vaguely vegetal flavour. To achieve this, it's important that the vegetables are cut small so that they cook quickly and don't lose too much colour and flavour. (In a meat stock that's cooked for several hours, on the other hand, you're not going to be able to hold on to the distinct characteristics of each vegetable, so it's less important that they're cut small.) By small I don't mean diced or cut into mirepoix. Some recipe books ask you to do this, but I think it's an unnecessary amount of work. The important point is that the vegetables are cut in a way that produces as much surface area as possible, so a fine slicing is what's needed. A mandolin (p.390) really comes into its own here: it'll cut thinner and more consistently than even the most practised cook. Just watch your fingers (use protectors, if provided), as a mandolin blade is extremely sharp.

Whether you're making a vegetable stock, or a fish or meat stock, you need to think about the flavour characteristics of the vegetables you're putting in the pot, and how they'll respond to cooking. Onions and carrots impart sweetness. Along with garlic they often form the base of a stock, though you don't necessarily have to include all of them. Onions and carrots have a dense texture, so except in the instances where they're being sliced finely and cooked quickly alongside all other vegetables, they probably need to go in the pot and soften for a while before the other vegetables are added.

To these core flavourings, you can add vegetables such as celery, mushrooms or leeks to bring depth and complexity and give the stock a particular character. Celery will provide lots of flavour, but it's strong and very distinctive and can overpower other ingredients. If you're after a relatively neutral stock, you may want to avoid it. Button mushrooms will provide an aromatic characteristic, as will leeks and fennel, though all three of these need to be cooked relatively briefly if they're to hang on to their aromas. Mushrooms and leeks go especially well in chicken and fish stock, and using mushrooms is a good way to introduce a meaty-like robustness to a vegetarian stock. The fragrance and earthiness of mushrooms, combined with a rigorous reduction, creates a concentrated, intense and extremely flavourful liquid (p.45).

For a fish stock, the vegetables used can vary but tend to be the same ones you'd find in a classic court-bouillon. (This is a very basic vegetable stock, in which fish is poached, p.174.) Onions, carrots, celery, fennel, thyme and parsley usually form the backbone, along with some white wine. To these you can add a variety of other flavourings. Leeks, button mushrooms and lemon zest often make an appearance, and you can play around with other herbs and spices, such as basil, tarragon, fennel seeds and saffron. Tomatoes can be used to introduce colour, if it's needed, and acidity.

For rich meat stocks, you might also want to include tomatoes, either lightly caramelized or in the form of a tomato purée or home-made tomato fondue sauce (p.212). They'll bring richness and meatiness, because they're full of umami (p.20), and also add some acidity. (If you use tomato purée, it needs to be 'cooked out' a little to bring out its aromas. Put it in with the softening vegetables for the last 5–10 minutes of cooking before water is added. Your nose will tell you when it's ready.)

Herbs and spices in stocks

Herbs and spices introduce greater flavour complexity to a stock. Among the commonly used ones are thyme, parsley, bay, peppercorns and, for more robust stocks, rosemary, sage and cloves. Fish stocks might well include fennel seeds and perhaps a strip of citrus zest. The hardier herbs, such as bay, thyme and rosemary, can be put in the pot near the start of cooking. (This doesn't preclude you from adding more of a herb towards the end to reinforce a particular flavour.) The more fragile ones, such as parsley, chives, tarragon, basil and chervil, should be added towards the end in order to capture as much of their aroma as possible. A good way of doing this is to add them once the stock has come off the heat and let them gently infuse into the liquid (p.24).

A classic way to bring flavour to a soup, stew, sauce or poaching liquid is to use a bouquet garni: a collection of herbs and spices that are added to the liquid as it's warmed and removed before serving. It usually includes a thyme sprig or two, a few parsley stalks and a bay leaf, but beyond that the choice of aromatics depends on what's available and what purpose the liquid will serve. For robust dishes you might add rosemary, sage or cloves; something lighter or fishier will benefit from a celery stick or leaves, some strips of leek or perhaps orange zest.

The traditional way to prepare a bouquet garni is to take all the flavourings except the bay leaf, hold them together (like a bouquet), wrap the bay leaf around them and then tie a piece of string around the leaf. Some people artfully tie up the aromatics using a strip of leek, which has a nice economy and aesthetic to it. At the other end of the scale, you can forgo the fiddle of assembly altogether and just put the ingredients in a little muslin bag. If the liquid is going to be strained after cooking, there's no need to secure all the bouquet garni ingredients together – just chuck them in the pot along with everything else.

Making stocks

Once the meat or fish and vegetables have been chosen and prepared, they need to be cooked in some form of liquid. Traditionally they're put in a stockpot, and covered with water, but only just – that way the flavour won't be too diluted. Bring the water to the boil, skim the scum from the top with a slotted spoon or a ladle and simmer for 20–30 minutes for fish and vegetable stocks that give up their flavour quickly, and anything up to several hours for meat stocks, where a slow cooking is needed to extract plenty of the all-important gelatine that will thicken and enrich the stock. (This is especially important if the stock is destined to be reduced to create a sauce. The gelatine will give the sauce body.)

Cooking from cold and heating slowly are key factors in making a stock this way. They allow the soluble proteins that escape from the solids to coagulate slowly and either settle at the sides and base of the pot, or rise to the surface, making them easy to skim off. (They would otherwise make the stock cloudy.) Leaving the pot uncovered is also important, helping to prevent the stock from boiling, concentrating the liquid and drying out the surface scum, which aids skimming.

There is nothing wrong with this method of stock-making, but you can make an even more flavourful stock by using a familiar, if somewhat neglected, piece of equipment – the pressure cooker. I know this might seem like a 1970s throwback, but pressure cookers have come a long way since then. As far as I'm concerned, it's the secret weapon for making great stock. Because the lid of the pressure cooker is sealed shut, it holds on to flavour that would otherwise simply evaporate, and because it cooks at a high temperature, it generates lots of flavour as well.

Normally a liquid boils when it has enough energy (from heat) to 'push up' with greater force than atmospheric pressure is 'pushing down' on it, allowing water molecules to escape in the form of steam. (At sea level, where the atmospheric pressure is greatest, water will boil when it reaches 100°C. On high mountains, where there is less pressure, water molecules need less energy

to escape and thus need less heat. The boiling point is around 72°C at the top of Mount Everest.) The pressure in a pressure cooker is greater than atmospheric pressure, so the molecules have to push all the harder in order to escape. The liquid reaches a temperature of 120°C without coming to the boil. (Go much above this and the pressure build-up will cause the relief valve to be triggered. This will bring the liquid to the boil, making the stock cloudy, and lots of volatile aromas will be lost along with the steam escaping from the valve.)

There are significant benefits to cooking the stock at this higher temperature. More flavour will diffuse from the ingredients, and you also get the benefit of Maillard reactions (p.136), which generally start to have an impact on food at 120°C, creating lots of deep, complex flavours. The result is a greater depth of flavour than can be achieved by the traditional slow simmering of a stock.

Once cooked, the stock – whether cooked in a pot or a pressure cooker – will need straining to remove all the bits from the liquid. It's not difficult but you need to be practical about it. Unless you're making a consommé (which needs filtering rather than straining, see p.53), you can either remove the larger bits with a slotted spoon or pour the contents of the stockpot into a colander set over a bowl. (Make sure you tip them into something reasonably large, otherwise it'll splash everywhere.) Press gently on the ingredients with the back of a ladle to extract as much flavour and juice as possible, and follow this with a further straining through a fine sieve set over a bowl and preferably lined with a double layer of wet muslin, or even a clean, wet J-cloth. (For some reason, wet muslin filters more effectively than dry.) This double straining through a large strainer and then a smaller, finer one might seem like overkill – a bit of a belt-and-braces job – but if you want a nice clean stock with no little particles left in it, this is the way to do it.

Then you have to store your stock. One of the great things about stock is that, so long as you've got a big enough pan, you can always make more than you need because it freezes well. However, if you're going to store a large amount – say, a couple of litres or more – don't

freeze it as a single block, which won't be very user-friendly if you're making a recipe that requires only a litre, say. One of the best methods of storage is to reduce the stock until it is extremely concentrated (see below), with a viscous, syrupy texture, and then pour it into ice-cube trays. Each ice cube can then be used more or less as if it were a little stock cube.

Maximizing flavour in stocks

In some stocks, particularly brown meat stocks, you will want to introduce lots of the big, complex flavours caused by Maillard reactions that take place when ingredients are seared on a high heat (also known as browning). You can do this by searing the meat and/or bones in a frying pan on the hob or in a roasting tin in the oven. (In many of my brown stocks, I do both.) The meat will have acquired flavours from this dry searing and roasting, which will benefit your stock, but you also want to take advantage of the sticky bits left in the bottom of the roasting tin or frying pan. This you do by deglazing, which is adding liquid to the pan, and heating, stirring and scraping, to get all the caramelized flavours into the liquid. This liquid can then be added back into the stock (or indeed any other dish). I use the deglazing technique in the beef, crab and lamb stocks in this chapter, as well as recipes elsewhere in the book.

Deglazing is a clever way of introducing extra layers of flavour and complexity to stocks and sauces. Often a pan is deglazed with alcohol, usually wine, or vinegar, but most liquids will work, so long as you choose something that will complement the dish. If a stock is destined for a rich sauce, such as port and red wine, you might deglaze with brandy and/or port or red wine. With a chicken stock, you can deglaze the pan with white wine. With fish, you might use vermouth or a touch of Pernod. A squirt of lemon juice works with a pan of fried chicken bits. A touch of rum is good for caramelizing banana.

Deglazing is also a great way to make a simple sauce. If you've roasted a chicken, for example, then while it's resting you can deglaze the meat juices in the pan over a high heat with wine, a touch of grain mustard and water, to make a basic gravy. With fried fish you can deglaze the pan with a little lemon juice, throw in a knob of butter, warm it through and then pour it on top.

Another excellent technique for boosting the flavours in a stock is to brown finely sliced onion with a small amount of star anise. I've always been impressed by how this spice enhances the flavour of Chinese spare-rib dishes, and a few years ago I began exploring its properties and trying it out in various dishes. The effect of browning onions with star anise was amazing – the two ingredients contain compounds that react to produce clove, cinnamon, thyme, black pepper and chilli notes that really work in a meat stock (or indeed onion soup), enriching it and accentuating the meaty notes.

One of the most common methods for boosting a stock's flavour is boiling it so that some of the water evaporates. Evaporation will drive off some flavour molecules along with the water, but it'll produce a stock with a less dilute and therefore more concentrated flavour. And as the stock is heated, compounds present in the liquid will continue to react to produce all sorts of new flavours.

During the process of reduction, impurities in the stock will cause a scum to form on the surface, which can cloud the liquid and possibly render it bitter. Therefore it's best to simmer it gently, which helps prevent the particles from dispersing through the liquid, but you'll also need to do what's technically known as *dépouillage*, which roughly translates as 'skimming the scum' – removing impurities using a slotted spoon or ladle. If the stock is at a simmer, most of the impurities should collect together and rise to the surface. If you position the pot so that it's partly off the source of heat, the scum will all gather on the cooler side of the pot, making it easier to skim.

How far a stock or other liquid needs to be reduced depends largely on what it's going to be used for. A stock being reduced for a glaze or concentrated essence destined for a sauce will need more reduction than a stock destined for a soup. Reducing a liquid intensifies flavour and thickens it, and how far you take this is often a question of balance. If, say, you've reduced a sauce to the desired level of flavour but it's not thick enough, reducing it further may not be an option because it'll make the liquid too salty and concentrated in flavour.

Sometimes, in order to intensify flavour further, chefs will make a second stock, using the first as the cooking liquid in place of water, in order to engineer a big depth of flavour, particularly if they're going to use the stock to make a sauce. At the Fat Duck, for some sauces, I take the second stock and use it to make a third – partly to get a particularly intense flavour, and partly so that the stock doesn't make the sauce too sticky. Sometimes when you boil down a stock to make a thick sauce, the gelatinous character can take over and give it a certain stickiness. If you want to avoid this, the triple-stock approach is a good (if time-consuming) way to do so.

White chicken stock

This is one of the most versatile stocks. It can form the basis of any risotto or soup and is perfect for subtle dishes like chestnut velouté (p.66) that would be overpowered by something stronger. It can also be used to make a great quick gravy for roast chicken (p.142).

The initial blanching of the chicken might seem like an unnecessary extra step, but it's an excellent way of removing impurities so as to produce a really clear stock.

Makes 2kg

1.75kg	Chicken wings
150g	Peeled and finely sliced onion (approx. 2 medium onions)
150g	Peeled and finely sliced carrot (approx. 2 large carrots)
100g	Finely sliced button mushrooms
60g	Finely sliced celery (approx. 2 sticks of celery)
50g	Cleaned and finely sliced leek, white and pale green parts only (approx. 1 leek)
2	Cloves of garlic, peeled and bashed with the flat part of a knife or by hand
10g	Flat-leaf parsley (stalks and leaves)
6	Sprigs of thyme
1	Bay leaf
5g	Black peppercorns

Place the chicken wings in a large saucepan and add enough cold water to cover them. Bring to the boil, skimming off the scum as it rises to the surface.

As soon as the water comes to the boil, remove the pan from the heat and drain immediately. Rinse the chicken wings thoroughly under cold running water, removing any residual scum.

Put the chicken wings into a pressure cooker, add 2kg cold tap water and bring to a simmer, skimming off any scum that rises to the surface.

Place the lid on the pressure cooker and bring up to full pressure over a high heat. Reduce the heat to low and cook for 1 hour.

Take the pressure cooker off the heat and leave to cool completely before removing the lid. Add the raw vegetables and garlic, and place the lid back on. Bring back up to full pressure over a high heat, then reduce the heat to low and cook for 30 minutes.

Take the pressure cooker off the heat again, and leave to cool completely before removing the lid. Add the herbs and black peppercorns and set aside to infuse for 30 minutes.

Strain the liquid through a sieve lined with two layers of wet muslin. Refrigerate overnight. Scrape the layer of fat from the surface before using or freezing for later use.

Brown chicken stock

In order to make a brown chicken stock rather than a white, the meat and some of the vegetables need to be browned, so the starting point for this stock is putting chicken wings in the oven to produce lots of deep colour and roasted flavours. The stock is used in a number of recipes in this book, including chicken with clams (p.200), truffle macaroni (p.216) and cocotte of pork with black pudding sauce (p.198). It can also be reduced to make a red wine sauce, or a glaze that can enrich any meat sauce (p.37).

Makes 2kg

2.5kg	Chicken wings
	Groundnut or grapeseed oil
150g	Peeled and finely sliced onion
	(approx. 2 medium onions)
75g	Peeled and finely sliced carrot
	(approx. 1 large carrot)
100g	Finely sliced button mushrooms
2	Cloves of garlic, peeled and bashed with
	the flat part of a knife or by hand

Pre-heat the oven to 200°C.

Rub the chicken wings with oil, then put into a roasting tray and place in the pre-heated oven for 1 hour, turning them every 20 minutes to ensure they are golden brown all over. Pour away the fat from the tray and set the wings aside. Add a little water to the tray and, using a wooden spoon, scrape the bits from the bottom of the pan. Reserve this liquid.

Heat a thin layer of oil in the bottom of a pressure cooker over a high heat. When the oil is hot, add the onions and cook until golden brown and caramelized, stirring frequently to prevent the onions from catching on the bottom of the pan (approximately 45 minutes).

Add the carrots and continue to cook until they are soft and caramelized before adding the mushrooms and garlic (approximately 20 minutes). Cook until the mushrooms are soft and cooked through (approximately 10 minutes).

Add the roasted chicken wings and the deglazing liquid. Cover with 2kg cold tap water and bring to a simmer, skimming off any impurities that rise to the top.

Place the lid on the pressure cooker and bring up to full pressure over a high heat. Reduce the heat to low and cook for 2 hours.

Take the pressure cooker off the heat and leave to cool completely before removing the lid.

Strain the liquid through a sieve lined with two layers of wet muslin. Refrigerate overnight. Scrape the layer of fat from the surface before using or freezing for later use.

Beef stock

This is a dark stock that's perfect for rich meat sauces and robust dishes like onion soup (p.57) and chilli con carne (p.156). It employs the technique of deglazing to add as much flavour as possible to the stock. If you are using bones to make it, be sure to ask the butcher to cut them small enough to fit in the roasting tray. This chopping also maximizes the surface area, which increases flavour extraction.

Makes 2kg

1kg	Chopped beef bones (ask the butcher), or use shin of beef if easier
350g	Oxtail, sectioned
	Groundnut or grapeseed oil
1kg	Diced shin of beef (or 2kg if using diced shin instead of bones)
500g	Peeled and finely sliced onion (approx. 7 medium onions)
1	Star anise
500g	Peeled and finely sliced carrot (approx. 6–7 large carrots)
375g	Red wine

Pre-heat the oven to 190°C.

Rub the beef bones and the oxtail pieces with a little oil and put into a roasting tray. Place in the pre-heated oven for 1 hour, turning them every 20 minutes so that they are golden brown on all sides.

In the meantime, heat a thin layer of oil in the bottom of a pressure cooker over a high heat. When the oil is smoking hot, brown the diced shin meat in batches, colouring deeply without burning. Remove the meat from the pan and set aside.

Pour a little water into the hot pan to deglaze it, and retain the liquid.

Wash the pan and return to the heat. Heat another thin layer of oil, add the onions with the star anise and stir to coat with the oil. Cook on a medium-high heat until the onions are lightly caramelized, stirring regularly to prevent the onions from catching on the bottom (approximately 45 minutes).

Add the carrots and continue to cook the vegetables until both are soft and caramelized (approximately 20 minutes).

Add the red wine and boil to reduce it to a thin syrup (approximately 30 minutes).

Add the roasted beef bones and oxtail, the browned shin, the deglazing water and 2kg cold tap water. Bring to a simmer, skimming off any impurities that rise to the top.

Place the lid on the pressure cooker and bring up to full pressure over a high heat. Reduce the heat to low and cook for 2 hours.

Take the pressure cooker off the heat and leave to cool completely before removing the lid.

Strain the liquid through a sieve lined with two layers of wet muslin. Refrigerate overnight. Scrape the layer of fat from the surface before using or freezing for later use.

Lamb stock

Chicken and beef make stocks with a rounded, relatively neutral flavour, whereas stock made from lamb has a much more distinctive flavour that's mainly suitable for lamb-based dishes, such as shepherd's pie (p.160) and slow-cooked lamb shanks (p.158). It can also be used to make a great sauce for a roast leg of lamb: deglaze the lamb roasting tray with white wine, add the lamb stock and reduce it to a syrupy consistency. Finish with a little grain mustard.

Bones are an economic way of introducing flavour and complexity to a stock, but if you can't get hold of bones you can always replace them with cheap cuts of the appropriate meat. We've used both meat and bones here, to maximize flavour.

Makes 1.75kg

1kg	Chopped lamb bones (ask the butcher)
	Groundnut or grapeseed oil
500g	Lamb mince
180g	Peeled and finely sliced onion (approx. 2–3 medium onions)
½	Star anise
180g	Sliced ripe tomato (approx. 3 medium tomatoes)
200g	Peeled and finely sliced carrot (approx. 2–3 large carrots)
50g	Finely sliced button mushrooms
40g	Finely sliced celery (approx. 1–2 sticks of celery)
3	Cloves of garlic, peeled and finely sliced
75g	White port
8	Sprigs of thyme
1	Sprig of rosemary
6	Tarragon leaves
1	Bay leaf

Pre-heat the oven to 200°C.

Rub the lamb bones with a little oil and put them into a roasting tray, then cook in the pre-heated oven for 45 minutes, turning every 15 minutes so that they are golden brown on all sides. When roasted, put the bones to one side.

Heat a frying pan until it is extremely hot, then add half the mince and fry it until it is well browned (approximately 5 minutes). Remove from the pan with a slotted spoon and add to the bones. Brown the remaining mince in the frying pan and also add it to the bones.

Lower the heat below the frying pan, add the onions and star anise and sweat until soft and lightly coloured (approximately 10 minutes).

Place the tomatoes in a pressure cooker over a medium heat, and cook until very soft and reduced by half (approximately 10 minutes).

In the meantime, remove the onions from the frying pan and add the carrots, mushrooms, celery and garlic. Cook until soft (approximately 20 minutes), then transfer all the vegetables to the pressure cooker.

Deglaze the frying pan with the white port, and pour it into the pressure cooker. Add the bones, mince, herbs and 1.75kg cold tap water.

Put the lid on the pressure cooker, and bring up to full pressure over a high heat. Reduce the heat to low and cook for 2 hours.

Take the pressure cooker off the heat and leave to cool completely before removing the lid.

Strain the liquid through a sieve lined with two layers of wet muslin. Refrigerate overnight. Scrape the layer of fat from the surface before using or freezing for later use.

Fish stock

A fish stock is usually destined for a seafood dish, so it needs a subtle, fragrant character that will complement maritime flavours. Fish bones are a key source of flavour and gelatine, but they need to be cleaned of all blood and viscera, otherwise the stock can end up cloudy and bitter-tasting. In general, unless you're looking for a strong fish flavour, it's best to use bones from mild white fish, like sole, cod and sea bass, rather than oily fish, like salmon and mackerel, which will be too strong. If you're including heads in your stock, the gills should be removed as they too will impart bitterness.

The rapid cooking here ensures the stock holds on to its fresh notes and won't acquire an overcooked characteristic. The stock also benefits from a gentle warm infusion (p.24) of lemon zest, herbs and mussels. The mussels really add something to the stock, bringing depth and a touch of sweetness, though you can of course leave them out if you're allergic to shellfish.

Makes 1.5kg

1.25kg	White fish bones (ask the fishmonger)
	Groundnut or grapeseed oil
150g	Peeled and finely sliced onion (approx. 2 medium onions)
75g	Peeled and finely sliced carrot (approx. 1 large carrot)
75g	Finely sliced celery (approx. 2–3 sticks of celery)
100g	Finely sliced fennel
100g	Finely sliced button mushrooms
1	Clove of garlic, peeled and finely sliced
150g	Sliced ripe tomatoes (approx. 2 medium tomatoes)
180g	Dry white wine
75g	Dry white vermouth
500g	Mussels, cleaned
¼ tsp	Saffron strands
½ tsp	Fennel seeds
50g	Flat-leaf parsley (stalks and leaves)
2	Sprigs of thyme
12	Basil leaves
6	Tarragon leaves
4	Strips of lemon zest, removed with a peeler

Chop the fish bones into small pieces and place them in a bowl of cold water. Leave them for 20 minutes. Drain the bones and pat dry on kitchen paper.

Heat a frying pan over a medium heat and cover the bottom of the pan with a thin layer of oil. Fry the bones for a few minutes without colouring, and set aside.

Heat a thin layer of oil in the bottom of a pressure cooker over a high heat. Add the onions, carrots, celery, fennel, button mushrooms, garlic and tomatoes, turn the heat to low, and sweat until soft (approximately 20 minutes).

Add the wine and vermouth, and boil until it has almost disappeared.

Add the fish bones and 1.5kg cold tap water, and put the lid on the pressure cooker. Bring up to full pressure over a high heat, then reduce the heat to low and cook for 15 minutes.

Take the pressure cooker off the heat and leave to cool completely before removing the lid. Place the pan over a medium-high heat, add the mussels, saffron, fennel seeds, herbs and lemon zest and heat until the mussels have opened (approximately 5 minutes).

Leave to cool before straining the liquid through a sieve lined with two layers of wet muslin. Refrigerate or freeze for later use.

Crab stock

In this book the crab stock is used only for crab risotto (p.220), but it has a fantastic sweet, nutty flavour that could also work well in a paella or bisque. Reduced and mixed with some chopped tomato, fresh chilli, basil and olive oil, it would make a great sauce to toss pasta in.

There's no way round the fact that, if you want a truly sublime crab stock, you have to kill a crab. Cooked crab will give up less flavour to the liquid, and it won't have the lovely, fresh juices either. Another key feature of this recipe is the use of the crab's shell, which is broken up and browned, then put in a pan with alcohol that is reduced and added to the other stock ingredients. A crustacean's shell is made up of proteins and sugars that have bags of flavour, particularly when they're roasted, which kickstarts all sorts of complex reactions. It's smart to take advantage of that concentrated flavour and, what's more, I think if you're going to kill a crab for your dinner, the least you can do is try to use every last part of it.

Makes 2kg

1	Live cock crab, weighing approx. 2kg
	Groundnut or grapeseed oil
400g	Dry white wine
150g	Dry white vermouth
300g	Peeled and finely sliced onion (approx. 4 medium onions)
2	Cloves of garlic, peeled and finely sliced
500g	Peeled and finely sliced carrot (approx. 6–7 large carrots)
150g	Finely sliced button mushrooms
90g	Cleaned and finely sliced leek (approx. 2 leeks), white and pale green parts only
50g	Finely sliced celery (approx. 2 sticks of celery)
75g	Finely sliced fennel
190g	Roughly chopped tomato (approx. 3 medium tomatoes)
1	Lemon, finely sliced
	Pinch of saffron strands
2	Star anise
3	Cloves

Kill the crab by driving a metal spike or screwdriver into its head through the mouth between the eyes. This will kill it instantly. Using a heavy knife or cleaver, chop the crab in half down the middle and allow the juices to drain through a sieve into a container. Discard the guts and gills from the body of the crab, retaining the brown crab meat and juices. Remove the claws and legs.

Bring a large saucepan of water to the boil and cook the claws and legs for 5 minutes. Drain and immerse them in iced water to cool them quickly. Place the brown meat, claws and legs in the fridge for use in the crab risotto.

Wrap the empty crab shells in a clean tea-towel and, using a hammer or rolling pin, bash until the shell is broken into small pieces, approximately 4–5cm in size.

Coat the bottom of a frying pan with oil, put over a medium-high heat and add the shell pieces. Fry them for 5–8 minutes until they are dark brown in colour. Strain the shells, reserving the oil for finishing the crab risotto. Return the shells to the frying pan and place over the heat.

When hot, add the wine and vermouth to deglaze the pan then, using a long match, set fire to the alcohol and stand back (see tip, p.153). Let it burn off until the flames disappear. Reduce the liquid by three-quarters before removing from the heat and mixing with the crab juices.

Heat a thin layer of oil in the bottom of a pressure cooker over a low-medium heat. When the oil is hot, sweat the onions, garlic, carrots, mushrooms, leeks, celery and fennel for 10 minutes, then add the tomatoes, toasted crab shells, juices and 2kg cold tap water. Put the lid on and bring up to full pressure over a high heat. Reduce the heat to low and cook for 1 hour.

Take the pressure cooker off the heat and leave to cool completely before removing the lid. Place the pan over a medium heat, add the lemon slices, saffron, star anise and cloves and heat for 5 minutes.

Strain the liquid through a sieve lined with two layers of wet muslin and refrigerate or freeze for later use.

Vegetable stock

This is a fresh, light and very fragrant stock for dishes like leek and potato soup (p.56) and mushroom spelt risotto (p.221). Between this, the bolder flavoured mushroom stock (opposite) and the intense Marmite consommé (p.70), you've got a range of liquids that can be used as substitutes for meat stocks in recipes.

Makes 2kg

50g	Unsalted butter
350g	Cleaned and finely sliced leek (approx. 7 leeks)
225g	Peeled and finely sliced carrot (approx. 3 large carrots)
200g	Peeled and finely sliced onion (approx. 3 medium onions)
200g	Finely sliced button mushrooms
100g	Finely sliced fennel
100g	Finely sliced celery (approx. 3–4 sticks of celery)
3	Sprigs of thyme
3	Bay leaves
30g	Flat-leaf parsley (leaves and stalks)

Melt the butter in a pressure cooker over a medium heat. Add the vegetables and sweat for 5 minutes, stirring occasionally.

Add the thyme, bay leaves and 2kg cold tap water, place the lid on the pressure cooker and bring to full pressure over a high heat, then reduce to low and cook for 20 minutes.

Remove the pressure cooker from the heat and allow to cool completely before removing the lid. Place the pan over a medium heat for 5 minutes, then add the parsley and allow to cool for 20 minutes.

Strain through a sieve lined with two layers of wet muslin and refrigerate or freeze for later use.

Mushroom stock

I'm a big fan of the much-underrated button mushroom, which has a lovely fragrance but can also deliver a punch of umami (p.20). This recipe captures that savoury taste, which is what you need for the mushroom jelly on p.105. And if you're giving a meat recipe a vegetarian makeover, it makes a great substitute for a brown chicken stock.

By the way, cooking lore has it that mushrooms should not be washed, because they will absorb water and become soggy. This simply isn't the case. Try weighing some mushrooms, washing them clean, then weighing them again. If they had absorbed water there would be a significant increase in weight, but it will have barely changed. Some kitchen wisdom is true – tomatoes really shouldn't be stored in the fridge because it affects their flavour – while other nuggets, such as the idea that searing 'seals' meat, are completely misleading (p.136). If you've reason to doubt some piece of received wisdom, test it out. The results are often surprising.

Makes 750g

100g	Unsalted butter
750g	Button mushrooms, halved
200g	Dry Madeira
8	Sprigs of thyme
5g	Black peppercorns

Melt the butter in a pressure cooker over a medium heat. Add the mushrooms, stir to coat in the butter and cook until golden brown. Lots of water will come out of the mushrooms but continue to cook until it disappears and the mushrooms begin to colour (approximately 20 minutes).

Deglaze the pan with the Madeira then, using a long match, set fire to the alcohol and stand back (see tip, p.153). Let it burn off until the flames disappear, then boil to reduce the liquid to a thick syrup.

Add 1.5kg cold tap water, the thyme and peppercorns to the pressure cooker, and put the lid on. Bring up to full pressure over a high heat, then reduce the heat to low and cook for 30 minutes.

Take the pressure cooker off the heat and leave to cool completely before removing the lid. Strain the liquid through a fine sieve into a saucepan, and reduce the liquid by half over a high heat.

Pass the reduced liquid through a sieve lined with two layers of wet muslin. Refrigerate or freeze for later use.

Soups

Soup is one of our most ancient dishes. Archaeologists have uncovered prehistoric evidence of pots containing traces of brothy concoctions composed of fish, nuts, wheat and summer fruits. The last meal of Tollund Man, who died about 2,400 years ago, was a gruel of barley and seeds. In the Middle Ages, these crosses between porridge and stew were known as pottage (after *potage*, a French word for something cooked in a pot) and eaten by all ranks of society. Another French word, *soupe*, which originally referred to the piece of bread added to a liquid to thicken it, arrived in Britain in the seventeenth century, at around the same time as we began serving thinner soups, and gradually it became the commonly used term for all varieties of flavoured liquid, thick and thin.

As you can imagine, a dish with such a long history has evolved into many forms – clear, thin, thick, chunky, hot, cold, rustic, refined – and can contain almost any ingredient. As Harold McGee puts it in *Keys to Good Cooking*: 'As long as it's fluid enough to eat with a spoon it can be a soup.' With such a protean dish, it's hard to make worthwhile generalizations, but there are a number of technical areas, such as stock-making (pp.29–45), liquidizing, thickening, straining and finishing – where you can control texture, create and intensify flavour and produce a soup with real interest and individuality.

If you base a soup on a proper stock, you're halfway to creating something with plenty of flavour and complexity. In fact, stock- and soup-making draw on lots of the same techniques, so with soups, as with stocks, you can deglaze a pan to capture the caramelized notes (p.36), reduce a liquid to drive off water and concentrate the flavours (p.37), sweat onions with star anise to boost meaty notes (p.37), and flame off alcohol to lessen the acidity (p.153). These are all techniques that can be used to introduce new flavours or enhance the existing ones.

People often think of soup simply as an ingenious way of using up leftovers, but a good soup can be incredibly complex, aromatic and satisfying. To achieve this, you need to think about precisely which ingredients you want in the soup and what effect you want from them. One of the keys is careful handling of the vegetables that are going to flavour the soup. Finely slicing the vegetables is just as important in soups as in stocks, maximizing the surface area and letting them to cook quickly, particularly with vegetables that will lose colour and flavour if cooked for too long, like leeks, fennel and mushrooms. In fact, for most soups, softening the vegetables in oil or butter over a gentle heat (so they don't brown or caramelize), followed by a fairly brief simmering in liquid, gets the best out of them, preserving colour and keeping the flavour fresh and distinct.

Of course there are exceptions to this – ones that make sense when you take into account the overall effect you're going for. The onion soup on p.57 needs lots of big flavour, so the onions are cooked for several hours in the oven, which is a much less aggressive cooking medium than a pan. (Air doesn't transfer heat very efficiently: while you can put your hand in a 100°C oven for a moment without coming to any harm, you can't do the same with a pan of boiling water.) Oven-cooked onions will have softened and browned but still have a bit of bite, which is exactly what I look for in an onion soup. With ingredients that respond well to roasting, such as root vegetables, it's often worth browning at least a portion of the vegetable in the oven and then adding it to the liquid to introduce layers of extra caramelized flavour. (See, for example, the pumpkin soup on p.61.)

On the whole, though, cooking soup vegetables for too long is a mistake. It is assumed that, in order to make a soup really smooth, you have to cook them until they're completely soft. But this often leads to them being overcooked and much less flavourful. Obviously they have to be soft enough to purée smoothly but, ideally, you want to reach this point and go no further. The briefer the cooking time the more those delicious smells coming from the simmering pan will stay in the soup. Indeed, sometimes getting the best out of ingredients means applying little or no heat. In the pea and ham soup on p.65 the peas are just warmed through during the re-heating, which helps them to hold on to their sweetness and bright green colour. And the seductive zing of the red cabbage gazpacho on p.63 comes from using ingredients that haven't been cooked at all, and so retain their raw, fresh characteristics.

Liquidizing and straining soups

More often than not, you'll need to blend a soup to thicken it and produce a smooth texture. This might seem a straightforward business – you just pour it in and hit the button, right? – but most of us have at some point managed to splatter the kitchen with the contents of the jug, even though it had a lid on, so it's worth following a few pointers.

For a start, soup is best liquidized in a blender rather than a food processor, because it has a smaller blade that spins faster, liquidizing more finely. The contents of the pan need to be transferred to the jug of the blender while still warm, as they'll liquidize more efficiently like that. That said, no matter how eager you are to get the soup done, resist the urge to pour it into a blender while it's still piping hot. If you put a hot liquid in the jug and close the lid, the heat can cause the air pressure to build to such an extent that, when you hit the switch, the soup forces its way out. So let it cool for a few minutes, then fill the jug no more than two-thirds full. Put on the lid but remove the small inner section, hold a folded tea-towel over the top, then press the button. Leave it for long enough that the contents are fully and evenly liquidized. Make sure that when you first add the soup to the blender, you pour in just enough liquid to blend the contents and no more. You can always stop and add more, to get exactly the consistency you want. But if you put the lot in and it's too diluted as a result, it's going to be difficult to remedy.

With thick, gutsy soups, a stint in the blender is usually all that's needed. But often I want a soup – particularly a dairy-based one – to have a light, velvety texture.

This is where the hand blender comes into its own. It's perfect for a final blitzing just before serving, to aerate the soup and give it a lovely light frothiness. Froths and foams are often viewed as whimsical and a little pretentious, but I don't see why. They are common in classic cuisine, producing a unique, delightful texture, and help to create lots of things we know and love, like soufflés, meringues, sponges and the foam on top of a cappuccino. You can froth up almost any soup but with the thicker ones, you'll probably have to loosen it with some liquid so the hand blender can aerate properly. This is a juggling act because if you add too much liquid, the soup becomes diluted and the flavour is muted. As always, the key is to add gradually rather than all at once, and taste continually, so that you can get the right balance of texture and flavour.

Before you froth your soup, though, you will probably have to strain it. Although some soups don't require straining, such as a hearty, rustic onion soup, most of the time you'll be passing the liquid through some form of filter. With clear, pure liquids like a consommé it's particularly important to remove all impurities, first by clarifying using egg white or ice (p.54), then by pouring into a sieve set over a bowl, which has been lined with two layers of wet muslin (wet seems to filter more efficiently than dry, for some reason). Simpler broths only need to be passed through a muslin-lined sieve or paper coffee filter.

Vegetable or other soups that have been liquidized need to be sieved, which will refine the texture. The purée is passed through a fine sieve set over a bowl, using the back of a spoon or ladle to press it down. It takes patience and a bit of elbow grease to do this but it can make a huge difference to the final texture, rendering it incredibly smooth and silky. A fine conical sieve (p.393) is probably the most hassle-free way of doing this, though you can use a flour sieve instead.

Thickening soups

Many vegetable soups will thicken perfectly once they have been liquidized. However, should you need them, various ingredients can be added to help thicken the mixture. One of the commonest is a starch such as cornflour, and since it has a fairly neutral flavour, it can be used in a wide range of soups. (Dilute it first in a little cold water, then whisk it into the hot soup.) But starch also masks flavour, so in general I tend to search out other ways to thicken soups.

There are plenty of classic alternatives, such as egg yolks, bread, potatoes and other root vegetables, cream and butter (though you need to be sparing with butter, or else the liquid will end up too oily). If you're using cream to thicken (as opposed to adding a swirl as a garnish), it's important to add it to the soup 5–10 minutes before the end and let it simmer with the other ingredients. This removes that lactic, raw-cream note that otherwise will make the ingredients seem unintegrated and spoil the flavour a little. (Double cream or high-fat crème fraiche are often the best choices for thickening by means of cream because they contain less milk protein and so won't curdle noticeably.) With egg yolks, too, you need to exercise a certain amount of control. Mix egg yolk with a little of the liquid first before adding to the bulk of the soup. Make sure that the temperature of the liquid into which it's put doesn't go above 85°C because it will start to scramble and make the soup grainy. Thickening with eggs is best done at the last minute. If they're heated for too long, the lovely silky texture they give the soup soon becomes impaired.

Alongside these classic thickeners are others that are perhaps not as well-known, but worth keeping up your sleeve. The red cabbage gazpacho on p.63, for example, is not only thickened by but gains a silkiness from the addition of mayonnaise. Indian cuisine often uses white poppy seeds or ground almonds to bring body to seafood soups. And in the chestnut velouté on p.66 the chestnuts provide all the thickening the soup needs.

Finishing soups

The finishing touches are your chance to bring the dish alive and set your stamp on it. Often it's these final details that transform a soup into something out of the ordinary. And there are plenty more options than just sprinkling on a few croûtons or swirling in a little crème fraiche.

First, this is the moment to adjust the seasoning. It's only at the end, once some of the liquid has evaporated and the soup has cooled slightly, that you can judge what's needed. The right level of salt is, of course, crucial here, as it'll draw out the flavours, so you need to taste and adjust accordingly. (See my soup cup test, described on pp.15–17.) Freshly ground black pepper might also be added now (it needs to be freshly ground so that it holds on to as much of its volatile flavour as possible), though with paler soups you may prefer to use white pepper to avoid dotting the surface with unattractive black specks. With thicker, starchier soups such as those with root vegetables or potatoes, it is also worth considering cayenne pepper as an alternative, which adds a welcome kick to what might otherwise be bland and homogeneous.

Most people's seasoning of soups doesn't extend much beyond salt and pepper, but I find that the addition of a little acidity can often enhance soup, particularly a rich one. So when you're tasting to check the levels of seasoning, think about whether the soup might benefit from a splash of vinegar – red, white or sherry can work well – or lemon juice, for example. With some soups, as well as tasting for seasoning you'll be monitoring the richness. This can be adjusted with a drizzle of oil – olive or sesame, perhaps, or a flavoured oil (as is used in the pea and ham soup on p.65 and the pumpkin soup on p.61). Or you might add a grating of cheese or spoonful of crème fraiche. I also sometimes like to add brown butter (p.204) to soups.

Finally, the finishing of a soup is a great opportunity to reinforce flavours and introduce textural contrasts that will make it more stimulating to the palate. Fresh herbs are easy, adding flavour and colour, and croûtons are a classic way to add a bit of crunch. But there are plenty of alternatives. Many of the ingredients that I singled out in the first chapter as having their flavour packed tightly into an encapsulated form (p.23) will bring liveliness and texture to the right soup: whole coriander seeds with a carrot soup; cumin seeds with something spicy; diced sautéed bacon with an earthy lentil soup; cubes of cucumber with a chilled summer soup. It's a good idea, too, to set aside a little of the main ingredient for a soup and then to use it (either grated or lightly cooked and then finely chopped) as a garnish for the dish. It'll accentuate the main flavour and provide a nice contrasting texture.

One of the soups that most takes advantage of these finishing touches is the pumpkin soup on p.61, which has pumpkin seeds to add texture and emphasize the pumpkin flavour, along with toasted hazelnuts, roasted pepper diamonds and a drizzle of red pepper oil to produce something that is both refined and exciting for the palate.

Consommés

A consommé is a real show-off dish. You're looking to create a liquid that is not only delicious but has a shimmering translucence, like amber. Clarification is the prime technique for creating very clear liquids. It can be employed in the making of juices, infusions and even gels (see for example the lamb jelly on p.98 and the mushroom jelly on p.105), but the most familiar use is for consommés. There are two ways of achieving the crystal clarity of consommés.

The traditional method uses egg whites to remove the impurities in the stock – mainly particles of fat – that scatter the light and make it look cloudy. When egg whites are heated they coagulate, setting into a network of strands that act as a sort of filter. This mesh comes to the surface to form a raft, which traps any impurities circulating within the stock. This approach has its uses, particularly for vegetarian dishes, but the 'egg raft' that removes impurities also removes flavour molecules, so wherever possible I prefer to use ice filtration. However, you have to start with a stock made with meat or fish, as the presence of gelatine is the key to the process. (Unless you *add* gelatine, as I have done in the mushroom jelly on p.105.) If you freeze a liquid that contains gelatine, which naturally forms into a fine network, you have in effect an in-built filter. Thaw the frozen block slowly in the fridge (which will usually take 24–48 hours, though if you're thawing a small amount it may be ready overnight) and the gelatine strands will trap the fat (which stays solid at fridge temperature) and the impurities. This might seem a long time, but it's an essential part of the process. Thaw too quickly and the fat melts into oil droplets which fall back into the consommé, undoing all your efforts and clouding it up. Thaw patiently, however, and what melts through is incredibly clear and flavourful.

You can test this for yourself by buying a small tub of clear chicken stock and following the instructions below. You'll be amazed by the difference in clarity before and after. The end result will look like white wine.

How to ice-filter stock

Ice filtration will produce a liquid of spectacular clarity that holds on to a lot more flavour than the traditional approach. And it's very simple: all you have to do is freeze the stock, then allow it to thaw.

1. Pour the chilled stock into a tray or freezer bags and place in the freezer. Once the stock is frozen, remove it from the freezer bags or tray (dipping the tray in warm water will help to loosen the block).

2. Put the block into a sieve or perforated tray lined with a double layer of muslin set on top of a bowl or other container. Cover the whole thing with clingfilm, and return to the fridge to melt gently for 24–48 hours. (The timing will depend on the quantity and density of the stock.)

3. Remove the muslin carefully. Pour the consommé into a clean saucepan and gently reheat.

How to egg-filter stock

The very thing that makes ice filtration work so well – a network of gelatine strands – means it can't be used to make a consommé based on a vegetable stock, which contains no gelatine. Here's where the classic method of clarification using egg whites comes into its own.

1. Put your cool stock in a pan on top of the stove.

2. Lightly whisk some egg whites until they're loose and have formed a few bubbles.

3. Add the egg whites to the pan. You can add crushed egg shell at this point, which helps coagulation. You can also add more of the key ingredients (i.e. raw cuts of meat to a meat stock, raw vegetables to a veg stock, or both), if you want, to introduce extra flavour. Mix them thoroughly with the egg whites before applying heat.

4. Heat the stock gradually. After about 30–40 minutes of very gentle simmering, an egg 'raft' will form and rise to the surface, attracting to it the fat and impurities.

5. Lift the raft out or move it to one side of the pan so that you can reach the liquid. (Or put the pan half-on, half-off the heat, so that the raft collects only on the cooler half of the pan, making it easier to access the liquid.)

6. Ladle the consommé from the pan into a fine sieve that is lined with a coffee filter paper or dampened muslin, set above a clean pan or storage container.

Leek and potato soup

This is my version of a classic soup. The potatoes give it a creamy consistency. The leeks give flavour. However, leeks lose a lot of their colour and flavour if cooked for longer than about 20 minutes, so it's crucial to slice them finely so that they cook as quickly as possible. (The onions and potatoes will need a longer cooking time to soften up: that's why they get a head start in the pan.) It's good to include some of the green part of the leek, too, because that gives a better colour.

You can use either vegetable stock (p.44) or, if you're serving to non-vegetarians, white chicken stock (p.38), which I think makes it even better. Remember to add the cream 5–10 minutes before the end, so that it has time to cook and lose its raw lactic note.

Serves 6

For the soup

180g	Peeled and very finely sliced waxy potatoes (approx. 2 medium potatoes)
120g	Unsalted butter
200g	Peeled and very finely sliced onion (approx. 3 medium onions)
750g	Cleaned and very finely sliced leek (approx. 15 leeks)
1	Bouquet garni (thyme, celery leaves and parsley, tied together with a strip of leek or a piece of string, see p.34)
1kg	Vegetable stock (p.44), or white chicken stock (p.38), warmed
100g	Double cream
50g	Semi-skimmed milk
	Salt

To serve

Chives

Rinse the sliced potatoes under cold running water for a couple of minutes to remove the starch which might otherwise make the soup thick and gluey.

Melt the butter in a large saucepan and sweat the onion and potato over a medium-high heat for 10 minutes. Add the finely sliced leek and cook for a further 5 minutes or just until the raw leek smell has disappeared.

Add the bouquet garni and the warmed stock to the pan, bring to the boil and reduce to a simmer. Add the cream and milk, and simmer for 10 minutes or until the potatoes are tender.

Remove the bouquet garni and liquidize the soup, then pass through a fine sieve into a clean pan. If necessary use a little more stock to thin out the soup.

Season with salt and warm through. Aerate the soup with a hand blender to make it frothy and light, then ladle into warm bowls. Chop the chives and garnish each bowl.

Onion soup

An amazing meaty effect is gained from caramelizing onions in the presence of star anise (p.37), and this recipe really showcases it. The technique is used both to make the stock and to sweat the onions.

A classic onion soup should have some form of bread topped with cheese floating in it. I like my bread fried and covered in really stringy cheese like Gruyère. For an even tastier topping, try replacing the Gruyère with the fondue recipe on p.231. Leave the fondue to cool and set, then place slices on the bread before grilling.

Serves 4

For the soup

	Groundnut or grapeseed oil
1kg	Peeled and finely sliced onion (approx. 5 large onions)
2	Star anise
30g	Unsalted butter
150g	Dry white wine
1kg	Beef stock (p.40)
2 tbsp	Dry Madeira, plus extra for finishing
	Salt and black pepper
	Sherry vinegar

To finish and serve

2	Slices of sourdough bread, halved
	Unsalted butter, for frying
	Dijon mustard
100g	Grated Gruyère cheese
1 tbsp	Chopped chives
2	Spring onions, finely sliced

Pre-heat the oven to 90°C.

To start the soup, heat a thin layer of oil in a casserole dish over a medium-high heat and sweat the onions with the star anise until lightly caramelized (approximately 15 minutes), stirring regularly to ensure they don't catch on the bottom.

Add the butter and 25g cold tap water, stir and put the casserole dish, covered, into the pre-heated oven for 7 hours, stirring occasionally.

After 7 hours, remove the star anise and discard. Place the dish over a high heat and deglaze the onions with the wine. Allow to reduce until almost dry.

Add the stock and simmer for 20 minutes.

Add the Madeira and simmer for another 20 minutes. Remove from the heat and season with salt, freshly ground pepper, more Madeira and sherry vinegar to taste.

When ready to serve, pre-heat the grill.

Fry the slices of sourdough bread in a little melted butter over a medium heat until golden and crisp. Spread each slice with Dijon mustard, then cover them with cheese and sprinkle with chopped chives and spring onions.

Ladle the soup into bowls and place a slice of the cheese-topped toast on top. Place the four bowls under the grill until the cheese turns golden brown.

Mushroom soup

Mushroom soup is a real nostalgia trip for me, as my mum used to give me canned mushroom soup when I was a kid. Mushrooms, like leeks, lose their fragrance if they're cooked too long. Once their aromas start to come off the pan, they're ready. So the onions and potatoes, which will take longer to cook, are softened a little in the pot first, and the leeks and mushrooms are added only 15 minutes before the stock.

The mushroom powder that garnishes this soup really makes a difference, introducing a powerful savoury taste, because it contains shiitake mushrooms, which are particularly high in umami (p.20). It's easy to make, can be stored in an airtight container for up to five months, and works well on any food that'll benefit from a boost of umami, like sauces and risottos, pasta and pizza, steak and omelettes. Keep it with your other condiments and use it as a seasoning and flavour enhancer.

Serves 4

For the mushroom powder

| 10g | Dried shiitake mushrooms |
| 10g | Dried porcini mushrooms |

For the soup

1.5kg	Vegetable stock (p.44)
160g	Unsalted butter
2	Onions, peeled and finely sliced
1	Small potato, peeled and finely sliced
2	Leeks, white part only, cleaned and finely sliced
800g	Button mushrooms, finely sliced
50g	Dry white vermouth
80g	Double cream
40g	Semi-skimmed milk
	Salt and black pepper

Pre-heat the oven to 150°C.

Roast the dried mushrooms for the mushroom powder on a baking tray for 5 minutes. Remove from the oven and allow to cool.

Blitz the dried mushrooms in a spice grinder or food processor and pass the powder through a fine sieve. Keep in an airtight container until ready to use.

To start the soup, gently heat the vegetable stock in a saucepan.

Melt the butter in another large saucepan over a medium heat and sweat the onion and potato without letting them colour (approximately 10 minutes). Add the leeks and mushrooms and cook until they begin to soften (approximately 15 minutes).

Turn the heat up to high and add the vermouth to the mushroom mixture. Allow it to reduce until almost all of the liquid has disappeared.

Pour the vegetable stock into the mushroom pan and add the double cream and milk. Bring to a boil and reduce to a simmer. Cook for a further 10 minutes. Remove from the heat and blitz in a blender until completely smooth.

Pass through a fine sieve and stir in salt and freshly ground pepper to taste. With a hand blender, aerate the soup for 60 seconds to make it light and frothy.

Ladle the soup into bowls. Sprinkle each bowl with a little of the mushroom powder just before serving.

Pumpkin soup

This is a silky, luxurious soup. Roasting half the pumpkin and sweating the other half in butter gives a more interesting range of pumpkin flavours. You need to search out a nicely ripe pumpkin, though, if you want it to really sing.

Almost any soup will benefit from elements that add flavour and texture contrasts. Here I've used hidden pumpkin seeds (for crunch and to extend the range of pumpkin flavours even further), roasted red pepper diamonds, toasted hazelnuts, red pepper oil (p.265) and brown butter (p.204). The latter is a fantastic way to finish off many dishes, bringing a delicious nuttiness.

Serves 6

For the soup

850g	Pumpkin flesh
	Olive oil
250g	Unsalted butter
3	Onions, peeled and finely sliced
400g	Whole milk
4	Sprigs of rosemary
	Pinch of cayenne pepper
40g	Sesame oil (or to taste)
40g	Balsamic vinegar (or to taste)
	Salt

To finish and serve

20g	Hazelnuts, toasted until golden brown
½	Sprig of rosemary
20g	Coarse dry breadcrumbs
1 tbsp	Melted brown butter (see tip, p.204)
1	Red pepper, de-seeded, roasted and peeled (see tip, p.157), then cut into diamonds
	Pumpkin seeds
	Red pepper oil (p.265)

Pre-heat the oven to 180°C.

To start the soup, thinly slice half of the pumpkin on a mandolin and cut the other half into large cubes.

Roast the large cubes of pumpkin drizzled with a little olive oil in the pre-heated oven for approximately 45 minutes or until soft and caramelized.

Melt 200g of the butter in a saucepan and sweat the onions and pumpkin slices for approximately 10 minutes.

In the meantime, in a second pan, heat the milk until almost simmering. Turn off the heat, add the rosemary, then allow to infuse for 20 minutes. Strain the liquid and discard the rosemary.

When the onions are translucent, add the rosemary milk, 600g cold tap water and the roasted pumpkin, bring to the boil and reduce to a simmer for 10 minutes until the sliced pumpkin is soft. Remove from the heat, liquidize and pass through a fine sieve. Season with cayenne, sesame oil, balsamic vinegar and salt.

When ready to serve, combine the toasted hazelnuts with the rosemary and blitz to a coarse powder. Combine with the breadcrumbs.

Brush the inside rim of the soup bowls with the brown butter and coat with the hazelnut and rosemary mixture.

Place some red pepper diamonds and pumpkin seeds in the bottom of each bowl.

Warm the soup, add the remaining 50g of butter and aerate with a hand blender. Ladle into the nut-encrusted bowls and garnish with drops of red pepper oil.

Red cabbage gazpacho

I serve a version of this at the Fat Duck, and diners love its fresh flavour and wonderful purpleness. The key to that flavour is juicing the final quarter of the cabbage into the soup at the last minute, so that you retain some of its peppery zing. It's served with mustard ice-cream (p.288), as cabbage contains mustard oil (where its pepperiness comes from). You could also serve the gazpacho – minus the ice-cream – as a summer appetizer in shot glasses.

Here I've used a red wine mayonnaise to help thicken the soup. The recipe will make more than you need (making less isn't really an option because you can't easily weigh out half an egg yolk), but the mayo will keep in the fridge for a week and it's superb with cold meats or in sandwiches. (For more about making mayonnaise, see p.118.)

Serves 4

For the red wine mayonnaise

1	Large egg yolk
10g	Dijon mustard
90g	Groundnut or grapeseed oil
10g	Red wine vinegar
15g	Red wine

For the gazpacho

1	Red cabbage
1	Slice of white sandwich bread, crusts removed
20g	Red wine mayonnaise (above)
30g	Red wine vinegar
	Salt

To finish and serve

¼	Cucumber, peeled, de-seeded and finely diced
4	Scoops of mustard ice-cream (p.288)

For the red wine mayonnaise, combine the egg yolk with the mustard in a bowl, then slowly whisk in the oil to form an emulsion.

When the emulsion is very stiff, stir in the vinegar and red wine until thoroughly combined. Cover with clingfilm and keep in the fridge until ready to use.

To start the gazpacho, remove the white core of the cabbage (which can be bitter), and juice three-quarters of the cabbage. Weigh out 250g juice.

Place the cabbage juice in a container with the bread and refrigerate for 2 hours.

Strain the juice through a fine sieve lined with muslin, using a ladle to press out as much juice as possible from the bread. (The bread releases starch into the juice, which will thicken it a little.) Discard the bread.

Just before serving, juice the remaining quarter of red cabbage and strain into the rest of the cabbage juice. Using a hand blender, mix the juice and the mayonnaise, then season with vinegar and salt.

When ready to serve, put a small mound of diced cucumber in the bottom of each bowl, then place a small scoop of mustard ice-cream on top. Pour the gazpacho around the ice-cream at the table.

Pea and ham soup

Some people might find it surprising that this recipe calls for frozen peas, but frozen peas are superior to all but the freshest of peas. Flash-freezing stops the breakdown of sugars, keeping the peas' sweetness. You also want to keep their vibrant green colour, which is best achieved by not cooking the peas at all, but simply adding them to the stock before liquidizing.

The recipe requires a fair bit of meat, not all of which makes it into the final dish. However, the cooking is easy – you just put the meat in the oven and forget about it for a few hours. This slow, low-temperature braising gives the gammon a nice soft texture and lots of flavour. Leftovers can be used in the toastie on p.232 or in the chicken and ham pies on p.143.

There's a lot of freedom with the stock. Instead of making a gammon stock from scratch, you could make the soup base using a vegetable stock (p.44) and adding pre-cooked shredded ham hock as you warm it ready for serving. Or, for a vegetarian version, use vegetable stock and leave out the gammon and bacon altogether.

Serves 4

For the soup

1	Small boneless gammon, weighing approx. 750g–1kg
1	Onion, peeled and sliced
1	Leek, white part only, cleaned and sliced
1	Carrot, peeled and sliced
900g	Frozen peas
65g	Unsalted butter
75g	Banana shallots, peeled and diced
1	Clove of garlic, peeled and finely chopped
160g	Unsmoked bacon, cut into lardons
	Salt and black pepper

To serve

Mint oil (p.265)

Pre-heat the oven to 85°C.

Place the gammon in an ovenproof saucepan with the onion, leek and carrot, then cover it with 1kg cold tap water. Bring to a simmer over a medium heat, then cover the pan and place in the pre-heated oven for 5 hours.

Allow the ham to cool in the stock, then remove and strain the stock into a bowl, through a sieve lined with two layers of wet muslin. Discard the vegetables and shred about 180g of the meat. Keep the rest chilled for another use.

In the meantime, spread the peas on a baking tray lined with kitchen paper and allow to defrost completely. (The paper absorbs the excess liquid that would otherwise dilute the pea flavour.)

Melt 25g of the butter in a saucepan and add the shallot, garlic and bacon. Cook for 5 minutes over a medium heat until soft but not coloured.

Add 750g of the ham stock, bring to the boil and simmer for 5 minutes. Add all but 75g of the peas and the remaining butter and remove from the heat immediately. Liquidize this mixture thoroughly, in batches if necessary.

Strain through a fine sieve, pressing through as many solids as possible, and pour into a clean pan. Season with salt and freshly ground pepper.

When ready to serve, gently reheat the soup. With a hand blender, aerate the soup until light and frothy, then add the ham and the remaining 75g of peas.

Carefully ladle the soup into four bowls and drizzle each bowl with mint oil.

Chestnut velouté with duck confit

Velouté means 'velvety' in French. Traditionally a velouté is thickened with a roux, but this can mute the flavour and make the soup a little heavy and starchy, so I look for other ways of thickening. Here the chestnuts do the job.

Serving the velouté with duck confit turns it into a wonderful dish. But starting your preparations a couple of days in advance, which confits demand, will not always be convenient, so you might want to leave the duck out. It's still a superb soup without it. You can serve it in espresso cups as an appetizer or at a party. And you could make a vegetarian version, using vegetable stock (p.44) instead of chicken, and leaving out the bacon.

Seasoning with a few drops of sherry vinegar at the end will make a real difference, cutting through the richness.

Serves 6

For the chestnut velouté

120g	Brown butter (see tip, p.204)
4	Slices of smoked bacon, roughly chopped
1	Banana shallot, peeled and finely sliced
1	Leek, white part only, cleaned and finely sliced
4	Sprigs of thyme
200g	Dry Madeira
250g	White port
1kg	White chicken stock (p.38)
400g	Vacuum-packed peeled chestnuts, roughly chopped
100g	Double cream
200g	Semi-skimmed milk
	Salt and white pepper
	Sherry vinegar

To finish and serve

	Duck confit from the potted duck (p.96), coarsely shredded
	A little duck fat
40g	Hazelnuts, toasted until golden brown and blitzed to a coarse powder

Melt the brown butter in a saucepan over a medium heat and reserve a little to coat the rims of the bowls (see below).

Add the bacon to the saucepan and cook for 5 minutes. Add the shallot, leek and thyme, and continue to cook, stirring regularly, until the bacon has browned and the vegetables are soft and translucent (approximately 7 minutes).

Increase the heat to high, add the Madeira and white port, and bring to the boil to reduce the liquid to a syrup.

Add the chicken stock and bring to a simmer. Reduce the heat to medium and add the chestnuts. Return to a simmer for 20 minutes, adding the cream and milk after 15 minutes.

Blitz with a hand blender, then pass through a fine sieve.

Season with salt and freshly ground white pepper (bearing in mind the duck confit is quite salty), and add a few drops of sherry vinegar.

To finish and serve, gently heat the duck meat in a little duck fat.

Brush the inside rim (about 2cm deep) of six soup bowls with the remaining brown butter and coat with the hazelnut powder.

Drain the duck meat and place a small amount in the bottom of each bowl. Using a hand blender, aerate the soup, then pour it over the duck and serve.

Szechuan broth with duck dumplings

This has lots of wonderful Asian flavours. It requires a bit of planning and preparation – you need to start at least two days in advance in order to ice-filter the stock (p.54) – but the end result looks and tastes spectacular. Of course you don't have to make the whole dish. The soup can be served on its own, garnished with the same sort of ingredients as the Marmite consommé on p.70, and the dumplings also work well on their own.

You will need a pressure cooker for this recipe.

Serves 8

For the consommé

1kg	Chicken wings
1.5kg	Pork ribs, cut into individual ribs
	Groundnut or grapeseed oil
1	Large onion, peeled and finely sliced
3	Star anise
180g	Shaoxing wine (Specialist ingredients, p.395), or Manzanilla sherry
75g	Peeled and finely sliced fresh root ginger
1 tsp	Szechuan peppercorns (Specialist ingredients, p.395)
1	Cinnamon stick (approx. 8–10cm)

To finish and serve

40g	Spring onions
	Salt
	Duck dumplings (below)

Pre-heat the oven to 200°C.

Rub the chicken wings and ribs with a little groundnut or grapeseed oil and place on separate baking trays. Roast in the pre-heated oven for 45–60 minutes, turning occasionally, until both wings and ribs have become golden brown all over.

Coat the bottom of a pressure cooker with a thin layer of oil and place over a medium heat. Add the onion with the star anise and sweat until soft and lightly caramelized (approximately 12 minutes).

Add the Shaoxing wine and boil to reduce by half. Add the ginger, Szechuan peppercorns, cinnamon stick, roasted ribs and wings and 1.5kg water, and bring to a simmer.

Place the lid on the pressure cooker and bring up to full pressure over a high heat. Reduce the heat to low and cook for 2 hours.

Take the pressure cooker off the heat and allow to cool completely before removing the lid. Strain the liquid through a sieve lined with two layers of wet muslin.

Filter the stock by ice filtration (p.54).

When ready to serve, pour the filtered consommé into a clean saucepan and gently heat. Finely slice the spring onions and add them to the consommé, then season with salt. Put a steamed dumpling (or more) in each bowl, pour over some consommé, and serve.

Duck dumplings

These delicious little dumplings would work just as well as a canapé or as part of a dim-sum style menu.

Makes 40 dumplings

For the Shaoxing jelly

180g	Shaoxing wine (Specialist ingredients, p.395)
6g	Leaves of gelatine, softened in cold tap water

For the Savoy cabbage

65g	Unsalted butter
180g	Savoy cabbage, washed and finely shredded

For the duck mixture

200g	Skinless duck breast, sliced
1 tsp	Salt
1½ tsp	Skimmed milk powder
6	Ice cubes
60g	Duck fat
1	Large egg

continued overleaf

40g	Light soy sauce (Specialist ingredients, p.395)
35g	Sesame oil
15g	Peeled and grated fresh root ginger
4	Spring onions, very finely chopped
½ tsp	Finely ground and sifted black pepper

To wrap the dumplings

40	Square wonton wrappers (Specialist ingredients, p.395)

For the jelly, place the Shaoxing wine in a small saucepan over a medium-high heat and, when simmering, flame off the alcohol (see tip, p.153).

Squeeze the softened gelatine, stir in to the wine until fully dissolved, then pour into a small, clean baking tray (20 × 30cm) and place in the fridge to set. When set, cut into 1cm cubes and keep refrigerated.

To cook the cabbage, melt half the butter in a frying pan over a medium heat. Add the shredded cabbage and sauté until it starts to wilt (approximately 5 minutes).

Add the remaining butter and reduce the heat to low. Cover the pan with a lid and leave to cook slowly for approximately 40 minutes, stirring occasionally to ensure that the cabbage doesn't catch on the bottom of the pan (add a little water if this starts to happen). The cabbage should be really soft.

Remove from the heat and allow to cool to room temperature before adding to the duck mixture.

When ready to start the duck mixture, place the mixing bowl and blade of a food processor in the freezer for 15 minutes or until very cold.

Place approximately 20g of the duck meat in the cold mixing bowl with the salt (this will help to extract the protein from the meat, which is necessary for a good texture), and blitz to a paste with the cold blade. Place in the fridge in the mixing bowl for 1 hour together with the food processor blade.

After 1 hour, add the remaining fresh meat and the skimmed milk powder to the salted meat in the cold mixing bowl. Purée this with the ice cubes.

Add the duck fat, egg, soy sauce and sesame oil, and blitz until thoroughly incorporated and the meat becomes a fine paste. Fold in the grated ginger, spring onions, the black pepper and the cooked Savoy cabbage.

To assemble the dumplings, lay the wonton wrappers on a clean work surface, then place a teaspoon of the meat in the middle of each wrapper and flatten it gently.

Place 2 cubes of the Shaoxing jelly in the middle of the meat. Wet the outer edge of each wonton wrapper with water, then gather the wrapper around the meat and jelly and pinch closed the top. Place on a tray covered with a damp paper towel and reserve in the fridge until needed, or steam immediately for 6 minutes (in batches if necessary).

Marmite consommé

Marmite – you either love it or hate it. I happen to love it for its big wallop of umami (p.20). Here it's the key ingredient for a very full-flavoured vegetarian soup. I originally developed this consommé as part of a Fat Duck recipe that took the elements of a classic meaty dish – pot au feu – and gave them a vegetarian twist.

But on its own it makes a terrific soup that you can take in all sorts of directions, simply by adding different garnishes at the end – blanched baby vegetables, wilted spinach, poached eggs, raw enoki mushrooms or indeed any sort of mushrooms, cooked pasta or noodles all work really well.

It's also a great addition to your vegetarian stock armoury, as it does not contain gelatine. (This is why the recipe employs the traditional 'egg-raft' form of clarification rather than ice filtration, see p.53.) The intense flavour of a Marmite consommé means that it's a good vegetarian substitute for beef stock in the onion soup on p.57.

You will need a pressure cooker for this recipe.

Serves 4

For the consommé

750g	Brown butter, strained (see tip, p.204)
1kg	Peeled and finely sliced onion (approx. 5 large onions)
1kg	Cleaned and finely sliced leek, white part only (approx. 20 leeks)
500g	Peeled and finely sliced carrot (approx. 6–7 large carrots)
750g	Red wine
3	Large egg whites

To finish and serve

10g	Sherry vinegar (or to taste)
½ tsp	Marmite (or to taste)
	Salt and black pepper

To start the consommé, melt the brown butter in a pressure cooker over a medium heat and sweat the onion, leek and carrot until soft (approximately 15 minutes).

In the meantime, bring the wine to the boil in a saucepan and flame off the alcohol (see tip, p.153). Boil to reduce by one-third to 500g.

Add 250g cold tap water and the reduced wine to the vegetables. Place the lid on the pressure cooker and bring up to full pressure over a high heat. Reduce the heat to low and cook for 1 hour.

Take the pressure cooker off the heat and allow to cool completely before removing the lid.

Strain the broth through a fine sieve into a bowl and place in the fridge overnight to allow the fat to separate from the broth. Remove the fat and reserve (this can be used to cook vegetables, melt over steaks or finish sauces).

Pour the broth into a clean pan, and filter using egg filtration (p.54).

When ready to serve, warm the consommé, add the sherry vinegar and Marmite, and season with salt and freshly ground pepper.

Garnish with your choice from the suggestions above.

Starters

Green tea and lime palate cleanser 82
Tea-smoked salmon 85
Soy-marinated roe 86
Blinis 86
Soused herrings 87
Konbu-cured halibut 89
Hay-smoked mackerel 90
Scallop tartare with white chocolate 93
Brûléed chicken liver parfait 94
Potted duck 96
Lamb jelly with cucumber salad 98
Bagna cauda 100
Lentils cooked in smoked water with peach and goat's cheese 102
Brûléed mushroom parfait 103
Mushroom jelly with mushroom cream 105
Scotch eggs 107

A starter doesn't have to satisfy hunger – that's the job of the main course. Its role is to whet the appetite and get the saliva going. It should be, in the most literal sense, mouthwatering. And so a number of the recipes in this chapter depend on traditional but under-used techniques like curing, pickling and smoking that create intense, sharp flavours to really stimulate the palate. I've made use of flavour encapsulation (p.23) in the soy-marinated roe (p.86) and the lamb and mushroom jellies (pp.98 and 105), to create dishes that give a nice burst of flavour – a perfect start to a meal. There's also a fantastic palate cleanser, as I've always liked the feeling of sitting down to eat with a mouth that is as neutral and clean-tasting as possible, ready for the flavours it's about to experience.

When cooking for a lunch or dinner party, if you're laying on a menu of three courses, you've got your work cut out, no matter how simple the recipes. So it's wise to have parts of the menu that buy you a bit of breathing space, and a lot of these starters can be made in advance. A number of them still involve techniques that need patience and precision – making chicken liver parfait (p.94) with a supremely smooth texture will require an extremely gentle cook in a bain-marie – but some of the work can be done beforehand, leaving you free on the day to concentrate on the intricacies of the main and dessert. Most of these starters can also easily be turned into light meals, accompanied by good bread or a salad.

Curing

Curing was originally a method of salting food in order to preserve it. However, it is also a superb technique for changing the texture and flavour of all kinds of food: Cheddar, chorizo and sauerkraut, for example, all have had a degree of salting. The most familiar products of curing are probably the wonderful hams – Bayonne, Parma, *pata negra* – created by salting pork, but it also has a transformative effect on fish, which is the focus of the curing recipes in this chapter.

What salt does is remove water from food (think of degorging aubergines), which firms up the texture and concentrates the flavours, as they are, literally, less watered-down. It's also a good medium for introducing extra flavours. Mix aromatic ingredients – spices, herbs, even citrus fruits or tea leaves – with salt, pack the mixture round some food and, as the salt draws moisture out, the aromas go into the food. Adding aromatics is a great opportunity for culinary creativity, though obviously you have to make sure the ingredients complement the dish. It needs to be subtly done because it's very easy to overpower delicate flavours.

Although salt is a major player in a cure mix, doing most of the work of drawing out the water, it can be combined with sugar, which also removes water and can generate extra flavours. The ratio of salt to sugar you use depends on how much sweetness you want the cure to impart and how much you want the salt to alter the flesh. The salt or salt-sugar cure can be incorporated with aromatics in a number of ways. In these recipes they're generally blitzed to a powder together in a food processor or spice grinder. But there are occasions when blitzing is best avoided. If you're using tea leaves in a cure, blitzing might extract too much bitterness. Instead they should be moistened to help flavour transference (but be careful: too much moisture will start dissolving the salt and sugar and ruin the cure). And if hardy herbs like rosemary or thyme are cut too much they can lose some of their fragrance and acquire an unwelcome damp-leaf characteristic. In these cases, it's better to increase the amount of herb you're using, pick the leaves and add them whole.

The length of time that the food stays in the fridge during curing is, like the cure mix, a variable to be adjusted according to the effect you want. A brief cure will keep the flesh tender but impart a limited amount of flavour. A longer cure will create more flavour and the food will keep for longer, but it'll also be denser, saltier and drier. So you need to consider what combination of characteristics you're looking for. It's a balancing act that may take a bit of experimentation before you come up with the timing that suits you for a particular dish.

Once the cure has done its work to the level you want, the food should be lifted out of it and as much of the mixture as possible scraped off the flesh. Rinse in cold water, pat dry and return it to the fridge, uncovered, so that it dries out a little. After which the food can be eaten, perhaps with a dressing, as with the konbu-cured halibut on p.89, or taken a step further and smoked, as with the tea-smoked salmon on p.85 and the hay-smoked mackerel on p.90, or cooked, as in the umami broth on p.183.

Smoking

Like curing, smoking is an ancient cooking technique that was originally used to preserve food. The smoke would dry the food and seal the surface, preventing it from going rancid, while some of compounds in the smoke would inhibit the activity of microbes and enzymes that would otherwise quickly spoil it.

But – again, like curing – smoking is also a fantastic way to introduce an extra flavour dimension. Most of you will be familiar with smoked salmon and kippers, but almost anything can be smoked: not just fish but poultry and other meat, sugar and salt (a pinch of smoked sea salt enhances a seared steak no end), fruit and vegetables, cheese, fat (I cook fennel in smoked duck fat, p.205) and even water (which I use to cook lentils, p.102). Smoking can, indeed, be very addictive, and you can find yourself experimenting to create all kinds of effects. For years I've been searching for the exact combination of ingredients that will produce the soft, smooth, ashy smell of the embers in a cottage hearth.

You can smoke food over an open fire – chucking a few rosemary branches under the lamb chops on a barbecue, for example, towards the end of cooking – but the technique works best in an enclosed space, so that the smoke is contained and concentrated. You don't even have to have special equipment to do this: you can simply put wood chips into a frying pan on the highest heat. Wait until the wood is smoking (you can speed this up by using a blow-torch as well), then put, say, a piece of fish in the pan on a small circular cake-rack, cover the pan with foil to ensure it's well-sealed, put the lid on and let it smoke for a while. But if, like me, you get hooked, it's probably best to invest in a smoker (a smoking tin or home smoking box). This needn't be expensive. The basic version, which looks rather like a lidded roasting tin with a small trivet inside, should work fine.

The most traditional combustible stuff used for smoking is wood which, when it burns, breaks down into compounds that have caramel, vanilla and clove aromas. Oak is commonly used in Britain because it has a good balance of the substances that give these characteristics, and fruit-tree woods are also popular, though I'm not yet convinced that their fruit flavours come through in the smoke. I've eaten Peking duck smoked by cherry-tree wood where I thought I could detect a fruity aroma, and that's about it. But you can decide for yourselves: many types of wood chip for smoking are available online, from apple, oak, maple and hickory to walnut and pecan.

Whatever contribution particular trees might make, they're only going to do so near the beginning of the process. The heated sap might possibly give a certain flavouring but once the wood has blackened to the point where it's like charcoal the only flavour it's going to impart is a carbonized one. (You can see the truth of this if you chuck those rosemary branches on the barbie. It's when the rosemary first begins to burn that all the aromas comes out. By the time the leaves are all shrivelled and blackened they're not giving off that resinous scent any more.)

You can use anything that'll create a pleasant aroma when smoked. Tea leaves are another option. Obviously you have to take into account the flavour characteristics of each tea, but at its best tea-smoking can introduce a delicate, almost perfumed note to a dish. For instance, lapsang souchong has a distinct smokiness even before it's set alight. A piece of salmon would stand up to this well, but for other foods lapsang might be overkill.

Another idea is to use an essential oil. Try smoking scallops like this. Put a frying pan on the highest heat until it's smoking hot. Put scallops on a circular cake-rack and place inside the pan, add a few drops of an essential oil you think might work (health-food shops stock a broad range, from the delicate to the pungent), then cover the pan with foil and a lid and leave for a couple of minutes, after which they can be cooked as normal.

Whatever combustible material you choose, there are two methods for smoking food: hot-smoking and cold-smoking. Hot-smoking is where you light the wood chips or tea leaves, and allow them to both flavour and cook the foodstuff. However, you don't always want the food to cook as it takes on its smoked flavour. If you're smoking a fish, for example, that has already been cured (p.76) or brined (p.170), it will have effectively been cooked already, so any further cooking would render it overdone. Then there are delicate things like a smoked mayonnaise, which won't stand much heat and ought not to be cooked anyway. This is where cold-smoking comes into its own. For both methods, however, the technique is the same, except for one detail: with cold-smoking, ice is added to the smoker to keep the contents cool. With hot-smoking, no ice is used. (Of course, you're not confined to cooking and smoking by means of hot-smoking. You can also cold-smoke food first and then cook it.)

It's important, too, to bear in mind that there are a number of factors that influence how much and how quickly a food is smoked. Size and density need to be taken into account: a small piece of fish with a delicate structure will take on smoke more readily than a duck or chicken breast. The size of the container and the amount of combustible material used will also affect the results. It's best to have as little empty space as possible in the smoker in order for the smoke to perform its magic properly.

In addition to these factors, the amount of time the food is subjected to the smoke is a variable that can be controlled in order to get the results you want. I've found that, in general, 30 minutes is the period of time that gets the most out of a smoking, but obviously the physical character of the foodstuff has to be factored in. I've smoked candyfloss, for example, which has so much surface area that it takes on flavour in seconds. This is an extreme, but popcorn takes only about 5 minutes. Smoking is a technique that lends itself to experimenting just to find out what happens. Smoke something for half an hour and see if it's got the flavour you want. If it's too mild, give it another 30 minutes and taste again. In my tea-smoked salmon recipe (p.85), the fish is smoked three times to get a decent build-up of smoke for just the right suffusion of jasmine.

How to smoke food

Whether you are cold- or hot-smoking, the process involves fire – and smoke. Smoke is very invasive, so to prevent alarms going off and your house smelling like it's fire-damaged, you should do smoking outdoors. (If inside, have the extractor hood switched on and plenty of doors and windows open.)

1. If cold-smoking, put a container of ice under the rack in a smoking tin or box. If hot-smoking, omit the ice. Place the food on the rack.

2. Put the smoking chips in a corner of the tin and set them alight. Seal the tin and leave for 30 minutes.

3. Repeat this process up to two more times, depending on the level of smokiness you want.

Pickling

Pickling (or sousing) began as a method of preserving food throughout winter by putting it in some form of acid, usually vinegar. (Originally verjuice, the juice of unripe grapes, apples or crab-apples, and the medieval forerunner of vinegar, would have been used.) Meats and fish were pickled, but the technique was applied mainly to vegetables. These sharp flavours might have been forced upon us through necessity, but our taste for that lovely lively acidity has remained – think of Branston pickle, Worcestershire sauce, mango chutney and, of course, tomato ketchup.

You can pickle pretty much what you want. Here you'll find recipes for soused herrings (p.87), pickled cucumber (p.268), pickled lemons (p.268) and a couple of chutneys (pp.270 and 271). But you can pickle other fruit and veg (butternut squash is delicious pickled, and mushrooms make an amazing ketchup), and you can pickle meat, herbs and nuts. Bear in mind that whatever you use has to be able to stand up to the sharpness and gutsiness of the pickling ingredients. Some vegetables might have to be gently cooked to soften them up a little, but a pickle should have a bit of texture to it, so don't overcook them. Other than a bit of chopping, things like cucumber and lemon are often pickled more or less as they are.

All manner of flavourings and aromatics can be infused into the acidic liquid to give it complexity – bay leaves, dill, allspice berries, juniper berries, pink peppercorns, thyme, cinnamon, ginger, curry powder and other typical curry spices. Obviously these need to be robust enough to make their presence felt, but not so powerful that during infusion they come to dominate the rest of the flavours. (Rosemary, for example, would be too strong.) Pickling is a great way to experiment with flavouring, and it needs no elaborate equipment. Put acid and sugar in a pan and heat them gently so that the sugar dissolves, then add the aromatics. The warmth of the liquid will encourage the herbs and spices to release their flavourings, and a long, steady infusion takes place as the liquid cools down. Then the food is placed in the pickle or souse for the desired length of time.

Cooking in a bain-marie

The bain-marie is a technique for cooking certain things very gently and evenly. You'll come across a stovetop form of it later in the book, as a way of melting chocolate (p.304), but in this chapter we're concerned with cooking custards in the oven.

Most of us think of custard as the pale liquid you pour on to fruit crumbles or hot puddings, but a custard can mean any egg-based mixture that is cooked until it has set. It can be sweet, as in a crème brûlée (p.326) or crème caramel, or it can be savoury, like the chicken liver parfait (p.94) and the mushroom parfait (p.103), but either way, the key to successful custard cooking is a low temperature and a moist environment. The classic method for doing this is a bain-marie. This is basically a deep roasting tray into which are placed uncooked custards in ramekins, and just-boiled water is then poured around them. The water needs to be just-boiled rather than cold because in a low-temperature oven it would take hours for cold water to reach the right temperature. Once this is done, the tray is tightly covered with foil and put in the oven.

Cooking the custards in a tray filled with water means that all the heat is applied to the food through the same medium – water – and at the same steady rate. And, since the oven's thermostat can be set to a specific temperature, it's easy to prevent the custards from overheating. Since you're going to some trouble to engineer that it's the water that cooks the custard, it's wise to make sure that the water level in the baking tray and the top of the custard in the ramekin are at about the same height, so the water can do the job efficiently. Setting this level about two-thirds of the way up the ramekins, once they are in the tray, is a practical measure, and also makes the tray easier to manhandle into the oven without slopping.

When cooking the chicken liver parfait (p.94), there are a couple of pitfalls to avoid before you get to the cooking stage. If the original ingredients aren't at the same temperature when they're combined, the warmer ones can start cooking the colder ones and the mixture might split or end up grainy. My solution is to put the ingredients in sandwich bags and place them in warm (50°C) water for 10 minutes. It adds an extra step to the process, but it's worth it as a precaution. Equally, it's important to pass the incorporated mixture through a fine sieve lined with a double layer of muslin. Again, this adds another step to the process, but it's essential in order to prevent the mixture going grainy.

The perfect baked custard should be set but completely smooth and creamy. This takes time and shouldn't be rushed. You can't really make a brûlée in the afternoon and serve it the same evening. Ideally, the custard needs to rest overnight in the fridge – that's the best way to gain the unique delicate texture you're looking for.

How to bake a custard in a bain-marie

As a further protection for the custards from the direct heat of the base of the roasting tray, you can line it with parchment paper with a few holes pierced in it.

1. Pre-heat the oven to 110°C. Have a deep roasting tray at the ready.

2. Pour the egg-based mixture into ramekin dishes so that they are two-thirds full. Place the ramekins in the tray and pour just-boiled water into the tray so that it reaches two-thirds of the way up the ramekins.

3. Cover the tray tightly with foil and place it on the middle shelf of the pre-heated oven. After 15 minutes, start checking to see if the custards have reached the right internal temperature by carefully removing the foil and inserting a digital probe into the centre of the parfait.

4. Once the correct temperature has been reached, remove the roasting tray from the oven, take the ramekins out of the water and allow them to cool at room temperature for 20 minutes before placing in the fridge to chill for at least 6 hours, but preferably overnight.

Green tea and lime palate cleanser

At the Fat Duck, we serve a palate cleanser similar to this right at the beginning of the tasting menu, but it works equally well as an appetizer on a hot summer's day. The refreshing, slightly icy granita (a sort of coarse sorbet, p.278) along with the light green tea foam creates a very nice contrast of textures and temperatures in the mouth. Green tea has amazing palate-cleansing properties, while the acidity of the lime juice gets the saliva going and makes the mouth water, whetting the appetite.

Serves 8–10

For the green tea syrup

200g	Fructose (fruit sugar)
15g	Pectin powder
30g	Green tea leaves
	Zest of 2 limes, removed with a peeler
½ tsp	Salt

For the green tea and lime foam

200g	Lime juice (approx. 10 limes)
120g	Egg whites (approx. 4 large eggs)
50g	Vodka
½ tsp	Matcha green tea powder (Specialist ingredients, p.394)

For the lime granita

90g	Fructose (fruit sugar)
45g	Lime juice (approx. 2–3 limes)

To serve

1 tbsp	Matcha green tea powder, wrapped in muslin, for dusting

For the green tea syrup, bring 1kg water to the boil in a saucepan.

Sift the fructose and the pectin together, add to the water and bring back to the boil. Simmer for 5 minutes, then remove from the heat and allow to cool completely.

When cold, add the green tea and lime zest (rolled between fingers to release the oils) to the syrup and leave to infuse for 2 hours. Pass through a fine sieve, discarding the zest, and set aside. Add the salt.

For the green tea and lime foam, mix 650g of the green tea syrup and the lime juice with the egg whites, vodka and green tea powder.

Pour this into a cream whipper charged with two N_2O gas charges (p.356). Place in the fridge for at least 20 minutes before using.

For the lime granita, place the fructose and 450g cold tap water in a saucepan over a medium-high heat and bring to the boil. Remove from the heat and allow to cool completely.

When cold, stir the lime juice into the syrup.

Pour the liquid into a small deep-sided baking tray and place in the freezer. Whisk the mixture with a fork every 20–30 minutes until it crystallizes (approximately 1 hour 30 minutes).

Meanwhile, place eight to ten shot glasses in the freezer for 30 minutes.

When ready to serve, put a tablespoon of the granita into each of the frozen glasses.

Top each glass up with a squirt of the foam, then dust the surface with the green tea powder. Serve with teaspoons.

Tea-smoked salmon

Salmon responds well to smoking (p.76) because of its oiliness. Fat holds on to flavour, so the fish can really take on a smoked aspect, and the fat also keeps the salmon from drying out too much.

You can of course buy smoked salmon in any supermarket, but smoking your own gives a much more individual, distinct flavour – and a real sense of achievement. The recipe uses jasmine tea to flavour the smoke but other teas can be used – Earl Grey, lapsang souchong, Darjeeling – each of which will bring a different character to the fish.

Serves 6–8

330g	Salt
165g	White granulated sugar
5g	Chopped dill
30g	Jasmine tea leaves
500g	Salmon, skinned, pin bones removed

To make the cure, mix the salt, sugar and dill together thoroughly.

Moisten 15g of the jasmine tea leaves with a little water and allow to stand for 5 minutes, then spread them all over the salmon.

Put a layer of the cure on the bottom of a container and rest the salmon on top. Completely hide the salmon with the remaining cure. Cover the container with clingfilm and put into the fridge for 16 hours.

Remove the salmon from the cure and rinse thoroughly. Leave to rest in the fridge for 2–3 hours until the fish is dry but a little sticky.

Place a small container of ice under a rack in a smoking tin. Place the fish on the rack.

Place the remaining jasmine tea leaves in the corner of the tin and set them alight. Seal the tin and leave for 30 minutes. Remove the lid and light the leaves again, then re-seal. Repeat this process one more time.

Slice the fish thinly with a very sharp knife and serve with brown bread or blinis (p.86), pickled cucumber (p.268) and soured cream butter (p.260). If not serving immediately, wrap tightly in clingfilm and keep in the fridge for up to a week.

Soy-marinated roe

Salmon roe have a wonderful burst-on-the-tongue texture to rival any jelly, making them a lovely way to garnish blinis (right) or prawn cocktail (p.125). The Japanese-style marinade is simple to do but gives the roe an incredibly sophisticated flavour. It's important to rinse the roe before adding them to the marinade because this removes the film on the surface, giving them a clearer, fresher flavour.

Makes enough for approx. 20 blinis

50g	Mirin (Specialist ingredients, p.394)
	Light soy sauce (Specialist ingredients, p.395)
50g	Salmon roe (sometimes called salmon caviar)

To serve

Blinis (right)
Crème fraiche
Chives

Pour the mirin into a small saucepan and place over a medium heat.

Once it begins to simmer, set the liquid alight in order to burn off the alcohol (see tip, p.153). As soon as the flames die away, remove the pan from the heat.

Weigh the mirin, then transfer it to a bowl. Weigh out the same amount each of cold tap water and light soy sauce and first add the water to the mirin in the bowl. Allow to cool to room temperature before adding the light soy sauce.

Gently rinse the salmon roe by placing in a fine sieve under cold running water until the water is no longer cloudy, then allow to drain.

Add the roe to the marinade a few minutes before serving. Drain, then place the roe on blinis with a little crème fraiche and garnish with freshly chopped chives.

Blinis

You can, of course, buy blinis from a shop, but nothing beats home-made ones. They're much plumper and lighter when they're freshly cooked, the perfect base for some soured cream, crème fraiche or mayo with a spoonful of soy-marinated roe (left), a piece of soused herring (opposite) with beetroot relish (p.269), a slice of tea-smoked salmon (p.85) with a dollop of vanilla mayonnaise (p.118), or shop-bought taramasalata.

It's very important to rest the blini batter for at least an hour to give it a lighter texture.

Makes approx. 40 blinis

140g	Plain flour
1 tsp	White caster sugar
¼ tsp	Bicarbonate of soda
½ tsp	Salt
3	Large eggs, separated (the recipe uses 2 egg yolks and 3 egg whites)
120g	Whole milk
50g	Unsalted butter, melted and allowed to cool, plus extra, for cooking the blinis

Put the flour, sugar, bicarbonate of soda, salt, two egg yolks, milk and melted butter into a mixing bowl and whisk together thoroughly to create a smooth batter. Allow to rest for at least 1 hour.

Whip the three egg whites until soft peaks form, then carefully fold a third of them into the batter using a spatula, followed by the remaining two-thirds.

Place a non-stick frying pan over a medium-high heat and add a knob of butter. When the butter is foaming, use a teaspoon to drop small amounts of the batter into the pan (they should each spread to 5–6cm in diameter).

When lightly brown on one side, flip the blinis over to brown on the other side. Remove from the pan and allow to cool on kitchen roll. Repeat this process for the rest of the batter. Use within a couple of hours, or you can freeze for up to 2 weeks.

Soused herrings

Dating back to Roman times, the technique of sousing is familiar throughout northern Europe. Originally a method of preservation, it is now used more as a way of flavouring fish, introducing a piquant, pickled characteristic. No heat is applied to the fish – it 'cooks' in the cold spiced vinegar.

Serves 8

18%	Brine (180g salt dissolved in 1kg tap water)
8	Herring fillets, skin on
600g	White wine vinegar
200g	White caster sugar
250g	Peeled and sliced onion (approx. 3–4 medium onions)
1	Bay leaf
10	Black peppercorns, crushed
2	Allspice berries, crushed
1	Sprig of thyme, leaves chopped

Pour the brine into a bowl and if necessary cool to room temperature before placing the herrings in the brine in the fridge for 3 hours.

After 3 hours, wash the herrings at least three times in fresh cold water. Discard the brine.

Put the white wine vinegar and sugar into a saucepan and bring to the boil. Put the onion, bay leaf, peppercorns, allspice and thyme into a container, and pour the boiling liquid over them. Leave to cool completely.

When the souse is cool, add the herrings, cover and leave in the fridge for at least 2 days.

Drain well and serve with beetroot relish (p.269).

Konbu-cured halibut

Curing white fish – allowing them to come into contact with salt before (or instead of) cooking – helps to improve the texture of the flesh, making it denser and moister. This simple cure is Japanese, using konbu (giant kelp) to enhance the umami taste (p.20) in the halibut. It's a delicious preparation that can be used to cure any other thick, meaty white fish, such as cod, brill and turbot. (For more about curing, see p.76, and salting and brining, see p.170.)

Serves 4–6

1	Halibut fillet, skinned and halved lengthways (to remove the bones), approx. 300–400g
4	Dried konbu sheets, soaked in cold tap water until soft (Specialist ingredients, p.394)
50g	Dried konbu sheets
110g	Salt
50g	White caster sugar

Place each half of the halibut fillet between two sheets of the soaked konbu and wrap tightly in clingfilm. Leave in the fridge overnight.

Pre-heat the oven to 100°C.

Place the 50g of dried konbu in the oven for 1 hour 30 minutes to 2 hours until it breaks in half easily. Put the dried konbu in a spice grinder or food processor and blitz to a powder. Remove approximately 10g of the powder and mix the rest with the salt and sugar for the cure.

Unwrap the fillets, reserving the konbu sheets, and dust both sides of the fish with the loose 10g of konbu powder.

Lay two sheets of clingfilm on the work surface, and place a sheet of konbu on each. Generously coat the fillets with the cure and lay them on the konbu sheets on the clingfilm. Top with the remaining konbu sheets. Roll up the clingfilm, leaving the ends slightly open for any juices to run out. Place the two rolls on a drying rack over a tray and place in the fridge for 30 minutes.

Unwrap the cured fillets, then rinse under cold running water and pat dry.

Slice thinly with a sharp knife and serve with ponzu sauce (p.266), wasabi mayonnaise (p.118) and salad leaves.

Hay-smoked mackerel

I like smoking foods (p.76), and I like smoking with hay, which is easily obtainable from a pet shop, and gives fish a lovely and delicate smoked flavour. It needs to be done outdoors as there'll be flames and smoke, so it's probably one for the summer.

Hay-smoking is a technique that can be used not just for fish but also chicken, sausages and other meats, cheese or anything else that can be put in a clamp and placed on a barbecue. (If you're feeling adventurous you could try smoking fruit – bananas work really well.) The hay will burn in seconds, creating plenty of smoke but little heat: it doesn't cook the food. So, unless the food you're smoking can be eaten raw (bananas, for example), it'll have to be cured first so it's ready to eat, or put on the barbecue after it has been smoked.

The cure in this recipe is a nice simple one that works for all oily fish. Here, because the mackerel fillets are so thin, it is only needed for two hours. (For more about curing, see p.76, and salting and brining, see p.170.)

Serves 4

1 tbsp	Coriander seeds
50g	White caster sugar
50g	Salt
	Zest of 1 lemon, finely grated
	Zest of 1 lime, finely grated
4	Fresh mackerel fillets, with the skin on

For the smoking

Meadow hay

Place the coriander seeds in a spice grinder or food processor and blitz thoroughly. Mix with the sugar, salt, lemon and lime zest.

Sprinkle the cure on to a tray and lay the mackerel fillets on top, flesh-side down. Cover with clingfilm and place in the fridge for 2 hours.

Rinse the fillets under cold running water to remove the cure, and dry well with kitchen paper.

Lay the fillets skin-side down on a board. Cut a small piece of flesh off the narrower tail end of the fillet, but don't cut all the way through. Remove this small piece and hold the flap of skin that remains attached to the fish firmly in one hand. With the other hand, use the knife to gently cut the flesh of the fish from the skin. This removes the tough outer membrane of the fish, but leaves the shiny silver pattern.

Line a barbecue fish clamp with plenty of meadow hay, ensuring it's not packed so tightly that air can't circulate. Wrap the fish fillets in damp muslin (if you want to avoid having to clean off bits of burnt hay from fillets), then place them in a single layer on the hay. Cover with more hay before closing the clamp. Either place the clamp on a lit barbecue or set the hay alight and allow to burn.

When most of the hay has burnt, remove the fillets from the clamp and unwrap from the muslin.

Serve with pickled lemons (p.268) and pea shoots, or a green salad dressed with mustard vinaigrette (p.119).

Scallop tartare with white chocolate

This recipe is based on a Fat Duck dish that has gone through several incarnations. It began life a decade ago as a disc of white chocolate topped with caviar. It gained a certain notoriety at the time because some people couldn't accept the amalgam of such unlikely ingredients. Since then, however, unusual flavour combinations have become more familiar, and this recipe is a prime example, an amazing pairing of rich, smooth chocolate and rich, briny seafood. (For more about flavour pairing, see p.20.)

Serves 6

For the prawn oil

200g	Olive oil
400g	Whole raw prawns, shell-on

For the white chocolate foam base

20g	Groundnut or grapeseed oil
150g	Peeled and finely sliced carrot (approx. 2 large carrots)
50g	Leek, white part only, cleaned and finely sliced
30g	Fennel, finely sliced
45g	Button mushrooms, finely sliced
½	Banana shallot, peeled and finely sliced
½	Clove of garlic, peeled and finely sliced
15	Black peppercorns
½ tsp	Coriander seeds
70g	Dry white vermouth
1	Sprig of flat-leaf parsley
200g	Fish stock (p.42), reduced to 50g
135g	Whipping cream
150g	Semi-skimmed milk

For the scallop tartare

6	Large cleaned scallops, cut in 5mm cubes
10g	Pickled lemon (p.268), cut into 2mm pieces (optional, can be replaced by lemon juice)
1½ tsp	Chopped chives
3 tsp	Walnut oil
¼ tsp	Sherry vinegar
	Salt

To finish and serve

30g	White chocolate, chopped, plus extra shavings
	Groundnut or grapeseed oil
6	Scallops, each sliced into 3 discs
	Caviar or salmon roe
	Pea shoots

For the prawn oil, heat the oil in a large saucepan until very hot. Drop in the prawns, remove from the heat, and shake the pan continuously until the prawns turn pink.

Allow the prawns to cool in the oil, then strain, reserving the oil. (The prawns can be placed on kitchen roll to drain off the excess oil, then peeled and eaten, or kept in the fridge for later.)

To start the foam base, heat the oil in a saucepan over a medium heat. Add the finely sliced vegetables, garlic, peppercorns and coriander seeds and sweat until the vegetables start to soften (approximately 15 minutes).

Pour in the vermouth, increase the heat to medium-high and reduce to a syrup.

Add the parsley, fish stock, whipping cream and milk and bring to a simmer. Turn off the heat and allow to infuse until cool. Strain into a clean pan.

To make the scallop tartare, combine the scallops with the pickled lemon (or lemon juice), chives, walnut oil, vinegar and salt. Using a small ring mould (approximately 5cm), pack the tartare into the centre of six shallow bowls.

When ready to serve, warm the foam base gently and stir in the chopped chocolate until it melts. Season with salt.

Pour a little oil on to a plate and dip the scallop discs in it. Season with salt, then sear them quickly on one side in a hot, dry pan.

Rest the scallop discs, seared-side up, on top of the tartare and garnish with caviar, pea shoots and shaved white chocolate.

Using a hand blender, froth the white chocolate foam and pour the foam around the mounds of tartare. Lightly drizzle the prawn oil on the foam, and serve immediately.

Brûléed chicken liver parfait

The idea of a chicken liver brûlée might seem unusual, but it makes a beautiful starter that surprises people (in a good way) and has nice textural contrast – the rich, silky-smooth, delicate custard topped with a brittle, caramelized, glass-like crust. Don't baulk at the large amount of alcohol required: it is reduced down to a very concentrated syrup and is key to the flavour of the dish. The Madeira, in particular, contributes a lot to the dish's character – the richer and nuttier it is, the better the end result – so it's vital to buy a top-quality product.

Ingredients that are to be mixed together will combine better, without splitting, if they are at the same temperature. This is why we put the main ingredients for the parfait – the chicken livers, eggs and butter – in separate sandwich bags in warm water. (For more about cooking custards in a bain-marie, see p.80.)

Serves 8

For the alcohol reduction

100g	Peeled and finely sliced shallot (approx. 2 banana shallots)
1	Clove of garlic, peeled and sliced
15g	Sprigs of thyme, tied together with string
150g	Dry Madeira
150g	Ruby port
150g	White port
75g	Brandy

For the parfait

400g	Chicken livers (stringy veins removed)
20g	Salt
4	Large eggs
400g	Unsalted butter, cubed and at room temperature
125g	Whipping cream
	Demerara sugar, for the top

Put all the ingredients for the alcohol reduction into a medium saucepan and place over a high heat. Bring to the boil and reduce to a thick syrup. Remove and discard the bundle of thyme, and put the reduction to one side until it is required.

To start the parfait, fill a medium saucepan with cold tap water and heat to approximately 50°C.

Combine the livers and salt in a sealable sandwich bag. Crack the eggs into another sandwich bag, with the butter in a third.

Remove the saucepan from the heat and place the bags in the water, being careful to keep the tops of the bags out of the water. Allow the bags to warm for 10 minutes so that all the ingredients are the same temperature before you start mixing them.

Pre-heat the oven to 110°C.

After 10 minutes, remove the bags from the water and put the livers and eggs into a tall container and add the alcohol reduction. Blitz smooth with a hand blender. Slowly add the melted butter to the liver mixture while blitzing as if making mayonnaise.

When all the butter has been fully incorporated, pass the mixture through a fine sieve lined with a double layer of muslin. Squeeze out as much of the mixture as possible, then stir in the whipping cream.

Pour the mixture into eight 8cm diameter ramekins so that they are two-thirds full. Place the ramekins in a deep roasting tray, and pour just-boiled water into the tray until it reaches two-thirds of the way up the sides of the ramekins. Cover the roasting tray with foil and place it on the middle shelf of the pre-heated oven.

After 15 minutes start checking the parfaits by carefully removing the foil and inserting a digital probe into the centre of a parfait. Once the temperature reaches 62°C, remove the roasting tray and take the ramekins out of the water. Leave them to cool for 20 minutes at room temperature before chilling in the fridge, for at least 6 hours or overnight.

About 30 minutes before serving, remove the parfaits from the fridge. Just before serving, sprinkle with a thin layer of demerara sugar and brûlée with a blow-torch to form a glassy top. Serve with char-grilled bread and date, fig and apple chutney (p.271).

Potted duck

This recipe combines two methods of preservation to produce what is in effect a delicious, rich, spiced pâté. First you make a confit, a traditional French technique, which involves curing (p.76) and cooking the duck legs in duck fat. After the meat is shredded it is then smoked (p.76) and potted, a historical British technique: the cooked meat is put in a pot and covered with a layer of fat to exclude air and prevent spoilage.

You need to start work on this recipe a couple of days in advance of serving. It's a good idea to make a double quantity, as the duck legs you don't pot will keep for a long time, stored in their own fat. When ready to use, remove from the fat, warm them through in a hot dry pan, and serve them with mashed potatoes or a potato salad; in summer you could put the legs on the barbecue.

If you have duck fat left over at the end of cooking, you can bring it to the boil, strain it and store it in a jar, ready to confit other foods, such as salmon, pork belly or even fennel (p.205).

Serves 6

9	Star anise
5	Juniper berries
2	Cinnamon sticks
5	Black peppercorns
2	Bay leaves
1	Sprig of thyme, leaves picked
	Zest of ½ lemon, finely grated
	Zest of ½ orange, finely grated
60g	Salt
2	Duck legs
500g	Duck or goose fat
2	Sprigs of rosemary

For the smoking

40g	Smoking chips (Specialist ingredients, p.395)

Pre-heat the oven to 180°C.

Place the star anise, juniper berries, cinnamon sticks, peppercorns and bay leaves on a tray and roast them for 5 minutes.

In a spice grinder or food processor, blitz the spices to a powder and mix with the thyme, lemon and orange zest and salt. Rub this mixture on to the duck legs and place in a covered container in the fridge for 24 hours.

Rinse the legs thoroughly and pat dry.

Pre-heat the oven to 75°C.

Melt the duck or goose fat and pour over the legs in a small casserole dish, making sure they are completely submerged in the fat. Add the rosemary, cover the dish and place in the oven for 18 hours.

Remove from the oven and allow to cool to room temperature. Remove the legs. Blitz the fat and cooking juices together with a hand blender and set aside.

Scatter the wood chips over the bottom of a saucepan or smoking box and place a rack or perforated tray inside. Cover and place the pan over a high heat. When the chips begin to burn and smoke, remove from the heat and quickly place the legs on the rack, skin-side up. Cover with the lid and leave to smoke for 30 minutes. (If the lid does not fit tightly enough, cover the pan with foil before replacing the lid.)

Remove the legs and shred the flesh, using two forks. Divide the shredded meat between six ramekins or a suitably sized Kilner jar, and pour a thin layer of reserved fat over the top. Leave to set for 2 hours in the fridge.

Serve with char-grilled bread and date, fig and apple chutney (p.271).

Lamb jelly with cucumber salad

This is a real show-off dish – it looks wonderful and the jelly has an unbelievable depth of flavour – but it is technically one of the more demanding recipes in this book. The jelly will take about three days to prepare, though most of this is taken up with the hands-off techniques of ice filtration (p.54) and infusing (p.24).

If chervil proves difficult to get hold of, use the smallest leaves of flat-leaf parsley instead.

Serves 6

For the lamb jelly

1.6kg	Lamb stock (p.41)	
1	Sprig of rosemary	
½	Sprig of tarragon	
4	Sprigs of coriander	
4	Sprigs of flat-leaf parsley	
	Salt	
7g	Leaves of gelatine (cut with scissors)	

For the lamb salad

200g	Lamb tenderloin
	Salt and black pepper
	Groundnut or grapeseed oil
65g	Cucumber, peeled, de-seeded and cut into small bayonets
18	Oven-dried tomato halves (p.269), cut into thin strips
	Mustard vinaigrette (p.119)
12	Small chervil leaves

To start the lamb jelly, filter the lamb stock by ice filtration (p.54).

Discard the muslin and its gelatinous content and pour the clarified stock into a clean saucepan. Boil to reduce by half over a high heat, leaving approximately 500g stock. Leave to cool.

Infuse the stock with the herbs for 12 hours, then strain and season with salt.

Soften the gelatine in cold water, squeeze dry, then add to a small saucepan containing approximately 100g of the stock. Heat just enough to dissolve the gelatine, then whisk the mixture into the rest of the stock.

Divide the finished stock between six medium bowls and refrigerate for at least 2 hours.

When ready to serve, season the lamb tenderloin with salt, and sear in a very hot, oiled pan on all sides. Allow the meat to rest for 10 minutes, and then cut into small cubes.

Gently mix the cucumber, tomato, lamb cubes, vinaigrette, salt and freshly ground pepper and pile on to the set lamb jelly. Garnish with chervil leaves.

Bagna cauda

Bagna cauda is a classic Italian dipping sauce of oil, garlic and anchovies. It's served fondue-style in a pot into which you dip raw or cooked vegetables. Traditionally it's served warm (the name means 'hot bath'), but I find it equally good cold, as an accompaniment to cold meats, smoked fish or barbecued pork, or even as the dressing for a Caesar-style salad.

Blanching the garlic four times might seem a hassle but it's worth it, otherwise the garlic will still retain some of its harsh, aggressive raw qualities.

How to blanch garlic

Blanching garlic in milk gives it a mild, sweet and slightly nutty character. First, you need to peel and de-germ the garlic cloves. Next, cover them with semi-skimmed milk in a saucepan and bring slowly to the boil over a medium heat. As soon as the milk starts to boil, strain the garlic and discard the milk. Rinse the cloves in cold tap water before returning to the pan, and repeating the process, with fresh milk, three more times.

Serves 4

130g	Cloves of garlic, peeled, halved and de-germed
800g	Semi-skimmed milk
15g	Breadcrumbs
100g	Anchovy fillets in olive oil, drained
75g	Olive oil
	Juice of ½ lemon

To serve

Raw and blanched seasonal vegetables
Sourdough bread

Blanch the garlic in 100g milk four times, using a fresh 100g milk each time (see tip, right).

Cover the blanched garlic with the remaining 400g milk and bring to a simmer. Cook for 10–12 minutes until the garlic is very soft and the milk has reduced in volume, taking care not to let it boil over. Remove from the heat.

Blitz the garlic and milk until smooth, using a hand blender or food processor, then add the breadcrumbs, 30g cold tap water and the anchovy fillets. Blend until smooth again.

Continue to blend while slowly adding the olive oil and lemon juice, then push the mixture through a fine sieve.

Put the bagna cauda in a small saucepan over a low-medium heat and warm through. Decant into a serving bowl, and serve with raw and blanched seasonal vegetables and char-grilled sourdough bread.

Lentils cooked in smoked water with peach and goat's cheese

It's not often that the key ingredient for a dish can be bought at the local garage, but this recipe is an exception. The best way of getting a subtle smoked flavour into lentils is to braise them in smoked water. For this you need water that has been de-ionized, which means it has been subjected to an electrical charge to remove mineral ions that make the water hard and prevent the lentils from softening up properly. De-ionized water is used in car batteries, so it's available in garages.

Serves 6

For the smoked water

400g	De-ionized water (Specialist ingredients, p.394)
25g	Smoking chips (Specialist ingredients, p.395)

For the bouquet garni

25g	Peeled and roughly chopped carrot (approx. 1 small carrot)
25g	Roughly chopped celery (approx. 1 stick of celery)
25g	Peeled and roughly chopped shallot (approx. ½ banana shallot)
1	Sprig of thyme
10	Black peppercorns
1	Bay leaf
5	Cloves

For the lentils

100g	Puy lentils
	Groundnut or grapeseed oil
50g	Peeled and finely diced shallot (approx. 1 banana shallot)
50g	Balsamic vinegar
25g	Clarified butter (see tip, p.286)
15g	Chives
	Smoked salt and black pepper

For the peach purée

200g	Peaches (approx. 4 peaches)
10g	Fructose (fruit sugar)

To finish and serve

125g	Goat's cheese with rind, sliced in 6 rounds
2	Bags mixed salad leaves
6	Radishes, finely sliced
	Mustard vinaigrette (p.119)

To smoke the water, fill a heatproof bowl with the de-ionized water and place inside a home smoking box. Put the smoking chips in the bottom of the box around the bowl and place the box over a medium heat until the chips begin to smoke. Cover the box tightly with the lid. After 5 minutes, turn the heat off. Leave the box covered for 40 minutes. Repeat this smoking process with the same chips twice more.

For the bouquet garni, loosely wrap all the ingredients in a piece of muslin and tie tightly.

To cook the lentils, fill a pan with the smoked water and bring to the boil over a medium-high heat. Add the lentils and the bouquet garni and simmer for 15 minutes with the lid on. Remove the bouquet garni. Strain the lentils.

Heat a little oil in the bottom of a saucepan and sweat the shallot until soft. Add the lentils and balsamic vinegar to the shallot, and cook over a low heat until the vinegar has been absorbed (approximately 10 minutes).

Add the butter, stirring until combined, then chop the chives and add them with smoked salt and freshly ground pepper to taste.

In the meantime, for the peach purée, peel and slice the peaches and place them in a small saucepan. Heat over a low temperature for a few minutes until warmed through then add the fructose and blitz with a hand blender. Strain the mixture through a fine sieve. Leave to cool and place in the fridge until required.

When ready to serve, pre-heat the grill. Warm the slices of goat's cheese under the grill until just beginning to melt but still holding their shape.

Dress the salad leaves and radishes with the vinaigrette, season with salt and freshly ground pepper, and pile into the centre of six plates. Place the lentils on the leaves and top with a little peach purée and a slice of goat's cheese.

Brûléed mushroom parfait

While the chicken liver parfait on p.94 has as its base an intense egg and liver custard, here mushroom duxelles is topped with an egg and mushroom custard, for a double hit of mushroom flavour and texture. The crisp brûlée topping adds yet more texture.

Serves 8

For the alcohol reduction

100g	Peeled and finely sliced banana shallot
2	Cloves of garlic, peeled and sliced
15g	Sprigs of thyme, tied together with string
150g	Dry Madeira
150g	Ruby port
75g	White port
50g	Brandy

For the mushroom duxelles

	Groundnut or grapeseed oil
15g	Peeled and finely chopped banana shallot
100g	Finely chopped button mushrooms
1	Sprig of thyme, leaves finely chopped
10g	Dry Madeira
	Salt and black pepper

For the mushroom parfait

450g	Unsalted butter, cubed, at room temperature
500g	Finely sliced button mushrooms
100g	Mushroom stock (p.45)
4	Large eggs
10g	Salt
	Unrefined caster sugar, for the top

Prepare the alcohol reduction as described on p.94.

To start the mushroom duxelles, heat a little oil in a frying pan and sweat the shallot for 5 minutes over a medium-high heat. Add the mushrooms and chopped thyme, and cook until all of the liquid has cooked out (approximately 15 minutes). Add the Madeira and cook until evaporated. Season with salt and freshly ground pepper. Divide between eight 8cm diameter ramekins, and set aside.

To start the parfait, melt 100g of the butter in a frying pan and cook the mushrooms over a high heat until they are caramelized and all the liquid has cooked out of them (approximately 15–20 minutes). Put them into a tall container. Add the mushroom stock and the alcohol reduction and blitz with a hand blender until as smooth as possible. Place the mixture in a sealable sandwich bag.

Fill a medium saucepan with cold tap water and bring to approximately 50°C. Remove the saucepan from the heat.

Crack the eggs and put them and the salt into a second sandwich bag. Put the remaining 350g butter into a third bag. Place the three sandwich bags in the saucepan, being careful to keep the tops of the bags out of the water. Allow the bags to warm up for 10 minutes so that all the ingredients are the same temperature before you start mixing them. This prevents the mixture splitting.

Pre-heat the oven to 110°C.

When the butter has melted, put the mushroom stock mixture into a bowl. Add the eggs to this and blitz again with a hand blender until smooth. Slowly pour in the melted butter while blitzing so it emulsifies.

Pour the mushroom and egg mixture into the ramekins over the duxelles. They should be no more than two-thirds full. Place the ramekins in a deep roasting tray, and pour just-boiled water into the tray until it reaches two-thirds of the way up the sides of the ramekins. Cover the roasting tray with foil and place it on the middle shelf of the pre-heated oven.

After 15 minutes, start checking the parfaits by carefully removing the foil and inserting a digital probe into the centre of a parfait. Once the temperature reaches 74°C, remove the roasting tray and remove the ramekins from the water. Leave them to cool for 20 minutes at room temperature before chilling for 6 hours or overnight.

About 30 minutes before serving, remove the parfaits from the fridge. Just before serving, sprinkle a thin layer of the sugar on the top of the ramekins and brûlée with a blow-torch to form a glassy top. Serve with apricot chutney (p.270) and char-grilled bread.

Mushroom jelly with mushroom cream

The base of this dish is a mushroom alternative to the lamb jelly on p.98. In the latter recipe the stock is ice-filtered (p.54) using the meat's own gelatine. However, since mushrooms don't contain gelatine, here it is added to the stock in the form of gelatine leaves. You'll have to start making this quite a time in advance, as the mushroom stock has to be clarified by ice filtration, which will take up to a couple of days, and then each layer of the dish has to be chilled for an hour or so before the next layer is added.

Serves 6

To fortify and clarify the mushroom stock

25g	Peeled and finely sliced banana shallot
95g	Dry Madeira
500g	Mushroom stock (p.45)
1½ tsp	Mushroom ketchup (Specialist ingredients, p.395)
12g	Leaves of gelatine, softened in cold tap water

For the mushroom purée (layer 1)

30g	Unsalted butter
50g	Peeled and finely sliced onion
50g	Cleaned and finely sliced leek, white part only
200g	Finely sliced button mushrooms
15g	Dry white vermouth
150g	Vegetable stock (p.44)
15g	Double cream
½ tsp	Mushroom ketchup
	Salt
6g	Leaves of gelatine, softened in cold tap water

For the mushroom jelly (layer 2)

	The clarified stock
6g	Leaves of gelatine, softened in cold tap water

For the Madeira and sherry cream (layer 3)

100g	Dry Madeira
100g	Oloroso sherry
100g	Double cream
	Enoki mushrooms, to garnish

To fortify and clarify the mushroom stock, place the shallot and Madeira in a small saucepan and reduce over a high heat to a thick syrup. Strain the liquid and discard the shallot. Combine the reduced Madeira with the mushroom stock and mushroom ketchup, and heat a small amount of this liquid in a pan. Squeeze the softened gelatine dry, then add to the liquid and stir to dissolve. Return the liquid to the stock, pour into a freezer bag or tray and freeze until completely solid.

Filter the stock by ice filtration (p.54).

For layer 1, the mushroom purée, melt the butter in a saucepan, add the onion and sweat until soft. Add the leek and mushrooms and cook until just beginning to soften. Add the vermouth and reduce until it has almost completely evaporated. Add the vegetable stock and cream, bring to a simmer and cook for 10 minutes.

Remove the pan from the heat and blitz with a hand blender until completely smooth. Add the mushroom ketchup and salt to taste.

When soft, squeeze excess liquid from the gelatine. Stir into a small amount of the warm purée until dissolved, then return this to the pan. Carefully pour a layer of purée (approximately 80g) into each of six glasses and refrigerate until set (approximately 1 hour).

For layer 2, the mushroom jelly, gently warm a small amount of the clarified stock and add the softened, squeezed gelatine leaves. Stir to dissolve and return the liquid to the rest of the stock.

Season with a little salt and carefully divide the stock between the six glasses, making a second layer on top of the set mushroom purée. Place in the fridge for 2 hours.

For layer 3, the Madeira and sherry cream, pour the Madeira and sherry into a small pan and reduce over a high heat to a thin syrup. Leave this mixture to cool to room temperature, then add the cream and some salt.

When ready to serve, make sure the mushroom jelly layer is completely set before putting a tablespoonful of the cream on top, tipping each glass around in a circle so the cream covers the top in a thin layer. Plant small enoki mushrooms in the jelly, and serve.

Scotch eggs

It's said that the department store Fortnum & Mason invented the 'Scottish Egg' in the mid-nineteenth century as a ready-to-eat luxury food. While most modern mass-produced versions are dense and stodgy, the Scotch egg can be a wonderfully refined food with lots of textural contrasts – a crunchy fried-breadcrumb exterior giving way to juicy meat and that final surprise of the egg with its still-runny centre. I like it served with a blob of mustard mayonnaise (p.118) or sauce gribiche (p.123).

Scotch eggs are great picnic food, but to ensure runny yolks you can't really make them much in advance. To be at their best, they should be served as soon as possible after leaving the oven. You can use any sausage meat here, but for me what works best is the kind used in a banger – something that has a bit of filler, which gives a smooth texture, rather than pure meat, which gives a coarser, drier texture. It's a good idea to keep the sausage meat very cold, as it will be easier to wrap around the eggs.

Makes 8

10	Medium eggs
450g	Sausage meat
1 tsp	Chopped thyme leaves
45g	French's mustard
½ tsp	Cayenne pepper
2 tbsp	Chopped chives
	Salt and black pepper
	Plain flour
50g	Whole milk
125g	Panko (Specialist ingredients, p.395), or coarse breadcrumbs, blitzed to a powder
	Groundnut oil, for deep-frying

Place 8 of the eggs in a large pan with enough water to cover the eggs by 2cm. Place the pan over a high heat. Bring the water to the boil; as soon as it starts to simmer, allow the eggs to cook for 2 minutes exactly.

Remove the eggs to a bowl and place under cold running water for 2 minutes. Let them cool for 10–15 minutes.

Meanwhile, place the sausage meat in a food processor with 2 tablespoons of cold tap water and pulse six times.

Turn into a bowl. Add the thyme, mustard, cayenne pepper, chopped chives and season with a little salt and freshly ground pepper. With clean hands, mix the spices into the meat and then divide into eight balls, approximately 55g per portion.

Once the eggs are cool enough to handle, carefully peel off the shells (see tip, below). Flatten each portion of sausage meat between two sheets of clingfilm into a circle, then remove the clingfilm. Place an egg in the centre of each sausage-meat circle. Wrap the sausage meat around the egg, pressing the edges in order to seal it but being careful not to press too hard. Place in the fridge for 20 minutes.

Pre-heat the oven to 190°C.

In the meantime, put enough flour to coat the eggs into a bowl and season with salt and freshly ground pepper. Beat the remaining eggs in a second bowl and stir in the milk. Put the Panko into a third bowl. Roll each egg in the flour, gently tapping off any excess, then dip it in the beaten egg. Finally, roll it in the breadcrumbs, making sure that all sides are coated.

Heat a deep fat fryer to 190°C or place a deep saucepan no more than half filled with oil over a medium-high heat until it reaches this temperature.

Fry the Scotch eggs two at a time for 2 minutes until golden brown. Remove from the oil with a slotted spoon and place on a drying rack over a baking tray. When all the eggs have been fried, place the tray in the oven for an additional 10 minutes. Serve immediately while the yolks are still runny.

How to peel a soft-boiled egg

Tap the top of the egg (the less pointy, more round end) carefully on the side of the sink to crack the shell. Hold the egg under a cold tap that is running very gently. Allow the water to get between the egg white and the shell and peel away the shell with your fingers, taking care not to pierce the albumen and break the egg.

Salads

Hot, cold, raw, cooked, simple, complex – the word salad covers such a wide set of characteristics that it's almost impossible to define, let alone lay down, general principles. Depending on its ingredients, a salad can be served as a starter, main, side or dessert – fruit salad, anyone? It can contain meat, fish, vegetables, pasta, noodles, grains, nuts and eggs. It will usually have some form of dressing, though even this term tends to evade attempts at definition, since it's used to describe everything from a simple vinaigrette or drizzle of good olive oil on a classic Italian tomato and mozzarella salad to the thick, creamy, mayo-based Marie Rose sauce for a prawn cocktail.

So there are few, if any, rules when it comes to salad-making. But since you're likely to be showcasing the fresh, raw qualities of at least some of the ingredients, it's important to seek out the best quality you can (though I'd say this should be your starting point whatever you're cooking). A salad should definitely be seen as an opportunity to celebrate seasonality: the peach and Parma ham salad on p.128 needs to be made in summer, when the peaches are at their ripest and best. Outside of this, though, the field is wide open.

The mixed bags of salad leaves sold in supermarkets often include incredibly peppery ones, such as mustard cress and some types of rocket, which will make a fine accompaniment to a rich meat stew but completely overpower anything with a gentler flavour. It's useful, therefore, to taste whatever leaves you're using in a salad (particularly if they're ones you don't recognize or are using for the first time) in order to get a balance of flavours you're happy with. Peppery and exotic leaves have become so fashionable that people tend to ignore more traditional varieties like little gem or iceberg. But these shouldn't be overlooked simply because they lack novelty value – the crisp crunch of an iceberg lettuce, for example, is still for me the perfect accompaniment to a nice juicy steak.

Whatever leaves you're using need to be washed in several changes of water to get rid of any dirt. Taking the trouble to compose an elaborate and beautiful-looking salad only to find it's ruined by a few specks of grit is very disappointing. I think it's also a good idea to rehydrate leaves before they go into the salad bowl, even if they're from a pre-washed supermarket packet, to freshen them up. You can do this by removing any tough outer leaves, cutting up the rest with a very sharp knife (using a blunt knife or simply tearing the leaves can bruise them, making them go limp) and placing them in a bowl of cold water (or iced water, which is even more effective) for a quarter of an hour. The plant cells will take in water to replace any that has been lost, making the leaves plump and crisp. At my restaurants we usually salt the water too – about half a tablespoon per kilogram of water – which in my experience helps to remove grit (though I haven't yet found a convincing scientific explanation for why this is the case), and also perks up the leaves.

Once done, make sure the leaves are spun in a salad spinner at least three times, because leaves need to be thoroughly dry before being dressed. Since water and oil don't mix well, wet leaves will repel the oil in a dressing.

The choice of ingredients to go alongside (or in place of) the leaves is limited only by preference and imagination. I don't use nuts and fruit (other than citrus fruits) much in salads, yet in the peach and Parma ham salad on p.128 and the pear and sherry salad on p.127, the fruit complements the other ingredients superbly because of compounds they have in common. Ingredients need to be selected with an eye on textural contrast, so that your salad keeps the palate stimulated. The sherry jelly cubes in the pear and sherry salad, for example, bring a burst-on-the-tongue excitement to the dish, as well as little intense hits of encapsulated flavour. The radishes in the green bean and radish salad (p.120) add a nice crunch as well as a peppery zing. Combining raw and cooked, sprinkling in chopped citrus segments or adding shavings of raw vegetables such as fennel or beetroot can give a salad an edge.

The need for textural contrast doesn't mean you have to include loads of ingredients, though. There's a Spanish salad I like that makes a virtue of simplicity: crisp iceberg lettuce with thinly sliced tomato and thinly sliced mild onion, dressed with a plain oil-and-vinegar vinaigrette. In the Basque region they make a salad of mild lettuce leaves, thinly sliced sweet onions and vinaigrette that goes incredibly well with a cut of beef. The softness of the leaves and the crisp firmness of the onion are the perfect foil for a juicy, char-grilled piece of meat, and the vinaigrette cuts through the richness of the meat and gets the saliva going, which makes it seem even more juicy and mouthwatering. And one of my favourite salads has to be pickled lemons (p.268), served with pea shoots and – if you want – a light dressing. Incredibly simple, but delightfully clean and refreshing.

Salad dressings

In a way, a salad only really becomes a salad once it's dressed. A dressing might include all kinds of ingredients – cream or crème fraiche if you want something rich and creamy, or perhaps the juices that you've saved from Sunday's roast for something robust and full-flavoured. Often, however, you'll find the best dressing for the job is a simple vinaigrette, with some oil for richness, some vinegar for a hit of sharp acidity, and perhaps a little mustard for piquancy. Combine these three, add seasoning and you'll have an incredibly versatile dressing that'll work with most salads (p.119). Just make sure you use it generously – the professional chef tends to add a lot more to a salad than the home cook does.

The acidity in the dressing is there in part to make the mouth water. It'll usually be provided by vinegar (though lemon juice is a good alternative if you want to add a citrusy flavour as well as a bit of tartness). Since it has a relatively neutral flavour, white wine vinegar is the best all-purpose choice, but all sorts of other vinegars – balsamic, tarragon, cider, sherry and red wine – can be used, depending on the ingredients. Red wine vinegar works well in the dressing for a salad that's going to accompany meat. (This is also a dressing that'll benefit from some of those reserved roasting juices I mentioned earlier – they'll really intensify the flavours of the dish.)

Sherry vinegar has a rich, nutty character that suits meat dishes and the earthy notes of lentils. Cider vinegar is a good stand-in for white wine vinegar, if you want a dressing with less acidity. Balsamic has a distinct aroma and attractive flavour but it can be unpredictable to work with, for while the top-quality ones are like a perfectly balanced syrup, some of the less expensive versions are all sweetness with very little kick of acidity.

There is of course an equally diverse range of oils you could use for a dressing: groundnut, grapeseed, argan, walnut, sesame and olive, to name but a few. A lot of people use only high-quality, estate-bottled, extra virgin olive oils for their dressings but, except in certain cases (a tomato salad, for example – olive oil works very well with tomatoes – or a salad with full-on Provençal flavours such as a Niçoise), I find that olive oil is too strong for a salad, and ends up dominating the other flavours. So I generally prefer to make a dressing with a more neutral oil, such as groundnut or grapeseed, though I might add a little sesame, olive or flavoured oil to it, if the dish needs a fuller-flavoured dressing. (The same goes for the oil used for making a mayonnaise. There are occasions when you might want a mayonnaise to have the distinctive flavour of olive oil, but in general I find it's too strong. And, in any case, some unrefined extra virgin olive oils actually contain substances that can destabilize an emulsion, causing it to separate within a couple of hours. So, once again, I prefer to use groundnut or grapeseed oil.)

Mustard's not essential for a vinaigrette, but it adds bite and gets the saliva going. And because it's an emulsifier (see below) it helps to combine the ingredients. Although there is as big a range of mustards as there are of vinegars and oils, I almost invariably use Dijon or wholegrain mustard in my dressings. Anything stronger might well overpower other flavours in the salad.

With leaf-based salads, it's essential that you add the dressing only at the very last minute, otherwise the leaves are likely to be limp and discoloured by the time they're served. People assume it's the vinegar that causes this. In fact, the oil is the culprit, seeping in through tiny cracks in the surface of the leaves. You can test this out for yourself by washing a small handful of leaves, then drying and dividing them into two groups. Put one in a bowl with some oil (any will do for this: it doesn't have to be olive oil) and the other in a bowl with some vinegar. After 5 minutes or so the leaves in the vinegar will still look fresh (like the left leaf in the picture opposite) while those in oil will be limp and distinctly unappetizing (like the right leaf).

Emulsions

Most salad dressings are some form of emulsion. The term describes a specific set of circumstances: a combination of two liquids (usually water, in the form of vinegar, and oil) that won't dissolve into one another and so keep their distinct identities, even when mixed. Some emulsions are trickier than others: a vinaigrette can be made with just a quick whisking with a fork, but mayonnaise needs a more methodical approach. By its nature, an emulsion is unstable. While this won't be too much of a problem with a vinaigrette – if it separates, you just whisk to re-combine the ingredients – it can be a headache when in the process of making a cold mayonnaise or a warm hollandaise, which can split or curdle.

Understanding the structure of an emulsion can help to avoid this. Liquids like oil and water that don't mix will naturally arrange themselves into separate masses. (Think of that rainbow-slick of oil floating on top of the water in a roadside puddle.) In order for the two liquids to combine, this tendency has to be stopped. So the first step towards emulsification is breaking the oil up into tiny droplets, because the tinier and more numerous and spread out the oil particles are, the less likely they are to find each other and join together in one large mass. That's why an emulsion requires vigorous whisking.

For a simple oil and vinegar vinaigrette, that whisking is enough to combine the ingredients long enough for their purpose. You're only mixing the ingredients so that they're reasonably evenly distributed, and the stability of the mixture's not really an issue – the vinaigrette should

be tossed through the salad at the last minute anyway, and it'll stay combined for as long as it takes to eat. So a vinaigrette emulsion can be made by just whisking all the ingredients together in a bowl, or putting them in a jar with a lid and shaking them.

For a lot of emulsions, however, we need to create a more stable mixture with a more viscous texture – a béarnaise that is not too runny, perhaps, or a nice firm mayonnaise. This requires the presence of an emulsifier, which is usually a substance that contains molecules that have a fat-compatible tail and a water-compatible head. Put an emulsifier in a mixture of water and fat droplets, and the tails will bury themselves in droplets, leaving just the heads showing. The surface of each droplet becomes covered with these protruding heads (in graphics of this process the fat droplets look like clove-studded oranges), which, since they repel fat, keep the droplets apart from one another. The fat can't join back into one large mass so it remains dispersed through the water.

This is how egg yolks emulsify fat and water, and they are very good at it. One yolk can emulsify at least two kilograms of oil – so you could make two kilograms of mayonnaise with just a single egg yolk, though it wouldn't be particularly rich. (Mustard, the other common emulsifier for dressings, particularly vinaigrettes, works slightly differently, coating the fat droplets with proteins and a gluey mix of carbohydrates, but the end result is the same: the droplets are kept apart.)

So an egg yolk can easily combine the ingredients for a mayonnaise and, in fact, mayonnaise isn't that difficult to make so long as you follow a few simple rules. The water-based ingredient and the emulsifier should be put in the container first and whisked together, then the chosen oil should be added very gradually. If the oil is added too quickly or in too large an amount, it's likely to group together in a separate mass. However, if this slow-but-steady approach is adopted, then the amount of oil added in a single dose can gradually be increased: once the liquid contains enough droplets to create a bit of friction, the droplets effectively work like grinders, helping to break each new addition of oil into droplets.

As the oil is added in this manner, the liquid into which the oil droplets are dispersed ends up absolutely crowded with them. That's what gives mayonnaise its wonderful creamy thickness, but it's also what makes it so vulnerable to splitting – it's literally full to bursting with tiny fat particles. This throng of droplets is also the reason why it's a mistake to try to thin a stiff mayonnaise by adding yet more oil. All you're doing is putting more droplets into an already overcrowded situation. On the other hand, adding more of a water-based ingredient, be it vinegar, red wine (as in the mayo that thickens the gazpacho on p.63), lemon juice or warm water, will give room for the droplets to move around in, and so will loosen up a mayo nicely. When an emulsion becomes stiff and unyielding, it's a sign that it's nearing the point where there are too many droplets. It'll need thinning if it's not to split.

Mayonnaise

People are often wary of trying to make their own mayonnaise, fearful that it'll split. However, if you're patient and follow the standard steps carefully, it's not that difficult to do, and it's an invaluable kitchen skill.

A well-executed, thick, creamy mayo will have a greater and more complex flavour, and a much more voluptuous texture, than any store-bought variety. It's also very adaptable – you can add many different flavourings to a mayonnaise that will change its character to suit all sorts of different dishes. Below, I've given recipes for wasabi, mustard and vanilla mayonnaises, and on p.63 a red wine mayonnaise is used to thicken red cabbage gazpacho. And, since mayonnaise is the basis for a number of classic sauces, once you've mastered it, you'll have acquired a lot of the basic know-how for making an aïoli, a tartare sauce, a sauce gribiche (p.123) or a rémoulade (p.120).

Before you start, make sure all the ingredients are at room temperature, which encourages emulsification. Use a hand blender that comes with its own jug, or an electric whisk or hand whisk with plenty of wires: one with big gaps in it will be no more effective than a fork. If not using the hand blender container, you'll need a heavy bowl that's large enough for whisking but not so large the eggs get lost in it. It also needs to have a rounded base so the mixture doesn't stick in the edges. Set it on a dampened tea-towel to keep it in place.

3	Large egg yolks
30g	Dijon mustard
350g	Groundnut or grapeseed oil
35g	White wine vinegar
½ tsp	Salt
	Small pinch of cayenne pepper

Add the egg yolks and mustard to your chosen container. Whisk these together until they are smooth.

Drizzle in the oil, only drop by drop at first, whisking continually. As the ingredients begin to emulsify, the mayonnaise will become thicker. Once it has thickened a little, the amount of oil can be increased to a thin but steady stream. Keep whisking continually as you pour.

When the mayo is stiff, and all the oil has been incorporated, whisk in the vinegar. This not only thins the mayo but also adds acidity to balance the richness of the oil and helps render the emulsion more stable.

Finally, season with salt and a pinch of cayenne pepper, which will help to cut the richness. Cover with clingfilm and keep in the fridge for no longer than a week.

Wasabi mayonnaise

Also known as Japanese horseradish, wasabi introduces some Asian flavours to mayonnaise and gives it a nice little kick. It goes really well with salmon or tuna.

2 tbsp	Mayonnaise (above)
2 tsp	Wasabi paste

Mustard mayonnaise

Adding a little French's or Savora mustard emphasizes and deepens the mustard flavour in the mayonnaise and introduces a bit of zing. Great with seafood or as a dip with a plate of steak and chips.

3 tbsp	Mayonnaise (above)
1 tbsp	French's or Savora mustard

Vanilla mayonnaise

This is a lighter mayonnaise than the master one above, because it uses the egg white as well. It is great with the liquorice poached salmon on p.187.

1	Large egg yolk
1	Whole large egg
15g	Dijon mustard
5g	Salt
	Seeds from 2 vanilla pods
350g	Groundnut or grapeseed oil
20g	White wine vinegar

Combine the eggs, mustard, salt and vanilla seeds in a bowl. Using a hand blender, blitz the ingredients together. Slowly add in the oil, a little at a time as described above. When the mayonnaise has emulsified, stir in the vinegar. Keeps for 2 days in the fridge.

Mustard vinaigrette

A classic vinaigrette consists of just oil and vinegar, but the addition of a little mustard brings a piquancy to it that makes it particularly mouthwatering. There are other vinaigrettes in this book, but this is the most versatile for dressing your day-to-day salads.

40g	White wine vinegar
40g	Dijon or wholegrain mustard
120g	Groundnut or grapeseed oil
	Salt

Combine the vinegar and mustard in a bowl and whisk together. Slowly add in the oil while still whisking. Season with salt. Keeps in the fridge for several weeks.

Mustard and caper vinaigrette

This vinaigrette is terrific tossed with diced (or crushed or sautéed) potatoes, as served with the cod on p.201. It's also a great dressing for cooked meats and, if you add a touch of cream to it, it makes a simple sauce to go with grilled chicken or fish.

Blanching the shallots first takes away the harsh flavour of raw onion.

20g	Peeled and finely diced shallot (approx. ½ banana shallot)
2 tsp	Wholegrain mustard
1 tsp	Runny honey
2 tsp	Capers, drained and chopped
1	Dill pickle, finely sliced
3 tbsp	Groundnut or grapeseed oil
1 tbsp	White wine vinegar
	Sea salt and black pepper

Fill a small saucepan with water and place over a medium heat. Bring to the boil and add the finely diced shallot for 20 seconds.

Drain the shallot and plunge immediately into a bowl or basin of iced water. Drain thoroughly and pat dry.

Combine the rest of the ingredients in a bowl, season with salt and freshly ground pepper, and whisk together thoroughly. Add the blanched shallot to the vinaigrette. Keeps in the fridge for up to a week.

Green bean and radish salad

This salad showcases two vegetables that I think are often underestimated, partly as a result of their recent histories. In the 1970s restaurants that considered themselves smart would invariably serve radish as an unimaginative garnish on the plate. As a result it has come to be seen as an unexciting vegetable, yet it has a wonderful crispness, freshness and peppery zing that can really enliven a dish.

Green beans acquired an undeserved bad reputation in the 1980s, when nouvelle cuisine spread like a virus through British restaurants and introduced the notion of cooking green beans only until they were *al dente*. This produced a firm texture but squandered flavour. The beans need to be cooked to the point where they're still firm but no longer have that squeak when bitten into. (For more on cooking green vegetables, see pp.242–3.)

Serves 4

200g	Green beans, topped and tailed
12	Radishes, trimmed and quartered
60g	Groundnut or grapeseed oil
20g	White wine vinegar
20g	Wholegrain mustard
1 tsp	English mustard
	Salt and black pepper

Bring a pan of salted water to the boil over a high heat. Add the beans and cook for 2 minutes, covered with a lid, adding the radishes after 1 minute. Remove them from the boiling water and plunge them immediately into a bowl of iced water to refresh them.

When cold, strain the beans and the radishes and place them in a bowl.

Whisk together the oil, vinegar and mustards and pour the dressing over the beans and radishes. Mix gently and season with salt and freshly ground pepper.

Celeriac rémoulade

Raw celeriac has a delightfully subtle celery flavour. One of the best showcases for it is celeriac rémoulade, which has a creamy sharpness that goes very well with steak, cold meats and smoked fish. You can also give it a different spin by stirring in some chopped black or green olives. It can be prepared using good-quality shop-bought mayonnaise, but a rémoulade made with fresh mayonnaise is a real pleasure.

Serves 4–6

300g	Celeriac
35g	Wholegrain mustard
1 tsp	Capers, rinsed, patted dry and finely chopped
25g	Cornichons, finely chopped
	Juice of 1 lemon
2 tsp	Flat-leaf parsley leaves
4	Sprigs of tarragon, leaves picked
150g	Mayonnaise (p.118)
	Salt and black pepper

Peel the celeriac and, using a mandolin or a very sharp knife, cut into fine slices. Cut these slices into fine shreds.

Place the shredded celeriac in a bowl and add the mustard, capers, cornichons and lemon juice.

Chop the herbs and add them to the bowl.

Stir in the mayonnaise and season with salt and freshly ground pepper.

Garden salad with sauce gribiche

Gribiche is a classic French sauce similar to tartare. It traditionally accompanies fish and chicken, and can also be used as a dip for chips (p.257) or Scotch eggs (p.107). Here, though, it forms the base layer of a miniature edible garden, complete with vegetables that appear to be bedded in soil. The idea of edible soil was first thought up by the Japanese chef Yoshihiro Narisawa and has since appeared in a number of restaurants, including René Redzepi's Noma in Copenhagen. I've used it to create a piece of horticultural visual trickery that will delight your guests as they eat with their fingers and warily taste the soil, only to find it's delicious.

The choice of vegetable can vary according to the season. In place of those below you might want to try radishes, baby leeks, baby turnips or baby fennel. (As a variation you can grill the vegetables instead of cooking them in oil or water. This will give them a nice barbecued characteristic – although you will lose the illusion that the vegetables are growing out of the soil.)

Serves 6–8

For the salad

200g	Pitted black olives in brine, drained and rinsed
25g	Grape-Nuts
8	Baby carrots
8	Brussels sprouts
8	Baby asparagus
8	Baby broccoli
8	Baby bok-choy

For the gribiche

1	Medium egg
130g	Mayonnaise (p.118)
35g	Cornichons, finely chopped
30g	Capers, rinsed, patted dry and finely chopped
15g	White wine vinegar
30g	Whipping cream
	Salt and black pepper
2	Sprigs of tarragon, leaves picked
10g	Flat-leaf parsley leaves
10g	Chives

Pre-heat the oven to 110°C.

To dry the olives, spread them on a tray lined with parchment paper and dry in the oven for 4 hours. Halfway through the drying process, roughly chop the olives so they dry more quickly.

Remove the olives from the oven and allow to cool before chopping very finely. Do not be tempted to chop the olives in a food processor because it will become a paste.

While the olives are cooling, increase the temperature of the oven to 180°C. Toast the Grape-Nuts on a baking tray for 10 minutes. Remove from the oven and allow to cool before crushing with a pestle and mortar to a coarse powder.

Mix the toasted Grape-Nuts with the dried olives and set aside.

To start the gribiche, lower the egg into a small pan of boiling water and cook for 10 minutes. Drain and cool under cold running water. Remove the shell (see tip, p.107), then separate the white from the yolk.

Finely chop the egg white and press the yolk through a sieve. Stir both into the mayonnaise with the cornichons, capers and vinegar.

Lightly whisk the cream to soft peaks and fold into the mixture. Season with salt and freshly ground pepper, cover with clingfilm and refrigerate until needed.

When ready to serve, cook the vegetables in oil or water, depending on the vegetable, or serve them raw. (For more on cooking vegetables, see pp.242–3.)

Just before serving, chop the herbs and fold them into the gribiche.

To construct the salad, put a layer of gribiche in the bottom of individual bowls or one large serving dish. Sprinkle the olive and Grape-Nut mixture in a layer on top and 'plant' the vegetables in neat rows in the soil.

Prawn cocktail

Confession time: prawn cocktail is my secret vice. When I get home late after working in the Fat Duck there's nothing I like better than to raid the fridge for prawn cocktail. Home-made, shop-bought – at two in the morning I don't really care. But given the choice, I'd go for the recipe below. You can make it with shop-bought mayonnaise, but it'll be at its best and most addictive made with fresh (p.118). And maybe garnished with some soy-marinated roe (p.86), as in the picture.

Being such a prawn cocktail addict, I'm deeply resistant to attempts to muck around with the ingredients, but putting a little chopped basil and tarragon into the mix introduces some fresh, lively extra flavour, as does scraping the seeds from a vanilla pod and adding them to the mayonnaise.

Serves 4

110g	Tomato ketchup
100g	Mayonnaise (p.118)
¼ tsp	Cayenne pepper
	Worcestershire sauce, 12 drops
10g	Lemon juice
	Salt and black pepper
400g	Cooked shelled prawns
1	Iceberg lettuce, finely shredded
1	Avocado, peeled and diced

Combine the tomato ketchup, mayonnaise, cayenne pepper, Worcestershire sauce and lemon juice in a bowl and mix thoroughly. Season with salt and freshly ground pepper. Add the prawns to the sauce and stir to coat.

Place the shredded lettuce on the bottom of four glasses or glass bowls, followed by the diced avocado, and then a generous spoonful of prawns and sauce.

Crab and pink grapefruit salad

Crab and grapefruit are a great combination in a salad. The acidity of the fruit balances the sweetness of the crab beautifully. I like a salad to contain flavour and texture contrasts that keep the palate surprised and stimulated. That's why the little cubes of grapefruit jelly are here, while the tiny pieces of grapefruit are like a natural version of the cubes, bursting on the tongue to release little floods of flavour. (For more on flavour pairing and encapsulation, see pp.20–24.)

Serves 4–6

For the pink grapefruit jelly

180g	Fresh pink grapefruit juice
1 tbsp	Fructose (fruit sugar)
1 tsp	Powdered gelatine

For the pink grapefruit vinaigrette

½	Pink grapefruit
10g	Dijon mustard
20g	White wine vinegar
60g	Groundnut or grapeseed oil
10	Chives
	Salt and black pepper

For the salad

300g	White crab meat
130g	Mayonnaise (p.118)
20	Chives
10	Tarragon leaves
	Salt
	Drizzle of truffle oil
½	Pink grapefruit
½	Iceberg lettuce, finely shredded
1	Avocado, peeled and diced

For the pink grapefruit jelly, heat the grapefruit juice in a small pan over a medium heat and add the fructose, stirring until it has dissolved. Sprinkle the gelatine into the pan and stir over a gentle heat until completely dissolved. Strain the liquid into a clean shallow container and allow to set in the fridge.

Cut the set jelly into 5mm cubes and keep in the fridge until ready to serve.

For the vinaigrette, take a pink grapefruit. Peel the whole fruit, then break it in half, reserving half the segments. Squeeze the other half through a sieve into a bowl. Mix the grapefruit juice with the mustard and vinegar and whisk together. Begin adding the grapeseed oil in a thin stream while whisking in order to form an emulsion. Season with freshly chopped chives, salt and freshly ground pepper.

For the salad, mix the crab meat with the mayonnaise. Finely chop the herbs and add most of the chives and all of the tarragon to the bowl. Season with salt. Add a small drizzle of truffle oil to the mixture, being careful not to use too much as it can be overpowering.

Separate the reserved half of the pink grapefruit into segments and remove the pith. Slice each segment into half lengthways, then each of these halves into about eight pieces.

When ready to serve, dress the lettuce with the grapefruit vinaigrette and divide half of it between four to six glass bowls or glasses. Add a layer of the crab mixture followed by a layer of grapefruit jelly cubes, the diced avocado and some of the grapefruit pieces, before adding another layer of the lettuce. Garnish with the remaining chopped chives and grapefruit pieces to taste.

Pear and sherry salad

I love using sherry in cooking. It's not a very fashionable ingredient – I guess it still tends to conjure up an image of the maiden aunt having a little pick-me-up. However, sherry is a complex wine containing compounds that can enhance the flavours of some foods, in particular certain cheeses, which is why I have included Stilton in this recipe (and why sherry is used in the fondue, p.231).

Pears are classically poached in red or white wine for dessert, but sherry could easily be used instead. Here they are sliced raw and briefly marinated in sherry for an aromatic crunch. The sherry flavour is accentuated further by the sherry jelly cubes, and the whole is brought together by a hazelnut vinaigrette.

Serves 4–6

For the sherry jelly cubes

150g	Oloroso sherry
20g	Unrefined caster sugar
10g	Powdered gelatine
50g	Sherry vinegar

For the hazelnut vinaigrette

20g	Dijon mustard
40g	Sherry vinegar
120g	Groundnut or grapeseed oil
20g	Ground hazelnuts
	Salt and black pepper

To finish and serve

2	Pears, peeled, halved, cored and sliced
30g	Oloroso sherry
1	Head of chicory (endive), trimmed and separated into leaves
1	Head of red chicory (endive), trimmed and separated into leaves
100g	Bag mixed lettuce leaves
120g	Stilton cheese, cut into thin slices

For the sherry jelly cubes, pour the sherry into a small saucepan over a medium-high heat and flame off the alcohol (see tip, p.153). Stir in the sugar.

Pour 60g cold tap water into another small pan, add the gelatine powder and gently warm until it has fully dissolved. Remove from the heat.

Add the reduced sherry and the sherry vinegar to the water and mix well. Strain into a clean shallow container and refrigerate until set.

Cut the set jelly into 5mm cubes and keep in the fridge until ready to serve.

For the hazelnut vinaigrette, place the mustard and vinegar in a bowl and whisk together. Begin adding the oil while whisking in order to form an emulsion. Stir in the ground hazelnuts and season with salt and freshly ground pepper.

Just before serving, put the pear slices in a bowl with the sherry and leave to soak for 5 minutes.

Drain and divide the pear slices between plates.

Toss the endive and salad leaves in a bowl with the hazelnut vinaigrette and season with salt and freshly ground pepper. Place a small pile of leaves on top of the pears and add the Stilton pieces and sherry jelly cubes just before serving.

Peach and Parma ham salad

This salad gets its edge from the combination of peach, cloves and Gruyère, which have an amazing affinity due to compounds they have in common. The peaches must be perfectly ripe, so this is a salad for summer, when the fruit are at their best. The ham adds flavour and texture.

Serves 4–6

For the vinaigrette

| | Mustard vinaigrette (p.119) |
| ½ tsp | Ground cloves |

For the peach salad

25g	Balsamic vinegar
180g	Parma ham slices
2	Ripe peaches
200g	Rocket leaves
	Sea salt and black pepper
80g	Gruyère cheese, shaved with a vegetable peeler

Combine the vinaigrette with the ground cloves.

For the peach salad, pour the balsamic vinegar into a small saucepan and bring to the boil over a medium heat. Let the liquid reduce to a syrup consistency (approximately 10 minutes), and remove from the heat. Allow to cool.

While the vinegar is reducing, place the slices of ham in the freezer for about 10 minutes. This will make them easier to cut. Chop the slices roughly.

Halve the peaches, remove the stones and slice the flesh into thin wedges.

When ready to serve, toss the rocket leaves in the vinaigrette and season with salt and freshly ground pepper. Add the peach slices, the Parma ham and Gruyère shavings and, using a spoon or squeezy bottle, drizzle the reduced balsamic over the top of the salad.

Meat

Roast chicken 142
Chicken and ham pies 143
Braised chicken with sherry and cream 147
Five-spiced duck breast 149
Beef tagliata 150
Oxtail faggots with celeriac purée 152
Slow-roasted rib of beef with bone-marrow sauce 155
Chilli con carne 156
Slow-cooked lamb shank and giant couscous salad 158
Shepherd's pie 160
Lamb steaks with tapenade 161
Roast leg of lamb with anchovy, rosemary and garlic 162
Braised pork belly with crackling 164

For me, meat is one of the most exciting ingredients to cook, because it's a real technical challenge, but when you get it right the results can be sublime – juicy, tender and full of amazing flavour. Meat's quality is influenced by many different factors: genetics, rearing, type of feed, the method of slaughter and post-slaughter handling. All of these can affect the texture and flavour of a steak or roasting cut long before you get your hands on it. Your control over this stage of the process rests mainly on developing a relationship with a butcher you can trust. Good-quality meat can make a huge difference to a recipe – it's worth the effort of seeking it out.

Meat presents a challenge because the flesh has to be cooked long enough so that it's soft and tender while still remaining moist. This can be difficult to pull off, because heat soon dries meat out. At 40°C proteins start to contract and squeeze out the moisture. By 70°C, most of the juices have gone. To put this in perspective, when the internal temperature of meat reaches 45°C, it's what the French call *bleu*. When it reaches 50°C, it's rare. At 55°C it's medium-rare and at 60°C it's medium. At 70°C it's what some people call well done – and I call leathery. During this process, as water evaporates from the meat, it loses its plump shape and shrinks dramatically.

Cooking a lean meat, such as steak, is always tricky, because the high heat needed to make a nice brown crust pushes the meat through that temperature range very quickly. But at least with a steak you know that in general the flesh is the same throughout and will respond to cooking in much the same way. Tougher cuts like oxtail will contain not just lean meat but also connective tissue, which is difficult to break down unless it's subjected to lengthy cooking – which might dry out and overcook the lean meat. To reconcile these opposites and cook meat well, you need to know a little about its structure and the cooking techniques for getting the best out of each cut.

For practical purposes, therefore, we can divide raw meat into two broad categories: tender and tough. Which category a cut of meat falls into depends largely on how much connective tissue it has. This fibrous substance – composed of elastin and collagen which, when heated, turn into gelatine – encases the muscles. It has great elasticity and tensile strength and, if not broken down properly by cooking, can make meat tough and chewy. The parts of an animal that do lots of work and have plenty of muscle – legs, shoulders, tongue – will contain lots of connective tissue. Those parts that have done less work – like loins and breasts – will have far less connective tissue and be more tender as a result. The two categories require different cooking strategies: generally, tender cuts need to be cooked quickly, while tougher cuts need a longer cooking time.

Ageing meat

If you establish a relationship with your butcher, this should give you the opportunity to cook with meat that has been aged. Many good butchers take pride in the meat that they buy and sell, and will accept that ageing it is part of their service. (This is less likely in sources of meat other than specialist butchers.)

The changes to meat's structure and flavour after ageing are due to the work of natural enzymes (proteins that act as catalysts, building, altering or taking apart other proteins). After slaughter, these break down largely flavourless proteins, fats and sugars into smaller, more flavourful units. (And, during cooking, these new units react together to create yet more flavours.) At the same time the enzymes start breaking down the proteins in connective tissue and other supportive structures, which helps tenderize the meat and keeps it juicy (since the weakened connective tissue is less able to squeeze moisture out of the meat during cooking). The result is especially tasty meat.

We're familiar with the concept of ageing from the practice of hanging game such as pheasant and venison, but in fact most meats will improve with ageing, though some respond better to the process than others. In meats that contain a fat that's relatively unstable (such as polyunsaturated fat), the fat will go rancid quite quickly and so the meat can't be stored for too long. Chicken is best aged for only a couple of days, and pork and lamb for only a week or so. Beef, on the other hand, has a very stable fat and can be aged for a long time. At Robert's Steakhouse in New York a few years back, I ate steak that had been aged for ten weeks and I was really impressed. The flesh was phenomenally tender, with a lovely nutty, buttery flavour. The head chef there regularly aged beef for twelve weeks, and he had even done so to eighteen weeks. The results, apparently, were really interesting. 'Ageing is nature's flavour enhancer,' he told me.

There are two ways of ageing meat, dry and wet. Dry-ageing is the traditional method: the cuts of meat are stored in a sealed room in which the temperature, humidity and air movement are constantly monitored and adjusted to provide the optimum environment for the enzymes to do their work, and to prevent bacteria and spoilage. The sophisticated technology and necessary attention to detail make this an expensive process. Dry-ageing isn't cost-effective for the producer, particularly since meat is priced by weight, and dry-aged meat loses water and shrinks during storage.

As a result, dry-ageing fell out of favour, and the rival process of wet-ageing, which was pioneered in the 1970s, became the more popular option, at least for the mass market. Here the meat is vacuum-sealed and stored in a fridge for a while. Many producers, supermarkets and restaurants took to wet-ageing enthusiastically because the meat develops a degree of aged flavour and tenderness relatively quickly. With wet-ageing there's far less wastage because it retains its water, and the vac-pac prevents spoilage and most bacteria, making the meat easier and cheaper to store and handle. Economically it makes sense, but wet-ageing imparts none of the wonderful tenderness or concentration of flavour that you get from dry-ageing.

You can explore some of the effects by ageing your own meat. Buy a top-quality piece of beef (a large roast is better than a steak or chop), remove it from the container and put it on a cake rack set on top of a plate or drip-tray. Place this in a not-too-full fridge, uncovered. So long as there's enough room for air to circulate, the cold, dry environment is good for this rudimentary method of dry-ageing. After a few days (larger cuts such as joints will obviously take longer than steaks), remove the meat from the fridge, trim off the exterior (which will have dried out in the dry atmosphere of the fridge – the longer you leave the meat, the more you'll have to trim off), and it's ready for cooking.

Brining meat

As well as ageing meat before cooking it, there's another process that will at this stage improve the flavour and juiciness of meat: low-level brining. We're all familiar with the practice of placing raw meat in a concentrated salt solution, which introduces salt to the flesh and dries it out at the same time, altering the texture and flavour so that beef becomes pastrami and salt beef, and pork becomes bacon and a variety of hams (p.76).

You can use the same technique with a lower concentration of salt to produce a subtler yet equally dramatic transformation in raw meat (and fish, for that matter, see p.170). A low-level brine doesn't draw water out of meat. Instead of 'hamming', low-level brining heightens the flavour and ensures it stays moist.

The salt in a low-level brine does two things. First, it breaks down muscle filaments, helping to tenderize the meat. (And, once the filaments have broken down, flavourings in the brine can be absorbed much more easily.) Second, it reacts with proteins to improve the water-holding capacity of muscle cells, which then absorb water (and flavourings) from the brine. This increased intake of liquid means the meat is far more able to withstand the moisture loss that occurs during cooking.

Many meats will gain something from sitting in brine for a while, particularly meats that dry out very easily, such as pork and poultry – it can really give a lift to Sunday's roast chicken or that Christmas turkey. It's featured in many of the recipes in this chapter, and you could also add a brining step to other recipes – the braised chicken with sherry and cream, for instance, on p.147.

Brining is certainly the best way of getting salt into large joints of meat that are otherwise difficult to season properly. It's also an effective method for getting flavours to really penetrate the meat, more or less as stowaways alongside the salt. Add a bag containing aromatics (thyme, rosemary, bay, star anise, coriander, juniper) to the brine for a pork belly, and these will subtly permeate the flesh and enrich its overall flavour. It's a much better method of getting flavour into a food than marinating. I once put a chicken breast marinated in yoghurt, garlic, chilli and spices into an MRI scanner to find out exactly how far the marinade would penetrate. After a full 14 hours it had travelled only about half a centimetre. Unlike a brine, which helps flavours penetrate into the flesh, a marinade only really adds a coating of flavour to the surface of a piece of food.

Brining needs only the most basic equipment – and some space in the fridge. An amount of salt is added to a large pan of water, usually somewhere between 6g and 15g per 100g water (in other words, 6–15 per cent), and then generally warmed so that the salt fully dissolves. If you are using solutions of 10 per cent or less, it may be enough to add the salt to cold water and whisk it in. However, if flavourings are also going to be added to the brine, then the water needs to be warmed so that the flavours infuse into it properly. The warm solution is then cooled to avoid the heat of the water beginning the cooking process. Once the brine is cold, food is added to the pan and then refrigerated for anything from 10 minutes for delicate things like fish, to perhaps a couple of days for a denser piece of meat.

How much salt is used and how long food is brined for depends largely on the composition and thickness of the flesh: a pork belly will need a stronger brine for a longer time than a chicken breast. If you increase the concentration of salt, then up to a point you can decrease the time it'll take to have the required effect. This can be particularly useful with something dense like a pork belly.

There are limits, though. It might be tempting to mix up a 20 per cent brine in the belief that'll it work twice as fast as a 10 per cent, but in fact, once the salt solution goes above a certain percentage, it acts like a cure, making the meat drier and more ham-like. These factors – time and salt concentration – are two of the main variables that you can experiment with to get the results you want.

The third variable is heat. Old-style recipes for corned beef would cook the meat in a salt solution, and a robust meat like ox tongue can certainly withstand a gentle heating in brine. But heat causes the salt to penetrate very quickly, making it more difficult to control the effects of the brine and easier to ruin the food, so it's less common than brining in cold water.

The final part of the brining process is rinsing off the excess salt and patting the food dry, so that it's ready for cooking. The most effective way to wash off the salt is to put the food in a pan, turn on the cold tap and leave it running for a while, but this is very wasteful. Instead, you can put the brined food in cold water for an hour, changing the water periodically – perhaps every 15 minutes. This causes a sort of brief reversal of the brining process, drawing out enough salt to bring about a suitably balanced seasoning. If there's any doubt about whether it's de-salted sufficiently, cut off a small piece, poach and taste.

After rinsing, the food should be patted dry very thoroughly, particularly if it's to be browned straight after the brining process, because moisture inhibits caramelization. If the water hasn't been removed from the surface of the food, you won't get any colour.

Searing meat

Searing – frying quickly in a pan over a high heat – is a key method of cooking meat (and other foods) because it's a superb way of generating colour and flavour. When protein-rich foods like meat are exposed to a high heat, amino acids begin to react with other compounds (principally sugars) to create a huge range of different flavours. The characteristic roasted flavours of coffee, chocolate, bread crusts and pan-fried meat all come largely from such reactions, which are called Maillard reactions, after the French biochemist who first identified the process in the early part of the twentieth century.

It takes a lot of energy to kickstart the Maillard reactions. They speed up as the temperature increases and the moisture content decreases, so they occur significantly only at around 120°C. Since metal is one of the best conductors of heat there is, putting meat in contact with the base of a frying pan, buffered by a thin layer of oil to prevent sticking and help conduct the heat, is a very good way to brown food and get the Maillard flavours going.

What searing doesn't do, incidentally, is 'seal in the juices', although you hear this said all the time, even by reputable chefs. When I first read this in Harold McGee's book, *On Food and Cooking*, I was amazed because up to that point I'd unquestioningly accepted the orthodoxy, just like most other people. Harold demolished the idea with the kind of irrefutable logic that makes you wonder why you hadn't worked it out for yourself. As he points out, that hiss and sizzle you hear when a steak hits the pan is the juices vigorously boiling away.

Searing can, therefore, be difficult to get right. The high heat that generates Maillard flavours also causes water loss and dryness. There's a risk that, by the time the centre of a piece of meat is cooked, the outside will be overcooked. With some lean meats, searing combined with careful use of a digital probe to monitor the level of 'doneness' will produce perfectly moist and tender flesh, especially if the meat is flipped regularly. This is the way I cook steak, such as the beef tagliata (p.150), and it's how the

136

five-spiced duck breast (p.149) is cooked too. However, with many cuts, it's often a good idea to think of searing as one part of a two-stage process – the meat is browned very quickly just to bring colour and flavour to it, then cooked through by a less aggressive form of heat (such as the oven) in order to hold on to the juices. The majority of the relevant recipes in this book employ this two-stage approach, because it gives you the best of both worlds.

Successful searing depends on getting the pan really hot and then maintaining that heat. One of the biggest mistakes cooks make is not getting the pan hot enough in the first place. So, put the pan on a high heat and leave it there for at least 5 minutes before you start searing. (When the oil goes into the pan it should begin to smoke. If it doesn't, your pan's not hot enough.) The pan should have a heavy base that will distribute the heat evenly and won't buckle at this kind of temperature.

It must also be big enough to accommodate comfortably the food going into it. For the meat to brown, it has to be in contact with the pan, so there should be no overlapping. If you add a large quantity of cold food to the pan at one time, this will lower the pan's heat so much that it no longer vaporizes the juices as they emerge from the meat. The meat will stew in these juices rather than fry, and it won't go very brown. This is why recipes advise you to brown meat for stews, say, in batches, which might seem like an unnecessary chore, but it makes a big difference.

How to fry a steak

The quicker a steak browns, the less moisture is lost. Harold McGee extensively tested every method of cooking steak and came up with a brilliant technique – flipping the steak very frequently during cooking. This effectively gives the steak continual little pulses of heat, which prevents it from overcooking. Just as the surface of the meat in contact with the pan is about to get too hot, it's flipped and allowed to cool slightly. The result is a very even cooking and a very juicy steak.

Buy the best meat you can. Rib-eye, rump and sirloin are all great cuts, but I'd choose by quality rather than cut (which again probably means cultivating a local butcher you can trust). Whatever looks best on the day is the one to go for. Ideally, it should be about a couple of centimetres thick. (With a steak that's much thinner than that, by the time the exterior is brown, the interior may well be overcooked.) The meat needs to be at room temperature when you start cooking. So, if it's been kept in the fridge, it should be taken out a couple of hours in advance. It also needs to be nice and dry, so if you've bought a vacuum-packed steak, remove it from the packaging at least half an hour before cooking, lay it on kitchen paper and turn it over once or twice on to fresh paper. As for serving, I sometimes choose to cut the meat into slices, especially with thicker cuts. (This is how the beef tagliata on p.150 is served.) Doing this allows you to season the steak very efficiently – and it gives you the opportunity to sneak a piece before serving, to check whether it's done to your liking.

1. Put a heavy-based frying pan on a high heat for at least 5 minutes.

2. Salt the meat generously. For an average steak I'd probably sprinkle a couple of good pinches per side. Don't add any pepper at this point as it will burn.

3. Pour some groundnut or grapeseed oil into the pan, wait until it smokes, then put the steak in. To avoid oil splashes, hold the steak up by one end and place the other end into the nearside of the pan first, so that when you let go, the steak falls away from you rather than towards you.

4. Cook the steak, flipping it every 15 seconds. A 2cm steak will take about 2 minutes to reach medium-rare.

5. Towards the end of cooking, use a digital probe to monitor how close the meat is to readiness. (You can see overleaf the temperatures at which meat is *bleu*, rare, medium-rare, etc.) Insert the probe into the thickest part of the flesh and make sure you don't push right through to the base of the pan. You'll need to take the meat out of the pan about 5 degrees before it reaches the exact temperature you want: the steak will carry on cooking after it's removed.

6. Rest the meat for 5 minutes before serving. This allows residual heat to finish the cooking, and lets the fibres relax, so that they hold on to more of their juices. Do this resting on a rack set over a plate: if you place the steak on to a hard flat surface, the heat can't escape from the underside and so might overcook it.

7. Cut the steak into slices if you want, and season with salt and freshly ground black pepper.

8. The white 'marbling' in steaks is evidence of fat that should provide plenty of juiciness. However, if it's not marbled, you might want to drizzle the meat with oil or butter. Or you can put butter or olive oil in the pan once it's cooled a little, stir and scrape to deglaze the sticky bits and the meat juices (p.36), and pour this over the steak.

Slow-roasting meat

Although you can cook small and tender cuts of meat at a low temperature, the usual cooking strategy is to heat these quickly but sufficiently briefly that they don't lose too much moisture. With bigger and tougher cuts, however, speedy cooking isn't an option: it takes time for heat to penetrate to the centre of a large joint of meat. But the longer the meat is cooked, the more likely it is to dry out, even if you're using gentle methods of cooking. One of the most common traditional methods is to put meat in an oven and roast it at a relatively high temperature, say 200°C, in order to bring the meat's internal temperature up to around 60°C. Since air isn't a particularly efficient method of heat transfer, this is a much less aggressive form of cooking than searing. Still, with the temperature climbing towards a whopping 200°C, it's all too easy for the meat to overcook and dry out.

To me this approach has always seemed crude and over the top, like using a flamethrower to light a cigarette. For years I experimented with alternatives, including turning meat frequently and spraying it periodically with liquid nitrogen to keep the heat under control. Eventually I came across the sous-vide process, which is the least complicated and most sophisticated and consistent method of cooking food slowly at low temperatures (pp.189–205). Before that, however, I developed a technique that produces excellent results and requires no special technology bar an oven thermometer and a digital probe. I pre-set the oven to exactly the temperature I wanted the meat to reach, and let that much gentler heat bring the meat up to temperature very gradually. This is exactly the approach I've used in the beef with bone-marrow sauce on p.155, putting it in an oven set to 60°C. The especially low temperature means the beef will take a lot longer to cook than normal – from 4–6 hours to cook all the way through – but it's far less likely to squeeze out all its moisture. You end up with a piece of meat that's extremely juicy.

Cooking at a low temperature doesn't only help meat hold on to its juices, though. It's also particularly efficient at breaking down the connective tissue that makes meat tough and chewy. So the low-temperature approach lets you take all sorts of neglected and underestimated cuts like brisket, skirt, tongue and cheeks and turn them into something truly melt-in-the-mouth delicious.

The key component of connective tissue is the protein collagen. It's this that needs to be broken down in order to make tough cuts of meat tender, and the most effective way to do so is to heat the collagen very slowly. Collagen is made up of three strands of gelatine, twisted into the form of a helix, like a tightly wound hawser (which is why collagen has such tensile strength). It's very robust, but if it's subjected to heat in the presence of liquid over a period of time, the tight-knit structure comes apart, separating back into strands of soft gelatine. (That's what the brown jelly under Sunday's roast chicken carcass is.) If the meat is cooked sufficiently gently, the gelatine doesn't all leak into the roasting tray, but remains in the flesh, keeping it deliciously moist and juicy. And even if some of the leaner meat is more cooked than is ideal, the presence of fat and gelatine will make it seem juicy rather than dry. It's a very forgiving form of cooking.

From bottom to top, pieces of a sirloin steak cooked to 45°C (*bleu*), 50°C (rare), 55°C (medium-rare), 60°C (medium) and 70°C (well done).

My low-temperature approach can also be applied to stews and braises: the meat is cooked gently in a pot with a braising liquid, as in the braised pork belly on p.164, the oxtail faggots on p.152, and the lamb shanks on pp.158 and 160. Obviously the lengthier cooking times involved in low-temperature cooking mean you have to plan ahead, sometimes to the point of beginning the preparations for a meal 24 hours in advance. But the moisture-retention benefits of long, slow cooking make it the best option for almost any meat.

There are, however, a couple of disadvantages to low-temperature cooking (though these are easily rectified). Because the juices stay in the meat, there's going to be very little in the roasting tray to make a gravy or sauce, and without gelatine, what juices there are won't have that thick, rich mouth-feel. So you will probably have to supplement the juices, or make the sauce separately.

The low temperature also means you won't get any browning of the exterior and all the lovely Maillard flavours that come with that. The solution is simple: sear the meat either before it goes in the oven or after it has come out and rested. Doing this beforehand has the advantage that it triggers Maillard reactions that, once they've started, tend to snowball: they continue for a while after the meat has gone into the oven, despite the low temperature. However, I often prefer to sear after the meat has rested because the flesh will have cooled down a little, and so is less likely to be damaged or overcooked by the sudden blast of high heat.

Carving meat

There's a lot of mystique surrounding carving, but as far as I'm concerned there are two main considerations when you're cutting up meat. It's important to have a truly sharp knife, so that you're not pressing down on the flesh and sawing away, squeezing out the juices. And it's important to cut across the grain because this actually makes the meat seem more tender. If you're biting across the grain in a slice of meat, it will be chewier and will appear tougher than a slice where you're biting into the grain.

Imagine for a moment chopping a large log for firewood. If you lay the stump horizontally and chop into the bark, the resistance is formidable and chopping is a slog. If, however, you set the stump vertically and chop into the top, following the grain, it splits naturally and easily. It's the same with meat: if you carve across the grain, you end up with a slice of meat that, as you bite in, splits readily along the strands of fibre.

So, with a leg of lamb, for example, after cooking and resting, place the meat on a chopping board. Grip the knob of bone that juts out of the meat with your left hand (reverse this if you're left-handed). Keeping the joint flat on the board, rounded side upwards, cut into the meat from the top downwards, until the knife meets bone, in slices of whatever thickness you prefer, all the way along the top of the meat. Then, while still gripping the bone, run the knife horizontally across the meat, just above the bone, separating the slices. Turn over and repeat on the other side.

With chicken and turkey you can make carving easier by removing the wishbone before roasting (though this may be a disappointment for your kids if they're in the habit of tugging it apart for luck). To do this, set the bird on a chopping board and pull back the neck skin, feeling with your fingers until you find the contours of the wishbone, which will be the first bone you come across. Run the blade of a small, sharp knife along the wishbone on each side of the V-shaped cavity. It can then be eased away from the breastbone and carefully pulled off.

Then, after roasting and resting, remove the legs by slicing down where they meet the breast, and splaying them outwards to expose the joint, which you can then sever. Remove the breast by running a sharp knife deeply into the flesh along one side of the centre bone that extends the length of the bird, making a deep vertical cut. Then cut horizontally through the flesh at the bottom of the breast, until the horizontal cut meets the vertical, separating the breast from the ribcage. Repeat the procedure on the other side of the centre bone. The breasts can then be laid cut-side down on the chopping board and sliced.

Roast chicken

A good roast chicken is one of the glories of the weekend. Whenever possible, on a Sunday evening I like to cook a dinner of roast chicken, roast potatoes, carrots, gravy and cauliflower cheese. (My youngest daughter loves cauliflower cheese so much she once had it on her birthday, with the candles stuck in it!)

However, the conventional method of roasting on a high heat risks drying out the meat. A better approach is to cook the chicken on a lower heat, using a digital probe to monitor it, then rest it, and finally put it back in the oven very briefly on a high heat, just to give the surface some colour and Maillard flavours. It's not essential, but I'd also recommend brining the chicken before roasting it, so that it stays juicy and moist. Cover the chicken in an 8 per cent brine overnight (p.135), then rinse and pat dry.

Serves 4–6

1	Chicken, weighing approx. 1.5–2kg
1	Lemon
½	Bunch of thyme
125g	Unsalted butter, at room temperature
	Salt and black pepper
6–12	Chicken wings or skin-on thighs
2	Carrots, peeled and roughly chopped
2	Cloves of garlic, peeled and bashed with the flat part of a knife or by hand
200g	Dry white wine
250g	Brown chicken stock (p.39)
1 tbsp	Dijon mustard
2 tbsp	Tarragon leaves
2 tbsp	Parsley leaves

Pre-heat the oven to 90°C.

Remove the wishbone and any trussing from the chicken (p.140). Open out the legs a little so air can circulate. Cut off the wingtips and parson's nose (if it has one) and reserve. Roll the lemon between your palm and the tabletop to soften it, then pierce it a few times with a fork. Put the lemon and thyme into the cavity of the bird. Rub butter into the skin. Season with salt and freshly ground pepper.

Place the chicken in a roasting tray with the chicken wings or skin-on thighs, wingtips and parson's nose. Add the carrots and garlic to the tray.

Place in the oven and cook until the internal temperature of the thickest part of the breast reaches 60°C. (With an average-sized chicken this should take 3–4 hours.)

Remove the chicken from the roasting tray and place it on a rack set over a plate so that it can rest for 30–45 minutes. Turn the oven temperature up to 230–240°C.

Put the roasting tray containing the wings or thighs, carrots and garlic on the hob over a medium-high heat and brown the meat and vegetables. Add the white wine and scrape and stir to deglaze the pan. Add the chicken stock and any juices from under the chicken, and cook until reduced to a sauce. Strain into a small saucepan.

After the chicken has rested, put it back in the roasting tray and return it to the oven for 5–10 minutes so that it browns, taking care that it doesn't burn. (To help browning you could melt some butter in a pan, add some wine and a few sprigs of thyme, bring it to the boil, then take it off the heat and use it to baste the chicken.)

Before serving, add the mustard to the sauce, warm through, then chop and add the herbs.

Serve with roast potatoes (p.254), glazed carrots (p.247) and Brussels sprouts (p.248).

Chicken and ham pies

When the ingredients for a pie are cooked together for a long time, the texture and flavours tend to become bland and amorphous. Here, as in the fish pie on p.176, the main components of the dish are cooked separately and brought together only right at the end. This helps preserve the character and integrity of each ingredient.

To intensify flavour, the chicken is placed in a brine (p.135) and left for 5 hours, during which time you can carry on with other parts of the recipe. Two hours after the chicken goes into the brine, pre-heat the oven for the ham. After the ham has been cooking for 3 hours, you prepare the chicken and place it in the oven as well.

I really like the flavour of cooked chicken skin, but in a pie, where it's not crisped up, it can be tough and chewy. So here the skin is removed from the chicken, rendered in a pan, and the fat is then used to soften the leeks, so you still capture that lovely chicken-skin flavour.

Again like the fish pie, this pie filling is thickened using the setting agent agar-agar, rather than a starch. But if you can't get agar-agar, use cornflour – it'll still be very tasty. This recipe will make six individual pies, but if you prefer, just make a large one to serve family-style.

Serves 6

For the chicken

8%	Brine (80g salt dissolved in 1kg tap water)
8	Boned and skinned chicken thighs (keep the skin)
500g	Brown chicken stock (p.39)

For the ham

1	Gammon joint, weighing approx. 1kg
1	Onion, peeled and finely sliced
1	Leek, white part only, cleaned and finely sliced
1	Carrot, peeled and finely sliced

For the leeks

2 tbsp	Groundnut or grapeseed oil
	Chicken skin from the thighs
300g	Leeks, white part only, cleaned and finely sliced

For the mustard sauce

200g	White wine
225g	Whole milk
225g	Double cream
150g	Brown chicken stock (from above)
2 tbsp	Agar-agar flakes (Specialist ingredients, p.394)
30g	Dijon mustard
40g	Wholegrain mustard
	Salt and black pepper

To assemble and cook the pies

5g	Tarragon leaves
10g	Flat-leaf parsley
250g	All-butter puff pastry
1	Medium egg, lightly beaten

Place the brine in a bowl big enough to contain the chicken thighs. Add the chicken and leave for 5 hours.

Rinse the chicken under cold running water for 5 minutes, then dry with kitchen roll. Store in the fridge until needed.

Two hours after you have started brining the chicken, pre-heat the oven to 85°C.

Put the gammon joint and vegetables in an ovenproof saucepan, and pour in enough cold water to cover the meat. Put a lid on the pan and place over a medium heat.

Bring the water to a simmer and then place the pan in the oven for 5 hours, or until the meat flakes. Allow the meat to cool in the liquid before removing and dicing.

When the gammon has been cooking for 3 hours, place the brined chicken thighs in another ovenproof saucepan and cover with the chicken stock. Bring the stock to a simmer over a medium heat, then place in the oven, along with the ham, for 1 hour 30 minutes.

Allow the chicken to cool in the liquid before removing and dicing. Keep 150g of the chicken stock for the mustard sauce that will bind the pies. (The remaining stock can be used for soups or sauces, or discarded.)

continued overleaf

Meanwhile, cook the leeks. Coat the bottom of a frying pan with the oil and place the pan over a medium-high heat. Add the chicken skin and render the fat from it for 10–15 minutes. Remove the skin and discard.

Reduce the heat to medium and add the leeks to the fat. Cook until completely soft (approximately 15 minutes), then allow to cool in the pan.

Now make the mustard sauce. In a saucepan, reduce the white wine by two-thirds. Add the milk, cream and chicken stock and cook for 10 minutes over a low heat while whisking. Sprinkle the agar-agar into the pan and whisk it into the sauce. Continue to simmer for 4 minutes. Allow to cool, then blitz thoroughly with a hand blender. Return the pan to a medium heat, stir in the Dijon and wholegrain mustards, and season with salt and freshly ground pepper.

When ready to assemble and cook the pies, pre-heat the oven to 215°C.

Mix the diced ham and chicken with the mustard sauce and leeks. Finely chop the herbs, add them to the mixture and adjust the seasoning. Pour into individual pie dishes, approximately 10cm in diameter (or, if you prefer, a family-sized dish, approximately 28cm in length).

Roll the pastry out on a lightly floured surface until approximately 5mm thick. Cut out six circles slightly larger than the diameter of the pie dishes (or cut to the right size for a single pie). Leave the pastry in the fridge to rest for about 20 minutes.

Lay the pastry discs over the pie dishes and fold the overhang around the lip of the each dish to seal the edges.

Crimp the edges of the pies with a fork for decoration. Make a few holes in the middle to release the steam. Using a pastry brush, coat the top of the pies with the beaten egg.

Place in the oven for approximately 15–20 minutes or until the pastry turns golden on top. (A large pie will take a little longer to heat through.)

Braised chicken with sherry and cream

Normally white wine would be used in a cream sauce for chicken, but here I have used sherry. It adds deep aromatic notes to what is basically a very simple dish. If you have time, you could brine the chicken thighs in an 8 per cent brine (80g salt per 1kg water) for 4–6 hours first – this will make the texture and flavour even better (p.135).

Serves 6

For the chicken

6	Chicken thighs, skin on
	Salt and black pepper
	Plain flour
150g	Unsalted butter
2	Onions, peeled and sliced
1	Leek, white part only, cleaned and sliced
3	Cloves of garlic, peeled and bashed with the flat part of a knife or by hand
300g	Palo Cortado or Amontillado sherry
500g	White chicken stock (p.38)
250g	Double cream
10	Baby onions, peeled (see tip, right) and halved
	Pinch of sugar
8	Sprigs of thyme, leaves picked
150g	Button mushrooms, quartered

To finish and serve

100g	Pancetta lardons
10g	Parmesan cheese, finely grated
10g	Gruyère cheese, finely grated
5g	Dijon mustard
1 tsp	White truffle oil
	Chives, tarragon and parsley

Season the chicken thighs with salt and freshly ground pepper, and dust with a little flour. Melt 30g of the butter in a casserole dish and sear the chicken until golden brown. Remove the chicken from the pan and set aside.

Add the onions, leek and garlic to the pan, and cook until translucent (approximately 15 minutes).

Pre-heat the oven to 100°C.

Pour the sherry into the onion pan and bring up to the boil. Set alight (see tip, p.153). When the flames have died away, reduce the heat, add the chicken stock and cream, and simmer for 20 minutes.

Return the chicken to the pan and bring to a simmer. Cover the casserole dish and place in the pre-heated oven for 45 minutes or until the chicken is completely cooked. Allow the chicken to cool in the liquid.

Once cool, remove the chicken from the pan. Strain the sauce through a fine sieve and discard the vegetables. Place the sauce back in the casserole over a high heat and boil to reduce by half, skimming off any impurities that rise to the surface.

In the meantime, in a frying pan, melt half of the remaining butter until foaming. Sprinkle the baby onions with salt, freshly ground pepper, a pinch of sugar and the thyme leaves, and brown on the flat side, then remove.

Add the remaining butter to the pan and caramelize the mushrooms to a golden colour, seasoning during the process (approximately 15–20 minutes).

Add the onions and the mushrooms to the casserole with the reduced sauce, and simmer for 2 minutes.

Wipe the frying pan and, over a medium-high heat, render the fat out of the lardons until they are soft (approximately 10 minutes). Remove the lardons and drain on kitchen paper.

To serve, add the Parmesan, Gruyère, mustard and truffle oil to the casserole. Season with salt and freshly ground pepper. Add the chicken thighs, stir, and place over a medium heat for 10 minutes to warm them through.

Garnish with the lardons and freshly chopped herbs.

How to peel small onions and shallots

Small onions and shallots are fiddly to peel, but you can make it easier by blanching them in boiling water first. Bring a pan of water to the boil, add the whole onions and blanch them for 1–2 minutes, covered with a lid. Remove with a slotted spoon and cool immediately in iced water. When cool, they should easily come out of their skins.

Five-spiced duck breast

This recipe uses a home-made five-spice powder (p.264), cooks the duck with eastern flavourings, and serves it with bok-choy and soya beans. The texture at the end is enhanced by the spring onion strips (iced water makes them curl extravagantly). The crunch of the puffed wild rice is probably the least authentic touch, but who gives a Lee Ho Fook?

The duck breasts are cooked using much the same technique as for steak (p.137), flipping the meat to ensure an even penetration of heat. However, because a duck breast has a thick layer of skin on one side which acts as a barrier against the heat, that side has to be cooked for longer than the other, unprotected side.

Serves 4

For the duck

4	Duck breasts
1 tbsp	Five-spice powder (p.264)
	Salt

For the vegetables

4	Cloves of garlic, peeled, halved and de-germed
400g	Semi-skimmed milk
	Groundnut or grapeseed oil
4	Baby bok-choy, trimmed and halved
50g	Mirin (Specialist ingredients, p.394)
100g	Light soy sauce (Specialist ingredients, p.395)
2	Red Thai chillies, de-seeded and finely chopped
10g	Fresh root ginger, peeled and finely chopped
50g	Frozen peas, defrosted
50g	Frozen soya beans, defrosted
2	Spring onions, finely sliced

To finish and serve

1	Spring onion, cut into strips and put into iced water
	Puffed wild rice (optional, p.374)

Score the skin of the duck breasts in a criss-cross pattern with a very sharp knife, and dust both sides with the five-spice powder and salt.

Heat a frying pan over a medium heat and, when very hot, place the duck breasts in the pan skin-side down. Allow the fat to render out. Cook for 3 minutes, then flip over and cook for 1 minute. Flip again back to the skin side and cook for 3 minutes, then flip over for 1 minute. Repeat this process two more times, then remove the duck from the pan and allow to rest for 7 minutes.

Blanch the garlic in 100g milk four times, using a fresh 100g milk each time (see tip, p.100). Finely chop the garlic and set aside.

To cook the vegetables, heat some oil in a clean frying pan over a medium heat and add the bok-choy. Cook until there is colour on one side (approximately 2–3 minutes), then flip over and colour the other side.

Add the mirin and cook until the liquid has almost disappeared, flipping the bok-choy to coat it. Make sure the bok-choy is thoroughly cooked, adding a little water to the pan if not.

In the meantime, combine the garlic with the soy sauce, chillies and ginger in a bowl.

Add the peas, soya beans and sliced spring onions to the bok-choy in the pan, but remove from the heat immediately. Coat everything in the soy mixture.

To serve, divide the vegetables between four plates. Slice the duck breasts diagonally and place the slices on top of the vegetables. Garnish with the drained and dried spring onion strips and, if you like, sprinkle with puffed wild rice.

Beef tagliata

The name comes from *tagliare*, the Italian for 'to cut'; tagliata is a dish of seared steak cut into slices and served with rocket and Parmesan shavings.

Searing is a great skill to master – you get a real sense of achievement from serving up a perfectly seared steak with a simple, well-dressed salad. The key is to have the pan extremely hot before you start. (For more on searing steak, see p.137.)

Serves 4

	Olive oil
2	Sirloin steaks, weighing approx. 400–500g each
	Salt and black pepper
3	Garlic cloves, peeled and bashed with the flat part of a knife or by hand
4–6	Sprigs of rosemary
2	Strips of lemon zest (use a vegetable peeler)
50g	Lemon juice (approx. 1 lemon)
60g	Rocket leaves
40g	Parmesan cheese shavings (use a vegetable peeler)
	Sea salt

Place a heavy-bottomed frying pan over a high heat, then add a thin layer of olive oil. Heat until it is smoking hot.

Season the steaks with a little salt and place them in the hot pan for 15–20 seconds. Then turn the steaks over and fry for a further 15–20 seconds. Repeat this, turning the steaks, for 2–3 minutes. Remove from the pan and allow to rest on a wire rack set over a plate to catch the juices.

Remove the pan from the heat and discard most of the oil (but don't clean the pan). Allow the pan to cool for a few minutes, then pour in 120g olive oil. Add the garlic and sprigs of rosemary to the oil. Rub the strips of lemon zest between your finger and thumb to release the oils, and add them to the pan too.

Allow to infuse for 5 minutes while the meat is resting, then squeeze in the lemon juice. Strain this dressing through a sieve and add any juices from the steak.

Slice the steaks thinly (5mm wide) with a sharp knife. Season with salt and freshly ground pepper and place on a serving dish. Spoon over half the dressing.

Mix the rocket leaves with the remaining dressing and place on top of the beef. Finish with the Parmesan shavings and a sprinkling of sea salt crystals.

Oxtail faggots with celeriac purée

The reward for carefully slow-cooking tougher cuts, like oxtail, is that you can produce something with lots of complex flavour and a lovely gelatinous texture that I really prize.

If, as here, you're cooking meat in a liquid that you're then going to reduce to make a sauce, don't remove the meat from the liquid as soon as it's cooked. If you do, the meat will steam, lose moisture and dry out. (This can be particularly damaging with a small cut of meat.) Keep the meat in the liquid until it has cooled.

In order for the faggots to keep their shape, they are wrapped in caul fat, which is the thin sheet of connective tissue surrounding the organs in the abdominal cavity of sheep and pigs. Caul fat is often used as a skin for sausage-like foods – think of French crépinettes and Greek sheftalia – as well as for wrapping lean pieces of meat such as venison, which can benefit from some added fat. When cooking with caul fat, make sure to baste it frequently during cooking to keep it moist, otherwise it might end up tough. And don't be tempted to brown it. While you're eating you should barely notice it's there.

Celeriac purée is a perfect accompaniment for this dish. It's lighter than a mash and less likely to suck up too much of the sauce.

Serves 4

For the faggots

900g	Oxtail (4–5 large pieces)
	Salt
	Plain flour
	Groundnut or grapeseed oil
200g	Peeled and finely diced carrot (approx. 2–3 large carrots)
200g	Peeled and finely diced onion (approx. 3 medium onions)
100g	Peeled and finely diced celeriac
3	Cloves of garlic, peeled and crushed
½	Star anise
250g	Port
100g	Brandy
750g	Red wine
750g	Beef stock (p.40)
2	Sheets of caul fat (ask the butcher), halved

For the celeriac purée

100g	Unsalted butter
500g	Peeled and finely sliced celeriac
200g	Whole milk

Season the oxtail with salt and coat each piece with flour. Cover the bottom of a casserole with a thin layer of oil and place over a medium-high heat. When the oil is smoking hot, brown the oxtail on all sides, in batches if necessary. Keep the oxtail to one side.

Pour away most of the fat in the bottom of the pan, leaving a thin layer, and return to a medium-high heat. Add the diced vegetables, garlic and star anise to the pan and cook until caramelized, stirring regularly (approximately 20 minutes). Once the vegetables are coloured, remove 150g from the pan and set this aside. Discard the star anise.

Pre-heat the oven to 90°C.

Add the port and brandy to the vegetables remaining in the pan and flame off the alcohol (see tip, opposite). Pour in the red wine and reduce over a high heat until most of it has reduced and the vegetables are a deep purple colour.

At this time add the beef stock and the oxtail and bring to a simmer. Cover and place in the oven for 9 hours.

Allow the oxtail to cool in the liquid, then take out and remove the meat from the bone, shredding it finely. Strain and reserve the braising liquid, discarding the vegetables.

Add the reserved 150g of vegetables and 100g of the cooking liquid to the meat, season with salt and mix well.

Divide the meat into four portions and wrap and seal each portion in caul fat, making a patty shape. Refrigerate overnight.

To cook, pre-heat the oven to 180°C.

Place the faggots in an ovenproof saucepan with enough of the reserved braising liquid to come about a third of the way up the patties.

Place in the oven, and baste the faggots with their liquid every 5 minutes for 20–25 minutes, or until the caul fat is translucent and the oxtail thoroughly glazed.

Meanwhile, for the celeriac purée, melt the butter in a wide-bottomed saucepan over a medium heat and add the celeriac. Cook for 8–10 minutes, stirring regularly. Add the milk and bring up to a simmer for 5 minutes.

Liquidize the mixture in a blender, then pass through a sieve into a clean pan. Warm over a medium heat and season with salt just before serving.

Remove the faggots from the pan. Add the remaining braising liquid to the pan and reduce on the stove top over a high heat until the liquid coats the back of a spoon. Season with salt.

To serve, place a faggot on a pile of celeriac purée and drizzle sauce around.

How to flame off alcohol

This technique, to drive off some of the alcohol content, is straightforward so long as you proceed with the caution appropriate for a process involving naked flames. Make sure there are no flammable items nearby. If you have an overhead extraction unit, turn it off before you start, or the flames will be sucked into the hood and could set it on fire. Put the alcohol in a pan, bring it to the boil, then light the vapour using a long match. Let the alcohol boil until the flames have died down naturally.

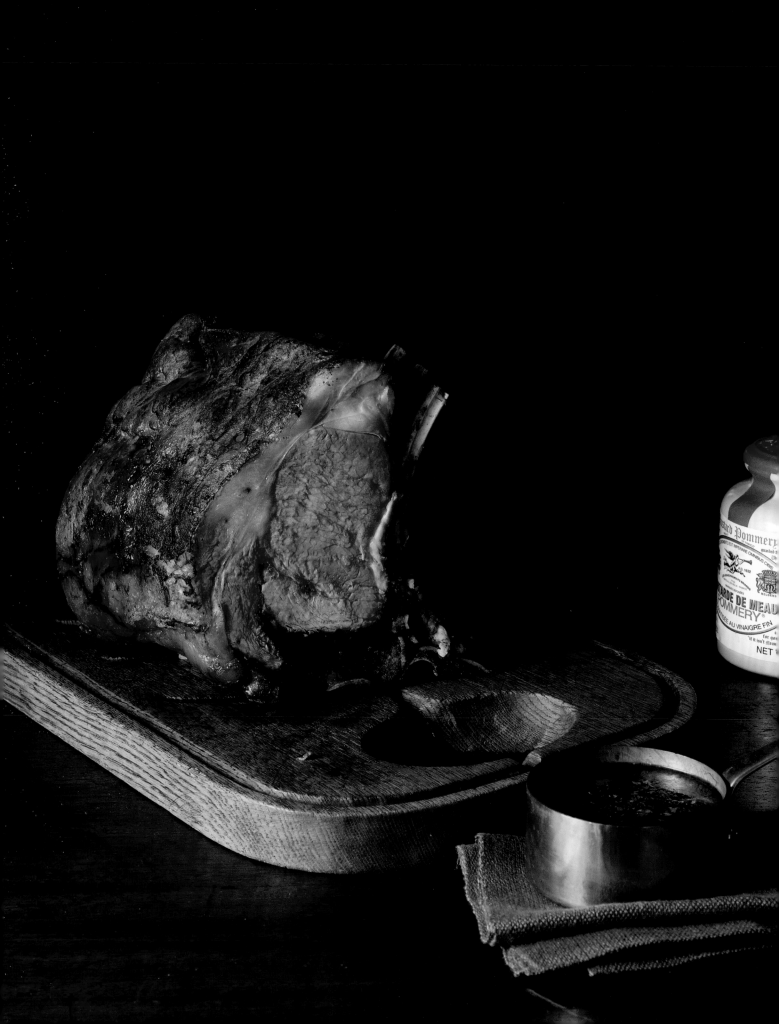

Slow-roasted rib of beef with bone-marrow sauce

This recipe is a prime example of low-temperature roasting (p.139), and you will have to start cooking at least 5 hours before you want to eat. It's a great showcase for dry-aged meat (p.134), if you can get hold of some, but it'll suit any good-quality rib of beef. I cook the meat to 55°C, which will make it medium-rare, but if you prefer it rarer or more done, refer to the photograph on p.138 for the appropriate temperature.

The bone marrow gives the sauce a rich, unctuous character, but if you can't obtain bone marrow, you can make the sauce without it.

Serves 6

For the beef

	Groundnut oil
1	Well-aged three-bone rib of beef (on the bone)
	Salt

For the bone-marrow sauce

2kg	Beef stock (p.40)
100g	Unsalted butter
250g	Peeled and finely sliced shallot (approx. 5 banana shallots)
150g	White wine
100g	Dijon mustard
10g	Sherry vinegar
15g	Lemon juice
100g	Bone marrow, rinsed and diced (ask the butcher)
20g	Flat-leaf parsley leaves
20g	Chives
10g	Tarragon leaves
	Salt and black pepper

Pre-heat the oven to 60°C.

Place a large frying pan over a high heat until it is smoking hot. Coat the bottom of the pan with a thin layer of oil and when it begins to smoke, season the beef with salt and brown on all sides.

Put the browned meat in a roasting pan and place in the oven until the internal temperature of the meat reaches 55°C (this should take 4–6 hours). When the core temperature reaches 55°C, remove the beef from the oven and leave to rest at room temperature for 1 hour.

To start the bone-marrow sauce, pour the beef stock into a large saucepan and place over a high heat. Bring to the boil and allow the liquid to reduce by three-quarters until 500g remains (approximately 25 minutes).

In the meantime, melt the butter in a medium saucepan and cook the shallots for approximately 7–10 minutes until they are light brown in colour. Add the wine and allow to reduce by three-quarters.

Remove the shallot pan from the heat and add the Dijon mustard. Stir thoroughly before adding the reduced beef stock.

Add the sherry vinegar and lemon juice and whisk until all the ingredients are fully incorporated.

Gently heat the sauce and when hot, add the diced bone marrow and remove the pan from the heat. The bone marrow should soften but not melt. Finely chop the herbs and stir them into the sauce. Season with salt and freshly ground pepper and pour into a warm jug.

When the beef has rested, cut the meat from the rib bones in a single piece by running a very sharp knife along the bones. Then run the knife along the chine (the other bone) so that all the bones have been removed. Carve the meat against the grain in 1cm slices. Serve with the sauce and roast potatoes (p.254).

Chilli con carne

The chilli cook-offs that take place across America each year are like a cross between charity fundraiser, barbecue and raucous street party, but the competitors take them very seriously. Each cook has their own secret ingredient or technique for elevating chilli to another level, from triple-rinsing diced pork to dusting cumin round the rim of the bowl.

In this chilli there are secret ingredients and techniques of my own. The kidney beans are brined overnight, which helps them to cook evenly and prevents the skins from splitting. The tomatoes are pressure-cooked, then reduced to an umami-rich concentrate, after which the vine is added and left to infuse because it has lots of raw tomato aroma. You can skip both these procedures and replace the beans and tomatoes with tinned varieties, but the tomato concentrate is an excellent way to enrich stews or any dish that requires tomato paste, so I'd just make a large batch and freeze some. The spiced butter (p.261) that finishes the chilli really gives it a lift (put some in the chilli and more on the table), and with this too you can make plenty and freeze some for use in other dishes.

In chilli cook-offs, competitors are cooking against the clock, but chilli is best made slowly, and the flavours develop if it's left to stand for a day or two.

You will need a pressure cooker for this recipe.

Serves 4

For the kidney beans

10%	Brine (50g salt dissolved in 500g tap water)
150g	Dried kidney beans
500g	Cherry tomatoes on the vine

For the chilli

	Olive oil
450g	Minced beef
1	Large onion, peeled and diced
2	Star anise
1	Large carrot, peeled and diced
3	Cloves of garlic, peeled and finely chopped
1	Green chilli, de-seeded and diced

30g	Tomato purée
375g	Red wine
50g	Spiced butter (p.261)
3	Medium tomatoes, diced
500g	Beef stock (p.40)

To finish and serve

2	Red peppers, de-seeded, roasted and peeled (see tip, opposite), then chopped
	Salt and black pepper
	Finely grated zest and juice of 3 limes
	Spiced butter (p.261)
	Grated cheese
	Soured cream
	Cornbread muffins (p.370)

Put the brine in a container, stirring until dissolved. Add the beans, cover and refrigerate for 12 hours.

Place the tomatoes and 50g water in a pressure cooker, reserving the vines. Put on the lid and place over a high heat. When it reaches full pressure, cook for 20 minutes.

Remove from the heat and allow to cool before taking off the lid. Place the pan over a high heat, stirring frequently until the liquid has reduced by half (approximately 10 minutes).

Leave the tomatoes to cool, then tip into a container, adding the vines to infuse a fresh tomato flavour.

To cook the beans, strain them and place in the pressure cooker. Remove the vines from the tomatoes and add the tomatoes to the beans. If necessary, add some water so that the beans are covered in liquid.

Put the lid on and place the pressure cooker over a high heat. When it reaches full pressure, reduce the heat and cook for 20 minutes. Leave to cool completely before opening. Add this mixture to the chilli when completed.

To start the chilli, coat the bottom of a large saucepan with olive oil and place over a high heat until smoking hot. Add the mince, in batches if necessary so that it browns rather than stews, and cook until evenly coloured. Remove and drain the meat.

Add a little water to the same pan to deglaze it, and tip the water and bits in with the drained meat so none of the flavour is lost.

Turn the heat down to medium and add another thin layer of olive oil. Add the onion and star anise and cook over a medium-high heat for approximately 7–10 minutes until the onion begins to colour, then add the carrot, garlic and green chilli. Cook for another 10 minutes or until the carrot is soft.

Add the tomato purée, stir and cook for another 5 minutes until everything turns a brick-red colour. Pour in the red wine and allow to reduce by two-thirds. Remove the star anise and discard.

Stir in the spiced butter (for mild-medium heat), the browned mince, diced tomatoes and stock, and simmer over a low heat for 2–3 hours, stirring occasionally.

To finish, fold the beans and chopped peppers into the chilli, and bring to a simmer. Season with salt and freshly ground pepper, lime zest and juice, and stir in more spiced butter to increase the heat. Serve with grated cheese, soured cream and cornbread muffins.

How to roast and peel red peppers

Cut the top and bottom off the peppers and remove the centre, seeds and white part. Cut the peppers in half and lay the pieces skin-side up on a baking tray. Brush the skins with groundnut or grapeseed oil. Place the tray under the grill until the skin has blistered and blackened. Put the peppers in a bowl and cover with clingfilm. When they are cool enough to handle, the skin will peel off easily.

Slow-cooked lamb shank and giant couscous salad

This is a delicious combination of shredded spicy lamb, herbs, onions, pomegranate seeds and giant couscous. Some of the dish's distinctive flavour comes from ras-el-hanout, a traditional North African spice mix available from ethnic stores or good supermarkets.

Pomegranate seeds are another traditional North African flavouring. The easiest way to remove them is to cut the fruit in half and, holding it over a bowl, hit the skin with a spoon, which should dislodge the seeds into the bowl.

Serves 6

For the spice mix

½ tsp	Ground ginger
1 tsp	Ground cinnamon
1 tsp	Ground coriander

For the vinaigrette

50g	Olive oil
1 tsp	Ras-el-hanout (Specialist ingredients, p.395)
20g	Sherry vinegar
5g	Dijon mustard
1 tsp	Spice mix (above)

For the lamb

1.5kg	Lamb stock (p.41)
2	Lamb shanks
2	Sprigs of rosemary
	Olive oil
200g	Giant couscous
1	Onion, peeled and finely diced
1½ tsp	Spice mix (above)
	Salt
½ tbsp	Ras-el-hanout

To finish and serve

5g	Parsley leaves
5	Mint leaves
5	Large basil leaves
1	Pomegranate, de-seeded

For the spice mix, simply mix the ground spices together thoroughly, and pass through a fine sieve.

For the vinaigrette, heat 10g of the olive oil in a small saucepan and add the ras-el-hanout. Heat gently for 3–4 minutes. Remove from the heat and stir in the remaining olive oil. Set aside to cool.

Whisk the sherry vinegar, Dijon mustard and 1 teaspoon of the spice mix together in a small bowl. Slowly drizzle in the ras-el-hanout oil while whisking.

To cook the lamb, pre-heat the oven to 100°C.

Pour 1kg of the lamb stock into a casserole and place over a medium-high heat. Bring to a simmer and add the shanks. Cover and cook in the oven for 4–5 hours.

Remove the pan and allow the shanks to cool in the liquid. When cool, shred the meat and set aside.

Reduce the braising liquid to 200g in a saucepan over a high heat. Remove the stock from the heat and add the sprigs of rosemary; allow to infuse for 10 minutes before straining and discarding the herbs.

Coat the bottom of a saucepan with a thin layer of olive oil and place over a medium heat. Add the couscous and sauté in the oil, stirring constantly, until the grains are golden. Add the remaining 500g of lamb stock to cover the couscous and bring to the boil. Cook for 6–7 minutes or until the couscous is cooked, then drain.

In the meantime, heat a thin layer of olive oil in a small frying pan over a low-medium heat. Add the diced onion and cook for 7–10 minutes. Sprinkle with ½ teaspoon of the spice mix and a little salt.

Mix the shredded lamb with the reduced stock, then sprinkle the meat with the ras-el-hanout and the remaining teaspoon of spice mix. Season with salt to taste.

When ready to serve, roughly chop the herbs and mix them with the drained couscous, meat mixture, half the pomegranate seeds and the sautéed onions, and season to taste. Stir through most of the vinaigrette and pile the couscous into a serving bowl. Drizzle with the remaining vinaigrette, and sprinkle with the remaining pomegranate seeds.

Shepherd's pie

Shepherd's pie is a much-loved English classic, so I didn't want to mess about too much with people's expectations of the dish. I've simply introduced a few techniques and ingredients that will create greater flavour complexity and make the dish a little more refined. The lamb shanks need a long, slow cook to tenderize them, so you'll have to start preparations a day in advance.

Generally, I like to thicken sauces using ingredients such as agar-agar rather than starch, as the latter can mute the flavours. Here, however, because the liquid to be thickened is such a small amount, cornflour is the best ingredient for doing so effectively.

Serves 6

For the lamb shanks

1kg	Lamb stock (p.41)
2	Lamb shanks

For the filling

	Groundnut or grapeseed oil
350g	Lamb mince
	Lamb stock, from the shanks (above)
15g	Sprigs of rosemary
15g	Sprigs of mint
170g	Peeled and finely sliced onion (approx. 2–3 medium onions)
200g	Peeled, halved and finely sliced carrot (approx. 2–3 large carrots)
½	Star anise
85g	Finely sliced celery (approx. 3 sticks of celery)
165g	Mushrooms, finely sliced
125g	Red wine
1 tsp	Cornflour
150g	Frozen peas, defrosted
	Diced shank meat (above)
	Salt and black pepper

For the topping

	Mustard pommes purées (p.258)

Pre-heat the oven to 85°C.

To cook the lamb, heat the lamb stock in a casserole dish over a medium heat until it begins to simmer. Add the lamb shanks, cover and place the casserole in the oven for 9 hours. Allow the meat to cool in the liquid.

Remove the shanks and roughly dice the soft meat. Set the stock aside for later use (see below).

To start bringing the filling together, cover the bottom of a frying pan with a thin layer of oil and place over a high heat. When smoking hot, brown the mince, in batches if necessary. Remove from the pan and leave to drain.

Strain the lamb shank stock into a saucepan and reduce by three-quarters over a high heat. Tie the herbs together with a piece of string and add to the reduced stock to infuse for 20 minutes, then remove and discard.

In a clean pan, sweat the onion, carrot and star anise in a little oil until soft (approximately 7–10 minutes). Add the celery and mushrooms and cook until all the moisture has evaporated. Remove the star anise, then add the red wine and boil to reduce to a thick syrup.

Take a small amount of the reduced stock and mix in the cornflour. Add this back to the rest of the stock before adding it to the vegetables in the saucepan. Add the mince, peas and shank meat and season well with salt and freshly ground pepper. Mix thoroughly and pour into a casserole dish.

Pre-heat the oven to 180°C.

Cover the meat filling with mustard pommes purées and bake in the oven for 20 minutes or until golden brown and bubbling.

Lamb steaks with tapenade

Lamb with olives is a classic Provençal combination, and this is an easy way to pair the two flavours. The tapenade has mint in it, which isn't classically Provençal at all, but I wanted to introduce just a hint of the British convention of serving lamb with mint sauce.

Here the steaks are seared, flipping them regularly (p.137), but you could use the same technique to barbecue the steaks instead. You can also cook a version of this dish sous-vide (p.197).

Serves 4

For the tapenade

170g	Black olives in brine (not pitted), drained and rinsed
70g	Capers in brine, drained
50g	Anchovy fillets in olive oil
10g	Mint leaves
15g	Basil leaves
40g	Olive oil
	Finely grated zest and juice of ½ lemon

For the lamb

1 tbsp	Olive oil
8	Lamb steaks, weighing approx. 100g each

To make the tapenade, remove the stones from the black olives by hand. Place the flesh in a food processor with the rest of the ingredients. Blitz together until a smooth paste, adding a little more olive oil if necessary.

To cook the lamb, warm the oil in a frying pan over a high heat until it is smoking hot.

In two batches, to avoid crowding the pan, add the lamb and flip the meat over every 15–20 seconds until cooked to medium-rare (approximately 3–5 minutes) or to your liking, before leaving to rest for 5 minutes.

Spread some of the tapenade on top of the lamb steaks, and serve with a green bean and radish salad (p.120).

Roast leg of lamb with anchovy, rosemary and garlic

Another recipe with classic flavours of Provence – lamb, rosemary and anchovies. Lamb and anchovies might seem an odd combination, but they work well together. The anchovies add savouriness without tasting at all fishy. The low cooking temperature (p.139) means there won't be much juice in the bottom of the roasting tray, but what there is will have lots of flavour.

A pommes boulangère made by cooking potatoes in lamb stock in a low oven (p.259) is a wonderful accompaniment for this dish that really accentuates the flavours.

Serves 4–6

For the roast lamb

1	Leg of lamb, weighing approx. 2kg
	Salt
3 tbsp	Groundnut or grapeseed oil
6	Cloves of garlic, peeled, halved and de-germed
400g	Semi-skimmed milk
12	Anchovies in olive oil, drained, rinsed and cut in half
4	Sprigs of rosemary
	White wine
½ tsp	Dijon mustard
500g	Lamb stock (p.41)

Pre-heat the oven to 80°C.

Season the lamb with salt.

Heat the oil in a heavy frying pan over a high heat. When the oil is smoking hot, add the lamb and sear until golden brown on all sides. Remove the lamb from the pan and place in a roasting tray.

Blanch the garlic in 100g milk four times, using a fresh 100g milk each time (see tip, p.100).

Cut the blanched garlic into slivers. Using a sharp knife, cut slits in the surface of the lamb at regular intervals. Use a small spoon to enlarge the holes and stuff them with an anchovy slice, a garlic sliver and a few rosemary leaves.

Place the lamb in the pre-heated oven for approximately 3–4 hours until the internal temperature of the meat reaches 55°C.

When cooked, remove the lamb from the oven, wrap it in foil and allow to rest for at least 30 minutes.

While the lamb is resting, place the roasting pan over a medium heat. Add a splash of white wine to deglaze, then add the mustard and stock, and reduce to a sauce consistency. Pour into a warm jug.

To finish and serve, remove the foil from the lamb and carve (p.140).

Braised pork belly with crackling

This recipe must be started a couple of days in advance: the meat is brined overnight (p.135), then slow-cooked for 18 hours (pp.139–40). You can do most of the preparation a day or two ahead, up to the point where you leave the braised pork to cool in the liquid.

Serves 4

1	Piece of pork belly, weighing approx. 500–750g
	Groundnut or grapeseed oil

For the curing brine (25% brine)

1	Star anise
15g	Coriander seeds
6	Cloves
6	Allspice berries
3	Juniper berries
	Zest of 1 orange
	Zest of 1 lemon
1	Sprig of rosemary
2	Sprigs of thyme
3	Bay leaves
2	Cloves of garlic, peeled and roughly chopped
250g	Salt

For braising the pork belly

1	Carrot, peeled and sliced
1	Onion, peeled and sliced
1	Leek, white part only, cleaned and sliced
1kg	Brown chicken stock (p.39)
	Salt and black pepper
	Groundnut or grapeseed oil

Pre-heat the oven to 180°C.

Toast the spices for the brine in the oven for 10 minutes, then blitz in a spice grinder or food processor to a coarse powder. Tie them in a muslin parcel with the zest, herbs and garlic.

Combine 1kg cold tap water and the salt in a large saucepan, add the muslin parcel and bring to the boil over a medium heat.

Using a very sharp knife, carefully remove the top skin of the pork belly, trying to keep it intact. Wrap the skin in clingfilm and keep in the fridge.

Remove the brine from the heat, pour into a bowl and allow to cool completely. Discard the spice bundle. Place the pork belly in the liquid, cover with clingfilm and place in the fridge for 12 hours.

After 12 hours, remove the meat from the brine and soak in cold water for 1 hour, changing the water every 15 minutes. When ready to braise the pork, pre-heat the oven to 70°C.

Place the brined pork in a large casserole with a lid, then add the vegetables and pour over the stock. Cover and cook over a medium heat until the liquid begins to simmer, then place in the oven for 18 hours.

After 13 hours, put the unwrapped pork skin on a drying rack on top of a baking tray and place in the oven while the pork is slow-cooking.

After 18 hours, remove the casserole dish and pork skin from the oven and increase the heat to 240°C.

Allow the braised pork to cool in the liquid. Once cool, remove the pork and set aside. Strain the liquid into a pan, discarding the vegetables.

Return the pork skin to the hot oven and cook for approximately 15 minutes until the skin has puffed up.

Set aside approximately 200g of the strained stock. Place the rest in a pan over a high heat and reduce by two-thirds. Season and keep warm.

When ready to eat, heat the 200g stock in a pan over a medium heat and add the pork belly, skinned-side up, being careful not to get the top wet. When warmed through (after approximately 20 minutes), remove the pork from the liquid and drain on kitchen paper.

Heat a thin layer of oil in a frying pan until smoking hot then place the pork belly, skinned-side down, in the pan and allow to colour for 30 seconds.

Combine the reduced stock with the liquid left over from warming the pork. Serve the pork in thick slices with mashed potato, sauce and a piece of the crispy skin.

Fish

Fish is one of the most evocative of foods. Many people's favourite eating memories, for example, involve fish eaten on holiday, whether just-caught snapper at a restaurant by the sea, or fish and chips on the promenade out of newspaper. My own fondest recollections include eating octopus marinated and cooked in olive oil and smoked paprika on a little wooden platform above the shingle beach at Cala Deia in Mallorca. Simple, fresh and fantastic.

Fish is often best cooked straightforwardly – grilled mackerel with just a squeeze of lemon is sensational – but it can also be turned into something refined, like sole Véronique or lobster ravioli. Yet cooking fish still makes people nervous, probably because it's very easy to overcook the flesh, and when this happens, there's little to hide behind. There's nothing pleasurable about eating a dry piece of fish.

The flesh of fish is more fragile than that of meat. Since they float, and don't have to support themselves against the force of gravity, fish don't need the tough connective tissue that land animals have. Their flesh is soft and delicate, and what connective tissue they have dissolves easily at around 50–55°C. And since the flesh is adapted for the relatively cold conditions of lakes, rivers and seas, applying heat has a swift and detrimental effect on it. Even at fridge temperature, fish flesh will already be breaking down. The best commercial fishermen go to great lengths to counter this. When the fish are caught, they're frozen immediately so that the flesh doesn't deteriorate, and it's done extremely rapidly so that the ice crystals are very small and cause the least damage. (Since water expands when it turns to ice, it can rupture cell walls, harming the flesh.) As you can imagine, if a fridge temperature of only 4–5°C breaks down fish, the heat of the cooking process is going to tenderize the flesh very quickly. At 20°C, connective tissue is already beginning to weaken. At 45–50°C, the fish begins to shrink and exude juice. By 60°C, there's little free juice left and the fish will be dry and fibrous.

Obviously physical differences between types of fish mean they will respond differently to heat: fish whose flesh is made up of loose layers of muscle (such as red mullet or cod) will heat up especially rapidly. Active fish that have dense flesh with plenty of protein – such as tuna and swordfish – will heat up less quickly because protein absorbs quite a lot of heat before its temperature rises. Fat absorbs heat even more slowly than protein, so fatty fish will come to temperature slower than lean ones. But, even given these differences, the temperature range for cooking fish is very small.

So the biggest challenge for the cook is producing fish that is still moist. Two of the most practical strategies for achieving this in a domestic kitchen are a very quick searing (see below), which will introduce some nice colour and lots of delicious Maillard flavours (p.136), or a very gentle poaching in a flavoured liquid (p.173), which is less aggressive on the flesh and produces a very moist fish with a lot of its natural flavour intact. (If you're prepared to invest in the technology, there's also the option of cooking the fish sous-vide, which just about removes the risk of overcooking, and will produce a fish that's exceptionally flavourful. For more on this, see pp.191–5.)

Whether searing or poaching, one of the best ways to guard against overcooking is to make use of a digital probe. Throughout this book I advocate employing one to take the guesswork out of cooking, but fish cookery is an area where it really comes into its own. A probe will tell you exactly how close a fish is to being ready, which is invaluable when the optimum temperature range is so narrow. And using a probe means you don't have to worry about what kind of flesh your fish has and how quickly it transfers heat, or jot down complicated calculations of weight multiplied by time: all you have to do is carefully monitor the progress of heat through the fish.

Using a probe is easy. To take an accurate reading, it should be inserted into the centre of the thickest part of the fish. (Make sure you don't push right the way through the fish and instead take a reading of the heat of the base of the pan.) Bear in mind that heat will continue to penetrate the flesh after a fish has been taken off the heat,

especially if you're cooking it fast. If a fish is cooked until the centre is at the required temperature, and then taken off the heat, it's likely to be overcooked by the time it reaches the table. A fish probed at 50°C in the pan could be 55°C by the time it's served, which for fish is a big difference, and it is likely to be quite dry. So if you want a piece of fish cooked to 50°C, take it off the heat when probing shows you that it has reached around 45°C, depending on the thickness of the fish. (Heat will shoot faster through a thinner fish.) Then let it rest for a couple of minutes or so – probably about the amount of time it takes to put the rest of the ingredients on the plate.

Salting and brining fish

One of my chefs once told me that his previous boss had insisted that there was no need ever to salt fish because they came from the sea! Far from it, the addition of salt can have a beneficial effect on both the texture and the appearance of most fish. It's used to preserve it, for example, by removing the moisture in which microbes might thrive, and it can give smoked fish a lovely colour. (Salt draws myosin proteins to the surface of the fish, which then react with the smoke to produce an attractive golden sheen.)

Lightly brining or salting fish – especially flakier ones, such as cod, haddock and flat fish – briefly before cooking can also make them denser and moister. Pre-salting is a common Japanese technique that's used there before a fish is steamed, fried or deep-fried to dry and firm up its outer layers. Salting has the added advantage of preventing the protein albumin from coming out of the fish as it cooks, speckling the surface with unattractive white blobs. You could do this using one of the cures in this book, such as the cure for the salmon in the fish pie on p.176 or for the konbu-cured halibut on p.89. (For more about curing, see p.76.)

Alternatively you can put fish in a 3–5 per cent brine (30–50g salt per 1kg water) for 10–20 minutes, then rinse it thoroughly before cooking. This works particularly well with salmon, and it's a great technique to play around with to create a particular texture. And see also the herring recipe on p.87, where the fish is brined first before being soused. (For more about brining, see p.135.)

Searing fish

Cooking fish over a high heat in a frying pan or on a barbecue is a risky business because the extreme heat can easily dry out the fish, if you're not careful. It's a high-wire act, but it has its rewards. Searing adds some nice colour and plenty of delicious, meaty Maillard flavours (p.136); also, if you like crispy skin – as I do – then this is the only way to get it. Have your digital probe ready.

Searing usually involves smaller fillets (with a whole or large piece of fish, it will take longer for heat to penetrate to the centre and the outside risks being overcooked, so it is probably better suited to poaching), and there are a few preparatory steps you should take to make sure they brown quickly and cook evenly. After the fillets are washed – as all fish should be before they're cooked, to make sure they're free of any innards and suchlike that could affect the flavour – they need to be particularly thoroughly dried, as excess moisture will prevent proper browning. If you have a fillet that is thicker in some parts than others, it's advisable to put a few slashes in the thicker part so that it cooks at the same speed as the rest.

How to sear a fillet of fish

First of all, you'll need a pan the right size and weight for the job – large enough to accommodate the fish comfortably and hold on to its heat, with a base heavy enough to spread the heat evenly. Overcrowding the pan must be avoided – anything that significantly cools it down will slow the searing process and, by the time the fish is brown on the outside, the inside will be overdone.

1. Put a heavy-based pan over a high heat for at least 5 minutes.

2. Season the fish fillets with salt on both sides. Don't add pepper yet, as it will burn.

3. Pour a thin layer of groundnut or grapeseed oil into the pan. When it is extremely hot, put the fish in the pan skin-side down. To avoid hot oil splashes, hold the fillet up by the thinner end and place it in the pan so the thicker end is facing towards you. That way, when you let go of the thin end, it will flop into the pan away from you.

4. The fish will soon start to contract and curl up. The temptation is to press down with a spatula to prevent this, but this can cause the skin to detach slightly from the fish and you end up with shrunken skin. A better approach is to place a small ramekin on top of the fish when it goes into the pan and let it rest there. The fish doesn't suffer the shock of being forced down, and it relaxes and flattens gently.

5. Once the skin is crisp and the fish has settled, you can turn it over and cook while testing with the digital probe until the flesh is cooked. However, the other side of the fish, which has no skin to protect it, is more vulnerable to the direct heat of the frying pan, so it's safer to take the pan and put it under a pre-heated grill instead. The layer of air between the grill's heat source and the fish means it's a less aggressive form of cooking than the conductive heat of the frying pan, so the fish is less likely to overcook.

6. One advantage of this method of cooking is that the searing and browning process gives you the basis for a sauce. At its simplest, once the fish is resting, pour a little of something acidic into the pan – lemon juice or wine work well – along with some butter. Warm through while deglazing the base of the pan to loosen all the sticky browned bits that hold lots of flavour. Pour the juices over the fish and serve.

Poaching fish

Poaching fish in liquid is a method of cooking that really suits its fragile structure, giving you a good degree of control over how much heat is applied. It's also a great way to introduce a restrained flavouring to the fish that enhances its subtle natural flavours, and doesn't overpower them. And it's very easy to do, particularly if you're using a digital probe. You heat the liquid to a temperature close to the one you want the fish to reach, add the fish to the pan and cook it – probing to monitor progress – until the flesh reaches the desired temperature. For me this is usually around 45°C, which gives a very moist, soft texture. However, you may discover that this is less firm than you like, in which case you can try out a range of temperatures to find the one that produces your preferred texture. The beauty of poaching and using a digital probe is that it makes it very easy to test and adjust until you've got precisely what you want.

A poaching liquid can be something fairly neutral, such as water or milk, or a mixture of the two, but also offers an opportunity to introduce complementary flavours to a fish by means of a hot infusion (p.24). Cooking the fish in a stock will contribute flavour: the traditional one for the job, known as a court-bouillon (p.174), adds aromatic vegetables, herbs and spices, vinegar or wine, and salt to the water. Since fish are cooked for a relatively brief period of time, the court-bouillon is usually prepared a little in advance so that its flavours have a chance to develop and can then, in turn, flavour the fish. The fish will also give up some of its gelatine to the liquid, which can be reduced to make a sauce, or simply kept and used as a fish stock in other recipes.

Another less well-known method of poaching employs olive oil (p.174). Before I discovered sous-vide, I used this technique all the time at the Fat Duck because it cooks the fish gently and evenly, holds in a lot of flavour and keeps the fish very moist. The texture of oil-poached salmon, for example, is amazing. It looks almost raw, but flakes perfectly and has a delicious gelatinous quality.

And the technique is no more complicated than poaching using a court-bouillon: the oil is heated to 50°C, then the fish is added to the pan and brought to a temperature of 45°C, using the digital probe to check progress. It might take a couple of goes to get a feel for the pace at which oil heats up on your hob. If you overshoot the desired temperature, it can take a while to bring the temperature back down, because oil retains heat so efficiently.

The technique does use a lot of oil but, once the fish has been removed, the oil can be heated to 100°C, strained and then re-used a couple of times.

From left to right, two pieces of salmon, one poached in a court-bouillon to 45°C, the other overcooked to 60°C.

173

Poached fish

Traditionally, the poaching liquid for fish consists of water and white wine plus flavourings, known as a court-bouillon. One of my favourite poaching liquids, though, is olive oil, which produces a superlatively moist fish with a delightfully gelatinous texture. Here are instructions for both methods of cooking.

For poaching in court-bouillon

2	Leeks, white part only, cleaned and chopped into large pieces
2	Carrots, peeled and sliced into 2.5cm rounds
2	Onions, peeled and roughly chopped
1	Bouquet garni (2 sprigs of thyme, 1 bay leaf, celery leaves wrapped in the outer leaves of a leek, see p.34)
10	Black peppercorns
400g	Dry white wine
100g	White wine vinegar
2	Lemons, halved

Place the vegetables, bouquet garni and peppercorns in a large saucepan and cover with 1kg cold tap water. Place the pan over a medium-high heat and bring to the boil.

Reduce to a simmer and add the white wine and vinegar.

Squeeze in the juice from the lemons and add the halves. Remove from the heat and allow to sit for 10 minutes. Strain and reserve for poaching the fish.

Warm the court-bouillon in a wide-bottomed saucepan over a medium-low heat until the temperature of the liquid reaches 50°C.

Place the fish in the liquid and bring the liquid back to 50°C. Maintain this temperature for approximately 10 minutes or until the internal temperature of the fattest part of the fish reaches 45°C.

Carefully remove the fish with a spatula and drain well.

For poaching in olive oil

Olive oil

Pour enough oil into a saucepan to completely cover the fish fillets when added, and place the pan over a medium-low heat until the temperature of the oil reaches 50°C.

Place the fish in the oil, and bring the oil back to 50°C. Maintain this temperature for approximately 20 minutes or until the internal temperature of the fattest part of the fish reaches 45°C.

Carefully remove the fish with a spatula and drain well on kitchen paper.

Fish pie

In most recipes for fish pie, the ingredients are all heated together for the majority of their cooking time. This approach will always be a compromise – there's no way a single time, temperature and technique is going to suit all the components of the dish – and these ingredients tend to lose their individual character. So here they are cooked separately, and then brought together briefly at the end to marry the flavours.

Fish pie sauces are generally made using a form of starch – flour, cornflour or arrowroot – but this can mask the delicate flavour of the fish and make the sauce seem heavy. So, the sauce here is made using a technique I developed for the Fat Duck, in which a liquid is set using agar-agar flakes, then blitzed to create what looks like a purée but is in fact a smooth, broken-up jelly.

You can make the components of the dish in advance, and finish it on the day. Make sure, though, that you only warm the ingredients through, or they'll end up overcooked.

Serves 4–6

For the cured salmon

125g	Salt
125g	White granulated sugar
250g	Salmon fillet, skin removed

For the confit onions

15	Baby onions
	Olive oil

For the sauce

15g	Unsalted butter
2	Medium onions, peeled and finely sliced
4	Cloves of garlic, peeled and finely sliced
40g	Dry white wine
20g	Dry white vermouth
50g	Smoked haddock, cut into 2cm pieces
200g	Fish stock (p.42)
125g	Whole milk
125g	Double cream
2 tbsp	Agar-agar flakes (Specialist ingredients, p.394)

For the pommes purées

	Pommes purées (p.258)
10g	Horseradish sauce
	Worcestershire sauce, 12 drops
15g	Wholegrain mustard

To finish and serve

16	Raw peeled prawns, cut in half lengthways
250g	Smoked haddock, cut into 2cm pieces
80g	Frozen peas, defrosted
5g	Chives
5g	Parsley leaves
5g	Tarragon leaves
5g	Chives
	Salt
	Sand and sea foam topping (optional, overleaf)

To cure the salmon, combine the salt and the sugar in a bowl. Place half of this in the base of a shallow container, and put the salmon on top. Cover with the remaining salt mixture, then with clingfilm, and place in the fridge for 6 hours.

Rinse off the cure thoroughly under cold running water and pat dry. Cut the fish into 2cm pieces. Keep to one side.

For the confit onions, trim the roots and peel them (see tip, p.147), then lay them in a single layer in a saucepan and cover them with oil. Place the pan over a medium heat and allow to cook until golden (approximately 15 minutes).

Drain the onions, discarding the oil, and allow to cool. When cool enough to handle, cut the onions in half. Keep to one side.

To start the sauce, melt the butter in a saucepan over a medium heat and sweat the onions and garlic until they become translucent (approximately 10 minutes). Deglaze the pan with the wine and vermouth, and boil to reduce to a thin syrup.

Add the haddock, fish stock, milk and cream and bring to a simmer for 20 minutes.

continued overleaf

Remove the pan from the heat and allow it to infuse for 20 minutes before straining into a clean saucepan without pushing through. Discard the onions and fish.

Add the agar-agar to the liquid and bring to a simmer over a medium heat. Allow to simmer for 4–5 minutes, whisking occasionally.

Allow to cool, then blitz thoroughly with a hand blender. Pass through a sieve and set aside until ready to use.

For the pommes purées, follow the recipe instructions on p.258, stirring the horseradish sauce, Worcestershire sauce and mustard through at the end.

When ready to serve, pre-heat the grill.

Heat the sauce in a large saucepan to a simmer and add the raw prawns; simmer until they are almost cooked through (approximately 1 minute).

Add the cured salmon, smoked haddock, confit onions and peas. Finely chop the herbs and stir them into the mixture. Season with salt to taste.

Warm the mixture through and pour into a pie dish. Cover the mixture with warm mashed potato – make a wave pattern, if you like – and place under the hot grill for 7–10 minutes or until the potatoes start to brown.

Sand and sea foam topping

For a bit of fun, you can cover the fish pie with this topping of sand and sea foam – an idea which takes its cue from my Fat Duck dish, 'Sound of the Sea' (p.26). It takes fish pie to the next level.

For the sand

	Groundnut or grapeseed oil
150g	Panko (Specialist ingredients, p.395)

For the sea foam

10g	Unsalted butter
20g	Peeled and finely sliced shallot (approx. ½ banana shallot)
1	Clove of garlic, peeled and finely chopped
10g	Dry white vermouth
20g	Dry white wine
200g	Fish stock (p.42)
400g	De-ionized water (Specialist ingredients, p.394)
5g	Dried konbu sheets (Specialist ingredients, p.394)
10g	Dried shiitake mushrooms
2	Parsley stalks
1 tsp	Soya lecithin (Specialist ingredients, p.395)

For the sand, heat 5cm of oil in a small saucepan over a high heat to 180°C.

Add the Panko and fry until golden brown. Strain the breadcrumbs through a sieve, and drain them on kitchen paper.

For the sea foam, heat the butter in a saucepan over a low-medium heat and add the shallot and garlic. Gently sweat for 4–5 minutes until translucent.

Add the vermouth and white wine to the pan and boil to reduce to a syrup consistency.

Add the stock, water, konbu, dried shiitake and parsley stalks and bring up to 65°C. Hold at this temperature for 30 minutes.

Pass the liquid through muslin and allow to cool. When cool, skim off any solidified butter.

To serve, remove the fish pie from the grill and cover half of the surface of the pommes purées with the golden breadcrumbs.

Warm the sea foam liquid in a saucepan over a medium heat. When warmed through, add the soya lecithin and blitz with a hand blender until light and frothy. Spoon a line of foam over the edge of the breadcrumbs to simulate the tide meeting the beach.

Haddock with leek and potato sauce

Whiter, less oily fish such as haddock, cod and halibut often benefit from a light brining or salting (p.170) before cooking, which firms up their texture and makes them less wet. If you do choose to brine or salt the haddock in this recipe, the fish won't need salting before it goes into the frying pan.

The sauce is a variation on leek and potato soup (p.56) and will suit any white fish, sautéed scallops, or lightly poached oysters or clams. You can also garnish the fish with cubes of sautéed potatoes, or with braised leeks. (Slice some leeks into a pan, add some butter and seasoning and a little bit of water or fish stock. Bring it to the boil on a high heat. Cook with the lid on at first to soften the leeks, then remove it to drive off moisture and help glaze them. They should be ready in 5–10 minutes.)

Serves 2

For the leek and potato sauce

50g	Peeled and finely sliced potato (approx. 1 small potato)
10g	Unsalted butter
35g	Peeled and finely sliced onion (approx. ½ onion)
160g	Cleaned and very finely sliced leek (approx. 3 leeks)
1	Bouquet garni (thyme, celery leaf, parsley and bay leaf, tied with a strip of leek or a piece of string, see p.34)
200g	Fish stock (p.42), warmed
10g	Whipping cream
10g	Whole milk
	Salt and white pepper

For the fish

	Groundnut oil
2	Haddock fillets, weighing 150–200g each, skinned
	Chives and tarragon, to garnish

For the leek and potato sauce, rinse the sliced potato under cold running water for 30 seconds, then drain well.

Melt the butter in a saucepan over a medium heat and cook the onion and potato for 10 minutes, stirring regularly. Add the leeks and cook for a further 5 minutes.

Add the bouquet garni and warm fish stock and bring to a simmer for 10 minutes or until the potatoes are tender. Remove the bouquet garni and liquidize the sauce before straining it through a sieve into a clean pan.

Add the cream and milk and warm through. Season with salt and freshly ground white pepper and keep warm.

To cook the fish, heat a thin layer of oil in a frying pan over a medium heat. Season the fish fillets on both sides with salt and place in the pan. After approximately 2 minutes, flip the fillets over, cook for 2 more minutes and remove from the heat.

Place the fillets on warm plates then, using a hand blender, froth the sauce and ladle it around the fish. Chop the herbs and sprinkle over the fish.

Crispy lemon sole with potted shrimps and cucumber

The 'crispy' in the title doesn't refer to the fish, but to the thin slices of bread on which the fish is fried, and under which it is then briefly baked and served. The fish is protected from direct heat, and what is in essence fried bread adds texture to the dish.

The potted shrimps make a delicious and incredibly simple sauce. It's vital, however, that the shrimps are only heated until they're just warmed through and no further, otherwise they turn into little bullets. The addition of cucumber to the shrimps gives crunch.

Serves 4

2	Slices of white sandwich bread
	Salt and black pepper
	Finely grated zest and juice of ½ lemon
4	Lemon or Dover sole fillets, skinned
2 tbsp	Groundnut oil
250g	Potted shrimps, shop bought
5g	Dill
½	Cucumber, peeled, de-seeded and sliced
	Pea shoots

Pre-heat the oven to 110°C.

Cut the crusts off the bread slices and place them between two sheets of clingfilm. Using a rolling pin, roll to a thickness of 2mm. Remove the clingfilm and season the bread with a little salt and a little of the lemon zest.

Place the fillets of fish on the rolled bread (two fillets on each slice) and trim the fish and bread to ensure that they are both the same size. You will have four pieces.

Heat the oil in a frying pan over a medium-high heat, then place the fillets, bread-side down, in the pan and sauté them until golden brown (approximately 3 minutes).

Remove from the pan and place the fillets, fish-side down, on a tray lined with baking parchment. Place in the oven for approximately 5 minutes.

Put the potted shrimps in a small saucepan and warm them gently over a low heat until the butter is completely melted. Finely chop the dill and add it to the shrimps with the cucumber, lemon juice and remaining zest, and season with salt and freshly ground pepper.

Place a spoonful of the potted shrimp mixture in the middle of each plate and put the lemon sole fillets on top, fish-side down. Drizzle some of the remaining shrimp butter around the plates and garnish with pea shoots.

Umami broth with poached mackerel

This broth is effectively dashi, a Japanese stock that's packed full of umami. To boost the umami even further, soy sauce, dried shiitake mushrooms and tomatoes are added to the dish, along with mackerel and bonito, which also contain umami compounds. Together, they really show off the magnified savoury effect of combining together different sources of umami (p.20).

Dashi is also a satisfyingly simple soup base. Follow the first two steps, omitting the soy and shiitake mushrooms, and you have a stock to which you can add tofu, chopped spring onion, seaweed and a spoonful of miso paste to create a delicious miso soup – a real taste of Japan.

Serves 4

For the umami broth

15g	Dried konbu sheets (Specialist ingredients, p.394)
10g	Dried shiitake mushrooms
25g	Bonito flakes (Specialist ingredients, p.394)
	Light soy sauce (Specialist ingredients, p.395)

For the roasted tomatoes

16	Small tomatoes, peeled (see tip, p.269)

To cure the mackerel

1 tbsp	Coriander seeds
50g	White caster sugar
50g	Salt
	Zest of 1 lemon, finely grated
	Zest of 1 lime, finely grated
4	Mackerel fillets

To serve

12	Fresh cherry tomatoes
6	Oven-dried tomato halves (p.269)
6	Spring onions, outer layer removed, halved, then very finely sliced lengthways
	Pinch of togarashi pepper flakes (Specialist ingredients, p.395)

For the broth, place 900g water, the konbu sheets and dried mushrooms in a saucepan over the smallest burner on the lowest heat. Bring the water to 60°C and hold at this temperature for 1 hour by checking every 10 minutes and removing the pan or increasing the heat.

Discard the konbu and mushrooms and raise the temperature of the water to 80°C. Remove the pan from the heat and add the bonito flakes. Stir and strain after 10 seconds. Season with a couple of drops of soy sauce.

To roast the tomatoes, pre-heat the oven to 200°C. Place the tomatoes on a baking tray and bake in the oven for 10 minutes or until the tomatoes start to colour.

Remove from the oven, and keep to one side. Cut in half and warm through slightly when ready to serve the dish.

To cure the mackerel, place the coriander seeds in a spice grinder or food processor and blend to a fine powder.

Mix with the sugar, salt, lemon zest and lime zest and sprinkle a layer into a shallow container. Place the mackerel fillets on the cure, flesh-side down. Cover with clingfilm and refrigerate for 25 minutes.

Rinse the fillets thoroughly under cold running water.

To finish and serve, pour 2cm of umami broth into a saucepan wide enough to hold the four mackerel fillets and place on low-medium heat. Add the fillets and poach for 5 minutes.

In a second pan, warm the remaining umami broth.

Take four of the fresh cherry tomatoes and cut into eighths for the salad garnish on top of the mackerel.

Take the remaining cherry tomatoes and slice in half vertically. Use a small spoon to gently scoop out the centres and seeds; you will use these around the mackerel. (Use the remaining tomato cups in salads.)

Divide the roasted tomato halves between four flat bowls in a line. Place the fish on top and ladle the warmed broth around. Place the tomato centres and seeds around the bowl in the broth.

Top with the oven-dried tomatoes, fresh tomatoes and spring onion. Sprinkle with the togarashi pepper flakes.

Sea bass with vanilla butter

People think of vanilla as sweet due to its associations with dessert, but as a matter of fact it's not sweet at all, and suits savoury dishes just as much as sweet ones. I first came across vanilla butter about twenty-five years ago at a restaurant in Paris. Served with lobster, I was bowled over by how well the flavours went together.

The fish fillets are so thin that they cook very quickly. If you have a digital timer with an alarm, I recommend that you use it to ensure they don't overcook.

Serve accompanied by broccoli with chilli (p.248).

Serves 4

	Groundnut or grapeseed oil
4	Sea bass fillets, skin on
	Salt
40g	Vanilla butter (p.263)

Cover the bottom of a frying pan with a thin layer of oil, and heat over a high heat until extremely hot.

Season both sides of fish with salt and place skin-side down in the hot pan to crisp for 90 seconds. Place a lightweight object such as a ramekin on top of the fish to keep it from curling as it cooks. Flip the fish over for a further 60 seconds and remove the fillets from the pan straight on to the serving plates.

Place 10g of vanilla butter on top of each fillet. As the butter melts, spoon it over the fillets to coat.

Liquorice poached salmon

The salmon is great served with asparagus (p.252) and vanilla mayonnaise (p.118). Garnish with grapefruit cells (or small bite-sized chunks of grapefruit, if separating citrus cells seems like too much of a chore), and some soy-marinated roe (p.86) or whole coriander seeds. (This is what I call flavour encapsulation, see p.23).

I tend to avoid mentioning specific brands in recipes, but the liquorice recommended here works very well, and is available in supermarkets.

Serves 4

For the liquorice stock

100g   Haribo Pontefract Cakes (liquorice)

For the liquorice jelly

4 tsp   Agar-agar flakes
        (Specialist ingredients, p.394)
200g   Liquorice stock (above)

For the salmon

4   Salmon fillets, skin off, weighing
        approx. 150g each
        Olive oil or court-bouillon (p.174)

To finish and serve

½   Pink grapefruit, segmented then separated
        into cells and drained on kitchen paper
        Sea salt
        Soy-marinated roe (p.86), or coriander seeds
20g   Balsamic vinegar, boiled to reduce by half
        and cooled
        Vanilla mayonnaise (p.118)
        Asparagus (p.252)

For the liquorice stock, place the liquorice and 500g cold tap water in a saucepan and allow to sit overnight so the liquorice dissolves completely.

The following day, bring the liquid to a simmer, whisk it well and then strain through a fine sieve.

For the liquorice jelly, pour 100g cold tap water into a small saucepan and sprinkle the agar-agar over it. Bring to the boil, then simmer for 4–5 minutes, whisking occasionally and making sure that all the agar dissolves. Add the liquorice stock, whisk to incorporate and simmer for another few minutes. Blitz with a hand blender for 1 minute, then remove from the heat.

Place a piece of clingfilm on a clean work surface and pour the liquorice stock through a sieve on to the clingfilm, letting it spread naturally. Allow this to set (approximately 1 minute), then cut the gel into pieces that are the same size and shape as the salmon fillets.

Poach the salmon in olive oil or court-bouillon until the internal temperature of the fattest part of the fish reaches 45°C, as described on p.174.

To finish and serve, put each piece of salmon on a warm plate sprinkled with the grapefruit cells, season with salt and place a liquorice 'blanket' on top of each one. Top the salmon with either a spoonful of soy-marinated roe or three coriander seeds and, at the last moment, dot the plate with the reduced balsamic vinegar. Serve with vanilla mayonnaise and asparagus.

Sous-vide

Sous-vide is a revolutionary cooking method that is set to transform the domestic kitchen. It's clean, efficient, versatile and user-friendly. It heats food to exactly the temperature you want so that it's perfectly cooked, with almost no risk of overcooking. And it holds on to all the juices, keeping food moist, succulent and full of flavour. What's more, sous-vide is so precise that you can do the same thing time and again. The consistency, convenience and precision of sous-vide has made it an indispensable part of many professional kitchens over the last decade. The technology is now becoming much more affordable and accessible – already it's making appearances on cooking shows like *MasterChef* – and I think it ought to have as big an impact on home cooking as the fridge and the gas cooker. It really is that good.

The technology itself is simple: a vacuum-packing machine and a water-bath. Vacuum-packing the food makes it easy to handle, protects it while cooking, ensures that it heats through evenly and prevents the juices from leaking out. The water-bath cooks the food efficiently (because water is a better medium for heat transfer than the air in an oven) and at a far more precise temperature than could be achieved with a pan on the hob.

Together, the vacuum-packer and the water-bath give the cook fantastic control. You can heat at the sort of low temperatures that really bring out the best in many ingredients. The use of a bag has misled some people into assuming sous-vide is simply an updated version of boil-in-the-bag, but nothing could be further from the truth. Boil-in-the-bag is essentially about convenience: the food is portioned and packaged in a form that is easy to handle, but is still subjected to a fairly aggressive cooking process. Boil-in-the-bag doesn't benefit the texture or flavour of food, nor does it give the cook any particular control over cooking temperature. While precise, low-temperature cooking is one of sous-vide's most significant benefits, it's far from the only one. The system is exceptionally well suited to cooking food in advance and reheating it. (Which makes it great for the time-strapped cook who needs to plan ahead, or the ambitious cook who wants to try out a complex multi-stage dish.) With conventional methods of cooking, although there are some dishes, like stews and curries, that can be reheated the next day, you wouldn't generally reheat a piece of steak, lamb or chicken, because it ends up with a 'cooked-out' characteristic that's far less appealing than the flavour of freshly cooked meat. (This deterioration is mainly down to exposure to the air, which oxidizes fat, creating 'old' flavours.) With sous-vide, on the other hand, since the meat is vacuum-sealed in a bag, no air is present and no air can get to it, so you can reheat the meat with absolutely no loss of flavour.

And the reheating is equally straightforward: the neatly vacuum-packed bags of food are removed from the fridge and put in a water-bath for long enough to warm through evenly. So long as the water-bath is set to the same temperature at which the food was originally cooked, there's very little danger of overcooking, even if you leave it in there a little longer than intended. It's a very streamlined, anxiety-free way of preparing food.

Vacuum-packing

Placing food in a special plastic bag before cooking it might seem strange, but there are two compelling reasons for doing so. First, air is a poor medium for heat transfer. (Think how cool a 100°C oven is compared to a pan of water boiling at 100°C.) Removing the oxygen allows the heat to penetrate and cook food far more directly and effectively. Second, being enclosed in a vacuum bag keeps the food from coming into contact with the water in which it is to be cooked (one of the key differences between sous-vide cooking and poaching). This prevents juices and flavours from being lost.

Vacuum-packing is largely a case of placing the bagged food in the machine, closing the lid and pressing a switch. You must, however, make sure that the food is at fridge temperature (3°C or lower), not just from a food hygiene

point of view, but to avoid overcooking it accidentally. In the low pressure of a vacuum, water will evaporate at a lower temperature than normal. If warm food is sealed in the vacuum-packer, then as soon as the air is removed, the water the food contains will start to boil, spoiling the texture and drying it out.

Cooking in the water-bath

Once vacuum-packed, the food is cooked in a water-bath – a metal reservoir that has a heating element and a temperature control. Again, because the heating medium is not air but liquid, food is cooked very efficiently. And it's cooked accurately – turn the dial to the optimum temperature, and it'll reach exactly that temperature and maintain it. This level of control makes cooking far easier and takes away a lot of the anguish about overcooking. Heating at a lower temperature means it's going to take longer for the heat to penetrate to the centre of the food and cook it through, so it takes a bit of patience, but the results are well worth the extra time.

Adding flavourings like oils or herbs or other ingredients to the bag alongside a piece of meat or fish can work, but it's complicated and often will involve trial and error. Because of the efficiency of the sous-vide process, including a slice of lemon and some dill with a piece of salmon, say, can have a very noticeable effect. And since you're cooking at low temperatures, it's important to consider whether what you're adding will cook properly. You can't include robust vegetables with a piece of meat or fish to be cooked at 60°C and expect them to soften to the right texture. One technique that does work well with many sous-vide recipes is brining. I've talked elsewhere about the benefits of a low-level brining of meat (p.135) and fish (p.170) to make them succulent, well seasoned and full flavoured. Brining is just as effective on ingredients destined to be cooked sous-vide.

The process of cooking food sous-vide is at its most impressive with tough cuts of meat, melting their strong, fibrous connective tissue into juicy gelatine (p.32), in much the same way a gentle braising might, but also

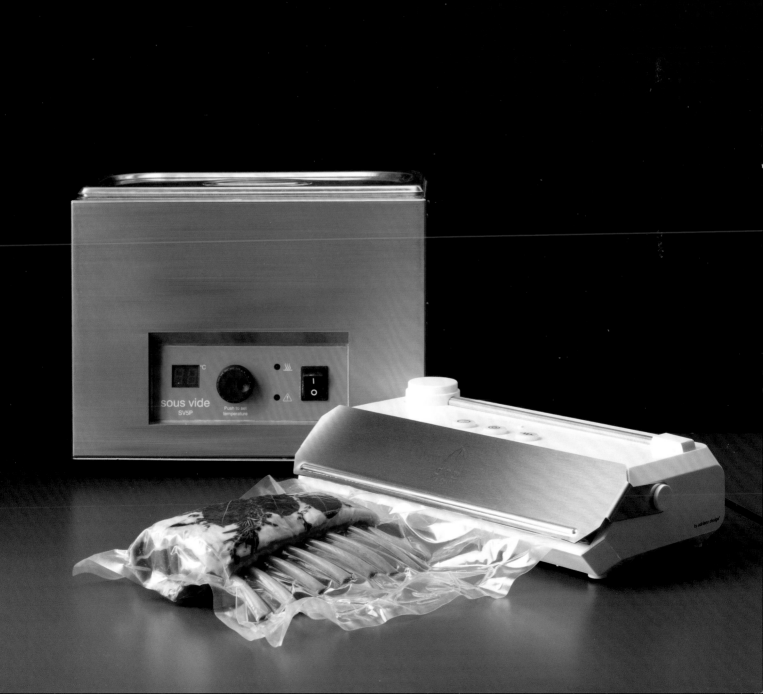

holding on to juices that would be lost during a braise. Leaner cuts, on the other hand, don't have a lot of connective tissue that needs breaking down. So, whereas with a tough cut you need to heat it until the internal temperature reaches, say, about 60°C and keep it there long enough for the flesh to soften (which can be a matter of several hours or more), with a leaner cut you simply need to heat it until it reaches the correct internal temperature, at which point it will be cooked.

One minor disadvantage of cooking meat sous-vide is that, because all the juices stay inside the meat, you'll have no roasting juices upon which to base a gravy or a sauce – it will have to be made separately. But as far as I'm concerned, this is a very small price to pay for moist, juicy meat.

With fish, cooking them sealed in a bag means they hold on to lots of flavour that would normally be lost, even with gentle cooking techniques like poaching. And some fish, such as salmon, end up with flesh that has a very voluptuous texture. (Try cooking the salmon fillet on p.202 and you'll see what I mean.) Sous-vide also takes the headache out of one of the biggest difficulties of fish cookery: preventing the fish from overcooking. In a water-bath, since the temperature won't go above what you've chosen, unless you leave the fish in far too long, it should come out cooked to perfection.

While sous-vide cooking produces meat and fish with an intense flavour and a lovely texture, it can't give them a nicely browned exterior and all the delicious Maillard flavours that are generated by searing. So sous-vide dishes that require browning will involve two separate processes: cooking in a water-bath until tender, followed by a quick searing on a high heat. The good thing is that, with sous-vide, since the inside is already correctly cooked, you can concentrate solely on bringing colour and flavour to the outside. But searing needs to be done with special care. Having used the sous-vide technique to ensure the food doesn't overcook, it would be a great shame to undo that at the last minute by searing clumsily or for too long. (For more on searing, see p.136 for meat and p.171 for fish.)

Slightly different considerations apply to cooking vegetables and fruit sous-vide. Plant tissues only begin to soften at around 60°C, and even then many vegetables are still relatively firm. It's often only as the tissue temperature approaches boiling point that the structure breaks down sufficiently to become tender. So sous-vide's value as an efficient form of low-temperature cooking isn't applicable. However, there are still benefits to cooking fruit and veg sous-vide. Once again the sealed bag means that they hold on to lots more flavour. And heating at a precise temperature can make the cooking process far easier. If you want to cook, say, carrots, you can put them in a bag with butter, thyme, garlic and orange juice and leave them to soften in the water-bath without worrying whether they will catch and burn. If you cook them for longer than you meant to, they'll just end up a little softer and sweeter. Obviously food can't be left in a water-bath indefinitely: although it won't burn, its flavour and possibly its texture will eventually deteriorate. But you have greater latitude than with traditional cooking methods.

Once cooked sous-vide, food shouldn't be allowed to stand at an ambient temperature for long. Although it's in a sealed bag, which protects it from some microbes, it should be handled as carefully as you would if cooked by more conventional methods. It mustn't spend too long at the kind of lukewarm temperature that provides a benign environment for microbes to multiply, so sous-vide food should be served straightaway or chilled.

Keeping sous-vide food suitably cold when it's not being cooked is an integral part of the cooking process. Proper chilling should be as precise a business as any other part of cooking – after all, it's one of the keys to good food hygiene. Putting the sous-vide bag under cold running water isn't good enough, nor is putting it in a bowl of water with a few ice cubes. Place the bag in a bowl containing at least 50 per cent ice, which should be topped up with more ice as the cubes begin to melt. The bag should also be moved around periodically to ensure it doesn't end up sitting in a pocket of warm water.

Rack of lamb

The recipe is a sous-vide variation of the lamb steaks with tapenade on p.161. Cooking rack of lamb sous-vide will produce beautifully tender meat and really capture the delicious Provençal flavours of this dish. After its slow cooking sous-vide, the meat is browned in a pan, but you can also do this on the barbecue for a lovely char-grilled exterior. As with the slow-roasted rib of beef (p.155), after cooking you can also slice the meat into thick chops and brown them in a pan or on the barbecue, following the instructions for frying steak on p.137.

Serve with a green bean and radish salad (p.120).

Serves 6

2	Racks of lamb, weighing approx. 500g each
	Extra virgin olive oil
16	Sprigs of thyme
4	Sprigs of rosemary
8	Bay leaves
	Salt
	Tapenade (p.161)

Pre-heat the water-bath to 60°C.

Place the racks in two individual sous-vide bags with 15g each of oil and the herbs divided between them. Seal the bags under full pressure, and place in the bath for 1 hour.

Remove the bags from the bath and remove the racks from the bags, discarding the herbs. Pat dry. (Alternatively, place the sealed bag in a basin of iced water at this stage and refrigerate until required.)

Season the lamb with salt. Coat the bottom of a large frying pan generously with olive oil and place over a medium-high heat. When the oil is hot but not smoking, add the lamb and cook for 4 minutes, flipping the rack every 15 seconds, until the meat is brown on each side. If the pan begins to smoke, lower the heat.

Remove the lamb from the pan and allow to rest for at least 5 minutes before coating with the tapenade. Divide into cutlets to serve.

Cocotte of pork with black pudding sauce

When I'm on holiday in France, I love cooking in a heavy cast-iron pot called a cocotte – simple one-pot stuff where the heavy lid helps to keep in all the lovely aromas that would otherwise evaporate away. The sous-vide system might look high-tech, but it's effectively the ultimate cocotte: the sealed bag means you hold on to as much flavour as possible.

This recipe also highlights a feature of the sous-vide system that's very useful for entertaining. You can cook the meat in advance, cool it in the bag and store it in the fridge, then reheat in the same bag – a neat, streamlined, hassle-free process.

The sauce is simplicity itself: reduced chicken stock with crumbled black pudding. It adds a very rich, deep flavour. Braised lettuce (p.252) is a good accompaniment.

Serves 4

1	Brined and rinsed pork belly, weighing approx. 500–750g (p.164)

For the black pudding sauce

500g	Brown chicken stock (p.39)
100g	Black pudding, skinned and crumbled
	Salt and black pepper

Pre-heat the water-bath to 60°C.

Place the pork belly in a sous-vide bag and seal under full pressure. Place the bag in the water-bath and leave it to cook for 18 hours.

Once the time has elapsed, remove the bag from the water-bath and place in a bowl or basin of iced water. Allow to cool for at least 1 hour or until completely cold.

When ready to eat, place the sous-vide bag in a water-bath pre-heated to 60°C for 15–20 minutes to warm through.

Meanwhile, make the sauce. Pour the stock into a saucepan and place over a medium-high heat. Bring to the boil and reduce the liquid by half (approximately 10–15 minutes). Remove from the heat, add the crumbled black pudding, and season with salt and freshly ground pepper.

Remove the pork from the bag and wipe away any jellied stock clinging to it. Remove and discard most of the fat, so that only a 5mm layer of fat remains. Using a sharp knife, cut lines diagonally across the fat side of the pork, making a criss-cross pattern. Pat the surface dry.

Just before serving, heat a sauté pan over a high heat and sear the skinned side of the belly for 30–45 seconds or until it turns golden brown.

Cut the pork into generous slices and drizzle with the black pudding sauce to serve.

Chicken with clams a la plancha

Chicken cooked sous-vide is incredibly tender, moist and flavourful, and I urge you to give it a go, even without the clams, if that seems like too much to take on at the same time. Brining will enhance the chicken's flavour and make it juicier (p.135), but you can forgo this, too, if you want. You should still end up with a really delicious piece of chicken.

A la plancha is the Spanish term for the technique of grilling food on a hot metal plate or in a frying pan. Here the clams are flamed open so that they gain a slightly charred note. The oil has to be hot enough so that the pan erupts into flames when you shake it. Flaming – whether as here, or driving off alcohol – is straightforward so long as you are careful (see tip, p.153).

Serves 4

4	Chicken breasts, skin on
8%	Brine (80g salt dissolved in 1kg tap water)
1kg	Clams
	Groundnut or grapeseed oil
500g	Brown chicken stock (p.39)
2	Sprigs of thyme, leaves picked
2 tsp	Sherry vinegar
1 tbsp	Brown butter (see tip, p.204)
	Salt and black pepper

Place the chicken breasts in the brine in the fridge for 1 hour.

Pre-heat the water-bath to 60°C.

Remove the chicken breasts from the brine, and soak for 30 minutes in two changes of clean water. Pat dry. Wrap each piece of chicken tightly in clingfilm to create a roll. Seal the rolls under full pressure in individual sous-vide bags and put in the water-bath for 45 minutes.

In the meantime, place the clams in a saucepan of salty water for 10 minutes to purge them of sand. Soak in a bowl or basin of clean water for 20 minutes, changing the water four times. Discard any that are cracked or don't close.

Heat a frying pan until it is smoking hot, then add a little oil and continue to heat until it is also smoking. Add the clams and shake the pan until the oil catches fire. Continue shaking the pan until all the clams have opened.

Remove the pan from the heat and when cool enough to handle, remove the clams from their shells.

Reduce the chicken stock in a small pan over a high heat by two-thirds to a sauce consistency. Chop the thyme and add to the sauce with the sherry vinegar and brown butter. Season with salt.

Take the chicken breasts out of the water-bath and remove them from the bags and clingfilm. Pat them dry with kitchen paper and season with salt and freshly ground pepper.

Heat a little oil in the bottom of a frying pan and quickly sear the chicken breasts until coloured (approximately 1 minute on each side). Remove from the pan and slice diagonally. Divide between four plates.

Re-heat the clams in the chicken sauce and pour over the chicken breasts.

Cod with mustard and caper vinaigrette

This recipe demonstrates the virtues of sous-vide, and is really easy if you're trying sous-vide for the first time. Cooking fish – particularly white fish – to the point where it's tender but still moist can be difficult, even for professionals. Using this method, you should be able to produce a perfectly cooked piece of cod that can match anything you'd find in a good restaurant.

You can brine the cod briefly beforehand (p.170) to give it a firmer texture.

Serves 4

1kg	Waxy potatoes, peeled and cubed (1cm cubes)
4	Fillets of cod, skin off
60g	Unsalted butter
	Salt
	Groundnut and grapeseed oil

To serve

Mustard and caper vinaigrette (p.119)

Pre-heat the water-bath to 50°C.

Rinse the potato cubes under cold running water for 5 minutes, then drain them well.

Place the cod fillets in individual sous-vide bags with 15g of butter in each bag. Seal under full vacuum and place the bags in the water-bath for 15 minutes.

In the meantime, place the potatoes in a saucepan, cover with water and add a pinch of salt. Bring the water to the boil, reduce to a simmer and cook for 10 minutes. Drain the potatoes and dress them with the vinaigrette while still hot.

Heat a thin layer of oil in a non-stick frying pan over a medium-high heat. Remove the cod fillets from the sous-vide bags and pat dry with kitchen paper. Season the fillets with salt and place them in the hot pan. Cook for approximately 30 seconds on one side until lightly golden, then remove from the pan and serve coloured-side up on top of the dressed potatoes.

Salmon with Bois Boudran sauce

Before I discovered sous-vide, I often used to poach fish in oil. It's a terrific technique that produces a tender, gelatinous fish, but there's no question that it does require a lot of oil (p.174). Cooking salmon sous-vide also produces fish with a wonderful texture, but uses hardly any oil.

Like the cod recipe on p.201, this is a good recipe to use as a first-time trial of sous-vide cookery. Putting the fillets in a 50°C water-bath for 15 minutes creates what is for me the perfect texture. But if that's a little undercooked for you, try a higher temperature or a slightly longer cooking time. One of the benefits of sous-vide cooking is that its precision makes it easy to adjust the process and see how that affects an ingredient.

The Bois Boudran sauce (p.267) goes particularly well with oily fish like salmon, because its acidic and bitter notes cut through the richness.

Serves 4

4	Salmon fillets, skin on
80g	Olive oil
	Groundnut or grapeseed oil
	Salt

To serve

| | Crushed potatoes (p.253) |
| 150g | Bois Boudran sauce (p.267) |

Pre-heat the water-bath to 50°C.

Place the salmon fillets in individual sous-vide bags with 20g of olive oil in each bag. Seal under full vacuum and place the bags in the water-bath for 15 minutes.

Heat a thin layer of oil in a non-stick frying pan over a medium-high heat. Remove the salmon fillets from the sous-vide bags and pat dry with kitchen paper.

Season the fillets with salt and place them, skin-side down, in the hot pan. Cook for approximately 30 seconds until the skin turns golden and crisp, then remove them from the pan.

Serve on top of crushed potatoes with 2 tablespoons of the sauce per portion.

Scrambled eggs with brown butter

This recipe shows how practical and adaptable the sous-vide approach is. Normally, professional-standard creamy scrambled eggs are cooked in a bain-marie, involving nearly half an hour's vigilant stirring. By contrast, cooking them to the same level of quality by the sous-vide method simply requires a gentle cooking on a low heat, and an occasional massaging of the bag with your hands to scramble the eggs.

Serves 2

6	Large eggs
25g	Whole milk
20g	Double cream
	Pinch of salt
20g	Unsalted butter, melted
20g	Brown butter (see tip, right), melted

Pre-heat the water-bath to 75°C.

In a bowl, blitz the eggs, milk, cream and salt with a hand blender or whisk, then stir in the melted butter.

Divide the egg mixture in half and pour into two sous-vide bags. Seal under full pressure.

Place the bags in the water-bath and allow to cook for 15 minutes, massaging the contents every 3–5 minutes by removing the bags and covering your hands with a tea-towel.

To serve, remove the scrambled eggs from the bags and drizzle with brown butter on the plate.

How to make brown butter

Brown butter – also known as beurre noisette – offers a great way to introduce richness and a lovely nutty flavour to all sorts of recipes. To make it, melt unsalted butter in a medium pan over a gentle heat, whisking continuously, until the solids turn golden brown and give off a nutty aroma. Take the pan off the heat immediately, strain the butter through a coffee filter and store in the fridge.

Fennel in smoked duck fat

This versatile side dish goes well with almost any fish or roast meat. It was inspired by a visit to the house of my friend the food historian Ivan Day, up in the Lake District. Ivan's house is a cross between a museum and a historical test kitchen, and I've visited often to talk ideas over with him and pick his brains. Once he served me a confit of smoked duck with fennel as a garnish. I really liked the combination, started playing around with the ingredients, and this is what I came up with, essentially a confit of fennel, but with a smoky flavour.

You can use the smoking technique in this recipe to flavour other fats, such as butter or olive oil. Fat is a great vehicle for smoke as it really absorbs the aroma molecules, which is why fattier foods like salmon and cheese are popular choices for smoking. (For more about smoking, see p.76.)

To cook the dish in a conventional way, simply place the sliced fennel in a casserole dish with 500g smoked duck fat and place in an oven pre-heated to 90°C for 6 hours.

Serves 6–8

100g	Duck fat
15g	Smoking chips (Specialist ingredients, p.395)
4	Fennel bulbs
	Salt

Put the duck fat in a small saucepan or heatproof bowl in a home smoking box.

Put the smoking chips in the bottom of the box around the pan or bowl and place the box over a medium heat until the chips begin to smoke. Cover the box tightly with the lid. After 5 minutes, turn the heat off.

Leave the box covered for 40 minutes. Repeat this smoking process with the same chips twice more.

Pre-heat the water-bath to 80°C.

Cut the fennel into 2cm slices, lightly season with salt and put into a sous-vide bag with 2–3 tablespoons of the smoked fat.

Seal under full pressure and put in the water-bath for 35 minutes. (After 30 minutes, check whether the fennel is cooked by taking the bag from the water-bath and, your hands covered with a tea-towel, testing it for softness.)

Remove from the bag, drain on kitchen paper and serve.

Pasta and grains

Grains like rice, wheat, maize, oats, millet and sorghum are the staples of a huge part of the world's population, and the ingredients of a vast range of foods, amongst them risottos, porridge, tortillas and bread. Rice and wheat are the two most cultivated cereals for human consumption, and they tend to overshadow all the others, but the more unusual grains can bring interesting flavours and textures to the most familiar of dishes.

For example, spelt makes a superb risotto with an appealingly springy texture (pp.221 and 223), and quinoa can be used in place of vinegared rice in sushi (p.217). Strictly speaking, quinoa isn't a cereal – it is the seeds of a plant related to beets and spinach. It can be used like other grains, though, cooked or added to liquids to thicken them or create texture. The tiny yellow spheres contain no starch and have a slight bitter note that makes them an excellent foil for rich, oily or sweet ingredients.

Breaking free of the idea that particular grains only go with particular dishes gives a cook the freedom to be creative. The parsley porridge on p.216 is a simplified version of the snail porridge that I serve at the Fat Duck. That dish came about when my head chef told me how, while in New York, he'd eaten fish porridge at a Chinese restaurant. It turned out to be the menu's translation of 'congee' – a rice gruel that is sometimes served with a fish garnish – but by then it was too late. I was busy thinking about porridge and how, even though oats are a grain, just like rice, we only ever eat them for breakfast. Why, I wondered, couldn't oats be used for a savoury dish…? My thoughts were interrupted by the day's delivery of snails, and they edged their way into the concept. When snail porridge first went on the Fat Duck menu in 2003, it was considered very radical. But the funny thing is, when I later began researching historical British cookery, I discovered several ancient recipes for savoury porridges, using such ingredients as herbs, cheese and onion.

Cooking pasta

It's not hard to see why pasta is such a global culinary success story: it pleases kids and adults alike, making it a great choice for a family meal, and it's easy to cook. But if you want to make a plate of pasta that's as good as you might find served in an Italian home, it's worth paying attention to the little details. It's these that can turn pasta from blandly satisfying to truly delicious.

To begin with, it's important to use good-quality pasta. Many of the mass-market dried brands adopt cost-cutting, output-upping practices – like using soft flour instead of semi-milled 'semolina', and speed-drying the strands – which produce pasta that has little flavour and a disappointing texture. You can tell good dried pasta by its surface texture. One that looks slightly rough and feels almost sandpapery to the touch is likely to have been prepared carefully. The roughness suggests it has been forced through traditional bronze dies rather than modern nylon or Teflon ones, and will hold on to a sauce far better as a result. And don't get sucked into thinking that fresh pasta is somehow superior to dried. In fact, for many dishes, the reverse is true. Dried pasta tends to produce a better *al dente* texture, which is the benchmark of a skilfully cooked pasta – the moment when the pasta's chalky centre has gone, but it still offers a bit of firmness and resistance, a bit of bite.

As important as the right choice of pasta is the technique for cooking it. Pasta needs plenty of water, in order to rehydrate it and dilute the starch that escapes from it; it needs a specific amount of salt for flavour; and it requires just the right amount of cooking to ensure an *al dente* texture. The key, easy-to-remember numbers are 1:10:100. You need 1kg of water and 10g of salt per 100g of pasta. This means you need a decent-sized saucepan, even if you're only cooking for a few people. If you're cooking for more, I'd use two or more pans rather than one giant one, which will be slow to come to the boil (which is frustrating and can throw your timing out), slow to come back to the boil (which might overcook the pasta), and isn't a very practical or safe way of lugging boiling water round a kitchen.

Some people advise you to add olive oil to the pasta-cooking water, which supposedly prevents the pasta from sticking. But it doesn't, it just puddles on the surface, doing nothing. Cooking the pasta in the right amount of water, with a quick stir when it first goes in, should help keep the pasta pieces separate.

The point at which pasta is *al dente* comes and goes quickly. I'd advise continual tasting to determine when the pasta is ready, rather than relying on the timing suggested on the packet. When it *is* ready, don't just dump the contents of the pan into the colander – you'll be sluicing the pasta with all the starch you've just carefully removed. Instead, lift the pasta out of the water into the colander using a slotted spoon, pasta spoon or pair of tongs. Draining the pasta this way also means you can hold on to the cooking liquid, which can be useful. If the pasta sauce needs moistening or thickening slightly, for instance, you can add a few spoonfuls of the cooking liquid. And if the cooked pasta isn't going to be used immediately, now is the moment to add some olive oil. Mix a little in after draining, to prevent the pieces sticking together.

Cooking risotto

Historians suggest that risotto started as peasant food, but it's come a long way – you're as likely to find it in a three-star restaurant as on the kitchen table. Done well, it can be a sublime experience, with the rice perfectly *al dente*, and the rice and its cooking liquid amalgamated into a runny, unctuous whole. In Milan they say a risotto should end up *all'onda*, or wave-like – the idea being that if you shake the pan when the risotto is ready, it will send a ripple across the surface. It's a description that's perhaps more romantic than realistic, but it gives some idea of the kind of loose texture you're looking for.

There are a number of variables that will help towards this ideal. Firstly the rice. There are character differences between the three main risotto rice types: arborio, the most common, breaks down easily to a fairly loose texture; vialone nano is firmer, takes longer to cook and absorbs more of the liquid; carnaroli falls somewhere between the two and has a nice creaminess to it. It's also worth trying to get hold of some rice that has been aged. They do this by storing it in temperature-controlled silos for a year so that the sugars present in the starch increase, and the lipids it contains oxidize, releasing fatty acids. The rice becomes sweeter and harder, which improves the flavour and makes it less likely to become sticky or overcook. It's becoming increasingly available online from producers like Acquerello.

The first step in making risottos is the *tostatura*, in which the grains are toasted in oil before adding the other ingredients. It prevents them from sticking, makes them absorb the liquid more evenly and introduces a delicate nutty flavour to the dish.

The next step is normally to add chopped onion and perhaps garlic. However, if you've toasted the rice first, there's a risk that, by the time the onions and garlic have softened, the rice will be overdone. (Reversing the process and softening the onion and garlic first merely presents you with a different problem: if the garlic is cooked for too long at this stage it can become bitter, and both the garlic and the onion might end up overcooked and tough, making the risotto lumpy.) You could of course cook garlic and onions separately from the rice and then combine the two, but another solution is to replace the garlic and onions with acidulated butter (p.260), added at the end of cooking.

Once the rice has been toasted, you can add some form of alcohol for flavour and acidity. White wine is the standard all-purpose choice. If you want to add a sweeter note, pour in some vermouth. (I often add a mixture of the two.) Pernod is superb with fish and seafood risottos and Madeira is fantastic with mushrooms. A risotto with asparagus, broad beans and other spring vegetables might suit a floral wine such as a Gewürztraminer.

After this, the cooking liquid is added. There are fiercely held opinions about how best to add this to the pot. Putting the lot in at the start; ladling it in a bit at a time and stirring it into the grains; pouring most in at the start and topping up occasionally – each of these techniques has its advocates. I've tested this extensively and found that the bit-by-bit approach and putting half in first and then topping it up will both produce excellent results.

The rice is usually cooked in a light stock or broth, but you can use other liquids instead. So long as it complements the other ingredients, you might choose to use beetroot juice (as in the beetroot spelt risotto on p.223) or leftover roasting juices, for example. Or you can simply add a little of one of these towards the end of cooking simply to make the flavour more complex. (With denser, more viscous liquids, like roasting juices or a wine reduction, they'll probably need to be added towards the end anyway, to ensure that the risotto retains a nice liquid consistency and doesn't become too thick.) And if you're making a seafood risotto that needs a fairly neutral base, you might decide just to use plain water. Whatever liquid you choose, it's important to have it already warm in a pan.

A risotto is ready when the rice and liquid are no longer separate but have amalgamated together. The rice should be soft but still have bite, and have lost all that chalkiness at the centre. The only way to establish whether the rice is properly *al dente* is to taste it regularly towards the end of cooking. At this stage, your main concern is preventing the rice absorbing too much liquid and becoming too soft, so during the last few minutes, add the liquid carefully and sparingly. The consistency needs to be slightly wetter than you intend serving it: it will have soaked up the excess by the time it reaches the table.

There's one final, crucial task before serving – the *mantecatura*. This is where butter (or acidulated butter if you're using it, p.260) and cheese (or possibly some mascarpone, olive oil or even lightly whipped cream) are stirred into the rice, which is then taken off the heat and left to stand for a few minutes. This procedure is as important to the final result as any other part of making a risotto, integrating the rice and liquid better and introducing extra creaminess to the dish.

Crab lasagne

In Britain, we think of lasagne as layers of ground beef, béchamel sauce and pasta, but it's often made with other ingredients – such as artichokes or mushrooms and ham, or seafood, which I think works particularly well. Here I've used crab meat to bring a welcome touch of lightness and sweetness to the dish.

One of the other main flavour components is an intense tomato fondue sauce that needs to be cooked for 4 hours. If this seems like a lot of work for one dish, make double the quantity: what you don't use here can be stored in the fridge, and will make a great sauce for other pasta dishes. You can also simplify the recipe by using sieved tomatoes (passata) to make a straightforward sauce instead. (Put a litre of passata in a pan, add olive oil, chopped herbs and garlic, and cook gently until reduced by three-quarters.)

In recipes that call for chopped tomatoes, most advise you to discard the pulp and seeds, but these have more umami taste (p.20) than any other part of the tomato, and it seems to me a shame to waste all that goodness. So, here's my approach. Peel the ripe tomatoes first (see tip, p.269). Then cut the tomatoes in half vertically and scoop out the insides with a teaspoon, over a chopping board. Roughly chop the pulp and seeds and tip them into a sieve set over a bowl. Sprinkle over a little salt and leave for 20 minutes to extract the juice. After this you can discard what's left in the sieve, reserving the juice to use alongside the tomato flesh.

Serves 4–6

For the tomato fondue sauce

115g	Extra virgin olive oil
1	Small onion, peeled and finely sliced
½	Star anise
2 tsp	Coriander seeds
1	Clove of garlic, peeled and crushed
1	Bouquet garni (thyme, celery leaf, parsley and bay leaf, tied together with a strip of leek or a piece of string, see p.34)
1.5kg	Tomatoes, peeled (see tip, p.269), de-seeded and chopped (reserving the juices)
	Tabasco sauce

	Worcestershire sauce
2 tsp	Tomato ketchup
20g	Sherry vinegar

For the crab filling

500g	Fish stock (p.42)
225g	Skinless cod fillet
400g	Cooked white crab meat, checked for bits of shell

For the sauce

	Grapeseed or groundnut oil
130g	Peeled and finely sliced shallot (approx. 2–3 banana shallots)
1	Clove of garlic, peeled and bashed with the flat part of a knife or by hand
¾ tsp	Fennel seeds
1	Bay leaf
200g	Dry white wine
1kg	Fish stock (p.42)
100g	Whipping cream
100g	Whole milk
20g	Cornflour
	Salt and white pepper
	Nutmeg

For the pasta

10g	Salt
10	Dry lasagne sheets

To finish and serve

20	Basil leaves
20	Tarragon leaves
50g	Parmesan cheese, finely grated

For the tomato fondue sauce, pour 90g of the olive oil into a wide-bottomed saucepan and place it over a very low heat. Add the onion, star anise and coriander seeds and sweat for 10 minutes.

continued overleaf

Add the garlic and bouquet garni and continue to sweat for another 5 minutes.

Add the chopped tomatoes, tomato juices, a few drops each of Tabasco and Worcestershire sauce, the ketchup and vinegar, and cook over a very low heat for 3–4 hours. When cooked the fondue should be dark red and almost jam-like.

Skim the separated oil off the top before liquidizing the fondue into a smooth sauce in a blender. (Keep this oil, as it has a terrific flavour, and can be used in vinaigrettes or tossed into pasta.)

Pass the sauce through a fine sieve, then stir in the remaining 25g olive oil.

For the crab filling, heat the fish stock in a small saucepan over a low heat until the liquid reaches 50°C.

Add the cod and, at this temperature, gently cook for 10–15 minutes until the fish is cooked through.

Remove the fish from the liquid with a slotted spoon and drain on kitchen paper.

When dry, flake the fish with a fork and mix with the crab meat.

To start the sauce, heat a thin layer of oil in a saucepan over a medium heat and sweat the shallots, garlic, fennel seeds and bay leaf for 10 minutes. Add the wine, increase the heat to high and allow the liquid to reduce in volume by two-thirds.

Add the fish stock and reduce by half. Strain through a fine sieve and discard the shallots, garlic and aromatics.

Return the liquid to the pan and add the whipping cream and milk. Place over a medium heat and when the liquid is warm, sieve in the cornflour and whisk over the heat until the sauce thickens (approximately 5 minutes). Season with salt, freshly ground white pepper and freshly grated nutmeg to taste.

For the pasta, bring 1kg cold tap water to the boil and add the salt.

When boiling, add the lasagne sheets one at a time. Cook for 8–9 minutes, stirring occasionally to stop the sheets sticking together. Using tongs, remove the pasta sheets from the water and set to one side on a tray.

To assemble and cook, pre-heat the oven to 180°C.

Chop 16 each of the basil and tarragon leaves. Spoon a thin layer of the tomato fondue sauce into a baking dish (20 × 30cm), then lay some of the lasagne sheets on top in a single layer. Add another layer of tomato fondue sauce followed by a layer of the crab and cod mixture, a layer of sauce and a sprinkling of Parmesan and herbs.

Repeat these layers until the baking dish is full, finishing with a layer of pasta covered with sauce and Parmesan.

Cook in the pre-heated oven for 25 minutes or until the edges are bubbling. Roughly chop the remaining herbs and sprinkle on top before serving.

My carbonara

Outside Italy a carbonara is often considered to be pasta with a ham and cream sauce. Italians would consider this a travesty, and I would agree with them. A carbonara sauce should consist of pancetta, garlic, beaten eggs and grated Parmesan (or perhaps Pecorino). Here I've added onions, chilli and peas for flavour, colour and texture.

You could also replace the pancetta with smoked or non-smoked bacon or a few anchovy fillets, and the peas with fresh soya beans, broad beans, thinly sliced runner beans or broccoli florets, all pre-cooked.

Serves 4

40g	Salt
75g	Olive oil
2	Medium onions, peeled and finely chopped
2	Cloves of garlic, peeled and finely chopped
1–2	Fresh red chillies (depending on how hot you want it), de-veined, de-seeded and finely chopped
250g	Pancetta lardons
400g	Spaghetti
6	Medium egg yolks
100g	Parmesan cheese, grated, plus extra for serving
250g	Frozen peas
	Salt and black pepper

Fill a large saucepan with 4kg cold tap water and add the salt. Cover with a lid and place over a medium-high heat to bring to the boil.

In the meantime, put the olive oil, onions, garlic and chilli into a large frying pan and place it over a medium-low heat for 5 minutes before adding the pancetta. Cook for a further 5 minutes or until the onion has lightly caramelized.

Once the water comes to the boil, add the spaghetti and stir it every few minutes to prevent it from sticking together. After approximately 7 minutes, whisk the egg yolks and Parmesan together in a bowl and add a ladle of the pasta water.

A minute or so before the spaghetti is cooked, take the pancetta and onions off the heat and add the frozen peas.

Drain the pasta (p.210) and return it to the pan. Add the contents of the frying pan along with the egg and cheese mixture, and mix together. Allow to sit for 2 minutes. Season with salt and freshly ground pepper to taste.

Stir thoroughly to incorporate everything, then serve with more grated Parmesan sprinkled on top.

Truffle macaroni

This versatile side dish is quite rich already, but to introduce even more flavour you could add a little brown butter (p.204), or even brown butter infused with sage leaves. (Roll sage leaves between finger and thumb, add them to the brown butter and heat for a few minutes. Remove from the heat and infuse for 5–10 minutes.) Chopped chives and a little tarragon are good added just before serving.

Serve with the braised pork on p.164, a pork chop or roast chicken. At the Hind's Head we sometimes serve the dish with a fried duck egg on top.

Serves 6–8 as a side dish

20g	Salt
200g	Macaroni
300g	Dry white wine
15g	Truffle oil
300g	Brown chicken stock (p.39), warmed
80g	Parmesan cheese, finely grated, plus 20g extra for sprinkling
10g	Cornflour
80g	Soft cream cheese

Pre-heat the grill to high.

Bring 2kg cold tap water and the salt to the boil in a large saucepan and add the pasta. Cook for approximately 7 minutes over a medium heat until *al dente*.

In a small saucepan, reduce the white wine over a high heat to 30g.

Drain the pasta (p.210) and toss with the truffle oil.

Add the warm chicken stock to the reduced wine. Mix the grated Parmesan with the cornflour and add to the pan. Stir until the cheese has been incorporated into the sauce, then add the pasta.

Cook over a medium heat until the pasta is warmed through, then stir in the cream cheese. Season with salt.

Put the pasta into an ovenproof dish, sprinkle with the remaining Parmesan and grill until the top is browned.

Parsley porridge

When I first developed my recipe for snail porridge for the Fat Duck, back in 2003, I had real trouble getting the right consistency. Even when the oats were cooked for no more than a minute, they still ended up a bit swamp-like. Eventually I figured out that the culprits were the oatflakes that had crumbled to powder at the bottom of the box. They cooked faster than the rest and released their starch more quickly, turning the mixture gluey. I started sieving the oats before cooking and that solved the problem.

The porridge makes an excellent accompaniment for the rib of beef with bone-marrow sauce on p.155.

Serves 4 as a side dish

120g	White chicken stock (p.38)
60g	Porridge oats, sieved to remove any powder
120g	Parsley butter (p.263)
	Salt and black pepper

Heat the chicken stock in a saucepan and add the oats.

Simmer until the oats have absorbed the liquid and are cooked but still retain their texture. This should take no more than 2 minutes – overcooking the oats will make them starchy.

Add the parsley butter. Stir until melted and mixed with the oats. Season with salt and freshly ground pepper.

Quinoa sushi

One technique – infinite fillings. This basic recipe makes sushi rolls with seasoned quinoa instead of rice, to which you can add a variety of different fillings. I've given three ideas for these using beef, crab and vegetables, but you can experiment with whatever Asian-inspired combinations you want. Using quinoa instead of the traditional rice makes the sushi lighter. They can be served with ponzu sauce (p.266) or horseradish cream (p.264) instead of the mayonnaise.

If you want your sushi to be neat and consistent, it's worth buying a sushi mat. This turns the process into a satisfying, hands-on experience – very Zen.

Serves 6

For the sushi

200g	Quinoa
¼ tsp	Salt
55g	Ponzu sauce (p.266)
15g	Miso paste (Specialist ingredients, p.395)
3 tbsp	Sesame seeds, toasted
1 tsp	Black onion seeds
10g	Chives
6	Nori seaweed sheets (Specialist ingredients, p.395)
2 tbsp	Horseradish cream (p.264)
	Filling of choice (below)

To serve

Wasabi mayonnaise (p.118)
Ponzu sauce (p.266)

Soak the quinoa in cold water for 15 minutes. Put 350g cold tap water into a saucepan and add the salt. Drain and rinse the quinoa well, and put into the pan of salted water.

Bring the water to a simmer over a medium-high heat, cover and reduce the heat. Cook for 15 minutes, then remove from the heat and allow to rest for 5 minutes.

Divide the quinoa in half and blitz half of it with a hand blender. Combine the two together again to make a sticky mixture.

Mix the ponzu sauce with the miso paste and stir this into the quinoa with the toasted sesame seeds and the onion seeds. Chop the chives and mix with the quinoa.

Trim 5cm off the top of one nori sheet and lay it flat on a sushi mat. Spread a thin layer of the quinoa mixture on the nori, meeting three of the edges. Leave a 3cm gap between the fourth edge and the quinoa. Position this gap furthest away from you on the mat.

Spread some horseradish cream along the quinoa on the edge closest to you. Place a strip of your chosen filling approximately 5cm from the edge nearest to you.

Using the sushi mat, roll the nori tightly round the filling. Brush the exposed nori with cold water to seal the roll.

Do the same with the remaining nori sheets, until you have six rolls.

Using a very sharp knife, slice each roll into individual pieces. Serve with wasabi mayonnaise and ponzu sauce.

Rare beef, shiitake and spring onion filling

A classic combination of flavours that you might find in an oriental stir-fry, but it works just as well as a sushi filling. You could use alternative mushrooms.

	Groundnut or grapeseed oil
350g	Feather steak
	Salt
15	Fresh shiitake mushrooms, halved
60g	Mirin (Specialist ingredients, p.394)
20g	Ponzu sauce (p.266)
10	Spring onions, trimmed of roots and dark green leaves

Coat the bottom of a heavy-bottomed frying pan with oil, and place over a high heat. Season the steak on both sides with a little salt and sear on each side, flipping the meat every 15–20 seconds (p.137) until the outside is well charred but the inside remains rare. This should take no more than 1 minute on each side. Set the meat aside to rest.

continued overleaf

Wipe out the pan with some kitchen paper and heat a little more oil over a medium-high heat. Fry the shiitakes until they are coloured on both sides. Add 40g of the mirin and allow to reduce and glaze the mushrooms. Remove from the heat, toss with 15g of the ponzu sauce and set aside.

Using the same pan, repeat this process with the spring onions and the remaining mirin and ponzu.

Divide the beef, shiitakes and spring onions between the six sushi rolls.

Crab, cucumber and horseradish filling
Crab and cucumber are a traditional pairing in Japanese *sunomono* dishes (vegetables and/or seafood in a vinegar dressing). Horseradish adds a bit of bite.

150g	Cooked brown crab meat
150g	Cooked white crab meat, checked for shell
50g	Horseradish sauce
50g	Mayonnaise (p.118)
	Salt
½	Cucumber, peeled and de-seeded

Combine the crab meats with the horseradish, mayonnaise and a pinch of salt. Cut the cucumber into long, thin batons.

Divide the crab mixture and cucumber batons between the six sushi rolls.

Cucumber, mango and avocado filling
The ingredients for a salsa or tropical salad: cucumber, mango and avocado offer contrasts of crunchy, soft and smooth textures and fresh, sharp and rich flavours.

1	Cucumber, peeled and de-seeded
1	Mango, peeled and sliced
1	Avocado, peeled and sliced

Cut the cucumber into long, thin batons.

Mix the batons with the mango and avocado, and divide the mixture between the six sushi rolls.

Crab risotto

Here I have used the sweet meat and stock from a live crab (p.43) – the flavour is unique – but you could use vegetable stock (p.44) and crab meat from the fishmonger or supermarket instead. By the way, seafood risottos rarely have Parmesan sprinkled on top – the strength of the cheese flavour drowns the delicacy of the fish. In season, asparagus spears are a lovely addition to this dish (p.252).

Serves 4

For the risotto

	Groundnut or grapeseed oil
150g	Carnaroli risotto rice
90g	Dry white wine
75g	Dry white vermouth
750g	Crab stock (p.43)

To finish and serve

	Mascarpone
60g	Mascarpone
45g	Acidulated butter (p.260)
150g	Cooked shredded white crab meat, and/or brown meat
15g	Basil leaves
15	Tarragon leaves
	Salt
	Crab oil (optional, p.43)

Add a thin layer of oil to a wide-bottomed saucepan and toast the rice over a medium-high heat, continually stirring, until it crackles and takes on a nutty aroma. Add the wine and vermouth and boil to reduce until the liquid has almost disappeared.

Warm the crab stock in a saucepan and add half of it to the rice. Stir and allow to cook for 10 minutes.

Continue adding stock one ladle at a time until the rice is tender and all the liquid has been absorbed.

Remove from the heat and gently stir in the mascarpone, butter and crab meat until well combined. Allow to rest for 4–5 minutes. Roughly chop the basil, finely chop the tarragon, and stir into the risotto. Season with salt before serving, and drizzle with crab oil, if using.

How to prepare risotto in advance

A risotto can be partly made in advance and finished later. Make in the usual manner but warm up only three-quarters of the stock. Chill the last quarter. When the risotto is about three-quarters through its cooking time, remove from the heat, pour the reserved cold stock on top and stir in. Tip the rice on to a tray and spread thinly, to cool it down quickly. Place the tray in the fridge, or in the freezer for half an hour before storing in the fridge. To finish, put the risotto in a pan and cook as normal, adding a little more warm stock if necessary.

Mushroom spelt risotto

Herbs and acidulated butter contribute their flavours to this risotto, which can also be used as a side dish. One of the key ingredients here is dried shiitake mushrooms, which are especially rich in the umami taste (p.20). It's worth having some in your storecupboard, so that you can add them to any dish where you want to enhance a mushroom flavour.

This is a vegetarian recipe, but you can use chicken stock as the cooking liquor if you want.

Serves 4

For the risotto

50g	Dried shiitake mushrooms
750g	Vegetable stock (p.44)
15g	Groundnut or grapeseed oil
100g	Peeled and finely chopped shallot (approx. 2 large banana shallots)
4	Cloves of garlic, peeled and finely chopped
200g	Pearled spelt
15g	Unsalted butter
200g	Button mushrooms, finely sliced
30g	Whipping cream
50g	Mascarpone

To finish and serve

60g	Acidulated butter (p.260)
40g	Parmesan cheese, grated
5g	Parsley leaves
5g	Tarragon leaves
	Salt and black pepper

Put the dried shiitake mushrooms into a saucepan with the vegetable stock and place over a high heat. Bring to the boil and allow to boil for 5 minutes. Remove the pan from the heat and allow to infuse for 30 minutes before straining into a clean pan. Set the mushrooms aside and gently warm the stock for using in the risotto.

Heat half the oil in a clean wide-bottomed saucepan over a medium heat and sweat the shallot and garlic (approximately 7–10 minutes). Remove when soft but not coloured and set aside.

Heat the remaining oil in the same saucepan, then add the spelt and toast over a medium-high heat for 3–4 minutes.

Pour in half of the warmed stock, stir and allow to cook for 10 minutes. Continue adding stock one ladle at a time until the spelt is tender and all the liquid has been absorbed.

In the meantime, melt the unsalted butter in a small frying pan over a medium-high heat. When foaming, add the button mushrooms and cook until caramelized in colour (approximately 10 minutes).

Add the caramelized mushrooms, shallots, garlic, cream and mascarpone to the spelt and cook for a further 4–5 minutes, stirring regularly.

Stir in the acidulated butter and, once melted, add the Parmesan and remove from the heat. Allow to rest for 3 minutes.

Roughly chop the herbs. Season the risotto with salt and freshly ground pepper and add the chopped parsley and tarragon just before serving.

Beetroot spelt risotto

The nuttiness of spelt complements the earthiness of beetroot. The spelt is cooked with beetroot juice, turning it a deep purple colour, and the texture and flavour of the finished dish are enhanced by sharp-tasting cubes of pickled beetroot, and the anise crunch of fennel shavings.

The risotto can be eaten on its own, but it also works really well as a side dish. It's good with roast game or fish, particularly smoked and oily fish, where the acidity of the pickled beetroot helps to cut their richness.

You can make a vegetarian version using vegetable stock in place of white chicken stock.

Serves 4

For the pickled beetroot cubes

200g	White wine vinegar
1 tsp	White caster sugar
½ tsp	Salt
100g	Peeled and cubed raw beetroot

For the risotto

200g	Beetroot juice (this is available in most supermarkets, but 500g raw beetroot will yield approx. 200g fresh juice)
	Groundnut or grapeseed oil
200g	Pearled spelt
100g	Dry Madeira
600g	White chicken stock (p.38), or vegetable stock (p.44), warmed

To finish and serve

30g	Parmesan cheese, grated
50g	Acidulated butter (p.260)
	Salt
1 tbsp	Crème fraiche
	Horseradish cream (p.264)
1	Fennel bulb, finely shaved with a mandolin
	Mustard vinaigrette (p.119)

For the pickled beetroot cubes, combine the vinegar, sugar and salt in a bowl and whisk together. Add the beetroot cubes and leave to marinate for at least 30 minutes.

To start the risotto, pour the beetroot juice into a small saucepan and place the pan over a high heat. Boil the liquid to reduce by half. Once the volume of liquid has reduced to 100g, remove the pan from the heat and set aside.

Coat the bottom of a wide-bottomed saucepan with a thin layer of oil and place the pan over a medium-high heat. Add the spelt to the oil and toast until lightly coloured, stirring continuously.

Add the Madeira to the spelt and cook until the liquid has reduced by three-quarters.

Pour in half of the warmed stock, stir and allow to cook for 10 minutes. Continue adding stock one ladle at a time until the spelt is tender and most of the liquid has been absorbed.

Add the reduced beetroot juice and continue cooking for another 5 minutes.

To serve, stir the Parmesan, acidulated butter, a pinch of salt and the crème fraiche into the risotto. When combined, remove from the heat and leave to rest for 3 minutes.

Divide the risotto between four plates and drizzle a little horseradish cream on top.

Dress the fennel shavings with vinaigrette and place a pile in the centre of each plate on top of the risotto. Drain the pickled beetroot cubes and sprinkle them around the plate before serving.

Cheese

Cheese is an ingredient with enormous range and complexity. The texture can be creamy, smooth and meltingly unguent, elastic, crumbly, firm or almost crunchy. It can contain several of the tastes at once, particularly salty, sour and umami. (Those little white crystals on the jagged face of well-aged Parmesan are pure monosodium glutamate.) And the flavour ranges from herbaceous, floral, fruity and buttery to milky, garlicky and earthy. As far as I'm concerned, Britain is second only to France in terms of the artisan cheeses it produces, and that's something we should be proud of. A piece of Stilton with a glass of oloroso sherry is one of the world's great pleasures.

So cheese offers a very refined eating experience. But some of my fondest memories of it spring from childhood and are anything but refined. I still love a baked potato with grated cheese on top, or just a Granny Smith with a chunk of Cheddar. (I remember, aged six, trying to hold chalk in one hand, cheese and an apple in the other, and write on a small blackboard. I took a bite from the wrong hand and ended up with a mouthful of chalk – the ultimate chalk and cheese experience.) For me, a burger isn't a burger unless it has a slice of cheese on top. And I relish the whole business of a cheese toastie – the way the cheese stretches to an impossible length as you remove the sandwich from your mouth after taking a bite; even the napalm heat of the cooked cheese that invariably burns your tongue.

So, although cheese is a versatile ingredient that can be eaten raw in a salad, heated to enrich a soup, or used for flavouring, for topping or for filling, in this chapter it's the nostalgic element that's to the fore. Macaroni cheese (p.234) is still one of my ultimate comfort foods, and fondue (p.231) will always remind me of the orange fondue sets everybody including my parents had in the 1970s, and of my first skiing trip when I was about twenty.

Making cheese

Although cheese has a complex flavour, the process involved in making it is essentially a simple one, and people have been doing it for thousands of years, since herdsmen somehow found out about the effect rennet has on milk. Rennet is a substance in the stomach of young milk-fed animals, usually calves; it transforms their mother's milk into curds, which can be digested more easily. This effect was probably discovered by chance, perhaps when milk was stored in a container or pouch made from a young animal's stomach.

If milk is left to stand, cream forms at the top and the rest naturally turns sour, as *Lactobacilli* and *Lactococci* bacteria already present in the milk convert the lactose that milk contains into lactic acid. (It's this acid that gives cheese its sharpness.) In such acidic conditions, proteins in the milk called caseins will gradually begin to clump together and curdle, and this is how simple soft cheeses were originally made and, to an extent, are still made today. However, when rennet is added to a milk already acidulated by bacteria, the milk will quickly separate into relatively firm solids (the curds) and a liquid (the whey). A skilled manipulation of this curdling is one of the foundation skills of the cheesemaker. By controlling how far and for how long the cheese is curdled by acid and then how far and for how long by rennet, the cheesemaker can achieve a particular texture. A simple curdling by means of acid will result in a soft moist cheese, such as cottage or curd. A quicker and more solid curdling due to the presence of rennet will help start the cheese's progress towards the harder texture we associate with Gouda, Cheddar and Parmesan.

After a cheese has curdled, the curds can be lifted out by slotted spoon to a mould and allowed to drain naturally of their whey (to produce fromage frais and cottage cheese etc). Most curds, however, are cut or sliced (or sometimes even milled) in order to separate out the whey as thoroughly as possible. The amount of separation, the time it takes and the temperature at which this is done determines the flavour and texture of the finished cheese. The curds are then put in some sort of mould or sieve and allowed to drain, after which the cheesemaker has a variety of options. The retained whey, which will still contain some milk proteins, can be re-boiled to make cheeses like ricotta (the whey by-product of Parmesan cheesemaking is fed to Parma ham pigs). The curds can be altered further by the addition of ripening microbes (e.g. *Penicillium* for Brie and Camembert, and blue cheeses such as Roquefort) or other flavourings, and they can also be heated to drive off more moisture (as in Emmental and Gouda). Most hard cheeses are then pressed, which will drive off yet more moisture.

Part of the cheesemaker's skill lies in balancing all these different considerations to make a cheese with exactly the character they want. Salt is added for flavour, and to help firm the structure and preserve the cheese. Depending on type, the cheese is then stored in a carefully controlled environment to allow enzymes from the milk, rennet and microbes to ripen or mature the cheese. Softer cheeses like Brie ripen quickly (within four to ten weeks), while harder cheeses like Cheddar are allowed to mature for six to eighteen months. Parmesan is matured for one to four years.

Cooking cheese

When cooking with cheese, your aim is usually to melt and integrate it fully with other ingredients. In these circumstances it's best to avoid the group of cheeses that readily form into stringy strands (notably Emmental, mozzarella and Cheddar), and it's a good idea to finely grate whatever cheese you choose so that when it's added to the pan, it disperses evenly.

However, your main focus of concern will be overcooking. The melting point for cheese runs from around 55°C for soft cheeses through 65°C for Cheddar, Gruyère and Emmental to 82°C for dry hard cheeses like Parmesan and Pecorino – at this point the proteins holding the structure together break down, making the cheese soft and runny. (Hard cheeses take longer because they have less moisture and the proteins are more tightly bonded together, so they don't flow as readily.) Go much above a cheese's melting point, however, and its proteins will start to tighten into clumps and squeeze out the fat they contain (rather like wringing water out of a towel), so that the cheese becomes grainy and oily. So controlling the heat during cooking is particularly important. Cheese should be exposed to heat as little as possible. Add it to a dish as late as you can and keep the temperature well below boiling.

There are, however, a handful of ingredients that are, in effect, the cook's secret weapons in the struggle to prevent cheese from going grainy and splitting out its fat. Chief among these are acidic ingredients like white wine and lemon juice, and starchy ingredients like flour and cornflour. So in the fondue recipe, a mixture of grated cheese and cornflour is added to a pan of heated wine and lemon juice and whisked until it's smooth. In most dishes I try to avoid using starch because it masks some of the flavour, but sometimes the benefits definitely outweigh the drawbacks.

There's also a substance that helps cheese to melt and blend effectively when it's cooked, but you're more likely to find it in a chemist than a food store. Sodium citrate is used by the medical industry as an anti-coagulant, but the commercial food industry has also long been aware of its thinning properties. Another of the difficulties with melting cheese to a nice runny mass is that as cheese melts the casein proteins and calcium it contains react together to create a tangle of rope-like fibres. However, if sodium citrate is present it disperses the calcium, preventing the reaction from taking place. So processed food manufacturers add sodium citrate to the scraps destined to be made into cheese slices, which helps them to melt into one another efficiently. The same science can be used to melt cheese to the perfect loose texture for a sauce like the one for cauliflower macaroni cheese (p.234). Just make sure that you use it sparingly, otherwise it can give a bitter taste to a dish.

However, there are dishes, such as fondue and cheese toasties, that make a virtue of cheese's capacity to form into fibres, creating a Dalí-esque molten stringiness. But making cheese stringy needs careful heat management

as well: if it's too hot, the cheese will be liquid rather than elastic; if it's too cool, it will firm up too much. The other secret to stringiness is beating the cheese as you warm it, which aligns and stretches the proteins to create the right elasticity. It's easy to judge when the cheese is ready. As you beat, lift the whisk every once in a while to see to see just how far you can draw strings of cheese out of the pan.

Stringy cheese just seems to suit some dishes, and it can be fun to make it truly super-stringy. While working on the cheese toastie, I couldn't resist finding out how far I could get cheese to stretch. In the Fat Duck car park my chefs and I produced a string about 5 metres long, which my pastry chef – hoping centrifugal force might stretch it even further – started whirling around his head like a lasso!

Finally, when finishing and serving a dish containing cheese, it's particularly important to taste before seasoning. Since cheese is often already quite salty and acidic, adding extra can overload it.

Cheese fondue with sherry and cloves

The fondue set is one of those classic wedding gifts that usually ends up at the back of a cupboard. This recipe is a great excuse to heave it out and dust it off. Done well, fondue is a lot of fun – a communal free-for-all that doesn't need a knife and fork. However, if you've never received a fondue set as a gift, you can still make the recipe. All you need is a Chinese-style plate warmer to keep the saucepan warm and the cheese mix nicely melted.

You want the cheese to be runny and stringy, not thick and stodgy, and the key to this is using cornflour and white wine to prevent the proteins in the cheese coagulating.

One of the other factors that gives this fondue its character is the combination of sherry and cloves, which go so well together because of a compound they have in common called eugenol. In tandem they help produce a richly flavoured mixture that needn't be confined to fondue. If it's left to set (in a baking tray lined with clingfilm), the fondue can be kept for a week in the fridge. It can be sliced to make an amazing cheese toastie (p.232) and it's equally good on burgers, on toast, in Welsh rarebit, or for topping the bread in onion soup (p.57).

In a bowl, mix the grated cheeses with the cornflour.

Bring the sherry to a simmer in a small saucepan over a medium-high heat. Add the thyme and garlic, remove from the heat and leave to infuse for 10 minutes. Strain and allow to cool.

Bring the wine and lemon juice to the boil together in a medium saucepan, and add the cheese, a handful at a time, whisking continuously until smooth and creamy.

Add the sherry, mustard powder and ground cloves to the cheese and wine, and continue to stir until the fondue thickens.

Transfer to a fondue pot and serve with cornichons, cubes of sourdough bread and crudités.

Serves 6–8

450g	Gruyère cheese, grated
450g	Comté cheese, grated
15g	Cornflour
30g	Manzanilla sherry
2	Sprigs of thyme
3	Cloves of garlic
500g	Dry white wine
20g	Lemon juice
5g	English mustard powder
	Pinch of ground cloves

To serve

Cornichons
Sourdough bread
Crudités

The ultimate cheese toastie

Like most kids of my generation I was excited by the Breville sandwich toaster when it first appeared in the 1970s. I remember the napalm-like heat of the cheese in the toasted sandwich, and the delicious browned crispiness of the bits of cheese caught at the edges of the machine. So I thought it would be fun to take the toastie and give it an upgrade.

A key part of that upgrade is an unlikely piece of kit: a washing-up sponge. One of the difficulties with toastie-making is producing a crisp, browned exterior without overcooking the filling. My solution is to do it in two stages. First you toast the slices of bread in the machine for 5 minutes, with a triangle of sponge inserted between them to ensure there's a decent cavity for the filling. Then you remove the sponge, put the filling in its place, and cook for a further 5 minutes.

It's more fiddly than just bunging a cheese sandwich in the Breville, but the results can be amazing. I always enjoy giving a humble dish a luxury makeover, so my filling has fondue cheese (p.231), shredded ham (p.65), onion compote (p.270) and truffle oil. But you can choose whatever ingredients you like and use the same process to make a toastie that's truly terrific.

Cut the sponge into two triangles to fit inside each half of a toasted sandwich maker. (The size of the sponge triangle will depend on the size and shape of your machine but the sponge should fit inside the triangle that the machine makes, leaving a 1cm gap around the edges.)

Pre-heat the toasted sandwich maker.

Spread one side of the bread with soft butter and place one slice butter-side down on the pre-heated machine. Place the sponge triangles where the filling should be and place the second piece of bread on top, butter-side up. Toast with the sponge inside for 5 minutes or until the bread is lightly golden.

Remove the sponge sandwich from the machine and cut open if sealed. Remove the sponge and spread a little softened butter on the inside of each half of bread and add slices of the cheese fondue, some shredded ham and a layer of onion compote, along with a few drops of truffle oil.

Close the sandwich and return it to the machine. Cook for 5 minutes more, until the toastie has sealed and the bread is golden brown. Be careful when biting into the toastie, as the contents will be piping hot and molten.

Serves 1

1	New washing-up sponge (without scourer)
2	Slices of white sandwich bread
	Unsalted butter, at room temperature
	Set fondue cheese (p.231), sliced
	Shredded ham (p.65)
	Onion compote (p.270)
	Truffle oil

Cauliflower macaroni cheese

You can create a really interesting dish by taking a single central ingredient, preparing it several different ways, then bringing them together. It's a wonderful method of showing off an ingredient and introducing a variety of textures. This macaroni cheese contains raw cauliflower florets, a cauliflower purée and deep-fried florets – the latter are optional, if you don't fancy so much work. (And I often add a pinch or two of curry powder to the purée. I don't know why it works, but it definitely adds something.) The sodium citrate helps thin out the cheese for the sauce (p.229).

Serves 6

1	Large cauliflower, broken into small florets
600g	Whole milk
30g	Salt
300g	Macaroni
	Groundnut or grapeseed oil, for deep-frying
240g	Gruyère cheese, coarsely grated, plus 50g extra for sprinkling on top
120g	Parmesan cheese, grated
12g	Sodium citrate (Specialist ingredients, p.395)
30g	Wholegrain mustard
90g	Brown butter (see tip, p.204)

Place most of the cauliflower florets (approximately 400g) in a saucepan, keeping some back for deep-frying and finishing, then cover with the milk. Place over a medium heat and simmer for 35 minutes.

Liquidize the mixture with a hand blender, then pass through a sieve into a clean saucepan. Keep to one side.

Bring 3kg cold tap water and the salt to a boil. Add in the pasta and cook until *al dente*, then strain. (For pasta cooking instructions, see p.210.)

Pre-heat the grill.

Heat a pan no more than half filled with oil to 180°C and deep-fry half of the raw cauliflower florets until golden brown.

Bring the cauliflower milk to a simmer, add the cheeses and sodium citrate and mix well. When the cheese has melted and the sauce is smooth, add the mustard, brown butter and salt to taste.

Fold in the cooked pasta, the deep-fried florets and the raw florets, and place in a casserole dish. Sprinkle the extra Gruyère over the top and place under the grill until golden brown and bubbling.

Tomato tart with basil mascarpone

This is a dish for the summer, when tomatoes are at their ripest. It's French-inspired, rather like the Provençal pissaladière, and draws on characteristic flavours of the south, like tapenade. The basil mascarpone adds a little richness and aromatic flavour just at the end. It's best served straight out of the oven, as the pastry is at its best when warm and crispy.

Serves 4

For the basil mascarpone

1	Clove of garlic, peeled
60g	Basil leaves
30g	Pine nuts, toasted
30g	Parmesan cheese, grated
	Salt
110g	Olive oil
200g	Mascarpone

For the tart

50g	Olive oil
60g	Unsalted butter
10	Small onions, peeled and finely sliced
5g	Thyme leaves
5g	Rosemary leaves
½ tsp	Dijon mustard
20g	Sherry vinegar
250g	All-butter puff pastry
	Tapenade (p.161)
35	Oven-dried tomato halves (p.269)
1	Medium egg, lightly beaten

For the basil mascarpone, put the garlic, basil leaves, pine nuts, Parmesan and a pinch of salt into a food processor or blender and blitz until smooth. Slowly add the oil until it resembles a wet paste.

Fold the mascarpone into this pesto and store in the fridge until needed.

To start the tart, heat the oil and the butter in a large saucepan over a medium heat. When the butter has melted, add the onions and cook for approximately 1 hour until they are very soft, stirring occasionally to prevent the onions from catching on the bottom of the pan.

When the onions are well caramelized, chop the herbs and add them to the pan with the mustard, vinegar and a pinch of salt and cook for another 10 minutes. Remove from the heat.

Pre-heat the oven to 200°C.

Roll out the puff pastry into one large (20 × 30cm) tart or four individual tarts (cut the pastry into four). It should be approximately 5mm thick. Lightly score a line in the pastry with a knife in a border 5mm from the edge. Prick the pastry inside this border with a fork.

Spread a generous layer of tapenade to the edges of the scored area. Cover with a layer of onions, then completely cover the onions with the oven-dried tomatoes arranged in neat rows.

Add a little water to the beaten egg and brush the edges of the puff pastry with this egg wash. Bake in the pre-heated oven for 15–20 minutes or until the edges of the pastry have risen and are a deep golden colour.

Spoon dollops of basil mascarpone over the tart before serving.

Quiche Lorraine

Quiche has a bad reputation, down to the fact that it often isn't very nice – the egg mixture overcooked and grainy, the pastry dense and soggy. To make a really good quiche, it's important to prepare the pastry properly and to blind-bake the pastry case (pp.301–3). The quiche should be made a day in advance, as this helps the custard filling to set properly after its carefully controlled baking. Finally, to show it to its best advantage, it should be served either warm or at room temperature.

Serves 6–8

For the pastry

230g	Plain flour
½ tsp	Salt
100g	Cold unsalted butter, cubed
25g	Egg, lightly beaten (approx. ½ large egg)

For the filling

40g	Unsalted butter
4	Large onions, peeled and finely sliced
200g	Bacon lardons
3	Large eggs, lightly beaten
300g	Whipping cream
40g	Grated Emmental cheese
40g	Grated Gruyère cheese
	Salt and white pepper
	Nutmeg

First make the pastry. In a mixer fitted with the paddle attachment, combine the flour, salt and butter until the mixture resembles breadcrumbs.

Change to the hook attachment and slowly add 30g cold tap water and the egg. Continue mixing until a smooth dough is formed.

Shape the dough into a thick disc, wrap it in clingfilm and rest in the fridge for at least 30 minutes.

For the filling, melt the butter in a wide-bottomed saucepan over a medium heat and sauté the onions until soft and golden in colour, stirring occasionally to prevent the onions from catching on the bottom of the pan.

This will take at least 1 hour. Drain the onions of any excess butter when cooked.

Fry the lardons in a frying pan over a low heat until just cooked but not coloured (approximately 5 minutes). Drain off any liquid and discard.

Place the pastry between two sheets of baking parchment and roll out to a thickness of 2mm. Place in the freezer for 30 minutes.

Pre-heat the oven to 180°C.

Line a 20cm tart tin with the pastry (pp.301–3), then prick the base all over with a fork to prevent air bubbles. Place the tin in the freezer for 10 minutes.

Cut a large circle of baking parchment and scrunch up. Lay it in the chilled pastry case and fill with baking beans or coins. Place the case in the oven for approximately 30 minutes before gently removing the beans or coins and parchment. Return the case to the oven and continue to bake for approximately 20 minutes until golden brown.

Remove the tart case from the oven and cool a little, then, using a sharp knife, cut the excess pastry from around the top of the tin. Reduce the oven temperature to 120°C.

Mix the eggs with the cream in a saucepan and then add the cooked onions, lardons and the cheeses. Season with salt, freshly ground white pepper and a pinch of freshly grated nutmeg. Place the pan over a medium heat and bring the mixture to 63°C.

Make sure the case is still warm when filling (reheat in the oven if necessary). Fill the case with the egg mixture and ensure the onions are evenly spread out.

Return to the oven for approximately 40 minutes. When the temperature of the quiche filling reaches 70°C, remove from the oven.

Allow to cool at room temperature for 20 minutes, then place in the refrigerator, preferably overnight. Bring back to room temperature or warm in an oven pre-heated to 150°C for 5 minutes before serving.

Sides and condiments

The British have never enjoyed a good reputation as far as side dishes are concerned. The French, Spanish and Italians think that all we serve are boiled vegetables, perhaps with a knob of butter. In fact, in classical French cuisine the technical term for boiling vegetables is *à l'anglaise*. There's some truth to this. When the Fat Duck first opened as a simple bistro in 1995, customers were sometimes a bit nonplussed if their vegetables formed part of a dish rather than being served separately.

That said, there's always a place for a simple vegetable side dish, simply cooked. And with a little precision and imagination, it can be turned into a fantastic accompaniment for a main course – cooking carrots with butter (p.247) produces something much more exciting than the same veg boiled in water. Sides are also an opportunity to showcase seasonality – asparagus and broad beans in season will have a wonderful freshness that doesn't want to be messed about with too much.

While vegetables are seen as accompaniment, condiments act more as the finishing touches for a dish. The term 'condiment' is in fact a broad category, covering everything from a spicy powder rubbed into meat at the start of cooking, to a flavoured oil added at the end, or a chutney that's virtually a side dish in itself. For example, pickled lemons (p.268) are fantastic alongside fish, but can also be the main ingredient of a great salad. Condiments often contain most of the five tastes – sweet, sour, salty, bitter and umami – and can help to emphasize those tastes. Some condiments can bring a dish together, adding finesse. Whisking cubes of flavoured butter (pp.261–3) into a stew or chilli con carne will make it rich and smooth, and give it a lovely glossy sheen. In some cases, a condiment can be used as a form of seasoning. A spoonful of apricot chutney (p.270) or a scattering of oven-dried tomatoes (p.269) will give a kick of acidity to many dishes.

Sauces can be used as condiments as well. Sauce-making is often seen as an elaborate process, but here I have given recipes for simpler sauces with plenty of flavour. The ponzu, barbecue and Bois Boudran sauces on pp.266–7 involve none of the raft of techniques – straining, clarifying, thickening and blending – that can make sauce-making seem daunting. Between them they will enhance a host of chicken, fish and grilled meat dishes.

What's more, many condiments such as chutneys, pickles and flavoured butters can be prepared ahead and kept for a while in the fridge or freezer. This would be perfect for midweek when you haven't the energy to do much more than grill a simple piece of fish. You can still reach into the fridge and find something delicious to go with it.

Cooking vegetables in water

Boiling might seem like a simple process, but in fact there are a number of steps you can take to ensure that what comes out of the pan is precisely cooked, full of flavour and has a nice vibrant colour.

First, it's important that you cut the vegetables to roughly the same thickness. Sceptics might think it's odd to cut vegetables so painstakingly and precisely, but it's the best way of making sure that everything cooks to the same degree. Although textural contrast is important to a dish, that doesn't include serving a thin, soft broccoli floret side by side with a thick rock-solid one.

The type of water that goes in the pan can have an influence on how the vegetables cook. It needs to be as neutral as possible. If you're in an area with hard water, acid and minerals such as calcium in the water can harden the vegetables. They may take longer to cook, which can affect the texture. Hard water can also dull chlorophyll, taking the edge off the attractive bright fresh green colour. (If this really is a problem, one solution is to cook vegetables in a mineral water that's low in calcium.) However, in general, keeping a careful eye on time and temperature should ensure success.

The speed at which the vegetables cook is crucial to their texture and appearance, so put them into a decent-sized pan full of boiling water. (A good rule of thumb is 1kg per 100g of vegetables: the same ratio as for cooking pasta, p.210.) A large volume of water should hold its temperature even when a quantity of cold vegetables is added to it, so long as they're cut into reasonably sized pieces. With a small volume of water, the addition of vegetables will bring it off the boil and it'll take longer to return to the boil, which might throw your timings.

There are keen debates about whether salt needs to be added to the water for vegetables. Since salting doesn't appear to me to harm them, and it does have some benefits – in *On Food and Cooking*, Harold McGee points out that a couple of tablespoons of salt per kilogram of water will help vegetables to hold on to their own sugars and salts – for the moment, I do salt the cooking water for vegetables. Bear in mind, though, that salting the water doesn't actually season the vegetables. I've blanched vegetables in water containing 80g salt per kilogram, which is a high percentage, and the vegetables still needed seasoning afterwards.

Despite many counter arguments, I think you should keep the lid on a pan of boiling green vegetables. When you're bringing the water to the boil in the first place it's a great waste of energy to leave the lid off, because it'll take much longer. And since the water needs to come back to the boil quickly once the vegetables have been added, it's a good idea to clap the lid back on to help things along. This is one job where a pan with a glass lid is invaluable, so that you can monitor what's going on in the pan.

The most critical moment during cooking is when the vegetables are ready and removed from the saucepan. The residual heat in the vegetables can carry on the cooking process, causing them to be overcooked and soft by the time they're served. So it's best to halt the process by draining them in a colander and plunging immediately into a bowl of cold (or, even better, iced) water. This works better than simply running the cold tap on to the pan, which won't cool the contents quickly enough, and the vegetables will start to lose their flavour and texture.

One advantage of this approach is that the vegetables can be cooked in advance and then warmed up later, either in a mixture of butter and water, or with a little butter and perhaps additional flavourings, such as chopped shallots or fresh herbs.

Alternatively, you can cook the vegetables until just before the point of readiness and let the residual heat finish the job. However, it takes a bit of experience to judge this correctly, so plunging the vegetables in cold water is probably the best way to ensure you achieve the perfect texture.

Cooking vegetables in fat

I often prefer to cook vegetables in butter or oil, which allows them to hold on to flavour that would leach out if they were immersed and boiled in water. This is different from frying and sautéing: in those techniques vegetables are cooked in fat on a high heat so that the moisture they contain evaporates instantly as it escapes, causing the surfaces to dry out and take on some caramelized flavours. Instead, vegetables are cooked gently in fat over a low heat in a pan with the lid on: this means they both fry and steam at the same time, in the moisture that comes from the fat and from the vegetable itself. The most important thing is to keep the heat low, so that the vegetables soften rather than brown, which would give them a very different flavour.

This technique is particularly suited to vegetables whose flavour molecules are soluble in water, such as carrots and asparagus, but it works well with other vegetables, too. Cooking Brussels sprouts (p.248) or cabbage in a mixture of butter and water gives the leaves a lovely buttery glaze and richness. And, although broccoli's flavour molecules are fat-soluble, which means it is best cooked in water, cooking broccoli in fat with the lid on gives it a nice roasted characteristic for which you might be inclined to sacrifice a little overall flavour (p.248).

When cooking vegetables by this method (or indeed any other), it's important that you cut them to roughly

the same thickness. It's also best to arrange the vegetables in a single layer in the pan, if at all possible, so that they cook evenly.

Cooking potatoes

You might think that giving background information on how to cook potatoes is unnecessary. After all, a potato's a potato, and even the most inexperienced cook has a pretty good idea of how to prepare it. And yet it's surprisingly easy to end up with gluey mash, limp chips or leathery roast potatoes. It turns out that the humble potato is quite a complex structure. If you want to get the best out of it, it's worth understanding that structure, and about how best to handle it to create lovely, silky mash, and chips and roast potatoes with a wonderfully crunchy exterior and a soft, fluffy interior.

First of all, a potato isn't just a potato. Behind that name lie hundreds of varieties – among them Anya, Charlotte, Desirée, King Edward, Marfona, Maris Piper and Pink Fir Apple. Each of these has a slightly different structure, which responds slightly differently to cooking. Choosing the right potato for the job will make a difference to the end result.

Although it looks like a solid knobbly lump, about three-quarters of a potato is water. The rest is known as 'dry matter', which is principally starch. It's the dry matter that gives a potato its flavour, and managing the dry matter is one of the key tasks in cooking good mash, chips and roast potatoes. Growing conditions have such an influence on dry matter that the amount present in a single variety can vary virtually from field to field, depending on the temperature, rainfall and drainage. It's not an exact science. That's why you can cook a particular variety perfectly one day, then find it responds badly next time around.

In general, floury potatoes like Anya, King Edward and Maris Piper have high dry matter, waxy ones like Charlotte and Marfona have less. You might therefore think it's a simple case of going for a potato with high dry matter. After all, maximizing flavour is what it's all about. But there's more to it than that. All starch granules are made up of a proportion of two molecules – amylose and amylopectin – which respond to heat and cooking in different ways. Amylose tends to form a strong, tightly knitted gel, whereas amylopectin coheres more loosely. I'm looking forward to the day when bags of potatoes come with information about dry-matter percentages and amylose-amylopectin ratios printed upon them. It'll really help cooks to find the perfect potato. For chips or roast potatoes you're looking for a variety that's high in dry matter and has a reasonable proportion of amylose to help keep the shape. For mash, on the other hand, too high a proportion of amylose is best avoided as it can lead to a gummy, gluey consistency.

When cooking roast potatoes (and chips, for that matter), I want an interior that's soft and fluffy, with a crisp, almost glass-like crust. Although you're often working towards the aims simultaneously, it's helpful to think of them as two separate tasks, each requiring a very specific process.

For that soft interior it's best to use a type of potato with a high dry-matter content and simmer carefully until it's almost falling apart. Be brave about this, because the outer crumbliness is the key to a good final crust as well as a soft inside. For the crust to be properly crunchy, the fat needs to pool and collect into little pockets that harden and crisp up. If you've simmered the potato until it's only just holding together, lots of cracks and fissures will have developed in the surface, and these are perfect places for the fat to collect. (Fat will penetrate the potato only where there is a crack.) To give the fat as many places as possible where it can catch and harden, it's best to choose large potatoes and cut them into quarters or, better still, eighths, so there are plenty of pointy edges where fat will also collect.

First rinse the cut potatoes in water for five minutes or so: this washes off surface starch, which would make the cooked potato less fluffy and crisp. The potato pieces for roast potatoes are then cooked in unsalted water – salt can occasionally make the crust a little chewy, so it's

safer not to add any. Potatoes with high dry matter fall apart more easily than those with a lower dry-matter content, so you'll need to keep an eye on progress during simmering. Appearances can be deceptive: a potato will often look as though it's firm right up to the moment where it falls apart, so you need periodically to remove a potato and check it.

When they're ready, the potatoes need to be lifted very gently out of the water with a slotted spoon into a colander (don't just tip them – which will almost certainly turn them to mush). Leave them to steam, which will ensure that moisture evaporates (it might otherwise make the crust soft or soggy), and that the potatoes firm up and are not too fragile to work with. Once cool the potatoes are ready for the roasting tray, and all the careful preparation in the early stages should guarantee a great roast potato. Make sure, by the way, that you hold on to any bits of potato that have broken off and put them in the roasting tray too. They will turn into lovely little nuggets of crispiness.

Since, for me, chips have to have a fluffy interior similar to a roast potato's, the first stages of cooking them are much the same: rinsing off surface starch, simmering the cut pieces until they're very soft but just holding together, with lots of little cracks in the surface. This requires a careful and regular checking of progress with a slotted spoon, and by the time the chips are ready they'll be fairly fragile and have to be handled delicately. (They'll become slightly more robust once they have cooled.)

As far as crisp chips go, moisture is the enemy. When I first discovered this, I went to extraordinary lengths to try to combat the problem – oven-drying chips or even individually pin-pricking them to get rid of excess moisture. The most practical solution for the home cook, however, is a concerted drying-out, drawing on the air-drying abilities of the freezer, both before and after the first session in the deep-fat fryer.

Double-frying is the other key to great chips. The purpose of the first session in the fryer, at a gentler temperature, is to make any starch left in the surface cells dissolve and combine to create a rigid outer layer that can withstand the higher temperature of the final frying, which will colour the chips golden. Skipping this can undo all the trouble you've taken to dry out the potatoes and drive off moisture. A single frying at a high temperature leads to a thin crust that can easily be rendered soggy by whatever moisture remains in the chip's interior. Although this first, low-temperature frying might seem a time-consuming process, once the chips have had it, they can be stored in the fridge for up to three days before their second, high-temperature frying.

As for mashed potato, you can, of course, make it simply by boiling and mashing some spuds. It might be a bit lumpy, but it'll work well enough to go with a couple of bangers. However, there are times when a dish calls for something more refined, and no less than pommes purées (p.258) will do. Creating a perfect, velvety texture requires a little more work, but it's worth it. The end result will be a real taste of luxury. The success of pommes purées is largely dependent on managing the starch present in the potato. Cooking has to break down the cell walls of potato without damaging the starch granules. If they're overcooked, the granules leak starch, turning the mash to a sticky, wallpaper-paste-like mass.

The key to preventing this is an initial 30-minute simmer at precisely 72°C, which alters a potato's structure so that it responds well to the subsequent boiling and mashing. Cooking the potatoes at this temperature kickstarts a process called 'gelatinization' in which the starch granules absorb water and swell to become a gel. (The process starts at 45°C and stops at around 75°C, hence the need for precision.) It also strengthens the potato's cell walls, so they're less likely to disintegrate. After this first simmer, it's essential to cool the potatoes completely, because this causes the starch molecules to firm up (an activity known as 'starch retrogradation'). At this stage, the potatoes will look uncooked but don't worry, they're now perfectly prepared for the final stage of cooking, which is simply softening by boiling in water as normal.

Using this two-stage cooking technique prepares potatoes perfectly for mashing. Nonetheless, it's vital that this final stage is done carefully so as not to undo all your work. Mashing is an invasive process and if it's done too aggressively there's a risk that, instead of neatly separating, the swollen starch granules will burst, leaking starch into the mash. Using a food processor to mash will just produce a gummy pulp, and even a masher is likely to cause some damage. For the smoothest pommes purées, it's better to use a food mill or potato ricer, which grinds the potato gently, rather than blitzing or squashing it, so the starch granules remain intact.

Glazed carrots

When boiled, carrots – like asparagus – lose a lot of their flavour to the water (p.243). Cooking them in fat, on the other hand, is an excellent way to lock in as much of the flavour as possible.

Up to a certain point, the longer carrots are cooked, the sweeter they will be. Obviously you don't want to end up with something unpleasantly soft, but it's worth pushing the cooking time a little in order to capture that sweetness. Once the carrots are cooked, you can turn up the heat to caramelize them. Instead of the thyme you could finish the carrots with ground coriander, or a touch of cumin and a little orange zest, or – my favourite – some ground caraway, or toasted caraway seeds.

Put the carrots and butter in a wide-bottomed saucepan over a low heat and sprinkle them with the salt, freshly ground pepper and sugar. Make sure the carrots form a single layer on the bottom of the pan.

Cover with a lid and cook for approximately 30 minutes, shaking the pan from time to time to ensure even cooking.

Add the thyme leaves and cook for a further 5 minutes until tender and glazed.

Serves 6

400g	Carrots, peeled and sliced into thick diagonal chunks of the same size
140g	Unsalted butter
	Salt and black pepper
1 tsp	White caster sugar
4	Sprigs of thyme, leaves picked

Broccoli with chilli

This is a very simple side dish that goes well with fish, pork and roast chicken; or you could toss it with pasta and a little grated Parmesan. You can also take it in a slightly different direction by adding some chopped salted anchovies halfway through cooking.

Serves 4

1 tbsp	Olive oil
400g	Tenderstem broccoli
1 tsp	Chilli flakes, or 1 red chilli (with or without seeds, depending on how hot you like it)
	Sea salt and black pepper

Heat the oil in a heavy frying pan over a medium-high heat and, when hot, add the broccoli. Cover with a lid and cook for approximately 5 minutes, shaking the pan from time to time to ensure even cooking.

Add the chilli flakes to the pan and toss the broccoli again. Season with salt and freshly ground pepper before serving.

Brussels sprouts with bacon

The key to this recipe is to separate the leaves of the sprouts. This might seem laborious, but if sprouts are cooked whole, by the time the interior is soft the exterior is overcooked. This way the sprouts are sweet and evenly cooked, and have no unpleasant boiled-cabbage characteristics. The recipe uses a simple technique in which the vegetables fry and steam at the same time, in butter, bacon fat and a little added water. You could also add some garlic and chopped chilli to the pan. And at Christmas, it's nice to add a few chopped pre-cooked chestnuts to the lardons too.

Serves 6

5	Slices of smoked bacon, cut into lardons
400g	Brussels sprouts
50g	Unsalted butter
	Salt and black pepper

Fry the bacon lardons in a frying pan over a medium heat until they are soft but not coloured (approximately 5 minutes). Remove from the pan with a slotted spoon and drain on kitchen paper. Set aside. Keep the bacon fat in the pan.

Slice the bases off the Brussels sprouts and carefully separate the leaves, pulling them off the sprout. Alternatively, shred them finely with a sharp knife.

Melt the butter with the bacon fat in the frying pan over a medium-low heat. When the butter is foaming, add the Brussels leaves and stir to coat them. Add 2 tablespoons of water and cover the pan with a lid.

Allow to cook for 5 minutes, stir in the lardons and season with salt and freshly ground pepper.

Choucroûte

Easy to make and store, and very healthy (it's packed full of vitamin C), pickled cabbage has been a feature of many countries' cuisine since the sixteenth century – there's the Alsace classic choucroûte garnie with pork and smoked streaky bacon, and in Transylvania they make a dish called sarmale by layering pickled cabbage, lard, smoked bacon, sausage, shredded pork, rice and allspice corns in an earthenware pot and cooking it in an oven for two hours.

Because of its health-giving properties, Captain Cook took plenty on board his ships, but he had trouble persuading his sailors to eat 'sour crout', because they weren't used to it. Yet it is an absolutely delicious dish – its pickled sharpness works particularly well with pork chops, grilled sausages and even a piece of white fish.

Serves 6

100g	Unsalted butter
400g	Peeled and finely sliced onion (approx. 6 medium onions)
1	Clove of garlic, peeled and chopped
1 tsp	Juniper berries, wrapped in a muslin bag
300g	Gewürztraminer wine
50g	White wine vinegar
	Salt and black pepper
1	Savoy cabbage
1 tbsp	Groundnut or grapeseed oil
30g	Smoked bacon lardons

Melt the butter in a frying pan over a medium heat. Sweat the onion, garlic and juniper berries until the onions are soft and lightly coloured (approximately 20 minutes). Remove the bag of juniper berries and discard.

Add the wine to the pan and boil to reduce to a thin syrup (approximately 50–100g).

Add the vinegar and reduce for 5 minutes. Season with salt and freshly ground pepper and remove from the heat. Strain the onion and reserve both onion and liquid.

Cut the cabbage in half and remove the tough core. Separate the leaves, and cut them into 5mm strips.

Heat the oil in a saucepan over a medium-high heat, then add the bacon and cook until lightly coloured. Using a slotted spoon, remove the bacon from the pan and drain on kitchen paper.

Add the cabbage to the pan and cook for approximately 7 minutes. Mix in the onions, bacon and reserved cooking liquid and continue to cook for 5 minutes, or until the cabbage is tender.

Season with salt and freshly ground pepper before serving.

Braised lettuce

Braised lettuce is a classic in French cuisine, and although we often think lettuce has texture rather than flavour, you'll be surprised at how flavourful this is. It's important, though, to blanch the lettuce in boiling water first, otherwise the leaves will lose a lot of colour during the brief braising that follows.

Little gem lettuces can be substituted for romaine. The water and butter emulsion used here to warm the lettuce is a good means of reheating many cooked vegetables.

Serves 4

100g	Brown butter (see tip, p.204)
	Salt
2	Romaine lettuces

Place 300g water in a small saucepan and bring to the boil. Remove the pan from the heat and add the brown butter, a little at a time, whilst blitzing with a hand blender to emulsify. Season with salt and put to one side.

Cut the lettuces in half lengthways then in half again, retaining the roots to keep the leaves together during the cooking.

Bring 1kg water with 5g salt to the boil over a high heat. In the meantime, prepare a bowl or basin of iced water for refreshing the leaves after cooking.

When the water is boiling, add the lettuce leaves to the pan for 15 seconds, remove with a slotted spoon and plunge immediately into the iced water.

Remove the lettuces from the cold water and drain on kitchen paper. Remove the root at this point.

Heat the water-butter emulsion in a wide-bottomed frying pan and add the lettuce leaves to the pan for approximately 1 minute or until warmed through. Remove the leaves from the pan and serve immediately.

Asparagus

You can roast, grill or barbecue asparagus, but one of the best techniques for holding on to the vegetable's flavour is to cook it in fat, because many of its flavour molecules are not fat-soluble (p.243). There's a widespread belief that thinner asparagus spears are better than thick ones. In fact the reverse is true – the thicker spears have more flavour because they get more nutrients from the ground. It's worth peeling the stems of thicker asparagus with a vegetable peeler – it removes bitter compounds contained in the skin and makes them cook more evenly.

Serve the spears by themselves with butter or hollandaise, or with a poached egg on top, or dip them into a soft-boiled egg. They are good as a side dish with fish, especially liquorice poached salmon (p.187) and crab risotto (p.220).

Serves 4

20	Asparagus spears
25g	Unsalted butter
	Salt and black pepper

Remove the woody part of the asparagus by snapping the ends off (they should break off naturally).

Melt the butter in a frying pan, then add the asparagus and cover with a lid. Place the pan over a medium heat for approximately 5 minutes or until the asparagus spears are *al dente*, shaking the pan from time to time.

Remove the pan from the heat and drain the asparagus on kitchen paper. Season with salt and freshly ground pepper before serving.

Crushed potatoes

New potatoes or Jersey Royals are cooked until soft, then dressed with a shallot and oil mixture before being crushed with a fork. It's a recipe with plenty of potential variations. You can add rosemary, thyme, onions, shallots, garlic or even smoked bacon to the cooking water – you'd be surprised how much flavour will infuse into the potatoes.

For a richer version, you can add a good knob or two of butter to the potatoes along with the shallot and olive oil mixture. At the end you could also stir in a tablespoon of horseradish sauce, some chopped anchovies or some chopped gherkins and capers.

Serves 4

750g	New potatoes, washed and halved
4	Cloves of garlic, peeled and bashed with the flat part of a knife or by hand
	Salt
4	Shallots, peeled (see tip, p.147) and finely diced
150g	Olive oil
2 tsp	Wholegrain mustard
15g	White wine vinegar
	Sea salt and black pepper
10g	Flat-leaf parsley leaves
10g	Chives
5g	Tarragon leaves

Put the halved potatoes and garlic in a saucepan, cover with water and add a teaspoon of salt. Bring to the boil, reduce to a simmer and cook until the potatoes are soft (approximately 20 minutes).

In a small pan, cook the shallots gently in the olive oil for 5 minutes and set aside.

When the potatoes are done, drain them, discarding the garlic. Place the potatoes in a bowl, and pour over the shallot and olive oil mixture. Add the grain mustard and vinegar and crush with a fork until the potatoes are roughly broken up but not fully mashed.

Generously season with sea salt and freshly ground pepper, then chop the herbs and stir them through. Serve warm or at room temperature.

Roast potatoes

This recipe will make roast potatoes just the way I like them – with a crisp, glass-like crust and a fluffy interior. I like to add garlic, rosemary and thyme for flavour, but if you prefer your potatoes plain (kids in particular often rebel against unusual flavours in their roast potatoes), you can leave them out.

It's important not to stint on the amount of oil you put in the roasting tray. The crispness on the outside of the potatoes comes from the fat that collects in cracks on their surface. So you need to provide plenty of fat so that it can do just that. Some people dust potatoes with flour before they go in the roasting tray, but I find this can lead to a chewier crust. That's why the potatoes are rinsed of any surface starch before they are boiled. (For more about roasting potatoes, see pp.243–4.)

Serves 6

1.25kg	Large Maris Piper potatoes
	Olive oil
8	Cloves of garlic, bashed with the flat part of a knife or by hand (optional)
30g	Rosemary sprigs (optional)
15g	Thyme sprigs (optional)
	Salt

Pre-heat the oven to 180°C.

Wash and peel the potatoes and cut into quarters. Put them into a bowl under running water for 5 minutes to wash the starch off.

Cover the potatoes with water in a large saucepan, bring to the boil and cook until very soft (approximately 25–30 minutes). Drain carefully and leave to cool in the colander.

Pour 5mm of olive oil into a roasting tray large enough to hold the potatoes in one layer. Place in the oven for 15 minutes. Add the potatoes to the tray with the garlic, if using. Stir to coat in the oil and place back in the oven for at least 1 hour, gently turning every 20 minutes.

After 1 hour, if using, add the rosemary and thyme to the pan and return to the oven for 15–20 minutes or until the potatoes are golden brown and crispy all over. Drain on kitchen paper and season with salt.

Triple-cooked chips

I became obsessed with chips around 1992, before I had even opened the Fat Duck, and this was probably the first recipe that I could call my own. It has since cropped up in restaurants and pubs all over the place. Achieving the crisp, glass-like exterior depends on getting rid of moisture from the potato and creating little cracks in the surface where the oil will collect and harden, making it crunchy. (For more about this technique, see pp.244–5.)

Serves 6

1kg	Maris Piper potatoes, peeled and cut into chips (approx. 2 x 2 x 6cm)
	Groundnut or grapeseed oil
	Sea salt

Place the cut chips into a bowl under running water for 5 minutes to wash the starch off.

Place 2kg cold tap water in a large saucepan and add the potatoes. Place the pan over a medium heat and simmer until the chips are almost falling apart (approximately 20–30 minutes, depending on the potato).

Carefully remove the cooked chips and place them on a cooling rack to dry out. Then place in the freezer for at least 1 hour to remove more moisture.

Heat a deep-fat fryer or a deep pan no more than half filled with oil (to a depth of around 10cm) to 130°C. Fry the chips in small batches until a light crust forms (approximately 5 minutes), remove from the oil and drain on kitchen paper.

Put the potatoes on a cooling rack and place in the freezer for at least 1 hour. (At this stage, if you don't want to cook and serve immediately, the chips can be kept in the fridge for 3 days.)

Heat the oil in the deep-fat fryer or deep pan to 180°C and fry the chips until golden (approximately 7 minutes). Drain and sprinkle with sea salt.

Pommes purées

Pommes purées is the ultimate rich, silky-smooth, buttery indulgence. It's not for every dish – there's something about bangers, for example, that cries out for a simple rough, fluffy mash – but a skilfully cooked pommes purées brings a real touch of refinement to a dish. The technique here, using waxy potatoes, and cooking them at a very specific temperature, is designed to hold on to the starch in the potatoes and prevent it from leaking and turning the potato gluey.

It's a useful recipe as you can prepare the potatoes up to the adding of the butter a few days in advance. Leave to cool, then store in the fridge. To reheat, put the potatoes through the sieve (for a really refined texture), then into a pan on a low-medium heat. Stir or beat in the warm milk. The mixture will look as though it's going to split, but the milk brings it all together.

For a super-indulgent version, increase the amount of butter to 500g per kilo of potatoes. However, you might need more warmed milk on hand at the end to help bring it all together. And of course you can vary the flavour of the purée – see the variations below.

Serves 6

1kg	Waxy potatoes, peeled
	Salt
300g	Unsalted butter, diced
240g	Whole milk, warmed

Bring a saucepan of unsalted water to 72°C over a medium heat.

Cut the potatoes into equal-sized pieces, put into the pan and bring the water temperature back up to 72°C. Hold the potatoes at this temperature for 30 minutes, removing the pan and adjusting the heat as necessary.

After 30 minutes, drain the potatoes and rinse them under cold running water.

Bring a saucepan of fresh salted water to the boil and add the potatoes. Cook until extremely soft and falling apart.

Drain the potatoes, then return them to the pan over a very low heat to dry them out.

Put the potatoes through a ricer on to the butter in a bowl, and mix together.

Put this mixture through a sieve, then add the warmed milk and salt to taste.

Mustard pommes purées
Stir in 30g wholegrain mustard with the milk.

Wasabi pommes purées
Stir in ½ teaspoon wasabi paste with the milk.

Horseradish pommes purées
Stir in 1 tablespoon horseradish sauce with the milk.

Pommes boulangère

Potatoes are sliced thinly, layered in a dish with butter and softened onion, covered with a warm meat stock, and baked in the oven until tender. The top will be golden and crisp, the interior meltingly soft. To maximize the colour on top, you could brush melted butter over the cooked boulangère and put it under the grill for a few minutes before resting.

This is a classic garnish for roast lamb (p.162) but, if you replace the lamb stock with chicken, fish or vegetable stock, it also makes an excellent accompaniment for other meat and fish dishes.

Serves 6

100g	Dry white wine
1.5kg	Lamb stock (p.41)
5	Sprigs of rosemary
2	Large onions, peeled and finely sliced
	Olive oil
50g	Unsalted butter
1kg	Potatoes, peeled and very finely sliced
	Salt and black pepper

Put the white wine in a large saucepan and reduce by one-third over a high heat. Add the lamb stock to the pan and reduce by half. Remove the pan from the heat, add the rosemary sprigs and leave to infuse for 20 minutes. Discard the rosemary.

In the meantime, place the sliced onion in a saucepan and cover with olive oil. Place the pan over a very low heat for 30 minutes or until very soft, stirring occasionally. Drain the onions, discarding the oil, and put to one side.

Pre-heat the oven to 150°C.

Grease the bottom of a casserole dish with a little of the butter, then line it with a layer of potato slices. Season with salt and freshly ground pepper, then scatter a few onions over the potatoes as well as a few curls of butter. Repeat this process with all the ingredients, making sure there is a little butter left over for the top.

Pour 750g of the warm lamb stock over the potatoes, cover with a piece of baking parchment and place in the pre-heated oven for 45–50 minutes. Check the potatoes every 10–15 minutes and press down the top layer with a spatula to ensure even cooking, adding more stock if the potatoes appear to be drying out.

Remove from the oven and allow to rest for a few minutes before serving.

Soured cream butter

This tangy butter is halfway between butter and cheese, composed as it is of butter, soured cream and cream cheese. Serve it with tea-smoked salmon (p.85), soy-marinated roe (p.86), on top of scrambled eggs (p.204) instead of brown butter, or with a baked potato with chopped chives on top.

100g	Unsalted butter
50g	Soured cream
50g	Cream cheese
	Squeeze of lemon juice
	Pinch of salt

Place 50g of the butter in a bowl and whisk over a pan of simmering water until softened.

Remove the bowl from the heat and whisk in the soured cream and cream cheese.

Put the bowl back over the pan of simmering water and whisk in the remaining butter until fully incorporated. The mixture may appear to split, but keep whisking over the pan of warm water and it will come back together.

Stir in the lemon juice and salt and decant into a small bowl. Keep in the fridge until required (for up to 2 days).

Acidulated butter

When I was researching the perfect risotto, I visited the kitchen of Gualtiero Marchesi, the first Italian chef to gain three Michelin stars and regarded by many as the father of modern Italian cooking. In his risotto Milanese, Marchesi didn't start by softening some finely chopped onion because, he said, he wanted to keep the flavour of the rice and saffron 'as pure as possible'. And so instead he added acidulated butter right at the end of cooking.

Acidulated butter is essentially a variant on the sauce beurre blanc. It's a fantastic way of finishing off risottos or poaching fish. The butter introduces a little sweetness, while the wine and vinegar bring in some acidity, helping to produce a balanced, well-seasoned dish.

100g	Peeled and sliced onion (approx. 1–2 medium onions)
185g	Dry white wine
300g	White wine vinegar
250g	Unsalted butter, cubed

Place the onion, wine and vinegar in a saucepan over a high heat and reduce the liquid by three-quarters (approximately 10–15 minutes).

Remove from the heat and whisk in the butter a little at a time until well emulsified.

Leave to infuse for 20 minutes at room temperature, then pass through a fine sieve, using a whisk to help push the solids through.

Roll into a log and wrap in parchment paper or put into a bowl. Keep in the fridge until required (for up to a week), or freeze for a month.

Spiced butter

I got the idea for this spiced butter when I visited a chilli cook-off in Washington DC. Everybody has their own special ingredient for finishing the chilli and giving it character – brown sugar, cocoa powder, peanut butter, banana, or even a slug of Jack Daniel's. This started me thinking about the classic French technique of finishing a sauce with butter to give richness and a glossy finish. So I developed this spicy, fragrant, umami-rich butter to complement a bowl of chilli (p.156), though it's just as good in braised mince, Bolognese sauce or a stew, or even simply tossed with pasta.

You can of course change the spices – making it less fragrant, for example, by cutting out the cumin and smoked paprika.

2 tbsp	Olive oil
1½ tsp	Ground cumin
1 tsp	Chilli powder
1½ tsp	Smoked paprika
1 tsp	Tomato ketchup
½ tsp	Worcestershire sauce
½ tsp	Marmite
125g	Unsalted butter, at room temperature

Heat the olive oil in a frying pan and lightly fry the cumin and chilli powder for a couple of seconds.

Pour into a bowl and add the smoked paprika, tomato ketchup, Worcestershire sauce, Marmite and butter. Mix together thoroughly.

Roll into a log and wrap in parchment paper or decant into a bowl. Keep in the fridge until required (for up to a week), or freeze for a month.

Blue cheese butter

This is fantastic with steak, which may not be surprising, since that's where I got the idea from. In New York there's a 'Gentlemen's Club' that serves some of the best steak in town. (I kid you not.) The secret is that the meat is first aged (p.134) so that it develops rich, almost Stilton-like notes. Serve a couple of slices of the blue cheese butter on top of a grilled or fried steak (p.137). You could also toss the butter with pasta, or serve it with a baked potato.

130g	Unsalted butter, at room temperature
260g	Stilton cheese

Place the butter in the bowl of a mixer fitted with a whisk attachment. Start mixing at low speed and crumble in the Stilton.

Continue to mix for approximately 3–4 minutes until well combined.

Roll into a log and wrap in parchment paper or decant into a bowl. Keep in the fridge until required (for up to a week), or freeze for a month.

Vanilla butter

This butter is excellent with grilled or fried fish, such as the sea bass on p.184. Don't discard the vanilla pods after adding the seeds to the butter – you can use them as a flavouring for sugar or oil.

3	Vanilla pods
125g	Unsalted butter, at room temperature

Halve the vanilla pods lengthways and, using a teaspoon, scrape out the seeds.

Mix the butter with the vanilla seeds, using a hand blender.

Roll into a log and wrap in parchment paper or place in a bowl. Keep in the fridge until required (for up to a week), or freeze for a month.

Parsley butter

This is an essential component of the parsley porridge on p.216, but it's good tossed with pasta, or added to a plain risotto after it comes off the heat. It also goes well with steak, grilled chicken or a piece of fish.

275g	Unsalted butter, cubed
40g	Peeled and finely chopped garlic (approx. 1 bulb of garlic)
5g	Lemon juice
25g	Dijon mustard
20g	Ground almonds
5g	Salt
120g	Curly parsley leaves

Melt 50g of the butter in a pan, add the garlic and sauté until pale gold and fragrant.

Add the lemon juice to the pan, then transfer to a food mixer fitted with the paddle attachment.

Add the mustard, ground almonds, salt and the remaining 225g unsalted butter and mix on a medium speed until thoroughly incorporated.

Chop the parsley very, very finely and sprinkle on top of the butter mixture and mix on medium speed for 5 minutes.

Remove the parsley butter from the mixer and roll tightly in parchment paper or place in a bowl. Keep in the fridge until required (for up to a week), or freeze for a month.

Horseradish cream

I prize the kick you get from mustard and horseradish, which can really enliven a dish. This simple horseradish sauce/garnish perks up so many things – soused herrings (p.87), tea-smoked salmon (p.85) and beetroot spelt risotto (p.223), as well as cured fish, steak, cold meats and baked potatoes.

100g	Crème fraiche
40g	Horseradish sauce
	Juice of ½ lemon
	Pinch of salt

Put the crème fraiche into a small bowl and stir in the horseradish sauce and lemon juice. Season with a pinch of salt. Keep in the fridge until required (for up to 3 days).

Five-spice powder

You can buy Chinese five-spice powder, ready ground, in jars, but I think it's fun to make your own – and it'll be infinitely more fragrant. It's a strong spice, so don't overdo it. It can be used as a rub for pork, chicken or duck (p.149) and, if mixed with salt, it could be a dry dip for Chinese or Vietnamese fried foods. It is also perfect for spiced nuts (p.377).

5	Star anise
½ tsp	Whole cloves
1 tsp	Whole fennel seeds
1 tsp	Szechuan peppercorns (Specialist ingredients, p.395)
1 tsp	Ground cinnamon

Grind the star anise, cloves, fennel seeds and peppercorns to a powder in a spice grinder or food processor.

Combine thoroughly with the ground cinnamon. Keep in an airtight container for up to 3 months.

Flavoured oils

Flavoured oils are a brilliant and easy way to finish and season sauces, soups and other dishes, and to create lively, interesting dressings for salads. They don't keep as long as ordinary oil, however: adding extra ingredients makes oil less stable and more liable to go rancid. So it's best to store flavoured oils in the fridge and to use them quickly. This also helps to guard against the botulism bacterium, which can be present in fresh herbs and spices and thrives in the airless environment of a bottle of room-temperature oil.

When flavouring oils, make sure herbs are rinsed and dried (on kitchen paper or a clean tea-towel) before use.

Mint oil

This oil is the perfect way to finish the pea and ham soup on p.65. It's also good with roast lamb or roast potatoes, even as part of a salad dressing.

| 25g | Mint leaves |
| 100g | Groundnut or grapeseed oil |

Bring a pan of water to the boil and drop the mint leaves in for 20 seconds. Remove the mint with a slotted spoon and submerge immediately in a bowl of iced water.

Remove the mint and dry the leaves in between two sheets of kitchen paper. Put the mint and oil in a liquidizer and blitz for 10–15 seconds.

Strain through a fine sieve and pour into a bottle. Keep in the fridge for 4–5 days only.

Red pepper oil

This is great in pumpkin soup (p.61). A few drops are a nice way to finish a gazpacho, and you could even drizzle some on a crab risotto (p.220) or roast vegetables.

| 1 | Red pepper, de-seeded, roasted and peeled (see tip, p.157) |
| 100g | Groundnut or grapeseed oil |

Put the pepper and oil in a liquidizer and blitz until fine.

Strain through a fine sieve and pour into a bottle. Keep in the fridge for 4–5 days only.

Ponzu sauce

This is a classic Japanese sauce traditionally served with grilled meat and fish, or as a dip for sashimi or sushi (p.217). It has a citrus note that normally comes from the inclusion of the zest of yuzu and sudachi fruits. These look like limes but have more of a mandarin character. You can buy them from Japanese food stores, but as they can be difficult to find I have used lemon zest instead.

20g	Chopped spring onions
70g	Light soy sauce (Specialist ingredients, p.395)
35g	Rice vinegar
10g	Unrefined caster sugar Zest of ½ lemon, finely grated
15g	Runny honey (see tip, p.359)
2 tsp	Peeled and grated fresh root ginger

Mix all of the ingredients together. Store in the fridge until ready to use, for about 2–3 months.

Barbecue sauce

You can use this sauce as a marinade, or spoon it over steak or a burger just before serving. It's also a great dip for chips (p.257). It keeps well in the fridge, so you can make it in advance.

15g	Groundnut or grapeseed oil
3	Cloves of garlic, peeled and finely chopped
1	Banana shallot, peeled and finely chopped
¼ tsp	Ground ginger
¼ tsp	Powdered allspice
¼ tsp	Mustard powder
¼ tsp	Cayenne pepper
¼ tsp	Smoked paprika
210g	Tomato passata
100g	Cider vinegar
120g	Demerara sugar
1 tbsp	Worcestershire sauce
1 tbsp	Golden syrup
½ tsp	Salt
¼ tsp	Black pepper

Heat the oil in a saucepan over a medium heat. Add the garlic and shallot and sweat until soft (approximately 7–10 minutes).

Add the dry spices, and continue to cook for 2 minutes, stirring to incorporate them.

Add the tomato passata, vinegar, sugar, Worcestershire sauce, golden syrup, salt and freshly ground pepper, and cook for 20 minutes.

Pour the contents of the saucepan into a blender and blitz for 30 seconds until smooth. Pass through a fine sieve and allow to cool. Keep in an airtight container in the fridge until needed, for 2–3 weeks.

Bois Boudran sauce

This spicy, herby, full-flavoured sauce was originally created for the Rothschild family by my good friend and neighbour Michel Roux Senior. A base of tomato ketchup, vinegar and Worcestershire sauce is given kick by soy sauce, chilli sauce and plenty of herbs. In the recipe, the shallots are blanched briefly in boiling water, but you could just as easily soften them by warming them in a pan with a little oil. The sauce has to be made a couple of hours in advance: the herb mixture is what gives it its essential character, and it needs time to infuse.

It's an excellent condiment for poached, grilled or barbecued chicken and salmon (p.202).

230g	Tomato ketchup
30g	Sherry vinegar
15g	Worcestershire sauce
10g	Light soy sauce (Specialist ingredients, p.395)
10g	Dijon mustard
95g	Olive oil
235g	Peeled and finely diced shallot (approx. 3–4 large banana shallots)
40g	Tarragon leaves
30g	Flat-leaf parsley leaves Tabasco chipotle pepper sauce

Place the tomato ketchup, sherry vinegar, Worcestershire sauce, soy sauce, mustard and olive oil in a bowl and whisk thoroughly to combine.

Bring a saucepan of water to the boil and add the diced shallot for 30 seconds to soften, then drain.

Chop the tarragon and parsley and add to the ketchup mixture, with the blanched shallot and a few drops of Tabasco, depending on how hot you like it. Leave to infuse for at least 2 hours.

Pickled lemons

These are lively and refreshing, and can be served with scallop tartare (p.93), hay-smoked mackerel (p.90), poultry and barbecued meat, or chopped and tossed into salads. Whatever you're serving them with, be sparing with the quantity – they're very concentrated, and a few go a long way.

750g   White wine vinegar
375g   White caster sugar
8   Unwaxed lemons

Place 1kg cold tap water, the vinegar and sugar in a large saucepan and bring to the boil. Stir to ensure that the sugar has melted and remove from the heat. Allow to cool to room temperature.

Slice the lemons as finely as possible with a mandolin or food processor, discarding the seeds.

Cover the lemon slices with the pickling liquid in a bowl, cover and place in the fridge for at least 4 days before using (the longer the better).

If kept airtight and in the liquid, the lemons will keep for 6 months in the fridge.

Pickled cucumber

Pickled cucumber is a very northern European taste. Originally a way of preserving the vegetable, it is now used as a tart accompaniment to smoked fish, such as the tea-smoked salmon on p.85.

1   Cucumber, peeled
50g   White caster sugar
100g   White wine vinegar
10g   Dill, plus a little extra for finishing
       Sea salt

Slice the cucumber lengthways down the middle, then slice very thinly on a mandolin or in a food processor.

Bring the sugar, vinegar and 150g cold tap water to the boil in a small saucepan over a medium heat. Allow to cool.

Chop most of the dill and mix with the sliced cucumber and pickling liquid in a container, cover and allow to marinate in the fridge for at least 30 minutes.

Drain the cucumber. Sprinkle with the extra dill, chopped, and salt to serve. Keeps for up to a week in the fridge.

Oven-dried tomatoes

Draining the tomatoes' seeds and pulp first means they can be dried for a shorter time than in most dried-tomato recipes. The cooking is long enough for them to lose their bitter notes, but short enough to remain soft, sweet and fragrant. For best results, you will need the ripest tomatoes you can find. They go really well with the lamb jelly on p.98, and are a key ingredient of the tomato tart on p.235.

1kg	Medium tomatoes
6	Cloves of garlic, peeled and finely sliced
	Bay leaves, finely sliced
	Thyme sprigs
	Salt
	Unrefined caster sugar
	Olive oil

Peel the tomatoes (see tip, below).

Cut the tomatoes in half lengthways and scoop out the pulp and seeds. Place them, cut-side down, on a tray or plate lined with kitchen paper. Allow to drain for 2 hours.

Pre-heat the oven to 100°C.

Transfer the tomatoes to a baking tray lined with parchment paper, cut-side up. On each tomato, place a slice of garlic and bay leaf and a small sprig of thyme. Sprinkle with a little salt and sugar. Drizzle with olive oil. Place in the pre-heated oven for 3 hours or until they are dry but still soft.

Once cooled, store them in a jar in the fridge, covered with olive oil. (You can leave the herbs in.) When the tomatoes have been eaten, the oil can be used to flavour dressings and pasta.

How to peel tomatoes

Bring a large saucepan of water to the boil. In the meantime, fill a bowl or basin with iced water. With a sharp knife, score a shallow cross on the bottom of each tomato. Lower the tomatoes into the boiling water and leave for 15–20 seconds or until the skins visibly split. Remove from the hot water and plunge into the iced water. Remove immediately and peel by hand.

Beetroot relish

I love the earthy flavour of beetroot. This relish is a perfect accompaniment for the soused herrings on p.87, but it also works well with grilled or other pickled fish, or curd or goat's cheese.

400g	Cooked beetroot, peeled and diced
30g	Crème fraiche
1 tbsp	Horseradish sauce
½ tsp	Peeled and grated fresh horseradish
	Salt and black pepper
	Juice of ½ lemon

Place the beetroot and crème fraiche in a bowl and mix until well combined and vibrant purple in colour.

Stir in the horseradish sauce.

Season with fresh horseradish, salt and freshly ground pepper to taste, and the lemon juice. Use within 2 days.

Onion compote

This fragrant onion mixture is delicious with cheese and cold meat, as well as adding zing to sandwiches and my cheese toastie (p.232).

50g	Unsalted butter
400g	Peeled and finely sliced onion (approx. 6 medium onions)
2	Cloves of garlic, peeled and finely chopped
4	Sprigs of thyme, leaves picked
	Groundnut or grapeseed oil
6	Slices of streaky bacon, cut into lardons
20g	Dry Madeira
	Salt and black pepper

Melt the butter in a large saucepan over a low-medium heat and add the onion, garlic and thyme leaves. Cook for 1 hour, stirring occasionally until well caramelized and dark in colour. If the onions start to catch on the bottom of the pan, add a little water and stir more frequently.

In the meantime, coat the bottom of a frying pan with a thin layer of oil and place over a medium heat. Add the bacon lardons and cook for 5–8 minutes until the bacon is soft and beginning to colour. Drain the bacon on kitchen paper and set aside.

Deglaze the pan of onions with the Madeira, and cook for a further 5 minutes. Add the bacon and season with salt and freshly ground pepper. Allow to cool.

Can be kept in a jar in the fridge for up to a week.

Apricot chutney

Apricots and mushrooms have a wonderful affinity. In fact, some wild mushrooms, specifically chanterelles, actually smell of apricots. So this chutney is a particularly tasty accompaniment for the mushroom parfait on p.103. It's also good with the chicken liver parfait on p.94, or you could just serve it on a cheeseboard.

175g	Dried apricots
1 tsp	Olive oil
1	Medium onion, peeled and diced
1	Clove of garlic, peeled and finely chopped
1 tsp	Peeled and grated fresh root ginger
150g	Orange juice
45g	Cider vinegar
¼ tsp	Chilli powder
35g	Unrefined caster sugar
	Pinch of salt

Boil enough water to cover the apricots in a bowl and let them soak for 3–4 hours or until completely soft. Drain the apricots and chop roughly.

Heat the oil in a saucepan over a low heat and cook the onion and garlic for 5 minutes or until soft.

Stir in the apricots, grated ginger, orange juice, cider vinegar and chilli powder and cook for 10–15 minutes until most of the liquid has been absorbed.

Stir in the sugar and cook for another 2 minutes, then add the salt.

Pour into a sterilized jar and store in the fridge, allowing the flavours to develop for at least 24 hours before serving.

Date, fig and apple chutney

Serve this dark, deep-flavoured chutney with chicken liver parfait (p.94), potted duck (p.96), or cheese.

100g	Groundnut or grapeseed oil
300g	Peeled and finely sliced onion (approx. 4 medium onions)
45g	Peeled and grated fresh root ginger
200g	Soft dried figs, diced
250g	Pitted dates, diced
350g	Peeled and diced apple (approx. 3–4 apples)
½ tsp	Ground ginger
½ tsp	Ground cinnamon
¼ tsp	Ground cloves
¼ tsp	Ground allspice
½ tsp	Finely ground black pepper
300g	Dry white wine
375g	Apple juice
	Zest of 1 orange, finely grated
	Zest of 1 lemon, finely grated
50g	Sherry vinegar
10g	Salt

Heat the oil in a large saucepan over a medium heat. Add the onion and ginger and turn the heat to low. Sweat for 30 minutes, stirring regularly.

Turn the heat up to begin to caramelize the mixture, then add the figs, dates and apple. Continue to sauté for 10 minutes, then add the spices and stir over the heat for 2 more minutes.

Add the wine to deglaze the pan, and bring to the boil. Boil to reduce the wine by half, then add the apple juice. Bring the pan to a gentle simmer and add the orange and lemon zest.

Cook until the mixture thickens and the fruit is soft (approximately 45 minutes). Finish with the sherry vinegar and salt, and stir to incorporate.

Pour into sterilized jars and store in the fridge, allowing the flavours to develop for at least 24 hours before serving.

Ices

On Sundays when I was a kid, my grandmother would drag me and my sister round the bric-à-brac stalls of Marylebone's Church Street market. Our reward for doing this without complaint was always an ice-cream in the Regent Snack Bar on Edgware Road. These days using this kind of bargaining strategy with children is considered bad practice, because it just demonizes further the very thing it's supposed to be rendering acceptable. All I know is that ever since, I've had a real passion for ice-cream. (And I've never been that keen on junk shops.)

I've also got a soft spot for ice-cream because it was one of the first foods that I investigated in depth at the Fat Duck. It was around then that I realized how a little scientific understanding could help me to achieve exactly the effects I was looking for. What I learned forms the basis of this chapter, and I hope it will have a transformative effect on your ice-cream-making.

Ice-cream bases

The starting point for ice-cream is creating the base mixture, to which you can add the flavours you want. The ingredients used for the base can vary widely, but the most important ones are fat, sugar and milk solids.

The fat content in an ice-cream usually comes from a combination of milk and/or cream, plus eggs. It's important, because it produces that lovely sensation of smoothness that's part of the pleasure of ice-cream. And, since fat is a relatively dense substance, it holds on to its temperature well (in much the same way that a thick overcoat holds on to warmth better than a thin T-shirt). This means it's good at preventing ice-cream from melting too quickly.

However, fat has some disadvantages. It coats the tongue and can blunt the flavour a little. Fat can also crystallize, causing an ice-cream to freeze into big crystals, giving it a crunchier texture. This can be a particular problem with domestic ice-cream makers because they freeze at around −5°C, which means they take 45 minutes to do what a commercial machine can do in 10. The slow speed of the freeze means it's more likely that the fat will crystallize, particularly if you are using egg yolks. So it's worth exploring alternative fats. These include yoghurt, soured cream and double cream or whipping cream. Whipping cream is used for nearly all the ice-creams in this book, because it has a fat content that will work with most types of ice-cream, so it's a very practical option for the home cook.

Fat is just one of a number of solids that give ice-cream its essential structure. The flavourings, milk solids (i.e., the things in milk and cream other than water and fat, such as proteins, lactose, minerals and vitamins) and sugar determine the body and texture of an ice-cream. If it's going to have the right structure and mouth-feel, there needs to be a good balance of solids to water in the base mixture. The amount of sugar is particularly important, because it's doing more than just sweetening the ice-cream. It balances the fattiness and it lowers the freezing point of the mixture (the sugar molecules hinder the water molecules' ability to order themselves into crystals), which means that a lower temperature will be needed to make the water solidify. This speeds up one of the most important parts of the ice-cream-making process, the development of ice crystals, as the lower the temperature gets, the more ice crystals form. (It's worth noting that when the ice-cream mixture is warm it will seem sweeter than when it's cold. You need to factor this in while tasting the ice-cream mix to gauge and adjust the level of sweetness.)

Milk solids (technically known as MSNF: milk solids, non-fat) provide a way to control the ice-cream's character and consistency. If you're inventing your own ice-cream rather than following a recipe in a book, and have a particular consistency you're aiming for, you'll need to choose ingredients that provide the appropriate percentage of total solids. (A standard vanilla ice-cream mix might have about 35 per cent total solids, made up of 14 per cent sugar, 11 per cent fat and 10 per cent MSNF.) Whipping cream is often used as a source of MSNF, but it contains a small amount of milk solids and a high amount of fat, so it can create a fattier ice-cream base than you want. By contrast, semi-skimmed milk powder is virtually all solids, and has no fat, so it's a good source of MSNF and can be added without you worrying about it adding to the amount of fat in the base mixture. I use semi-skimmed milk powder a lot in my ice-cream, because it's an easy way to add the necessary amount of MSNF without making the mix fattier.

So the amounts of fat and solids in an ice-cream base can be juggled to create different effects, as long as you bear in mind that each ingredient has a distinct role to play. Reducing or increasing any one will have consequences. Too many total solids and, once churned, the base will resemble frozen powdered milk. Too much sugar will prevent the mix from freezing properly, resulting in a sludge. Too much fat and an ice-cream ends up dense, too little and it will melt almost instantly. In the end, preparing an ice-cream base is a balancing act.

Churning and freezing

If you take a mixture of milk, cream and eggs (technically known as a custard) and simply freeze it, you'll end up with something relatively solid rather than a nice smooth and melting consistency. So when making ice-cream (or indeed a sorbet or granita) a key task is to prevent the mixture from crystallizing into a solid block.

One of the ingredients in ice-creams and sorbets is water, which is present in any number of the ingredients. (Milk, for example, is more than 80 per cent water.) Water is what forms into the ice crystals that give ices their frozen character. But that freezing has to be managed. If you pour water into a container and put it in the freezer, it will form a rock-hard, interlocking crystalline structure. For ice-cream, you need to engineer it so the water forms into lots of little ice crystals, evenly distributed through the mix, and separate enough that they don't fuse together. By the time the ice-cream base is put in the machine, you'll have already taken the first steps to ensuring this happens. The solids you've incorporated into the base will lower the freezing point at which the water solidifies into ice and ensure that, even at sub-zero temperatures, there's still some liquid present in the mixture.

To capitalize on this it's important that the mixture is frozen quickly. The faster an ice-cream is frozen, the smaller the ice crystals that develop, and the smoother the end result. Usually, with the more expensive domestic machines, what you're paying for is the speed at which it will freeze the mix. It's worth getting the best you can afford – or using dry ice, which, because it's super-cold, makes amazing ice-cream (see below).

But it's also important to introduce some air to the mixture to make it light. Churning (also known as stir-freezing) is basically just a way of getting air into the ice-cream mix – in much the same manner as whisking egg whites – while at the same time breaking down the ice crystals to make sure they're small.

I find that one problem with churning in a domestic machine is that it still allows some large crystals to develop, coarsening the end result. So I've developed a technique to counter this. Once the ice-cream is churned, remove it from the machine, blitz it with a hand blender for 10 seconds, and then put it back in to churn for another 10 minutes. It's a simple little thing, but it makes a huge difference to the final texture, turning it much smoother than it would otherwise be. The blitzing breaks the crystals down into tiny particles and, since the mixture is already partially frozen, it re-freezes faster and smaller than before.

However, there are some circumstances in which the slow freezing speed of the domestic ice-cream machine simply won't do a proper job. Egg-based ice-creams are one example because the fat freezes first, growing big ice crystals that spoil the texture. Ices in which alcohol plays a key note in the flavour (such as the whisky ice-cream on p.290) are another. Since alcohol freezes at a lower temperature than water – 80° proof vodka freezes only at around –27°C – its presence in any more than the smallest amount can prevent the mixture from freezing properly. This can be used to advantage – through trial and error you can develop the skill of adding a certain amount of alcohol to an ice base to create a lovely soft texture – but using alcohol as an ingredient definitely presents a technical challenge.

Anyone who wants to create great ices using eggs or booze will soon be looking for an alternative to the domestic machine. And, to be honest, anyone who gets hooked on ice-cream-making and begins to experiment with different types of fats and solids is probably going to find they eventually outgrow the capabilities of the domestic churner, too. One option is to buy a professional machine. The one at the Fat Duck is a boxy countertop job that cost the best part of £10,000. But I've come up with another, more realistic solution – dry ice or, to give it its proper name, frozen carbon dioxide.

'Cooking' with dry ice might seem like an incredibly specialist technique – I can see that the idea of handling a scientific-sounding substance that is shockingly cold takes some getting used to and raises all kinds of questions. How do I get hold of it? How do I store it?

How do I handle it? But in fact the process is very simple. You can obtain it from several suppliers online. It can be stored for a short while in the foam container in which it's sold (rather than the freezer, which at a mere −18°C isn't going to be very effective at preventing a −80°C solid from evaporating), but it really should be used pretty soon after purchase. So you will need to plan ahead a little before using it. Maybe make a weekend of it: prepare a bacon and egg ice-cream (p.289) *and* a whisky ice-cream (p.290) *and* a blackcurrant sorbet (p.292).

As for handling it, you should take exactly the same precautions you would with naked flames, hot pans and baking trays straight out of the oven: don't let it come into direct contact with your skin or you'll get a nasty burn. And you need to ensure that all the dry ice used to freeze an ice-cream mix has dissolved before you serve up the ice-cream. Take these simple precautions and you'll find that dry ice offers such an easy way of making amazing ice-cream that you might end up freezing all your ices like this. It also gives the opportunity for a great piece of theatre at dinner: you can bring the mixer to the table and make the ice-cream in front of your guests, creating the perfect texture in seconds in a flurry of billowing vapour, like a magician or mad scientist.

Sorbets and granitas

Sorbets and granitas are both water-based ices, but a sorbet is churned to a smooth texture while a granita is frozen with minimal stirring to produce a looser, coarser texture. (This looser granita texture means it's more forgiving to work with and, as the recipes on p.294 will show, makes few demands on the home cook.) Sorbets and granitas are different from ice-cream in that they are icier, and the base is made not from milk or cream but from a sugar syrup (water with some form of sugar dissolved into it).

Since a sorbet base consists of just sugar, water and flavourings, the sugar is the main solid doing the work of lowering the freezing point and ensuring the texture is smooth and the ice crystals small. You need therefore to have the right balance of sugar to water. If the ratio of sugar to water is too high, there won't be enough water to do an effective job of freezing the mixture. The mix won't churn well and you'll end up with something that's smooth but chewy and overly sweet. Conversely, too low a ratio of sugar to water means there'll be large ice crystals, making the sorbet lumpy and crunchy.

The traditional sugar used for ices is some form of sucrose (granulated sugar, caster sugar, icing sugar). However, I generally use fructose instead. Fructose is a natural sugar found in fruits and honey. It dissolves very easily into a sorbet mix to create a nicely homogeneous texture, but perhaps its greatest advantage is that it significantly intensifies the impression of 'fruitiness'. Fructose is easily obtainable from supermarkets and health stores, and it's well worth tracking some down because it can really enhance a sorbet's flavour. (Bear in mind, though, that fructose is noticeably sweeter than sugar and so you'll need to add less than you would if you were using sucrose.)

Judging the right level of sugar can be a tricky business because the amount of sugar a fruit contains can vary enormously – and fruit is very often the principal flavouring in a sorbet. A very ripe, in-season strawberry is likely to contain significantly more sugar than an unripe one. If you use unripe strawberries to make a sorbet, the chances are that it will end up grainy because there wasn't enough sugar in the base mixture for it to churn to a good consistency. So in order to make a successful sorbet, you need to have a method of determining exactly how much sugar the fruit you're using contains, and adjust accordingly.

With experience, you can get a feel for how ripe fruit is and how much you might have to adjust the sugar level. But you can also use a refractometer (p.393), which is an invaluable and inexpensive piece of kitchen kit that effectively measures how much sugar is present in a liquid and gives a reading on the Brix scale. This probably sounds very technical, but in reality all you do is place a drop of the sorbet base under the lens, which then gives a reading in degrees Brix. All the sorbet bases in this book are 26° Brix, so if you invest in a refractometer, you should be able to adapt the recipes to other sorts of fruit, using the refractometer to ensure that the purée has the right sugar content to make a good sorbet.

There is, however, a way of obtaining the right sugar ratio that relies neither on experience nor on technical equipment: you can use a commercial fruit purée instead, as I do for the blackcurrant sorbet (p.292). There's a general consensus in the food industry about the levels of water and solids that constitute a purée, so it should already be the right density for making a sorbet. No need to mess around with checking sugar levels, you can just add the purée to the sugar syrup, blitz and churn.

This doesn't mean you should do away with purée-making altogether. It's a very worthwhile skill to develop and there will be circumstances where you need to make your own for a sorbet – perhaps because there's no commercial version of the fruit you want to use. For the rhubarb sorbet on p.291, the purée has to be cooked because although a stem of rhubarb might feel fairly solid, it is in fact almost all water. A lot of this has to be cooked off, otherwise the ratio of water in the mixture will be too high and the end result after churning will be loose and grainy.

A well-made sorbet should be smooth, with a balance of sweetness and acidity. Because it contains no fat, a sorbet is seen as particularly fresh and light – a real showcase for the fruit it contains. One way to allow the purity of the fruit to shine in a sorbet is to heat it as little as possible. In the strawberry sorbet (p.290) and the blackcurrant sorbet (p.292), the only cooking involved is the initial warming of the sugar syrup. In the strawberry sorbet the fruit is blitzed to a smooth purée with a hand blender, then strained and added to cooled sugar syrup. It's incredibly simple, which means it's a great entry-level sorbet: if you've never made an ice before, try this one.

With other fruit, you'll have to take into account their physical characteristics and adjust the amounts of sugar and water accordingly. Fruits that are dense, such as mango, or dense and starchy, such as banana, or with

high levels of pectin, such as peaches and apricots, may involve a bit of trial and error before you find a mixture that churns well.

How to make ice-cream or sorbet with dry ice

Dry ice is the stuff used to create that spooky graveyard effect on stage, which is in fact the CO_2 evaporating. At $-80°C$, dry ice is spectacularly cold, so it can freeze spectacularly fast, creating the small ice crystals you need if ice-cream or sorbet is to have a truly smooth texture.

1. Put the dry ice in a clean tea-towel and fold the towel around it.

2. Using a rolling pin, gently bash the dry ice into small crystals. It's essential to do this for texture – big lumps will spoil the smoothness – and for safety: a large lump of $-80°C$ ice in the mouth is a very bad idea.

3. Put the ice-cream or sorbet mix in a food mixer fitted with a paddle attachment. (Don't use the whisk attachment as this will incorporate too much air.) Switch it on to medium speed and then gradually add the crushed dry ice.

4. Make sure all of the dry ice has dissolved. It should take no more than 30–60 seconds for the mix to become frozen. If it takes longer, add more dry ice as required.

Cinnamon and vanilla ice-cream

The starting point for this recipe was a scientific paper on a phenomenon called 'odour adaptation', which is when the brain stops us smelling something, even though the odour is still there. This process helps us to detect whether an aroma is getting stronger or not, and saves us from sensory overload.

You can explore the effects of odour adaptation for yourself using this ice-cream. (It works with about 85 per cent of people.) Take two squeezy bottles that are big enough to produce a good whoomph of air when you squeeze them, and place two vanilla pods in one of the bottles. Bash two cinnamon sticks to release their aroma and place them in the second bottle. Eat a spoonful of the ice-cream, then take a good sniff of the vanilla bottle. Now eat another spoonful of ice-cream – you'll find it only has a cinnamon flavour! And if you eat the ice-cream after sniffing the cinnamon squeezy bottle, it will seem to be pure vanilla.

It seems like magic but it's just odour adaptation at work. When the brain gets a surfeit of cinnamon, it masks it and concentrates on the vanilla, and vice-versa. I urge you to make the ice-cream, because it's absolutely delicious, but you don't need it to try the experiment. In place of the ice-cream you can use a third squeezy bottle filled with cinnamon *and* vanilla.

Serves 6–8

6	Vanilla pods, halved lengthways
360g	Whole milk
200g	Unrefined caster sugar
35g	Semi-skimmed milk powder
840g	Whipping cream
2	Whole espresso beans
1	Large cinnamon stick

Scrape the seeds from the vanilla pods and add them and the pods to the milk in a saucepan. Add the sugar and milk powder and place over a medium heat, stirring continuously until all the milk powder has dissolved.

Add the whipping cream, espresso beans and cinnamon stick and bring to the boil, stirring occasionally. Once boiling, remove from the heat and pour the mixture into a container. Allow to cool to room temperature by placing the container in a bowl or basin of iced water, then cover and place in the fridge for 2 hours to infuse.

Turn your ice-cream machine on at least 20 minutes before using it (it is vital to get the mixing bowl really cold before churning).

Strain the ice-cream mixture through a fine sieve. While straining, keep the mixture moving with a wooden spoon to ensure the vanilla seeds get through the sieve.

Pour the base into the ice-cream machine with the paddle turning. After approximately 20 minutes, the machine will start labouring as the ice-cream gets thicker. When the machine can no longer turn the paddle, remove the mixing bowl.

Using a hand blender, blitz the ice-cream for 10 seconds then replace the mixing bowl in the machine and churn for a further 10 minutes.

Decant the ice-cream into a sealable container and place in the freezer for at least 1 hour before serving.

Caramel ice-cream with mini cones

Caramel works really well in an ice-cream. It gives it a lovely colour and a grown-up flavour – less sweet, more caramelized – that nevertheless manages to evoke childhood memories of toffees, Caramac and butterscotch. On top, a caramel sauce would be wonderful, as would some crystallized nuts (p.377).

Fills 16 mini cones

250g	Unrefined caster sugar
360g	Whole milk
35g	Semi-skimmed milk powder
840g	Whipping cream

To serve

Mini cones (right)

To start the caramel ice-cream, place the sugar in a stainless-steel saucepan over a medium-high heat to make a dry caramel (p.307).

When the caramel is dark brown, add the milk a little at a time, whisking continuously, until the caramel has dissolved in the milk. Reduce the heat to low-medium.

Add the semi-skimmed milk powder and the whipping cream. Continue to whisk until the milk powder has dissolved. Remove the pan from the heat. Let the mixture cool completely over a bowl or basin of iced water.

Turn your ice-cream machine on at least 20 minutes before using it (it is vital to get the mixing bowl really cold before churning). Pour the base into the ice-cream machine with the paddle turning. After approximately 20 minutes, the machine will start labouring as the ice-cream gets thicker. When the machine can no longer turn the paddle, remove the mixing bowl.

Using a hand blender, blitz the ice-cream for 10 seconds, then replace the mixing bowl in the machine and churn for a further 10 minutes. Decant the ice-cream into a sealable container and place in the freezer for at least 2 hours before serving. Pipe into the cones.

Mini cones

The dusting of caster sugar on these cones makes them sweet, and gives them a powdery surface that reminds me of eating doughnuts as a kid. The recipe makes 16 cones.

200g	Clarified butter (see tip, below)
125g	Icing sugar
	Pinch of salt
4	Sheets of brik pastry (Specialist ingredients, p.394)
	White caster sugar

Pre-heat the oven to 150°C.

Put the butter in a pan, add the icing sugar and salt and heat until the sugar has dissolved. Using a hand blender, blitz the mixture for 30 seconds until all the ingredients are well combined.

Brush a clean chopping board with the butter and sugar mixture, then place a sheet of the pastry on it and brush the top with more of the mixture.

Using a 12cm ring cutter, cut out two discs. Cut each disc in half and roll into a cone shape. Place these in the holes of a cooling rack resting on an ovenproof saucepan so they keep their shape. Repeat this process with the remaining sheets of pastry.

Carefully place the pan and cooling rack in the oven and bake for 15 minutes or until golden brown. Remove from the oven and allow to cool.

Dust the cones with caster sugar before piping ice-cream into each one.

How to clarify butter

Heat unsalted butter in a medium pan over a gentle heat, whisking continuously. When the water is driven off by the heat, milk solids begin to coagulate on the surface of the fat. When these fall to the bottom of the pan, the butter is clarified. To separate the clear butter fat from the solids, pour through a coffee filter, carefully, into a clean container. Clarified butter is excellent for sautéing and searing, as it can be heated to a much higher temperature than normal butter.

Vanilla ice-cream

I spent years trying to recreate the distinctive flavour of the vanilla ice-cream I regularly ate as a kid in the Regent Snack Bar in London. Nothing seemed to work. It was only when I went to an ice-cream parlour run by a man who used to serve at the Regent that the puzzle was finally solved – my memory had been playing tricks on me. I saw him putting a scoop of vanilla plus a scoop of coffee in a tub, and suddenly recalled that that's what I used to have. So this recipe uses a coffee infusion to give you a taste of my childhood. You can leave out the coffee if you wish, or even use a little instant coffee instead.

Serves 6–8

5	Vanilla pods, halved lengthways
360g	Whole milk
175g	Unrefined caster sugar
840g	Whipping cream
2	Whole espresso beans

Scrape the vanilla seeds out of the pods. Put the milk, sugar, whipping cream, vanilla pods, seeds and espresso beans into a saucepan. Place over a medium heat and bring to the boil.

Remove the pan from the heat immediately, and pour the liquid into a bowl resting in a bigger bowl or basin of iced water. When the mixture has cooled, cover and place in the fridge for 24 hours.

Turn your ice-cream machine on at least 20 minutes before you are going to use it (it is vital to get your ice cream machine really cold before churning).

Strain the ice-cream mixture through a fine sieve and pour it into the ice-cream machine with the paddle turning. After approximately 30 minutes, the machine will start labouring as the ice-cream gets thicker. When the paddle can no longer turn, remove the pot.

Blitz the ice-cream with a hand blender for 10 seconds and return the mixture to the ice-cream machine for a further 10 minutes. Decant into a sealable container and place in the freezer for at least 2 hours before serving.

Mustard ice-cream

This has a wonderfully savoury flavour, and it works really well with the red cabbage gazpacho (p.63) because it brings out the peppery note of cabbage, which comes from the mustard oil it contains. But the ice-cream is also great with a tomato gazpacho, or as a garnish for cured fish, tea-smoked salmon (p.85) and pickles or potted meat.

Serves 6–8

360g	Whole milk
140g	Unrefined caster sugar
840g	Whipping cream
35g	Semi-skimmed milk powder
120g	Wholegrain mustard
10g	English mustard

Place the milk, sugar, whipping cream and milk powder in a saucepan over medium heat and whisk until the milk powder has completely dissolved.

Remove from the heat and pour the mixture into a container. Place the container in a bowl or basin of iced water to cool.

Once cold, add the two types of mustard and whisk well to incorporate.

Turn your ice-cream machine on at least 20 minutes before using it (it is vital to get the mixing bowl really cold before churning).

Pour the base into the ice-cream machine with the paddle turning. After approximately 20 minutes, the machine will start labouring as the ice-cream gets thicker. When the machine can no longer turn the paddle, remove the mixing bowl.

Using a hand blender, blitz the ice-cream for 10 seconds then replace the mixing bowl in the machine and churn for a further 10 minutes.

Decant the ice-cream into a sealable container and place in the freezer for at least 2 hours before serving.

Bacon and egg ice-cream

This ice-cream came out of one of those 'What if?' experiments that are such valuable catalysts for culinary creativity. (Just don't try them out on friends until you've road-tested the results yourself!) I cooked an egg-based ice-cream custard beyond the traditional temperature cut-off point, puréed and sieved the results, then churned them. The flavour took me back to childhood treats of boiled eggs with soldiers or fried eggs and bacon. I began exploring what other breakfast ingredients might go well in an ice-cream, and ended up with a Fat Duck classic.

In the restaurant we prepare it at the table using liquid nitrogen, which actually makes the mixture look like scrambled eggs. Although it won't have quite the same effect, freezing the ice-cream using dry ice will give it a scrambled appearance. (Dry ice is also the best way of ensuring that an ice-cream containing eggs – which can affect the way ice crystals develop – freezes to a really smooth texture.) Served with pain perdu and caramelized bacon (p.334), it will look amazing – a sort of breakfast-as-dessert *trompe l'oeil*.

Serves 6–8

400g	Sweet-cured smoked back bacon
1kg	Whole milk
30g	Semi-skimmed milk powder
24	Large egg yolks
120g	Unrefined caster sugar
1kg	Dry ice pellets
	(Specialist ingredients, p.394)

Pre-heat the oven to 190°C.

Lay the bacon slices on a parchment-lined baking tray, and place in the oven for 25–30 minutes.

When the bacon is cooked, drain on kitchen paper and cut it into strips. Place in a bowl, pour over the milk, then leave to infuse for at least 12 hours.

After 12 hours, place the milk and bacon in a saucepan, add the milk powder and bring to a gentle simmer. Remove the pan from the heat.

In the meantime, blitz the egg yolks and the sugar together using a hand blender.

Add some of the warm milk to the egg yolks and sugar and whisk thoroughly. This will bring the temperature of the egg yolks up to that of the milk mixture and prevent the eggs scrambling. Add the milk, egg and sugar mixture to the rest of the milk in the pan and place over a medium heat, stir thoroughly and continue to stir until the temperature reaches 85°C.

Once this temperature has been reached, remove from the heat and pass the ice-cream base through a fine sieve into a clean container, pushing the mixture through with the back of a spoon or ladle. Cool immediately by placing the container in a bowl or basin of iced water.

When cold, blitz the liquid with a hand blender until smooth.

When ready to make the ice-cream, follow the instructions for using dry ice on p.279.

Eat immediately or decant the ice-cream into a sealable container, and store in the freezer for up to 5 days.

Whisky ice-cream

Alcohol has a lower freezing point than other ingredients, so this recipe employs dry ice to freeze the mixture, which helps ensure that it develops a firm, smooth texture.

The ice-cream's character will depend on what whisky you choose. If you want a mild, fruity flavour, use one like Oban. For a smoky note, I'd pick Laphroaig.

Serves 6–8

500g	Whole milk
6	Large egg yolks
175g	Unrefined caster sugar
270g	Soured cream
40g	Malt whisky
1kg	Dry ice pellets (Specialist ingredients, p.394)

Pour the milk into a saucepan and bring to a gentle simmer. Remove the pan from the heat.

In the meantime, blitz the egg yolks and sugar together using a hand blender.

Add a little of the warm milk to the eggs and sugar and stir well, then pour the mixture into the pan and place over a medium heat. Stir thoroughly, then whisk until the temperature reaches 70°C. Hold the temperature for 10 minutes, whisking occasionally.

After 10 minutes, remove from the heat and cool immediately by pouring into a clean container and placing the container in a large bowl or basin of iced water.

When cold, add the soured cream and whisky and blitz with a hand blender until smooth.

When ready to make the ice-cream, follow the instructions for using dry ice on p.279.

Eat immediately or decant the ice-cream into a sealable container, and store in the freezer for up to 5 days.

Strawberry sorbet

Just three ingredients – what could be simpler? The strawberries need to be as ripe and sweet as possible, so this is a recipe to be enjoyed in the summer, when the strawberry season is at its peak.

Serves 6–8

400g	Fructose (fruit sugar)
2kg	Strawberries, hulled
10g	Vodka

Place 400g cold tap water and the fructose in a saucepan over a medium-high heat and bring to the boil.

Once boiling, remove the pan from the heat and place the pan in a bowl or basin of iced water. Allow the syrup to cool completely.

In the meantime, place the strawberries in a bowl and, using a hand blender, blitz them to a smooth purée. Pass the purée through a fine sieve to eliminate the seeds and then mix with the cold syrup and the vodka.

Turn the ice-cream machine on at least 20 minutes before using (it is vital to get the mixing bowl really cold before churning).

Pour the purée into the ice-cream machine with the paddle turning. After approximately 20 minutes, the machine will start labouring as the sorbet gets thicker. When the machine can no longer turn the paddle, remove the mixing bowl.

Using a hand blender, blitz the sorbet for 10 seconds, then replace the mixing bowl in the machine and churn for a further 10 minutes.

Decant the sorbet into a sealable container and place in the freezer for at least 1 hour before serving.

Rhubarb sorbet

I've loved the flavour of rhubarb ever since I was a kid, when I used to eat it raw, dipped in sugar. This recipe produces a sorbet that has a marvellously intense rhubarb flavour without any trace of bitterness, and I've used it as a garnish for a number of different dishes at the Fat Duck, from macerated strawberries with shortbread to a galette of rhubarb with crystallized coconut.

To capture the intense, fresh flavour of raw rhubarb, some freshly juiced rhubarb is added to the purée just before churning. The same approach can be used to boost the fresh flavour of any fruit purée, but you'll need to have some idea of how watery your fruit is before you start adding more liquid.

Serves 6–8

800g	Rhubarb, washed and roughly chopped
380g	Fructose (fruit sugar)
320g	Grenadine
250g	Rhubarb juice, passed through a fine sieve (approx. 500g rhubarb)
10g	Vodka

Place the rhubarb pieces, fructose and grenadine in a large saucepan over a medium-high heat. Allow to cook until reduced to a purée weighing approximately 700g.

Pour the purée into a blender and blitz until smooth. Push through a fine sieve into a bowl and allow to cool.

Before churning, mix the purée with the fresh rhubarb juice and the vodka.

Turn your ice-cream machine on at least 20 minutes before using it (it is vital to get the mixing bowl really cold before churning).

Pour the purée into the ice-cream machine with the paddle turning. After approximately 20 minutes, the machine will start labouring as the sorbet gets thicker. When the machine can no longer turn the paddle, remove the mixing bowl.

Using a hand blender, blitz the sorbet for 10 seconds, then replace the mixing bowl in the machine and churn for a further 10 minutes.

Decant the sorbet into a sealable container and place in the freezer for at least 1 hour before serving.

Blackcurrant sorbet

You can make your own purée for this recipe but it can be tricky to cook blackcurrants to the right consistency, so I've suggested using a commercial fruit purée (or coulis) instead. There are some excellent, natural ones on the market now.

This sorbet is good served with many soft fruits. It also goes well with the mint granita (p.294) and the mango terrine with green peppercorns (p.333).

Serves 6–8

180g	Fructose (fruit sugar)
45g	Lemon juice
750g	Blackcurrant purée
10g	Vodka

Place 450g cold tap water and the fructose in a saucepan over a medium-high heat and bring to the boil.

Once boiling, remove the pan from the heat and place the pan in a bowl or basin of iced water. Allow the syrup to cool completely, then add the lemon juice.

In a blender, blitz the blackcurrant purée and the vodka with the fructose syrup for 5 minutes. Pass the purée through a fine sieve and keep chilled.

Turn the ice-cream machine on at least 20 minutes before using (it is vital to get the mixing bowl really cold before churning).

Pour the purée into the ice-cream machine with the paddle turning. After approximately 20 minutes, the machine will start labouring as the sorbet gets thicker. When the machine can no longer turn the paddle, remove the mixing bowl.

Using a hand blender, blitz the sorbet for 10 seconds, then replace the mixing bowl in the machine and churn for a further 10 minutes.

Decant the sorbet into a sealable container and place in the freezer for at least 1 hour before serving.

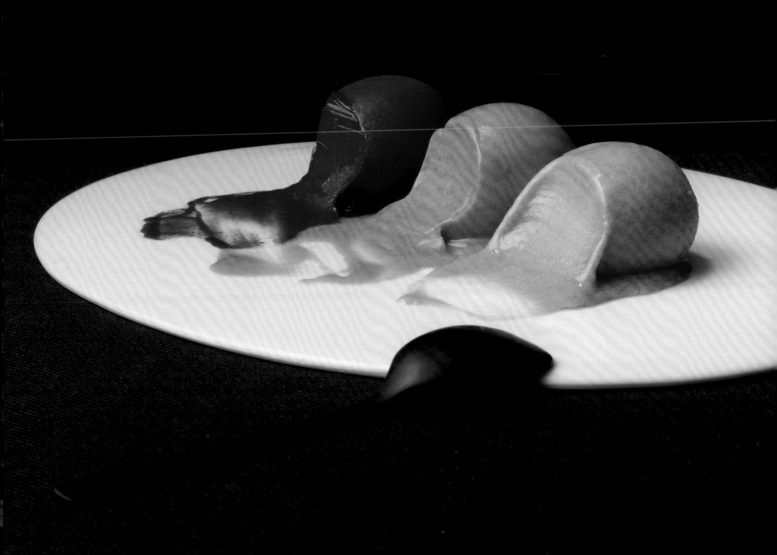

Orange and ginger granita

This is an adaptation of a recipe from one of my culinary heroes, Agnes Bertha Marshall (1855–1905), a visionary cook who invented an early ice-cream churner and recommended the use of 'liquefied air' in cooking a hundred years before people like me started experimenting with liquid nitrogen.

In her book *Fancy Ices* (1894), Mrs Marshall serves a mixture of this granita with apple ice-cream in a cornet, and you could do the same, using the cones on p.286. Alternatively you might serve it with orange segments, a fruit salad or macerated strawberries, or with chocolate ice-cream for a twist on Terry's Chocolate Orange.

Serves 8–10

14	Oranges
240g	White caster sugar
30g	Fresh root ginger, peeled and roughly chopped

Remove the zest from 8 of the oranges with a vegetable peeler in large pieces. Juice all the oranges (approximately 800g juice in total).

Place 550g cold tap water and the sugar in a saucepan over a medium-high heat and bring to the boil. Simmer until the sugar has melted.

Remove the pan from the heat and add the pieces of orange zest. Allow the liquid to cool completely over a bowl or basin of iced water.

When cool, remove the zest and pour the syrup into a blender with all the orange juice and the ginger. Blitz for 5 minutes to extract the flavour from the ginger.

Pass the liquid through a fine sieve lined with muslin, then pour into a small, deep-sided baking tray or metal bowl and place in the freezer.

Whisk the mixture with a fork every 20–30 minutes until it crystallizes (approximately 1 hour 30 minutes).

Decant the granita into a sealable container and place in the freezer for at least 1 hour before serving.

Mint granita with apple juice

A granita offers a great introduction to ice-cream-making because you don't need to use a machine. The key piece of equipment is a container made of metal rather than plastic, because plastic doesn't get as cold as metal and will take longer to freeze the mixture. This fresh, vibrant granita is here served with freshly pressed apple juice, but it also goes very well with blackcurrant sorbet (p.292).

Serves 8–10

For the mint granita

250g	Mint, leaves picked
80g	White caster sugar

For the apple juice

10	Granny Smith apples

Place a saucepan of cold tap water on the stove and bring to the boil. In the meantime, prepare a bowl or basin of iced water for refreshing the mint leaves.

Once the water has come to a boil, add the leaves for 10 seconds, then immediately transfer them to the iced water using a strainer or a slotted spoon.

After 5 minutes in the cold water, remove the leaves, squeeze out the excess water and place them on a tray lined with kitchen paper.

Place the blanched mint leaves with 500g cold tap water and the sugar in a blender and blitz for 3 minutes. Pass the mixture through a sieve and place the liquid in a small deep-sided baking tray or metal bowl in the freezer. Whisk the mixture with a fork every 20–30 minutes until it crystallizes (approximately 1 hour 30 minutes). Decant the granita into a sealable container and place in the freezer for at least 1 hour before serving.

For the apple juice, cut the Granny Smith apples into thirds and put them through a juicer. Pass the juice through a sieve.

Place a spoonful of the granita in the bottom of chilled glasses and pour over freshly squeezed juice.

Desserts and sweets

In eighteenth-century France, *le dessert* at the tables of the rich was an elaborate affair, with pyramids of fruit interspersed with extravagant table decorations and architectural fantasies – classical temples, rotundas and bridges – made out of marzipan, pork fat, pastry and spun sugar. This theatrical approach caught on in Britain, and the term 'dessert' adopted here too. It derives from the verb *desservir*, meaning 'to clear the table', which neatly captures the sense of occasion that surrounds desserts – the stage is cleared for the final act.

Moreover, by the 1800s, Britain's colonial expansion had provided more sources of sugar. It had become cheaper and easier to obtain, and had begun to feature heavily in recipes, edging out the practice of elaborate spicing, which had previously done the job of enlivening food and masking bitterness. Both rich and poor relished sugar, and sugar sweetness became an integral part of the dessert course.

Although dessert can now mean anything from cakes, pastries and puddings to ice-cream and raw or cooked fruit, it has a spirit of indulgence attached to it. There's also something quite nostalgic about desserts. We all have a sweet tooth when we're kids, and sweet dishes tend to loom large in the memory. I have great affection for Black Forest gâteau, even though most of the examples I ate during the 1970s were poor imitations of the real thing. It wasn't the flavour that captivated me, it was the excitement of the dish, the drama of its presentation. Perhaps that's why desserts so often involve showmanship – it's an attempt to re-ignite that childlike delight.

The desserts and sweets in this chapter capture, I think, a lot of these characteristics. There's certainly plenty of indulgence in the buttery pastry and caramelized flavours of the arlette and tartes tatin, and in the rich chocolate in the rosemary and bay truffles, chocolate tart and liquid centre chocolate pudding. The latter introduces a lovely moment of theatre when you dig in with your spoon and warm runny chocolate oozes from the centre. There's also plenty of nostalgia, from childhood favourites like strawberry sundae and marshmallows and even sherbet (remember dip-dabs and fountains?) to traditional dishes like Eccles cakes and lardy cake, and trattoria and bistro classics like tiramisù and a sharp lemon tart with just the right amount of wobble. That wobble is another example of the showmanship that goes into desserts. With the lemon tart (or the panna cotta or the crème brûlée), there's a sense of anticipation as you take your first spoonful. Will the filling be set to perfection?

I tried here, too, to trigger a little of that childhood delight by taking some familiar dishes and giving them a twist. So the panna cotta, crème brûlée, tartes tatin and marshmallows have flavours that may well be unexpected. And my take on wine gums interprets the premise of the sweets literally and flavours them with alcohol. A dessert is definitely an opportunity to be playful, and make your guests go *wow!*

Pastry

Some of the pastry recipes in this book use puff pastry. The aim of puff pastry is to form multiple layers of extremely thin pastry that are incredibly light and easily flake apart in the mouth. Making it is an elaborate process, however, involving several stages of rolling, resting, folding and chilling. So for the home cook, the most practical option is a shop-bought all-butter puff pastry, and that's what I suggest using for the tartes tatin (pp.312 and 314), arlette (p.315) and Eccles cakes (p.319).

Shortcrust pastry, on the other hand, is one of the most versatile types of pastry and often one of the most forgiving to make. Also known as *pâte brisée*, it is perfect for quiches, savoury tarts and pies. And by adjusting the recipe slightly, you have a suitable pastry for desserts, like the lemon tart (p.310).

Although pastry comes in a wide range of textures, from chewy croissants and shard-like strudel to crumbly tart cases and flaky pie crusts, it generally contains the same core ingredients – flour, fat and some form of liquid (e.g., water or dairy products) – plus perhaps eggs, salt and/or sugar, depending on the type of pastry and what it's going to be used for. It's the choice and balance of these ingredients, and the method and order in which you mix them, which determine the particular character of a dough.

With any dough, including pastry dough, the structure comes in part from the reaction of flour's gluten proteins with water. The more you expose gluten to water, and the more you work and massage and encourage it, the more elastic your dough will become. While this property is essential for bread-making, with pastry the ideal is usually a texture that is much crumblier or flakier. One of the pastry-maker's prime concerns, therefore, is generally to limit the development of gluten in the dough. The amount of liquid in a pastry is generally kept low so that the dough doesn't become too elastic, and it can have a decisive effect on the final texture. As little as 3g variation of water in 120g flour might make the difference between a crumbly texture and a tough one.

Fat also contributes to the overall texture (as well as providing flavour) by preventing the dough from developing too extensively. The fat coats the flour and acts as a barrier to the water, slowing down gluten development. Butter is most frequently used because it provides a delicious rich flavour, but it can be difficult to work with unless it's at 15–20°C. Too cold and it tends to be too solid to manipulate (although cold is good when using a processor); too warm and it soon becomes too soft to handle. The former problem is best solved by thinking ahead, if making by hand, and softening the butter in advance; the latter can often be remedied by returning the butter or pastry dough to the fridge. There are also other fats that can be used for pastries: lard or solid vegetable fats, in particular, are simple to use because they can be handled over a wide temperature range, though what you gain in practical ease you lose in terms of flavour.

Eggs are often added to these basic ingredients to bind them together, provide some of the liquid and to introduce richness, colour and flavour. In a sweet pastry, sugar can play a key role, not just sweetening the mixture but helping to limit gluten development by absorbing moisture, creating a more tender texture. Salt is often added to pastry, whether savoury or sweet, to enhance flavour.

One of the basic ways of limiting gluten development is to choose flour with a relatively low protein content, such as plain flour. (In general, strong or bread flour has 12–15 per cent protein; plain has around 9–11 per cent.) Another is to limit flour's contact with water. If you're aiming for a short pastry, a good strategy is to combine the flour, fat and dry ingredients before the wet ingredients, as mentioned above. Bear in mind, though, that butter is about 15 per cent water, so if this is the fat you're using, it will begin the process of gluten development. Lard and vegetable fats, which don't contain water, won't kickstart gluten development, but they can't simply be substituted for butter as they'll give a pastry a very different flavour. You'll have to weigh up the pros and cons of using one or the other.

One of the things that's often underestimated during pastry-making is how much heat can mess up the process. In a warm environment, or after the dough has been worked for a period of time, thus warming it up, the fat and other solids in the dough melt, so it becomes difficult to work with and the texture deteriorates. And if the pastry is at this point when it goes into the oven, there's a risk that its water will evaporate too quickly and it'll shrink. The pastry should be cold when it is heated, so that it takes a while for the fat and solids to soften to melting point.

So, success depends on keeping the pastry as cold as possible. Before starting a pastry-making session, it's worth putting all the equipment – bowl, rolling pin, pastry board – in the fridge for a while. Mixing needs to be done quickly and briefly: working the dough hard will warm it up too much. If mixing by hand, use your fingertips only, or the heat of your hands will transfer to the mixture. Once brought together, wrap the newly formed dough in clingfilm and place it in the fridge so that it can rest and chill for 30–60 minutes.

Before rolling it's a good idea to sandwich the pastry between two sheets of greaseproof paper, baking parchment or clingfilm, which makes rolling a tidy, trouble-free process (no dough sticking to the pin and tearing) and protects the dough. (After you've worked the pastry a bit, it might adhere to the paper, but a cooling stint in the freezer will separate the two again.)

The dough should be rested in the freezer once it has been rolled, in order to relax the gluten. A rolled dough becomes firm and taut, because the protein molecules have aligned into a tight-knit mass. However, if it's left for half an hour or so in a cold environment, this tension slackens off and the dough becomes much easier to work with. And if it's relaxed and not quite so elastic, the dough is less likely to shrink and crack after it's placed in a tart tin. The dough needs another rest in the freezer for 10 minutes after it has been put into the tin.

How to blind-bake a tart case

If you put a filled tart straight in the oven, there's a distinct possibility that the pastry crust won't cook through because the filling prevents heat from reaching the pastry. (And a wet filling is likely to soak into the pastry, breaking it down before it has time to harden.) You end up with a casing that's pale and soggy rather than brown and crisp. The way round this is to blind-bake the casing: cooking it on its own for a while, lined with baking parchment or greaseproof paper, then with baking beans, dried pulses or coins. Unusually perhaps, I prefer the latter because their flat shape means they cover the base evenly, weighing the pastry down well and stopping it from rising and the sides from collapsing. They also conduct heat efficiently.

Even a tiny, almost imperceptible crack in pastry can be enough to leak out lots of a liquid filling before it begins to set. The traditional way of guarding against this is to brush egg all over the base of the pastry case. Instead I use a neat invention of mine that I call 'liquid pastry' –

raw dough that has been blitzed with an egg with a hand blender. Using a paste made with a combination of eggs and dough allows you to stop up any cracks without altering the flavour of the pastry dough.

1. Place the tart tin on a baking sheet.

2. Place the pastry on top of a piece of greaseproof paper. Cut off a small portion of the dough and reserve in case it's needed to patch holes. Place another piece of greaseproof paper on top of the pastry, then roll the pastry flat, moving the pin from the centre outwards, and turning the pastry through 90 degrees every few rolls, until it is 2mm thick. Put the pastry in the freezer for 30 minutes to relax the dough and ensure the paper doesn't stick to it.

3. Remove the dough from the freezer, peel back the top layer of greaseproof paper and trim the pastry to 5–10cm larger than the diameter of the tart tin. Wind the pastry on to the rolling pin, removing the other layer of paper as you go.

4. Unwind the pastry over the tart tin and gently push it into the base and edges, allowing the excess to hang over the sides. (This might look untidy but it has a couple of important benefits. The weight of it helps prevent the pastry from shrinking, and even if it does shrink, since your pastry extends well beyond the edges of the tin, you'll still be able to trim it to fit perfectly after baking.) If you need to, use some liquid pastry (see above) to mend any cracks.

5. Pre-heat the oven to 180°C.

6. Prick the base with a fork to help prevent the pastry from puffing up. Put into the freezer for 10 minutes.

7. Remove the pastry from the freezer. Take a new piece of greaseproof paper, scrunch it up a couple of times (this makes it easier to manoeuvre into the edges and corners) and place it over the pastry base. Put baking beans or coins on top of the paper and put the tray and pastry-lined tin into the oven to bake for 30 minutes.

8. Take out of the oven, remove the baking beans or coins and greaseproof paper, and return the empty pastry case to the oven for 10 minutes, until golden brown.

9. Remove the tin from the oven. Once the pastry is cool enough to handle (but not yet too brittle to work with), take a sharp knife and run it round the top of the tart tin to remove the excess pastry, then leave the pastry to cool completely, or use warm, depending on the recipe instructions.

Cooking with chocolate

In the hands of a good producer, chocolate can have an amazing flavour range, from fruity and floral through milky and nutty to spicy and earthy. (Chemists have discovered more than six hundred volatile molecules in chocolate, making it one of the most complex-flavoured foods.) The fat brings a lovely richness and smoothness to dishes, and the acidity and bitterness balance rich, sweet ingredients really well. And, despite what people think, by and large it's a forgiving substance to work with.

However, like mayonnaise and vinaigrettes, chocolate is technically an emulsion – a mixture of liquids that would otherwise naturally separate. (For more on emulsions, see p.115.) In chocolate's case, fat molecules and sugar and starch molecules are held together by the emulsifier lecithin, which acts as a kind of bridge, linking them to one another. But, like all emulsions, it's a fragile union, and it can be upset. For most recipes involving chocolate, you'll have to melt it first, and heat that is too high can make it split or 'seize', go grainy or burn. Water, too, can make chocolate split, so make sure that your bowls and utensils are bone dry.

These caveats tend to make people wary of working with chocolate, but there are several effective techniques for melting it. So long as you follow one of these, rather than just putting the chocolate in a pan over direct stove heat (which is do-able, but a bit of a tightrope act), it's easier than you might think. If you have a microwave, this is one of the best uses for it: put the chocolate in the microwave for 1–2 minutes on high power, stirring every 30 seconds and keeping a watch on it to make sure it doesn't overheat. And if you're making, say, a chocolate tart (p.324) or chocolate mousse that involves warming a liquid such as cream, you can use the warmed liquid to melt the chocolate. Simply heat the liquid, take it off the heat and allow to cool a little, then add the chopped chocolate and stir to incorporate.

Another option is to use a bain-marie. You've come across this already as a technique for cooking egg-based custards, such as parfaits and brûlées, which involves putting custard-filled ramekins in a tray of water (p.80), then baking in the oven to set. However, since here we're concerned with a careful melting rather than the more precise business of setting, a simpler version of a bain-marie can be set up on the stove top rather than in the oven.

How to melt chocolate in a bain-marie

A stovetop bain-marie is usually composed of a saucepan with a bowl placed on top of it so that it rests on the mouth of the pan and is suspended within the pan. However, you could also use a double-boiler, a tailor-made saucepan that works on much the same principles.

1. Cover the base of a saucepan with a few centimetres of water and place a bowl on top of it. The base of the bowl should not touch the water beneath. (The bowl should fit snugly on the top of the pan, as you do not want escaping steam to overheat the chocolate, causing it to 'seize', rendering it grainy.)

2. Turn the heat to its lowest setting and bring the water to a simmer.

3. Chop up the chocolate: it's a poor conductor of heat so melts best if broken into small pieces. Put it into the bowl.

4. Keeping the water at a very gentle simmer, let the chocolate melt, stirring occasionally with a plastic spatula, until it's smooth and glossy. Never cover the bowl with a lid, as drops of condensation might drop into the chocolate.

Once melted, chocolate is often destined for some form of ganache, the chef's term for a mixture of chocolate and cream (and, sometimes, water as well, as in the liquid centre chocolate pudding on p.322, where it helps the ganache to melt as it bakes). Even if you don't know the name you'll be familiar with it as the basis of chocolate truffles, though in fact a ganache can be used in lots of chocolate preparations.

Varying the ratios of the two ingredients produces different textures: the more chocolate used, the harder the mixture will set. So two parts chocolate to one part cream will give a firm set; equal parts cream and chocolate give a firm, pliable ganache; and one part chocolate to two parts cream will give a soft, mousse-like texture. As a result, ganache can be used for firm truffles, poured over a cake to give a smooth, glossy, chocolate 'icing' – as in a Sachertorte – or even served as a dessert in its own right. Ganaches also feature in the chocolate tart (p.324) and the chocolate chip cookies (p.360).

Traditionally, a ganache is made by bringing cream just to boiling point and then pouring it over the chocolate to melt it. But you will get a specially smooth, creamy ganache by melting the chocolate as above, and then adding the hot cream (or cream and water, as in the chocolate pudding) in three separate stages, stirring each addition until it is properly incorporated and looks smooth and homogeneous before adding the next. This ensures that the chocolate is gradually and properly integrated with the other ingredients.

The cooling of the ganache can also affect its character. If put in the fridge to cool and set, it's likely to be too soft when it returns to room temperature and might become grainy. It's better, therefore, to let the ganache stand at room temperature for about 4 hours so that it cools down evenly and gradually. This lets the cocoa butter form into stable crystals that don't soften and melt so readily. It can then be put in the fridge and allowed to set.

Ganaches are fun to experiment with. Both chocolate and cream are good at taking on flavour, so you can use infusion (p.24) to incorporate the flavours you want.

The fact that you have a choice of liquids for the infusion increases your freedom to try out different ingredients. If a recipe calls for citrus peel, for example, whose acid would make the cream split, it can be infused into the chocolate instead. When infusing dry ingredients such as herbs, seeds or spices, add them to the cream in a pan or to melted chocolate in a bain-marie, warm gently, then allow the mixture to infuse, tasting regularly until you have the depth of flavour you're looking for. When you are satisfied, strain the mixture and it's then ready to be incorporated with cream or chocolate as appropriate, in three stages, as suggested.

Making a caramel

When sugar is heated, an amazing change takes place. What was largely sweet and odourless becomes richly aromatic and develops acidic and even bitter notes as it turns a shade of brown. Caramelization engineers an effect similar to that of the Maillard reactions (p.136), but although both involve browning and have an extraordinary transformative effect on the flavour of food, they are in fact quite different processes that produce very different groups of flavours.

The meaty, earthy, savoury Maillard flavours come principally from the breakdown of amino acids in proteins. Caramelization breaks down sugar molecules into hundreds of different flavour molecules, ranging from fruity, nutty, buttery characteristics through butterscotch and caramel to dark, bitter and roasted notes. It generally takes place at a higher temperature than Maillard reactions – from around 165°C rather than around 120°C – although this depends on the type of sugar being used. Glucose caramelizes at 170°C and fructose at 105°C.

The alchemy of caramelization takes a bit of skill and care. For a start, 170°C is an extremely high temperature and you can get burnt if you don't proceed with caution. Until you're pretty experienced, it's probably best not to caramelize a pan of sugar while you've got the distraction of a lot of other pans on the go. I'm forever trying to

persuade cooks to read through and visualize recipes and techniques before actually starting on them, and this is particularly good advice where hot sugar is concerned. Think through the moments where you're going to be moving or transferring the hot contents of the pan and make sure all the necessary equipment is ready and accessible in advance.

Unless you've got a probe that measures up to 170°C (many domestic versions don't) you'll need a proper sugar thermometer. Even then you don't want to be dipping it in and out of the liquid too often, which increases the risk of getting splashed with hot caramel (for safety's sake, you might want to wrap your hand in a tea-towel for protection). Minimize the need for this by developing a feel and instinct for the stages at which caramelized sugar is ready for particular types of dessert.

The character and intensity of the caramel's flavour, and the balance of sweetness and bitterness, depends on how dark you take it, but caramelization is always a little like a culinary game of chicken: you have to learn how to prevent it from burning and judge exactly when it's ready. And the only way to do that is to get in the kitchen and try it out. In most cases you want to stop cooking when the caramel takes on a dark brown colour: any darker and it might become bitter. However, in some dishes, such as fruit-based ones (fruit contains a lot of water that will temper the bitter notes), you can take the caramel until it's almost black, which will produce a really intense flavour. When it works, the flavour it brings to a dish is very seductive.

Traditionally, there are two ways to melt the sugar for a caramel or caramel sauce: the dry method and the wet method. With the dry method the sugar is warmed on its own in the pan. With the wet method the sugar is mixed with water, then heated. The wet method has certain benefits: the presence of water means you can cook the sugar on a higher heat from the outset without it burning, and it lengthens the time it takes to caramelize the sugar, allowing greater flavour development. But it's worth trying out both ways to see which you're most comfortable with. Whichever method you choose, the heat under the pan

needs to be medium to medium-high. If the heat is too low, the sugar will probably take too long to caramelize and begin to clump up. If it's too high, on the other hand, the bottom layer of sugar heats up more quickly than the rest and begins to burn.

Having a cup of water and a brush to hand during the wet caramelization process is very important. When the contents of the pan begin to melt and bubble, you'll see crystals of sugar sticking to the side of the pan. If these aren't dissolved they can cause the mixture to crystallize. Instead of a panful of smooth liquid caramel you'll have a clump of small white gritty sugar shards.

The choice of sugar can also influence the caramelization process, as well as the character of the end result. For example, unrefined caster sugar has an interesting molasses characteristic and melts and becomes a caramel particularly quickly, so you need to watch it attentively to make sure it doesn't burn. But this can be turned to advantage in dishes like crème brûlée, where its speedy caramelization means you can brown the top without heating the cream underneath.

How to make a wet caramel

A wet caramel starts off as a solution of sugar and water, becoming syrupy as the liquid evaporates, and then taking on colour to become a caramel. Sugar syrups of various concentrations are used in many desserts, primarily for poaching fruit and as the base for sorbets and granitas.

1. Fill a small bowl with cold water and place it and a pastry brush by the hob. Have a sugar thermometer or digital probe ready.

2. Put the sugar and water in a heavy, meticulously clean stainless-steel saucepan over a medium to medium-high heat.

3. As the sugar dissolves and the syrup comes to the boil, brush the inside of the saucepan with the pastry brush dipped in water to prevent sugar crystals from crystallizing the syrup.

4. When the syrup reaches the right temperature and colour take the pan off the heat. At 165°C a sugar syrup begins to caramelize and by 170°C it will have acquired a light golden colour. From this point on it browns, becomes less sweet and develops a more intense caramel flavour: 180–182°C produces a medium caramel and 188–190°C a dark caramel.

5. You can, if you want, place the base of the pan in a bowl of ice-cold water for a few seconds to prevent it cooking further.

How to make a dry caramel

In general a dry caramel is usually used immediately – poured on to a baking mat, added to other ingredients or has pastry dipped into it.

1. Put the sugar in a heavy, meticulously clean stainless-steel saucepan over a low heat. As the sugar starts to melt, shake the pan from time to time.

2. Once most of the sugar has become liquid, use a plastic spatula to work in the rest of the sugar so that it cooks evenly and there are no hot spots. Don't overstir, however, or the sugar will clump together.

3. When the caramel reaches the appropriate colour and temperature (see wet caramel instructions), remove from the heat. Because it is used straightaway, a dry caramel does not need to be cooled in a bowl of water.

From left to right, light (170°C), medium (180–182°C) and dark (188–190°C) caramel colours.

Making jellies

I've always loved jelly. When I was a kid my mum would take three different-flavoured packets of Rowntree's and set them, one on top of the other, to produce a fantastic multi-striped concoction. But there's more to jelly than kids' desserts. I use jellies a lot at the Fat Duck, particularly in savoury dishes, often as a garnish in the form of tiny cubes, because it's an excellent way to introduce textural contrast to a dish and – as the cube gradually gives way and melts on the tongue – a brief but intense flood of flavour that really stimulates the palate. A jelly is a great form of flavour encapsulation (p.23).

Gelatine is the most common setting agent used to create a jelly. A protein present in meat and fish, gelatine is a component of collagen, the tough, fibrous protein in animals' connective tissue (p.32). It has a property that's particularly valuable to the cook. When warmed, its molecules unwind from their natural helical shape into something looser and more free-form. As the liquid cools, however, the molecules begin to kink back into their helical shape, and the kinks tend to catch and mesh together into a rigid network that traps water molecules, creating a soft, spongy consistency. It doesn't take much gelatine to do this: a gel will form if the concentration of gelatine is 1 per cent of a liquid's total weight. So it's useful not just for making jellies but for thickening and enriching liquids such as stocks and sauces.

Originally, cooks had to make their own gelatine by boiling pigs' and calves' feet (and bones, cartilage and tendons). It was a smelly and time-consuming business, which meant that jellies and aspics were a relatively specialized area of cuisine. The advent of a commercial product made jelly-making much more accessible. Commercial gelatine is usually made from pig skin that is soaked in acid, then placed in several changes of warm water that are subsequently filtered, purified, evaporated and dried into sheets or powder. Using either as a setting agent is simple as long as you follow certain steps. Both types should be moistened first (a process known as 'blooming', after Oscar Bloom who invented the device for measuring gelatine's rigidity).

In the case of powdered gelatine, moistening helps prevent clumping when it's added to warm or hot liquid. (If this clumping does occur, it is salvageable, though it needs patience and physical graft. You have to stir continuously until the clumps dissolve, which can take quite a while.) The usual approach is to pour a small amount of cold water or the liquid to be set into a bowl (2 tablespoons of liquid per teaspoon of gelatine), then sprinkle the powder over the surface and leave it to absorb the water for 5–10 minutes. Alternatively, you can bloom it directly in the liquid that you are going to use (as in the whisky gums on p.340).

With gelatine sheets, place them in a bowl, cover with cold water, leave until totally soft (which will take no more than 5–10 minutes, possibly less), then remove and squeeze out the excess liquid and dissolve the sheets as the recipe directs. I prefer to use gelatine sheets rather than powdered, as they simply soften in the water, so are easier to work with, and tend to produce a clearer jelly. Make sure, however, that you do squeeze the sheets dry after soaking, otherwise you can end up inadvertently adding too much water to the recipe and affecting the end result.

Once the gelatine has been bloomed, it is stirred into the liquid that's going to be set. This liquid needs to be warmed so that the gelatine is evenly dispersed before it cools and gels. However, gelatine loses its setting power if it's exposed to high or prolonged heat: if you're adding gelatine to the hot ingredients, do so only once they are cooked and ready to set. One of the safest approaches (and one I often use in this book) is to add the softened gelatine to just a small amount of the liquid that you want to set, warm that gently until the gelatine has fully dissolved, and then stir this into the rest of the liquid.

The firmness of the set depends in part on the amount of gelatine you add. The lower the concentration, the less likely it is to set. A high concentration will make a chewier, more rubbery jelly. You can, of course, juggle the amount to get exactly the set you want. Some ingredients can also affect the set, so if you're experimenting you need to be aware that sugar strengthens gels, and a low concentration of alcohol will strengthen a gel but a high concentration will weaken it. Salt and acidic ingredients like fruit or vinegar will soften jellies, and there are some fruits and spices that ordinarily prevent setting completely, like pineapples, peaches, mangoes and ginger. This is because they contain protein-eating enzymes that break down the gelatine. The enzymes are, however, destroyed by heat so if you cook the fruit first or use tinned fruit (since the canning process involves heat), they can be turned into jellies.

Bear in mind, too, that even after they've set, gelatine molecules continue to bond together to try to form as stable a network as possible. (This is how my mum could achieve her striped-jelly trick. The gelatine molecules on the surface of each stripe would bond with the next.) It's best to serve a jelly as soon as it's set. The longer you leave it, the more rubbery it will become.

Gelatine has a delightful melt-in-the-mouth texture that's unmatched by almost any other setting agent, which is why it's generally the cook's first choice. However, there are circumstances where gelatine isn't viable. For one thing, since it's made from pig skin it's not suitable for vegetarians. And, since its melting point is low, it can't be used for something that'll be served warm or on a warm plate, as it might melt. So you must find an alternative.

One of my favourite setting agents is gellan gum, because it creates a gel with a clean mouth-feel and a spectacular flavour release. However, it is difficult to get hold of. When I first started working with gellan in 2001 it wasn't used in restaurants. Suppliers were used to dealing in industrial quantities and I had to buy my gellan in 25kg drums – enough to set the water in an Olympic-sized swimming pool! Since then, the number of chefs using gellan has increased, and more realistic supply lines have been set up, but even so it's still hard to obtain outside the catering industry.

A more readily available alternative (though its mouth-feel isn't as good as gelatine or gellan) is agar-agar, which comes from several types of red algae or seaweed and forms a clear, hard, brittle gel upon cooling. Agar-agar sets at 32–40°C and melts only between 85 and 95°C, so it's valuable in a situation where you need a heat-resistant gel.

Although not quite so useful as those above, another gelatine alternative is pectin. This is a soluble fibre, a natural setting agent, which is found mostly in the skin, seeds and cores of fruit. When combined with sugar and acid, pectin forms a bond that causes liquids to set. It is used mostly in the making of jams and jellies, but also in sweet-making, such as the pastilles on p.342. Many fruits are rich in pectin – apples, citrus fruits, currants and gooseberries – but pectin needs to be added to preserves made from low-pectin fruit such as strawberries. Commercial pectin, available as a powder or liquid, and sometimes mixed with sugar as a specific preserving sugar, is made using citrus skins or apple solids (pomace), both by-products of juice manufacture.

Lemon tart

Crisp pastry, the velvety filling, the brisk citrus sharpness as you bite in – not much beats a good lemon tart. For me the key to this tart is making the filling as smooth as possible: it has to be at the point where it's just set and no more. If the custard is overcooked it will be too heavy and if it's undercooked it will collapse.

Reaching that precise level of set can be tricky. In the early days at the Fat Duck I became a little obsessed with making sure that each tart we served was just right. The conventional way to check for this is the 'Wobble Test' – shaking the tart to see whether it's firm enough. But how do you describe this in a recipe? The answer is a digital probe (p.389). If you use a probe to take the filling to 62°C and then 70°C, it should be spot-on.

Serves 10–12

For the pastry

120g	Icing sugar
3	Large egg yolks
300g	Plain flour
150g	Unsalted butter
½ tsp	Salt
	Seeds from ½ vanilla pod
	Zest of ½ lemon, finely grated

For the filling

	Finely grated zest and juice of 5 lemons
300g	Double cream
390g	White caster sugar
9	Large eggs
1	Large egg yolk

To finish and serve

80g	Unrefined caster sugar
	Crème fraiche

To start the pastry, blitz together the icing sugar and egg yolks in a tall container with a hand blender.

Use a mixer fitted with a paddle attachment to mix the flour, butter and salt on low speed until it resembles fine cornmeal (approximately 2–3 minutes). Add the vanilla seeds and lemon zest, then add the egg yolk mixture and continue to mix on low speed until fully combined and a very soft dough has formed (approximately 3–5 minutes).

Mould the dough into a flat rectangle and wrap it in clingfilm before placing in the fridge for at least 1 hour.

Roll the pastry between two sheets of greaseproof paper to a thickness of 2mm, then place in the freezer for 30 minutes.

Pre-heat the oven to 180°C.

Line a 26cm tart tin (2.5cm deep) with the pastry as per the instructions on pp.301–3, prick the base with a fork, then place back in the freezer for 10 minutes.

Line the pastry case with scrunched greaseproof paper and beans. Place in the oven to blind-bake for 30 minutes.

After 30 minutes, remove the paper and its contents, and return the tart case to the oven for a further 10 minutes. Take the tart case out of the oven and allow to cool a little. Trim the overhanging pastry by running a sharp knife round the top of the tart tin and discard. Leave to cool completely.

When ready to bake, pre-heat the oven to 120°C, and place the baked pastry case in the oven to warm up.

Place all the filling ingredients in a bowl and mix together using a spatula. Place the bowl over a saucepan of simmering water and allow to warm up until the temperature reaches 62°C. At this point, strain the mixture through a fine sieve into a jug. With a spoon, remove the bubbles from the surface of the liquid.

Slide the oven rack out a bit, then pour the mixture into the warm pastry case inside the oven. Fill the case to the top, slide the rack carefully back in, and bake the tart for approximately 25 minutes or until the temperature of the filling reaches 70°C. Allow to cool completely at room temperature.

Just before serving, sprinkle a thin layer of sugar on top of the tart. Using a blow-torch, gently caramelize the sugar while continuing to sprinkle further sugar on top. Serve with crème fraiche.

Peach and rosemary tarte tatin

With its deep, rich caramelized flavours, tarte tatin is now part of the classic French repertoire, but legend has it that it was created by accident at the end of the nineteenth century when one of the two sisters who ran the Hotel Tatin placed an apple tart in the oven upside down.

Whether or not the story is true (*Larousse* says that an upside-down tart made of apples or pears is an ancient speciality of the Sologne area of France), it highlights the role played by chance in culinary creativity – a mistake can, sometimes, produce something amazing.

Serves 6

400g	Unrefined caster sugar
185g	Unsalted butter, cubed
6	Large ripe peaches, peeled and cut into 3 wedges around the stone
500g	All-butter puff pastry
125g	Double cream
5	Sprigs of rosemary
200g	Whipping cream
30g	Icing sugar

Put 200g of the sugar into a straight-sided ovenproof frying pan (approximately 24cm in diameter) and place the pan over a medium heat. Allow the sugar to begin caramelizing but do not stir until most of it has turned to liquid, then mix in the unmelted sugar with a spatula. Add 100g of the butter and mix until the sugar and the butter are well combined. Allow to cool slightly.

Arrange the peach wedges, cut-side up, around the pan, trying to pack them as tightly as possible. Allow to stand for 5 minutes.

Pre-heat the oven to 190°C.

In the meantime, roll the puff pastry into a circle between two sheets of baking paper to a thickness of 4mm and about 3cm larger than the diameter of the pan. Roll the edge of the pastry backwards to approximately 2cm in – this will give a nice, crispy edge. Place the puff pastry, rolled-edge-side up, on top of the peaches, making sure to tuck the pastry down the edges inside the pan.

Place the pan in the pre-heated oven for approximately 30 minutes or until the puff pastry is brown in colour.

While the tatin is in the oven, place the double cream in a small pan with the rosemary over a medium heat. Allow to come to a simmer, then remove from the heat and allow to infuse for 15 minutes. Remove the rosemary.

In the meantime, put the remaining 200g of sugar into a saucepan over a medium heat. Allow to caramelize as above, then add the remaining 85g butter. Mix until well combined. Add the infused cream in three stages, making sure the cream is fully combined after each addition.

Remove the tatin from the oven and let it sit for 5 minutes – this will allow the caramel to thicken up, making it easier to turn. Place a plate that is just larger than the diameter of the pan on top and turn the pan over, being careful of the hot caramel that may spill out. Remove the pan and allow the tatin to sit for 5 minutes.

Pour the whipping cream into a bowl, add the icing sugar and whisk until medium peaks form. Serve a portion of the tatin with a dollop of whipping cream and a drizzle of some of the rosemary-infused caramel over the top.

Pear and frangipane tarte tatin

Although the best-known tarte tatin is made with apples, it's a very adaptable dish that works just as well with prunes, quinces, plums, pineapple and rhubarb, among others. (There are even fennel and onion tartes tatin.) Here I've used pears, but I've also piped frangipane into them to introduce a delicate almond note that really enhances the caramelized fruit.

Serves 6

For the pears

500g	Unrefined caster sugar
250g	Unsalted butter, cubed
500g	Pear (or apple) juice
	Zest of 1 lemon, removed in strips with a vegetable peeler
	Zest of 1 orange, removed in strips with a vegetable peeler
3	Black peppercorns
2	Star anise
2	Cinnamon sticks
2	Vanilla pods, split down the middle lengthways
40g	Runny honey (see tip, p.359)
6	Pears, peeled and cored

For the frangipane

120g	Unsalted butter, softened
120g	Icing sugar
2	Large eggs, beaten
120g	Ground almonds
25g	Plain flour

To assemble

120g	Unrefined caster sugar
50g	Clarified butter (see tip, p.286), softened
250g	All-butter puff pastry

To start the pears, place the sugar in a deep stainless-steel saucepan over a medium heat to make a dry caramel (p.307). Once the caramel turns dark, mix in the butter, making sure that it melts completely.

Add the juice to the pan and stir thoroughly to make sure that any bits of hard caramel that form dissolve completely.

Add the zest, peppercorns, star anise, cinnamon, vanilla pods and honey. Reduce the heat to medium-low and bring to a gentle simmer. Simmer for 20 minutes but do not allow to boil.

Remove the pan from the heat and allow to cool to room temperature. Strain the mixture and reserve the liquid. Discard the spices.

Place the liquid back in a saucepan over a medium heat. Place the pears in the liquid and poach them over medium heat until they are soft to the touch but still firm. Allow the pears to cool in the liquid completely.

Remove the pears from the poaching liquid and place them upright on a board, discarding the liquid. Using a sharp knife, cut across the cored middle of each pear, stopping halfway down. Repeat twice at equal intervals around the pear. Each pear will now have six equal 'petals'. Reserve in the fridge until needed.

For the frangipane, place all the ingredients in a bowl and, using a whisk, mix them together until well combined. Place in a piping bag and keep in the fridge until ready to use.

When ready to cook, pre-heat the oven to 190°C.

Mix the sugar and the butter in a bowl, then place approximately 25g of the mixture in the bottom of each of six individual 7.5cm tatin dishes.

Roll the puff pastry to a thickness of approximately 2mm. Using a round pastry cutter, cut circles that are 1cm wider than the diameter of the tatin dishes.

Place each of the pears on to a circle of puff pastry, and pipe the frangipane right into the centre of each pear, filling the core. Turn the pears over, petal side down, on to the tatin dishes, pastry-side up, making sure to tuck the pastry tightly inside the rim of the dish. Place in the oven and bake for 35 minutes.

Remove the dishes from the oven and allow to cool for 2 minutes, then turn the tatins out on to plates to serve.

Arlette with pressed apple terrine

An arlette is puff pastry dough, thinly rolled out with icing sugar, which is then baked between two baking sheets to keep it flat. It caramelizes to crisp sweetness, and forms very thin, delicate sheets which in this recipe hold layers of poached apple, apple gel and rosewater cream. This is one of the more involved dishes in the book, but well worth the effort.

Serves 8–10

For the apples and poaching syrup

550g	Unrefined caster sugar
250g	Unsalted butter, cubed
500g	Apple juice
10g	Pectin powder
12	Braeburn apples, peeled and cored

For the apple gel

375g	Apple poaching syrup (above)
25g	Unrefined caster sugar
5g	Pectin powder
15g	Lemon juice

For the arlette

200g	All-butter puff pastry
100g	Icing sugar

For the vanilla salt

	Seeds from ½ vanilla pod
5g	Sea salt

For the rosewater cream

30g	Icing sugar
200g	Crème fraiche
100g	Whipping cream
	Rosewater, 3 drops

For the crystallized fennel seeds

10g	Fennel seeds
10g	Unrefined caster sugar

To assemble and serve

20g	Crumbled arlette pieces
1	Granny Smith apple, cut into small cubes

To start the apple poaching syrup, place 500g of the sugar in a deep saucepan over a medium-high heat. Allow the sugar to begin melting while gently shaking the pan from time to time. Once half of the sugar has melted, use a dry spatula to stir. Allow a dark colour to develop.

Add the butter and, using the spatula, mix until all of the butter is well combined. Add the apple juice a little at a time while mixing in order to incorporate thoroughly and ensure any hard bits of caramel melt into the liquid. Allow to come to a simmer.

In the meantime, mix the pectin with the remaining 50g sugar in a small bowl using a fork. This will ensure that the pectin is evenly dispersed. Add the pectin mixture to the saucepan and bring to the boil. Remove from the heat.

Pre-heat the oven to 90°C. Place a sheet of baking parchment on a baking tray of approximately 20 × 30cm.

Slice each apple in half from top to bottom and, using a mandolin, slice the apples vertically to a thickness of approximately 2mm. Begin layering the apples in overlapping rows on the tray by placing each slice on top of the bottom half of the previous slice.

Once an entire layer is complete, using a pastry brush, brush the top of the apples with the poaching syrup. Repeat these steps until all the apples have been used. Keep the remaining syrup to one side.

Place another sheet of parchment on top of the apples and place a heavy object on top in order to weight the slices down during the cooking process. Place the tray in the oven for 12 hours.

After the time has elapsed, remove the weight and the top layer of baking parchment. Increase the oven temperature to 120°C and bake the apples for an additional 90 minutes.

continued overleaf

315

Remove from the oven and allow to cool completely. Once completely cold, cut into rectangles measuring approximately 3 × 8cm. Reserve in the fridge.

For the apple gel, place the poaching syrup and 125g cold tap water in a saucepan over a medium-high heat and bring the liquid to a simmer.

In the meantime, line a baking tray (approximately 20 × 30cm) with baking parchment.

Mix the sugar with the pectin in a small bowl using a fork. Add the mixture to the water and poaching syrup. Heat to a temperature of 108°C, or to a reading of 69° Brix, if you are using a refractometer (p.393).

When the syrup has reached 108°C, remove the pan from the heat and whisk in the lemon juice. Pour the mixture into the parchment-lined tray and allow to set at room temperature for approximately 1 hour.

Once set, cut into rectangles measuring approximately 3 × 8cm. Reserve between sheets of parchment in the fridge.

To start the arlette, pre-heat the oven to 200°C.

Place the pastry on a large sheet of baking parchment and roll it out as thinly as possible, dusting frequently with the icing sugar. When the pastry is paper-thin, cut it in half. One piece at a time, place another sheet of baking parchment on top and sandwich the piece of pastry between two heavy baking trays.

Bake in the oven for approximately 15 minutes until golden brown and the icing sugar has caramelized. Do the same with the second piece of pastry.

Remove from the oven and, working quickly, cut each piece of pastry into rectangles measuring 3 × 8cm. You need 32–40 pieces. Allow to cool.

Once completely cold, store in an airtight container until needed. Any broken edges can be reserved and crumbled into small pieces to be used for garnish.

For the vanilla salt, simply mix the vanilla seeds with the salt in a bowl.

To start the rosewater cream, using a whisk, mix the icing sugar with the crème fraiche.

In a separate bowl, whisk the whipping cream and rosewater until soft peaks form. Mix this together with the crème fraiche and icing sugar and whisk until well combined, being careful not to over-mix.

Place the cream in a piping bag fitted with a 0.5cm nozzle. Place in the fridge.

To crystallize the fennel seeds, place a non-stick pan over a medium-high heat, add the fennel seeds and toast for approximately 1 minute. Sprinkle in the sugar and, as it melts, mix it with the fennel seeds using a spatula. Transfer to a tray that has been lined with parchment and allow to cool.

To assemble and serve, place an arlette rectangle on a plate, with an apple gel rectangle on top followed by another arlette rectangle.

Carefully place the apple rectangle on top, followed by another arlette rectangle and pipe the rosewater cream in small mounds, making two rows. Place a final arlette rectangle on top.

In a bowl, mix the crumbled arlette pieces, crystallized fennel seeds and vanilla salt and sprinkle on top of the last arlette. Place 4–5 apple cubes on top of each arlette, and serve.

Eccles cakes with potted Stilton

Eccles cakes – or 'dead fly pies', as they're sometimes affectionately known – are named after Eccles in Lancashire. No-one knows who invented them, but they have been sold in the town since the 1790s at least. Traditionally, they're served with Lancashire cheese, but they go very well with potted Stilton, too.

The cakes are at their best when freshly baked, so serve them pretty soon after they come out of the oven.

Makes 16 mini Eccles cakes

For the Eccles cakes

100g	Unsalted butter
150g	Unrefined caster sugar
200g	Currants
25g	Red wine vinegar
5g	Ground allspice
500g	All-butter puff pastry
	Egg wash (1 egg yolk beaten with 2 tsp milk)

For the potted Stilton

100g	Stilton, at room temperature
50g	Mascarpone
75g	Unsalted butter, at room temperature
½ tsp	Salt
30g	Pedro Ximénez sherry
½ tsp	Sherry vinegar

To start the Eccles cakes, melt the butter in a saucepan over a medium heat, then add the sugar and heat until the mixture begins to bubble. Remove the pan from the heat and stir in the currants, vinegar and allspice. Allow to cool completely.

Portion the mixture into 16 × 25g balls, put on a tray and place in the freezer for 1 hour.

Roll out the pastry to a thickness of 3mm, then cut out 16 circles using a pastry cutter (approximately 9cm).

Brush the circles with egg wash, then place the frozen filling in the centre of the circles and wrap the pastry around it. Press together the overlapping edges to seal, and roll between your hands to form a perfect ball. Turn each cake over so the join is on the bottom and slash the top with a knife three times.

Place the cakes in the freezer for at least 30 minutes (they can be left in the freezer at this stage if making them in advance of serving).

Meanwhile, for the potted Stilton, put the Stilton, mascarpone, butter and salt into a bowl and blitz with a hand blender until smooth.

Gently warm the sherry, 55g cold tap water and the sherry vinegar together in a small saucepan until almost simmering.

Slowly add the sherry and water to the cheese and mix carefully until well combined. Decant into small ramekins or a single bowl and place in the fridge to set (approximately 1 hour).

To bake the cakes, pre-heat the oven to 200°C.

Brush the surface of each cake with egg wash and bake in the oven for 20–25 minutes or until the pastry turns golden brown.

Take the potted Stilton out of the fridge 10 minutes before serving with the warm Eccles cakes.

Lardy cake with butterscotch sauce

Traditionally made around harvest time, and thought to have originated in Wiltshire (where pigs are bred for bacon), lardy cake is a bread dough rolled around a rich filling of mixed peel, currants, sugar, syrup – and plenty of pork fat or lard. As Jane Grigson says in *English Food*, lardy cake is 'very good, very fattening. The more lard, sugar and fruit you cram in, the better, so that the dough is layered with brown sweet richness.'

Serve the cake with whisky ice-cream (p.290) as well as the butterscotch sauce.

Serves 10

For the bread dough

460g	Strong white bread flour
280g	Lukewarm water
2 tsp	Dried yeast
10g	Salt
5g	Lard

For the filling

200g	Mixed peel
250g	Currants
200g	Apple juice
30g	Cognac
100g	Unrefined caster sugar
250g	Lard, at room temperature
150g	Golden syrup (see tip, p.359)

For the butterscotch sauce

140g	Demerara sugar
115g	Golden syrup
115g	Double cream
30g	Unsalted butter
¼ tsp	Salt

For the bread dough, put the flour and water into the bowl of a mixer fitted with a paddle attachment and mix at low speed for 3 minutes. Cover the bowl with a tea-towel and allow to rest for 30 minutes.

Add the yeast, salt and lard and mix on low speed for 8 minutes. Remove the dough from the mixer. Cover the surface of the dough with a sheet of lightly oiled clingfilm and allow to prove for 1 hour 30 minutes at room temperature.

Meanwhile, make the filling. Put the mixed peel, currants, apple juice and Cognac into a saucepan and place over a medium heat. Cook until the liquid has almost completely evaporated (approximately 10 minutes), then remove from the heat and allow to cool.

Using a mixer fitted with a paddle attachment, cream the sugar, lard and golden syrup on medium speed until light and creamy (approximately 5 minutes). Decrease the speed to low and add the cooled currant mixture. Continue to mix for 2 minutes until the currants and peel are fully incorporated.

When the dough has proved, knock it back, and roll it out on a lightly floured surface to a rectangle of 50 × 30cm. Spread the currant mixture all over the rolled-out dough, leaving a 2cm gap at the top. Roll the dough from the bottom into a tight cylinder, place on a parchment-lined tray, then allow to rest for 30 minutes in a warm place.

Pre-heat the oven to 180°C.

Put the cake on to a baking tray and place in the oven for 30–35 minutes, basting the top of the cake with the lard from the tray every 10 minutes, until golden brown.

Meanwhile, make the butterscotch sauce. Place the ingredients in a saucepan over a medium heat and bring to the boil. Whisk until the sauce reaches 120°C, then remove the pan from the heat.

Remove the tray from the oven and place the cake upside down on a cooling rack, turning a couple of times until cool. To serve, cut the cake into 1cm slices. Melt a little extra butter in a frying pan and fry the slices for approximately 30 seconds on each side. Serve with a tablespoon of warm butterscotch sauce.

Liquid centre chocolate pudding

The traditional way to make a chocolate pudding with a runny centre is by baking a mixture of eggs, butter, sugar, chocolate and a little flour until the outside forms a crust but the inside remains gooey. This recipe takes a completely different approach, putting a frozen chocolate ganache inside the cake mixture. This ensures that the centre melts to the perfect runny consistency at exactly the point when the exterior is cooked through.

If you want to skip making the ganache, you could use a scoop of good-quality chocolate ice-cream instead.

Serves 6

For the water ganache

155g	Whipping cream
160g	Dark chocolate, chopped (minimum 60% cocoa solids)
25g	Unsalted butter

For the pudding mix

120g	Dark chocolate, chopped (minimum 60% cocoa solids)
110g	Unsalted butter
50g	Plain flour
¼ tsp	Salt
175g	Eggs (approx. 7 large eggs)
75g	Unrefined caster sugar

For the water ganache, place 55g cold tap water and the cream in a saucepan over a medium heat and bring to a simmer.

In the meantime, place the chocolate in a bowl over a pan of simmering water and allow it to melt completely.

Once the chocolate has melted, add the water and cream mixture to it in three additions and mix thoroughly with a spatula after each addition. Stir in the butter. Allow to stand until it reaches room temperature, then stir one more time.

Pour the ganache into a deep-sided container until it reaches 3cm deep. Place the tray in the freezer for 2 hours or until fully set. Meanwhile, have ready six 7cm diameter ramekins.

Using a 3cm ring cutter, cut cylinders out of the ganache, and place one in the centre of each ramekin. Return to the freezer.

To make the pudding mix, place the chocolate and the butter in a bowl over a pan of simmering water and melt completely. Remove from the heat and allow to cool.

In the meantime, sieve the flour and salt together into a bowl. When the chocolate is cool, add the flour and salt and mix thoroughly.

Using a mixer fitted with the whisk attachment, whisk the eggs and sugar for approximately 8–10 minutes or until light and creamy.

Fold a third of the egg mixture into the chocolate, being as gentle as possible. Add the remaining egg mixture and fold until well combined.

Half fill each ramekin with the mix and tap the ramekin a few times on the work surface to ensure any big air bubbles disappear, then continue to fill to the top. Place the ramekins back in the freezer for 1 hour.

When ready to serve, pre-heat the oven to 180°C.

Place the ramekins in the oven. Bake for 18–20 minutes until the pudding mix is fully set. Serve immediately.

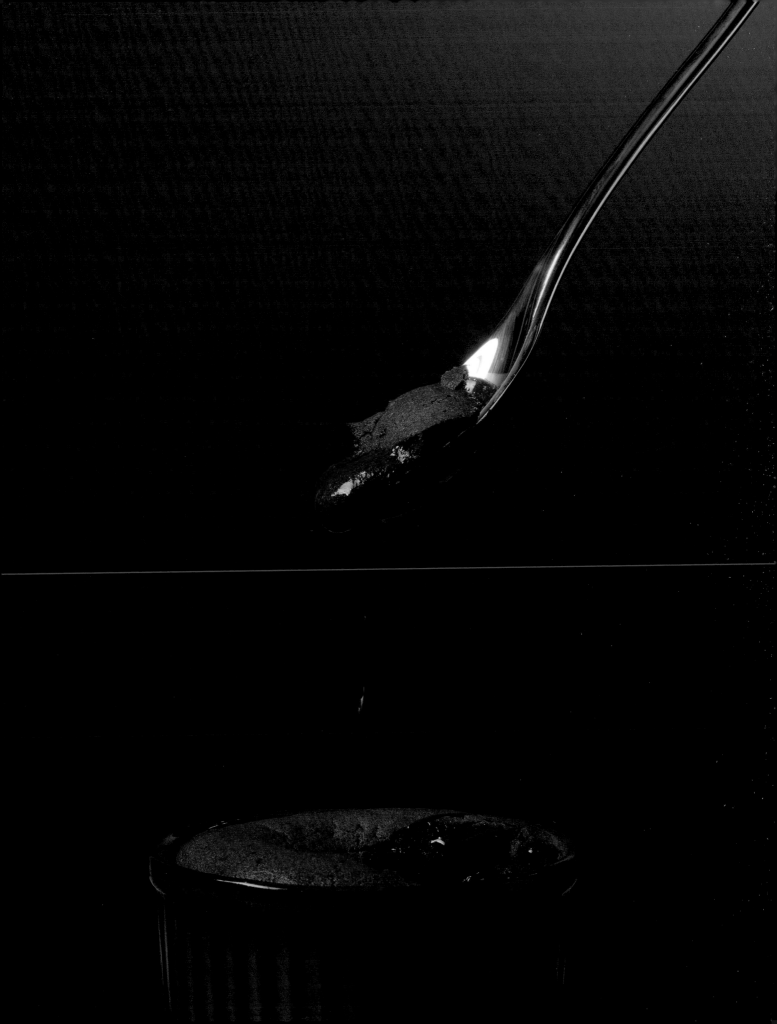

Chocolate tart

This tart is very rich, so you'll only need to offer small slices. Rather than baking the base and filling together, as in some tart recipes, here you prepare the biscuit base and the ganache filling separately. You then pour the chocolate ganache on to the baked tart base, and let it stand at room temperature for an hour before it goes in the fridge, so that it sets to a wonderful silky smoothness.

Serves 10

For the base

135g	Plain flour
10g	Cocoa powder
½ tsp	Bicarbonate of soda
115g	Unsalted butter
130g	Unrefined caster sugar
½ tsp	Salt
	Finely grated zest of 1 orange

For the ganache

225g	Whipping cream
⅛ tsp	Salt
100g	Dark chocolate, chopped (minimum 60% cocoa solids)
40g	Milk chocolate, chopped (minimum 30% cocoa solids)

To start the base, sift the flour, cocoa powder and bicarbonate of soda into a bowl and set aside.

In the bowl of a mixer fitted with the paddle attachment, cream the butter and the sugar together.

Add the flour and cocoa powder mixture, scraping the sides of the bowl with a spatula in order to incorporate everything into the mixture. Mix at medium speed for approximately 1 minute.

Add the salt and continue to mix for 2 minutes. Add the orange zest and mix for an additional 2 minutes.

Place the dough on a sheet of clingfilm. Form a thick disc. Wrap in clingfilm and place in the fridge for 1 hour.

Pre-heat the oven to 190°C.

Take the dough out of the fridge and place between two sheets of parchment. Roll to a thickness of 2mm, then place in the freezer for 30 minutes.

Remove the top layer of parchment and place the dough on a flat tray. Place the tray in the oven and bake for 10 minutes.

Remove from the oven and, while still hot, using a ring measuring approximately 12cm in diameter, cut a disc out of the biscuit, leaving the ring in place. Remove the baked dough from around the ring. (Eat this if you like.)

To make the ganache, place the cream and salt in a small saucepan and bring to a simmer over a medium heat. Remove from the heat and keep warm.

In the meantime, place both the dark and milk chocolates in a bowl over a pan of simmering water. Allow to melt completely. Once melted, remove from the water and add the cream in three stages, mixing well with a spatula after each addition in order to incorporate well.

To assemble the tart, using a pastry brush, brush the inside edge of the pastry ring between the metal and the tart base with a little of the ganache. Place the base in the freezer and allow to set for 10 minutes – this will prevent the ganache leaking out.

Pour the rest of the ganache into the ring and allow to set at room temperature for 1 hour, then place in the fridge for at least 3 hours.

Remove from the fridge. Wait 10 minutes before serving. To remove the pastry ring easily – if the chocolate is sticking – heat the outside very briefly with a blow-torch.

Tiramisù

Many classic Italian dishes have a long and illustrious history that usually involves a member of the nobility, a wedding or Marco Polo. Tiramisù comes with its own tall tale: it's said to have been invented in a brothel to energize flagging clients (the name translates as 'pick-me-up'). However, it turns out that the dessert actually originated in a restaurant in Treviso, near Venice, in the 1970s or early 1980s.

One of the secrets of my version is the hidden, wafer-thin disc of chocolate to give some textural contrast – a bit of brittle crunchiness. You'll need to get hold of a couple of sheets of acetate from a stationery shop in order to do this. The other key ingredient is the alcohol – it's important to buy the best Marsala you can.

Serves 4

For the base

3	Large eggs
75g	Unrefined caster sugar
300g	Mascarpone
200g	Whipping cream
60g	Marsala
1.5g	Leaf of gelatine (cut with scissors), softened in a little cold water

For the sponge fingers

24	Sponge fingers
150g	Ground coffee brewed in 400g water
100g	Marsala

For the dark chocolate layers

250g	Dark chocolate, chopped (minimum 60% cocoa solids)

To assemble

75g	Grated dark chocolate
50g	Cocoa powder, mixed with 50g grated chocolate

To start the base, whisk the eggs with the sugar until thick and creamy.

In a separate bowl, whisk the mascarpone, whipping cream and Marsala until soft peaks form. Fold the cream mixture into the sugar and eggs in three additions.

Place 5 tablespoons of the cream mixture in a small saucepan. Squeeze the excess water out of the gelatine leaf, add it to the pan and warm up the mixture just enough to melt the gelatine. Whip back into the bulk of the cream base.

To soak the sponge fingers, place them in a flat tray. Mix the coffee with the Marsala, and drizzle some of this over the top. Allow to soak for approximately 1 minute, then turn the sponge fingers over and drizzle with the remaining coffee mixture.

To make the dark chocolate layers, break the chocolate into pieces and melt in a bowl over a saucepan of simmering water.

Pour the melted chocolate over a sheet of acetate. Place another sheet of acetate on top and then place a heavy chopping board on top to create a thin even layer. Place in the freezer for 10 minutes.

Using a pastry cutter roughly the size of the inside of your serving bowls or glasses, cut out four discs. Store in an airtight container in between sheets of parchment in the fridge.

To assemble the tiramisù, place three soaked sponge fingers in the bottom of four bowls or glasses and spoon some of the tiramisù base on top. Sprinkle a layer of grated chocolate on top of this. Place three more soaked sponge fingers on top of the chocolate and add more tiramisù base. Place a chocolate disc on top and cover with more tiramisù base. Place in the fridge for at least 6 hours.

Before serving, dust with the mixed cocoa powder and grated chocolate.

Golden syrup crème brûlée

A crème brûlée is essentially a rich baked custard made with cream and eggs and topped with caramelized sugar. The custard is an adaptable mixture that works with savoury ingredients, such as chicken livers (p.94) or mushrooms (p.103), as well as sweet ones, and can encompass all sorts of variations, such as the coffee and jasmine ones below.

For me, the perfect brûlée custard should be just set and completely smooth. To achieve this, it needs to be cooked in a bain-marie (p.80) and it's important here that the custard has a depth of no more than 2cm. Use wide shallow dishes rather than high-sided ramekins.

Serves 4–6

400g	Double cream
100g	Whole milk
50g	Golden syrup (see tip, p.359)
5	Large egg yolks
50g	Unrefined caster sugar

Pre-heat the oven to 140°C.

Pour the cream, milk and golden syrup into a saucepan and place over a medium heat. Bring to a simmer.

In the meantime, place the egg yolks and 10g of the sugar in a bowl and whisk until light and creamy in colour. Once the cream mixture has reached a simmer, add a small amount to the egg yolk mixture in order to temper them (bring to the same temperature). Add the rest of the warm cream mixture and mix well using a spatula.

Strain the mixture through a fine sieve into a shallow bowl. Using kitchen roll, skim the surface of the custard in order to get rid of any bubbles. Pour the mixture into brûlée dishes to a depth of 2cm and get rid of any remaining bubbles with a blow-torch.

Place the dishes in a deep roasting tray. Fill the tray with just-boiled water until it reaches two-thirds up the sides of the dishes. Cover the tray tightly with foil and place in the oven. Bake for approximately 30 minutes or until the custard is set but still wobbles in the centre.

Take the dishes out of the water and allow to cool at room temperature for 15 minutes before placing them in the fridge. Allow to set for at least 6 hours in the fridge, or preferably overnight.

Just before serving, sprinkle a thin layer of caster sugar on top of each dish. Using a blow-torch, gently caramelize the sugar while continuing to sprinkle some of the sugar mixture on top. Serve immediately, as the sugar will start absorbing the moisture from the custard and go soft.

Coffee crème brûlée

450g	Double cream
150g	Whole milk
3 tbsp	Ground coffee
5	Large egg yolks
50g	Unrefined caster sugar

Pour the cream, milk and coffee into a saucepan and place over a medium heat. Bring to a simmer.

Follow the instructions for the golden syrup crème brûlée above, but make sure you strain the mixture through a piece of muslin as well as a fine sieve to get rid of all the ground coffee.

Jasmine crème brûlée

250g	Whole milk
40g	Jasmine tea leaves
400g	Double cream
5	Large egg yolks
50g	Unrefined caster sugar

Put the milk and jasmine tea leaves into a saucepan over a medium heat and bring to 60°C. Remove the pan from the heat and allow to infuse for 10 minutes.

Strain the milk through a sieve and weigh out 150g, discarding any excess. Place the infused milk and cream in a saucepan and bring to a simmer over a medium heat.

Follow the instructions for the golden syrup crème brûlée above.

Chamomile panna cotta

The base recipe for this panna cotta and the variations that follow is the same: it's only the infusion instructions that change. So you can easily experiment with all kinds of flavourings, using the base recipe as a starting point.

It might seem odd that the recipe tells you to infuse 350g milk and then weigh out and use only 250g. The reason for this is that tea absorbs a lot of moisture and you need to ensure you have the right amount of liquid for the quantity of gelatine. It's advisable not to make the panna cottas more than a day in advance as the gelatine will make them firm up too much – the set should be very delicate.

Serves 6

3	Chamomile tea bags
350g	Whole milk
250g	Double cream
100g	Unrefined caster sugar
6g	Leaves of gelatine, softened in a little cold water
30g	Fructose (fruit sugar)

To serve

20	Strawberries, hulled and sliced

Put two tea bags and the milk into a saucepan and place over a medium heat. Allow the liquid to come to a simmer then remove from the heat and allow to infuse for 15 minutes. Remove the tea bags and discard.

Weigh out 250g of the infused milk and discard the remaining liquid.

Warm the cream, infused milk and sugar in a saucepan over a medium heat. Do not allow to boil.

Squeeze the water from the gelatine and add it to the saucepan. Remove the pan from the heat and stir until completely dissolved.

Strain the liquid through a fine sieve into a bowl above a pan of simmering water. Stir the liquid occasionally until it has a thick custard-like consistency.

Pour the liquid into six moulds (approximately 7cm in diameter) and allow to set in the fridge for 8 hours.

To de-mould the panna cottas, fill a small bowl with warm water, and place the container with the panna cotta in the water for approximately 10 seconds. Remove each mould from the water and place a plate on top. Turn the mould upside down and allow the panna cotta to fall from the mould.

To make the chamomile sugar, mix the fructose with the contents of the remaining chamomile tea bag. (The sugar is great sprinkled on other soft fruits, too.)

To serve, sprinkle a little of the chamomile sugar on top of the sliced strawberries and arrange them around the panna cotta on the plate.

Earl Grey panna cotta
Substitute the two chamomile tea bags with two Earl Grey tea bags. Continue as for chamomile panna cotta, but omit the chamomile sugar.

Coffee panna cotta
Substitute the chamomile tea bags with 50g ground coffee. Warm the milk in a small saucepan and add the coffee. Remove from the heat and allow to infuse for 5 minutes before straining through a piece of muslin as well as a fine sieve. Continue as for chamomile panna cotta, but omit the chamomile sugar. Serve with the chocolate sauce on p.366.

Basil panna cotta
Infusing the panna cotta with basil takes it in yet another direction – giving it a fresh, summery character.

250g	Double cream
250g	Whole milk
100g	Unrefined caster sugar
80g	Basil leaves
6g	Leaves of gelatine, softened in a little cold water

Warm the cream, milk, sugar and basil to a simmer, turn off and allow to stand for 15 minutes. Continue as for chamomile panna cotta. Serve with fresh strawberries.

Strawberry sundae

You can use shop-bought ice-cream for this dish, or make the vanilla ice-cream on p.288.

Tapenade might seem an unusual ingredient in a dessert, but it came out of a fairly logical thought process. I had begun playing around with the classic Italian combination of strawberries and black pepper, which got me thinking about pairing strawberries with other peppery ingredients, such as olive oil. From oil I moved on to olives themselves and they seemed to suit strawberries very well. For me summer, strawberries and cricket are inextricably linked, so I particularly liked the fact that the slight leathery flavour of olives brought to my mind the smell of a wicket-keeper's gloves.

Serves 6

For the strawberry syrup

500g	Strawberries, hulled and quartered
100g	Fructose (fruit sugar)
¼ tsp	Red wine vinegar

For the sweet tapenade

150g	Pitted black olives
30g	Fructose (fruit sugar)
2g	Laphroaig whisky
3g	Olive oil

To assemble

12	Strawberries
150g	Fructose (fruit sugar)
300g	Whipping cream
100g	Icing sugar
	Vanilla ice-cream (p.288)
	Crystallized pistachio nuts (p.377)

For the strawberry syrup, combine the strawberries and fructose in a bowl and cover with clingfilm. Place the bowl over a pan of simmering water for 40 minutes.

For the sweet tapenade, blanch the olives until they lose their bitter taste. To do this, bring a pan of water to the boil and add the olives for 30 seconds. Drain and repeat this process twice more.

Using a hand blender, blitz the olives with the fructose and push through a fine sieve. Season the purée with the Laphroaig and olive oil.

Strain the strawberries through a piece of damp muslin, collecting only the juice, do not squeeze the pulp through.

Place the juice in a pan over a high heat, add the red wine vinegar and then boil to reduce by half. Allow to cool and then keep in the fridge.

When ready to assemble, slice the strawberries in half and place them, cut-side down, on a plate coated with fructose. Allow to sit for a minute.

Place a non-stick pan over a medium-high heat, then place the strawberries, fructose-side down in the pan, and allow to cook for approximately 30 seconds or until a syrup starts to seep out of each strawberry.

Remove the pan from the heat and allow the strawberries to cool upside down on a plate.

In the meantime, place the whipping cream in a bowl and whisk to soft peaks. Add the icing sugar and whisk to medium peaks. Place in a piping bag and keep in the fridge until needed.

Divide the strawberries between six sundae glasses. Place a little of the sweet tapenade on top of the strawberries, then drizzle with some strawberry syrup. Fill the glass with scoops of vanilla ice-cream, then pipe some of the whipped cream on top. Drizzle with more syrup and garnish with crystallized pistachios.

Banana Eton mess

Most people associate this utterly English dish with strawberries but, according to the great ice-cream expert Robin Weir, when it was originally served in the tuck shop at Eton College it was with either strawberries or bananas. Neither is more authentic than the other.

Serves 6

For the meringue

125g	Egg whites (approx. 4 large eggs)
125g	White caster sugar
125g	Icing sugar

For the hazelnut brittle

100g	Whole blanched hazelnuts
100g	Unrefined caster sugar
	Pinch of salt

For the banana purée

250g	Unrefined caster sugar
6	Bananas, peeled
25g	Rum
	Juice of 1 lime

For the lime cream

300g	Double cream
	Juice of 4 limes

To serve

2	Bananas, peeled, sliced into quarters lengthways and roughly chopped
	Finely grated zest of 2 limes

To start the meringues, pre-heat the oven to 100°C. Place the egg whites in the bowl of a mixer fitted with a whisk attachment. Whisk on medium speed until soft peaks form.

Add the white caster sugar a little at a time and continue to whisk for 5 minutes. Add the icing sugar a little at a time and whisk for a further 5 minutes. The meringue mixture should be glossy and smooth.

Pour the mixture into a piping bag with a small plain nozzle, and make small meringue shapes (approximately 4cm in diameter) on a baking tray lined with baking paper. Place the tray in the oven and allow to dry for 4 hours.

After 4 hours, remove the tray from the oven and allow to cool. Cut each meringue into four. Keep any small pieces that break, as you want them for decoration. Set aside.

To make the hazelnut brittle, pre-heat the oven to 180°C.

Place the hazelnuts on a baking tray and put into the oven for 10 minutes.

In the meantime, put the unrefined caster sugar and 30g cold tap water into a frying pan and place the pan over a medium-high heat until the sugar dissolves and the liquid becomes a dark brown caramel (p.307). Add the toasted nuts and salt to the pan and stir until the nuts are coated, then pour the mixture on to a baking tray lined with baking paper. (The caramel is extremely hot so be careful when pouring.) Allow to cool and harden.

Once cold, wrap the hard caramel in a clean tea-towel and bash it with a rolling pin to break it into smaller pieces. (These pieces of hazelnut brittle will keep in an airtight container for at least a month.)

To make the banana purée, put the unrefined caster sugar in a large clean frying pan over a high heat and let it melt (p.307). Once it is dark in colour, add the whole bananas, turning them over in the caramel so they are completely coated, then add the rum to the pan in order to deglaze it.

Put the caramelized bananas into the food processor with the lime juice, and blitz until smooth. Pour into a bowl, cover and place in the fridge to cool completely.

To make the lime cream, combine the double cream and the lime juice in a bowl and whisk until very soft peaks are formed, being careful not to over-whisk.

To assemble and serve, combine approximately 20g of the hazelnut brittle pieces with the banana purée and the lime cream. Gently fold in the chopped fresh banana and the larger meringue pieces and divide between six plates. Garnish with extra brittle and the smaller pieces of meringue and then sprinkle the lime zest over the top.

Mango terrine with green peppercorns

The combination of mango and peppercorns is a good example of the concept of flavour pairing: developing a dish by exploring compounds that different ingredients have in common (p.20).

The idea of putting the two together originated from a discussion with the brilliant flavourist François Benzi about terpenes. These are compounds with pine-like, leafy and citrus notes that are found in pine needles, citrus fruits, nutmeg, mint and woody herbs like sage, rosemary and thyme. 'Smell the stone of a mango,' François encouraged me, 'it has an aroma of green peppercorns.' I did, and was so impressed by that shared terpene characteristic that I began developing a dish structured around these ingredients. The fruity, resinous and slightly sharp terpenes give the dish a real lightness and freshness.

Serves 6

3	Ripe mangoes
1 tbsp	Fructose (fruit sugar)
	Juice of 1 lime
10g	Green peppercorns in brine, drained and finely chopped

To serve

Blackcurrant sorbet (p.292)

Peel and slice the mangoes in half lengthwise, discarding the stones. Slice the flesh into thin strips.

Lay the strips in a serving bowl and sprinkle them with the fructose. Cover and place in the fridge for 20 minutes.

When ready to serve, drizzle the lime juice over the mango and divide the slices between six plates.

Sprinkle the mango with a few chopped green peppercorns and place a ball of blackcurrant sorbet on the side.

Pain perdu

A sweet French version of eggy bread, pain perdu is the perfect accompaniment for bacon and egg ice-cream (p.289), served with a slice of caramelized bacon as a sort of breakfast-cum-dessert. But it's also delicious with other ice-creams, caramelized apples or any cooked fruit.

The bread is refrigerated for 12 hours, because cold speeds up the rate at which bread stales. Starch granules crystallize at around 4°C, and these granules help the bread to keep its shape during cooking and allow it to hold on to more of the soaking liquid, making for a richer pain perdu.

Serves 6

1   White loaf, crust removed

For the pain perdu mix

1   Vanilla pod
280g   Whole milk
30g   Unrefined caster sugar
4   Large egg whites
3   Large egg yolks

For the bacon

125g   Unrefined caster sugar
¼ tsp   Salt
25g   Maple syrup
6   Slices of smoked streaky bacon

To serve (per portion)

50g   Clarified butter (see tip, p.286)
2   Bread triangles
100g   Unrefined caster sugar
         Bacon and egg ice-cream (p.289)
1   Slice of caramelized bacon

Cut the bread into six slices, each 2cm thick, lay them in a container, cover with clingfilm and refrigerate for 12 hours.

For the pain perdu mixture, slice the vanilla pod in half lengthways and scrape out the seeds, reserving the pods to use in another recipe or to flavour sugar.

Combine the seeds with the milk, sugar, egg whites and yolks. Stir until the sugar has completely dissolved, then refrigerate until needed.

To start the bacon, pre-heat the oven to 180°C.

Boil the sugar, 100g cold tap water and the salt together and allow to cool.

When cool, add the maple syrup. Brush one side of each bacon slice with the syrup, then place brushed-side down on a heavy baking tray. Brush the top of the bacon with more syrup, then place a sheet of baking paper on top. Cover with a second heavy baking tray to keep the slices flat during cooking.

Place the bacon in the oven for 8–9 minutes or until the bacon has caramelized. Remove the bacon from the tray and allow to cool completely before placing in an airtight container between pieces of parchment paper.

When the bread is dry, cut each slice to a 10cm square, then cut these squares into two triangles. Place in a container and cover with the pain perdu mixture. Cover with clingfilm and place in the fridge for 20 minutes until the bread has soaked up all the liquid.

Remove the bread triangles from the liquid, place on a cooling rack and allow to drain for 3–4 minutes.

To finish and serve, heat the clarified butter in a non-stick pan over a medium heat, then fry the bread until both sides are golden brown. Remove from the pan and trim off any frayed edges. Drain the pan and wipe clean.

Add enough sugar to coat the bottom of the pan and heat until it starts to caramelize. Quickly add the bread and coat each side with the sugar. Remove from the pan and place on a silicone mat. Using scissors, snip off any stray caramel around the edges. Repeat this step with a second batch of two triangles but clean the pan and make a new caramel for the next two batches and so on.

Transfer the bread triangles to a plate, two per plate, and place some bacon and egg ice-cream on top. Finish with a slice of caramelized bacon.

Rosemary and bay truffles

A truffle is essentially a ganache: a mixture of warmed cream and melted chocolate that has been allowed to set (p.304). By adding flavourings to either the cream or the chocolate, you can incorporate all sorts of flavours into truffles. Here are rosemary and bay, thyme, ras-el-hanout and caraway options. As you can see, it's pretty much a blank canvas waiting to be filled by your imagination.

Makes 25 truffles

25g	Rosemary sprigs
3	Bay leaves
300g	Whipping cream
275g	Dark chocolate, chopped (minimum 65% cocoa solids)
1 tsp	Salt

To finish

Cocoa powder, or crispy chocolate coating (right)

Put the rosemary sprigs, bay leaves and whipping cream in a saucepan and place over a low heat to warm for 10 minutes. Turn the heat off and leave the pan to stand for 30 minutes.

While the cream is infusing, line a deep-sided container or baking tray, 20 × 30cm, with parchment paper and set aside.

Strain the infused cream, discarding the herbs, and return it to the saucepan. Place the pan over a medium heat and bring up to a simmer.

Melt the chocolate in a large bowl over a saucepan of simmering water.

When the cream is simmering, remove the pan from the heat, add the salt, and add to the melted chocolate a third at a time, making sure that the cream is thoroughly incorporated after each addition. Allow to cool slightly.

Pour the chocolate mixture on to the lined tray and leave to stand at room temperature for 4 hours, then place in the fridge for 5–6 hours or until set.

Using a small melon baller, scoop balls of the chocolate out of the ganache, or cut into cubes, then roll in cocoa powder or the crispy chocolate coating below.

Thyme truffles
Proceed as for rosemary and bay truffles, replacing the rosemary and bay leaves with 20g thyme leaves.

Ras-el-hanout truffles
Proceed as for rosemary and bay truffles, replacing the rosemary and bay leaves with 10g ras-el-hanout spice mix (Specialist ingredients, p.395).

Caraway truffles
Proceed as for rosemary and bay truffles, replacing the rosemary and bay leaves with 50g toasted caraway seeds. The caraway seeds will absorb lots of cream during the infusion, so use 400g whipping cream instead of 300g.

Crispy chocolate coating
This lovely effect is produced by means of sugar crystallization (p.357). By adding chocolate to a sugar syrup at the right moment, you can 'shock' the sugar into forming crystals, creating a powdery, sandy texture that's just right for a truffle coating.

100g	White caster sugar
40g	Dark chocolate, roughly chopped (minimum 60% cocoa solids)

Put 75g cold tap water and the sugar into a saucepan and place the pan over a high heat. Bring to the boil and continue to heat until the temperature of the liquid reaches 135°C or until the syrup at the side of the pan begins to colour.

Remove from the heat and immediately add the chopped chocolate. Whisk to incorporate the chocolate and continue to whisk until the liquid has completely crystallized.

Pour the chocolate crystals on to a parchment-lined baking tray and allow to cool. They can be kept in an airtight container in the freezer for up to a month.

Salted butter caramels wrapped in edible cellophane

I once went on a kind of pilgrimage to Brittany, in search of the salted butter caramels of Henri Le Roux, maker of legendary French sweets. I really like the chewy-but-giving texture of these caramels, and they suit all kinds of flavourings. I've given apple pie and barley variations overleaf, but I've made tomato, violet and even black pudding caramels in my time.

The edible wrappers aren't hard to make, but you'll need lots of clean 9cm Petri dishes. (These are inexpensive and easy to buy online.) And you have to use powdered gelatine rather than sheets, because it's easier to weigh out the precise amount of gelatine needed. Obviously you can make the caramels without the wrappers, but they do add something to the presentation, and everybody always loves the idea that you can eat the whole thing. The recipe makes more wrappers than you'll need, but since it requires just a single drop of glycerine, it's not really possible to halve the wrapper quantity.

Makes 100 caramels

For the caramels

400g	Double cream
380g	Whole milk
380g	White caster sugar
375g	Liquid glucose
300g	Unsalted butter
10g	Salt

For the edible wrappers

	Glycerine, 1 drop (Specialist ingredients, p.394)
5g	Powdered gelatine

Line a baking tray (approximately 20 × 30cm) with parchment paper and set aside with a sieve for later use.

Pour the double cream into a small saucepan and place it over a low heat to warm gently.

Put the milk, sugar, liquid glucose, butter and salt into a stainless-steel saucepan and place over a medium-high heat, stirring occasionally with a wooden spoon until the sugar, glucose and butter have melted.

When the temperature of the sugar and glucose liquid reaches 100°C, swap the wooden spoon for a balloon whisk and whisk the mixture continuously as the caramel begins to thicken and change colour.

As soon as the temperature reaches 154°C, remove from the heat and add the warm cream a third at a time. (Be careful of the hot steam released when the cream is added.) After the final addition, stir thoroughly to make sure the caramel has come together.

Pass the caramel through the sieve straight on to the baking tray. Allow to sit at room temperature for 2 hours before placing another sheet of parchment on top. Allow to set for an additional 12 hours before cutting into small rectangles and wrapping in edible wrappers.

For the edible wrappers, place 400g cold tap water in a saucepan, and add the glycerine and gelatine. Heat the mixture over a medium-low heat, stirring constantly with a spoon to melt the gelatine.

Spread out 20 Petri dishes, or as many as you require, on a flat surface. Weigh out 5g of the gelatine solution into each dish, swirling the liquid to coat the bottom evenly and tapping the dish to break any air bubbles.

Place the dishes on a shelf and cover lightly with baking parchment to prevent any dust from settling on them. Leave in a warm place for 20–25 hours, or until the wrappers are completely dry.

When needed, carefully peel the wrappers off the dishes and wrap immediately round the caramels. Twist the ends like a Christmas cracker.

continued overleaf

Apple pie caramels

Introducing apple pie flavour just seems to add to the Alice in Wonderland fantasy element of these sweets.

280g	Double cream
13g	Instant yeast
420g	Apple juice
420g	White caster sugar
420g	Liquid glucose
320g	Unsalted butter
3.5g	Cream of tartar
13g	Salt

Proceed as for the salted butter caramels, replacing the milk with apple juice. Blitz the yeast into the warm cream and add the cream of tartar with the salt.

Barley caramels

Apart from barley sugar and barley water, barley is now a relatively unfamiliar flavouring, yet it has a malted characteristic that works really well in a caramel.

For the barley water

500g	Pearl barley

For the caramels

280g	Double cream
420g	Barley water (above)
420g	White caster sugar
420g	Liquid glucose
320g	Unsalted butter
13g	Salt

For the barley water, place the barley in a container and cover with 1kg cold tap water. Cover and leave to ferment in a cool, dark room for 3 days. Strain and discard the barley.

Then proceed as for salted butter caramels, replacing the whole milk with the barley water.

Whisky gums

This is my take on wine gums. They sprang out of a question: what if I actually made wine gums with wine? I tried red wine, port and dessert wine, which all produced interesting results, but it was only when I moved on to whisky that the idea really took off. Making the gums with some form of wine involved a lot of reducing, which altered the natural flavours. Whisky, on the other hand, was already very concentrated, making it easier to harness its flavour characteristics. And since the cooking process causes the alcohol to evaporate, you encounter that flavour without the big punch of alcohol.

You can use whatever whisky you like. At the Fat Duck I've served tiny bottle-shaped gums of Highland Park, Glenlivet, Laphroaig and Oban to give an idea of the flavour profiles of whiskies from different parts of Scotland. (I've also made a gum with Jack Daniel's Single Barrel for a bit of fun, which tasted superb.) Laphroaig is a good one to begin with, because of its distinctive smoky flavour, but if you prefer something more fruity, try using Oban instead.

The gums will look really professional if they're made in chocolate moulds. These look like silicone ice-cube trays and are available online and in kitchen stores. However, you can simply pour the liquid into a lightly greased plastic tray or baking tray lined with parchment and cut it to shape once it's set. A chocolate mould's not a bad investment, though, as you can also use it to make many other sweets, including the pastilles on p.342 and the chocolate truffles on p.336.

Lightly grease a chocolate mould tray with a little groundnut or grapeseed oil. If you don't have moulds, line a 20 × 30cm baking tray with parchment paper.

Pour 130g of the whisky into a small saucepan and add the gelatine. Warm the pan over a low heat until the gelatine has dissolved in the liquid. Remove from the heat.

Put the remaining whisky in a different saucepan with the glucose, caster sugar and cream of tartar. Place over a high heat and heat until the temperature of the liquid reaches 124°C.

Remove the pan from the heat and allow the liquid to cool to 100°C before adding the whisky and gelatine mixture. Mix the liquids together with a spatula until the gelatine is fully incorporated, then pour the mixture into the lightly greased moulds or on to the parchment-lined baking tray.

Place the moulds in the fridge and leave to set for at least 6 hours before unmoulding.

Carefully remove the gums from the moulds, or cut the jelly on the tray into cubes. (You could also use a 1.5–2cm pastry cutter to cut out the gums.)

Once unmoulded, place the gums in a bowl with the granulated sugar and roll around until coated on all sides.

Makes 20 sweets

	Groundnut or grapeseed oil
200g	Laphroaig whisky
30g	Powdered gelatine
200g	Liquid glucose
150g	Unrefined caster sugar
½ tsp	Cream of tartar
100g	White granulated sugar, for dusting

Passionfruit pastilles

Like the whisky gums on p.340, these are a twist on a classic kids' sweet, making them more refined and introducing different flavours. If you don't have chocolate moulds, use a parchment-lined baking tray, and cut the pastilles to shape with a small pastry cutter.

When a fruit-based recipe requires sugar I usually opt for fructose, as it enhances the fruitiness. Here, however, you have to use sucrose instead. Fructose caramelizes at too low a temperature for this dish, causing the fruit to go dark and change flavour. The pectin powder helps the pastilles to set.

Makes 30 pastilles

	Groundnut or grapeseed oil
500g	Passionfruit juice (approx. 12 passionfruits)
350g	White caster sugar
1 tbsp	Pectin powder
100g	Liquid glucose
15g	Lemon juice (approx. ½ lemon)
100g	White granulated sugar, for dusting

Lightly grease a chocolate mould tray with a little groundnut or grapeseed oil. If you don't have moulds, line a 20 × 30cm baking tray with parchment paper.

Slice the passionfruits in half and, using a spoon, scoop out the pulp and the seeds into a bowl. Using a hand blender, blitz the seeds and pulp to a liquid.

Thoroughly mix the sugar and the pectin and put into a saucepan with the glucose and the passionfruit juice.

Place the pan over a medium heat and bring the temperature of the liquid to 108°C, or to a reading of 69° Brix, if you're using a refractometer (p.393), stirring from time to time until the sugar and glucose have completely melted. Remove the pan from the heat and stir in the lemon juice.

Pour into the moulds or on to the baking tray and allow to set at room temperature for 4 hours.

Carefully remove the pastilles from the moulds, or cut the jelly into cubes. (You could also use a 1.5–2cm pastry cutter to cut out the pastilles.) Place the pastilles in a bowl with the granulated sugar. Roll them around until coated on all sides before serving.

Blackcurrant fruit pastilles
Proceed as for passionfruit pastilles, replacing the 500g of passionfruit juice with 500g blackcurrant purée.

Caramelized apple pastilles
Flavouring the pastilles with caramelized apple gives them a marvellous tarte tatin quality. The caramelizing takes a bit of work but it produces a really rich, dark, deep flavour.

275g	Unrefined caster sugar
125g	Unsalted butter
250g	Apple juice
10g	Pectin powder
15g	Lemon juice (approx. ½ lemon)
100g	White granulated sugar, for dusting

Place 250g of the sugar in a deep stainless-steel saucepan over a medium heat to make a dry caramel (p.307).

Once the caramel turns dark, add the butter and stir with a wooden spoon until well combined. Add the apple juice and continue to stir. When fully incorporated, weigh out 375g of the liquid, discarding the excess.

Add 125g cold tap water and bring to the boil. Mix the remaining caster sugar with the pectin and whisk into the boiling syrup.

Continue to heat until the temperature of the liquid reaches 108°C, or to a reading of 69° Brix, if you're using a refractometer (p.393), then whisk in the lemon juice.

Mould the jelly as in the passionfruit pastille recipe, allow it to set, then roll in the granulated sugar.

Pineapple marshmallows

The basis of marshmallow is a type of Italian meringue, which is set with gelatine. These are fun to make – the sort of thing that brings out the kid in everyone – and there are plenty of ways you can set your own stamp on them. I've given recipes for pineapple, orange-blossom and rosewater marshmallows, but you can try any flavour you like. Kids love them chopped up and mixed with cereal or ice-cream. Or you can serve them with a frothy hot chocolate (p.384).

Makes 30 marshmallows

100g	Cornflour
100g	Icing sugar
130g	Pineapple juice
200g	Egg whites (approx. 7 large eggs)
400g	White caster sugar
170g	Liquid glucose
9g	Leaves of gelatine, softened in cold tap water

Mix the cornflour and icing sugar together in a bowl. Using a sieve, dust the bottom of a deep baking tray with some of the mixture (reserving the rest for the surface).

Put the pineapple juice into a saucepan, place over a medium heat and bring to the boil. When boiling, remove the pan from the heat.

In the bowl of a mixer fitted with a whisk attachment, begin to whisk the egg whites on a low speed.

While the egg whites are whisking, add 100g cold tap water, the caster sugar and glucose to the pineapple juice saucepan and place over a high heat. Bring up to the boil without stirring and allow the temperature to reach 128°C. Use a wet pastry brush to stop sugar crystals forming on the sides of the pan (p.307). Once the syrup has reached 128°C, increase the mixer speed to medium and continue to whisk the egg whites until medium peaks form.

When medium peaks form, begin to add the syrup to the egg whites in a thin, steady drizzle to one side of the bowl. (This will ensure that the egg whites don't cook as you add the hot syrup.) Once all the syrup has been added, squeeze the water out of the gelatine sheets and add them to the bowl. Increase the speed to high. Whisk until the mixture has cooled to room temperature.

Pour the mixture into the dusted tray and spread it to an even thickness with a spatula. Sprinkle the surface with more of the icing sugar and cornflour mixture and rest uncovered for 1 hour.

Cover the tray with clingfilm, then leave to set at room temperature for 10 hours. Slice into cubes and toss them in any remaining cornflour and icing sugar.

Orange-blossom marshmallows
Replace the pineapple juice with cold tap water (making a total of 230g water) and add 2 teaspoons of orange-blossom water to the syrup.

Rosewater marshmallows
Replace the pineapple juice with cold tap water (making a total of 230g water) and add 2 teaspoons of rosewater to the syrup.

Carrot (or beetroot or tomato) lollies

The carrot lolly actually started life as a carrot purée that I served with veal shank. One day I was making a batch at the restaurant and had an idea. I held off adding butter, spread a little on a baking sheet and stuck it in the oven to harden. The results were promising, so I made some more purée, fashioned a rectangular stencil to go on top of the baking sheet, 'painted' the purée on to it, stuck a stick in it, baked it – and out came a savoury lolly.

A silicone mat – a flexible, non-stick, silicone baking sheet – is useful for making these, but you can simply use a baking sheet and parchment paper instead: lay an 8 × 2cm stencil cut from the lid of a margarine tub or a piece of cardboard on top. (Or you can forgo the stencil altogether and simply smear the purée on to the silicone mat or paper and cut to shape. It might end up a little uneven towards the edges but it will still work.)

Makes 50 lollies

For the candied orange zest

105g	Fructose (fruit sugar)
90g	Liquid glucose
1	Orange

For the lollies

5 tsp	Agar-agar flakes (Specialist ingredients, p.394)
250g	Carrot juice (or beetroot or tomato juice)
30g	Icing sugar
20g	White caster sugar
	Groundnut or grapeseed oil
50	Cocktail sticks

To start the candied orange zest, place 560g cold tap water, the fructose and liquid glucose in a pan and bring to the boil. Add the orange and simmer, covered, for 2 hours 30 minutes. Remove from the heat and allow to cool. Wrap the orange tightly in clingfilm and place in the freezer for 2–3 hours or until hard enough to grate the zest.

Pre-heat the oven to 60°C.

Finely grate the zest of the frozen orange. Place the zest on a baking tray lined with parchment and put in the oven to dry for 2 hours. Store in an airtight container until needed.

To start the lollies, mix the agar-agar with 150g of the juice in a medium saucepan.

In a different container, mix the remaining juice with the icing and caster sugars, then add this to the saucepan. Place the pan over a medium heat and bring to the boil.

Using a hand blender, blitz the mixture for 1 minute. Remove the pan from the heat and let the mixture cool thoroughly. Once cool, blitz again until completely smooth.

Pre-heat the oven to 90°C.

Put a silicone mat on a baking tray. Drop a couple of drops of oil on the mat and wipe the surface with kitchen paper. Using a stencil and a palette knife, drag some of the puréed mixture evenly across the stencil to create a rectangle, circle or triangle. Repeat until you have as many lollies as you require. Sprinkle each of the lollies with the candied orange zest.

Place the baking tray in the oven for 10 minutes. After 10 minutes, remove the tray from the oven and place a cocktail stick into the centre of one side of each shape. Press very gently into the set mix. Return the tray to the oven and cook for 1 hour.

When cooked, delicately lift the lollies from the mat using a palette knife. Place them on a flat surface to rest for a couple of minutes before serving.

Raspberry sherbet

Remember sherbet fountains – those yellow cardboard tubes full of sherbet with a stick of liquorice poking out of the twisted paper at one end? Or sherbet dip-dabs, where a paper packet of sherbet came with its own lolly for dipping? They're a great nostalgia trip for me, and I've actually made my own mini-version of the fountain to serve at the Fat Duck. It gives people a real thrill when they see and taste something they won't have had since childhood. Serve this raspberry sherbet with liquorice sticks at the end of a meal and watch your guests' faces light up.

Serves 6–8

5g	Freeze-dried raspberries (Specialist ingredients, p.394)
50g	Icing sugar
1 tsp	Bicarbonate of soda
1 tsp	Citric acid (Specialist ingredients, p.394)

To serve

Liquorice sticks

Place all of the ingredients in a liquidizer and blitz for 45 seconds or to a fine powder.

Pass through a fine sieve, and keep in an airtight container for up to 2 weeks.

To serve, put into individual little jars or glasses, or into a bowl in the middle of the table, and dip in your liquorice stick.

Biscuits, snacks and drinks

Finally, here's a collection of recipes that don't have to be served at a mealtime. They're all favourites of mine and you could say they represent a lot of the typical characteristics of my cooking. There are some touches of nostalgia, like the banana and bacon cookies (p.358) that were inspired by a childhood holiday in South Africa; interesting spins on familiar dishes, such as my flavoured popcorn; and some products of my travels, like the puffed spelt (p.374) that I thought up as I drove through northern Italy searching for the perfect risotto. There are some that I just couldn't resist including: the Negroni, with its kick of astringent Campari, makes a great palate-cleansing aperitif (p.380); the cornbread muffins (p.370) go well with chilli con carne; and the millionaire shortbread (p.368) would be an excellent elevenses.

Many of these recipes involve baking, which has always been popular, probably because the process is so relaxed, and produces such delicious results. Biscuit-making involves quite a few of the same ingredients and techniques as pastry-making, but the process can be complicated, so I've included a few pointers on how to get the best out of your dough. There are also another couple of techniques that take advantage of science, like creating foams (p.356) that are perfect for topping a cool drink, or inducing an abrupt and almost magical crystallization of sugar (p.357).

Since they aren't tied to a meal, the recipes in this chapter allow you to play around in the kitchen without the pressure of juggling timings and courses. They're an opportunity to cook something that's fun and can be served with a flourish, like tandoori popcorn (p.373), or homemade pork scratchings (p.370) that'll knock spots off any pub version, or a Pimm's with crystal-clear ice cubes containing cucumber and borage flowers (p.379).

Cookie and biscuit doughs

The American equivalent of the British biscuit is 'cookie', which comes from *koekje*, the Dutch word for 'little cake'. (And 'biscuit' comes from the French '*bis-cuit*', meaning twice baked.)

One of the beauties of biscuit-making is that you can use the same set of ingredients and techniques to create a variety of biscuits, simply by making a few adjustments to the basic process, or adding an extra ingredient or two. The chocolate biscuits and the banana and bacon, golden syrup, Earl Grey and chocolate chip cookies are all effectively 'drop-cookies', made by spooning portions of dough on to a baking sheet, which then spread during their time in the oven. They have the slightly chewy characteristic that we expect in an American-style cookie. The shortbread, millionaire shortbread and caraway biscuits take more or less the same ingredients in a different direction, producing what we think of as traybakes (bar cookies in the US), which have the classic crumbly shortbread texture. Madeleines, made with an egg batter rather than dough, are so soft in texture they have to be made in a mould. And florentines – dense with nuts, dried fruit and peel – are in a category all of their own.

The core ingredients for most biscuit doughs are flour, sugar, eggs, fat and perhaps a raising agent, plus a little salt to help bring out the flavour. Between them they determine the flavour, texture and structure of the biscuit. Flour is of course a key ingredient for making a dough. It reacts with the water contained in some of the other ingredients (mainly the eggs) to produce a homogeneous, workable mass. The most practical choice for biscuit-making is plain flour: a strong flour might make the dough too elastic, and self-raising takes away from your control of ingredients. It's less complicated to add raising agents separately, if you need them.

Butter gives richness, moistness and flavour, but it's also the key to two processes that influence a biscuit's structure. When butter is creamed (i.e. mixed vigorously) with sugar it creates a mixture that contains a lot of air, and this ensures the biscuit has a texture that's light rather than dense. And when the dough is cooking in the oven, the water that the butter contains turns to steam, producing more air bubbles that help the dough to rise. (That's why my recipes specify that the butter should be cold when it's creamed: you don't want the butter to become so warm that its water content leaks out before the dough goes in the oven.)

Sugar is the other essential ingredient of the creaming process, helping to introduce air, but it also introduces colour, sweetness and flavour. (In these recipes I use unrefined caster sugar, because it has a nice sugar-cane characteristic.) And, once the dough has been in the oven, the warmed sugar will give biscuits a certain crispness, as it cools and sets.

Eggs contain most of the water that reacts with flour to form a dough (which is why, as you'll see, the choice of when you add eggs to a biscuit mixture is a major factor in its final texture and character). Eggs are also a source of richness and flavour, and if you're using whole eggs (rather than just the yolks), the whites will trap air during the mixing process (as they do in meringues), which will raise the dough and give it a light texture. (The shortbread recipes and the caraway biscuits use only egg yolks, because they don't want to be as aerated as the cookies.) The fat in eggs provides moistness, too – the more eggs you use, the more cake-like the texture will be.

Air is introduced to a cookie dough when butter and sugar are creamed and when whole eggs are mixed in, but, where desirable, this process can be given a boost by the addition of a raising agent, commonly baking powder and/or bicarbonate of soda. Baking powder contains an alkali and an acid that when added to liquid ingredients dissolve and react together to produce carbon dioxide, which becomes trapped in the dough and expands when it is heated in the oven. Bicarbonate of soda is an alkali that reacts with acidic ingredients (honey, brown sugar, flour) to produce carbon dioxide. Both will raise the dough to create a nice light texture, but bicarbonate of soda has the extra advantage that it can improve the colour of some biscuits. Acidic ingredients can prevent a biscuit from developing a nice brown colour; the alkali in bicarbonate of soda, however, can neutralize the acid sufficiently that it takes on colour after all. The presence of bicarbonate of soda in my biscuit recipes is, therefore, as much for colour as it is for raising. (The chocolate biscuit uses only bicarbonate of soda because it's designed to be a rich, dense biscuit, so it doesn't need to rise as much as the other biscuits.) The reactions of bicarbonate of soda and baking powder generally take place quickly, so if a raising agent is being used, it's best to prepare the mixture and put it in the oven as soon as possible. Bear in mind, too, that these products can have an adverse effect on a biscuit dough if the wrong amount is used. Too little and the texture ends up flat and dense. Too much will lead to a coarse texture and harsh flavour.

For the drop-cookies and shortbreads in this book, the ingredients are all combined in four stages. The first two are sifting the dry ingredients and creaming the butter and sugar. Sifting ensures none of the dry ingredients clump together. Creaming, as I said, introduces air to the mixture. It isn't difficult (it's definitely easier in a food mixer than by hand), and once you've done it a few times, you get a feel for it. What you're looking for is a mixture where the colour has lightened and the sugar is barely visible. Experience will help you avoid a heavy-looking, under-creamed mixture (which will affect the final texture, because the butter and sugar won't have integrated properly) and an overly light, over-creamed mixture (which might cause the fat to come out during baking, making the dough spread more than you want).

Stages three and four are adding the dry ingredients (flour and salt, plus perhaps a raising agent) and the wet ingredients (principally eggs) to the creamed butter and sugar. But the order of these two stages depends on whether you want a slightly elastic texture, as in a cookie, or something more brittle, like a shortbread. If you add the flour to the creamed ingredients first, the fat coats the flour particles, forming a sort of barrier around them. When the eggs are added, the water they contain will react with the flour to make a dough, but fat prevents the flour and water from developing too much elasticity. So, adding dry ingredients first produces a crumbly shortbread. If, on the other hand, you add eggs to the creamed butter and sugar, followed by the flour, then the water and flour have a greater opportunity to interact and create a slightly more resilient dough that's suitable for cookies.

The dry ingredients should be added to the food mixer on a low speed (to avoid them being flung around the kitchen by the mixer paddle), and allowed to blend together for 2–3 minutes. Halfway through this process, it's sometimes a good idea to stop the machine and scrape the sides and base of the mixing bowl: the paddles of many mixers don't reach the extremities of the bowl very efficiently, and any bits that aren't fully incorporated can prevent the mixture from cooking evenly.

When adding the wet ingredients, you still want to avoid under- and over-mixing: the former might lead to lumps, the latter can drive out some of the moisture and lessen a mixture's ability to rise (because it's the moisture turned to steam by the heat of the oven that helps this happen). So keep the paddle going just long enough to combine the ingredients. It should be obvious when the mix is ready – it'll be smooth and uniform.

Because cookies are small and thin, with a high sugar content, they can brown quickly during cooking, particularly on the base and at the sides while the centre cooks through. It's a good idea to use an oven thermometer to make sure you're heating at the optimum temperature, and best to monitor progress closely during cooking. The drop-cookies are designed to spread as they bake, so make sure that there is enough space between them on the tray before they go into the oven. After you take them out of the oven, leave the cookies on the tray for a couple of minutes before removing them with a spatula and placing them on a rack to cool completely. This will help them to keep their shape.

A shortbread-style dough needs a little more work than a cookie dough so that it holds its shape and structure as it cooks. After it has cohered into a ball, the dough needs to be rested for at least 2 hours in the fridge, otherwise the butter might come out of the dough, making it wet and unworkable. Once the dough has relaxed, it can be rolled but, once again, working the dough will have 'stressed' the butter, so it's best to put it in the freezer for a quick 20-minute cooling-off. After this it should be in good shape for cooking – place it in the oven and bake, taking care to turn the tray round once towards the end, to make sure that the biscuits colour evenly. (Ovens – especially older ones where the door isn't well insulated – sometimes have hotspots that can affect the development of colour.)

Foams

The use of foam in cuisine gets a lot of stick. It's often viewed as whimsical and pretentious – an indulgent bit of froth. But in fact foam is an integral part of lots of foods we know and love. A cappuccino isn't a cappuccino and a milkshake's a bit of a disappointment if it hasn't got a nice frothy foam on top. Foams may have been over-used by chefs and familiarity has bred contempt, but that's not the fault of the foam.

Technically, a foam is very similar to an emulsion (p.115) except that, where an emulsion is a dispersal of one fluid in another, a foam is the dispersal of a gas into a liquid or solid in the form of bubbles. The process is invaluable to the chef in a number of ways. First, foam is a very effective thickener. Incorporating air bubbles into a sweet or savoury sauce not only gives volume but also a certain viscosity, because the bubbles impede the easy flow of the water molecules, making it less runny. Second, a foam is a great carrier of flavour. Because it has a large surface area in contact with air, it really helps to convey aromas – a key part of what gives food its flavour – to the nose. Third, the foam's unique airiness makes it a fantastic textural component of a dish, whether it's incorporated with the other ingredients to produce an overall lightness, or presented as a fragile, surf-like garnish on the plate.

That airiness, however, presents a problem. A foam is living on borrowed time, as the air inside the bubbles rises up, and gravity tugs down the liquid in the bubbles' walls. The liquid drains off until eventually the walls are too thin to contain the air and they pop. This can be

prevented, or at least delayed, by adding a stabilizer to the ingredients. Proteins and emulsifiers, such as lecithin (which is present in eggs), have sections that are water-soluble (hydrophilic) and sections that are water-insoluble (hydrophobic). The water-soluble section will rest in the bubble wall while the water-insoluble section rests in the air inside, providing a structure that reinforces and stabilizes the foam. It can be a tricky thing to pull off: if the liquid's too thick it won't foam; if it's too thin it won't hold the bubbles. Too much stabilizer can render a foam gummy. Too much fat will kill it completely.

One very effective way of making a foam employs a cream whipper (also known as a whipped cream dispenser or creamer), which is very similar to a traditional soda siphon. It uses pressurized cartridges to force a gas – either N_2O (nitrous oxide) or, if you're looking for a bit of fizziness, CO_2 (carbon dioxide) – into a mixture, where it dissolves. When the liquid is released the gas forms bubbles, turning it into a foam. The combination of gas, pressure and a relatively unfamiliar piece of kitchen equipment makes home cooks wary of using a creamer, but it's not a complicated or particularly difficult process, and the results can be very rewarding.

You can make a very pure foam by aerating an unadulterated juice or purée, but it won't hold for long and won't have much body, so it's a good idea to combine the liquid with a stabilizer such as egg whites, which are blitzed into the liquid with a hand blender, to get plenty of air in there. The texture of these foams can range from thick and mousse-like through meringue to a viscous liquid, depending on what proportion of ingredients is used and how long the foam is rested (see below).

The liquid is then strained into the cream whipper so that it's very smooth (a funnel makes this easier and less messy), making sure that it fills only about three-quarters of the available space: if it's too full, there's no room for the bubbles to expand. Recipes usually require one or two cartridges (don't try to use more than a recipe advises). I generally use two and keep the second one screwed into the creamer rather than taking it out. This means that, as the amount of liquid in the creamer goes down, more gas goes into it to fill the new space, which ensures that the liquid stays aerated and continues to come out of the creamer forcefully and evenly.

However, before the liquid is sprayed out, the creamer and its contents need to be put in the fridge to cool for at least 20–30 minutes, and up to 2 hours. This allows the mixture to develop body and also to settle, which makes it come out more easily. Once the foam's ready, after its chilling, it's best to work quickly as, even if it contains a stabilizer, a foam is a fragile structure that will only hold together for a while. Hold the creamer upside down and press the lever very gently until the foam comes out.

Foams contribute to a number of dishes in this book, notably the green tea and lime palate cleanser on p.82, which has to be as light as possible – something that vanishes almost as soon as you put it in your mouth, leaving behind just a refreshing, cleansed feeling. Only a foam has the right lightness for this. And I like to finish a soup by frothing it with a hand blender to give it a velvety texture.

I also like foam on top of drinks, like Pimm's (p.379) and Negroni (p.380). It adds a lovely contrast of texture that is light enough not to interfere with the liquidity of the drink, and it's a great opportunity to add in extra flavours as well. The Pimm's foam, for instance, has a fresh, lively cucumber flavour, while the lime granita for the palate cleanser has a refreshing green tea foam on top, along with a dusting of the same flavour. Using foams really opens out the ways in which a cook can be creative with a liquid.

Crystallizing sugar

I'm a sucker for little moments of magic where the culinary and the uncanny meet. Crystallizing sugar is one of these moments. You heat a sugar syrup in a pan and, when you add, say, nuts to it, all the liquid seems to disappear, leaving just the nuts, now coated in sugar. The process behind this is called 'supersaturation'. Sugar molecules like to order themselves into solid masses called crystals.

When they're dissolved in water, as they are in a conventional sugar syrup, the water molecules get in the way of this ordering process. However, if you heat up a sugar syrup, as water evaporates it becomes more difficult for the remaining water molecules to keep the sugar molecules from bonding together, and they start to crystallize. At a certain point in this procedure the solution is said to be saturated: the tendency of the sugar to bond to itself is exactly counterbalanced by the water's capacity to stop it doing this.

Saturation happens when the solution is warm: heat is needed to animate the water molecules sufficiently that they can keep sugar molecules dissolved. Cold, slow water molecules are much less good at this. So as soon as a hot saturated solution is cooled, it becomes supersaturated, holding more sugar than it normally could at that temperature. At this finely balanced point, anything that touches the sugar will cause crystals to grow. When you're cooking a syrup or caramel, this phenomenon can ruin it (which is why we have to paint the insides of the pan with water, to get rid of sugar crystals, p.307). But it can be used to spectacular and delicious effect. Throw nuts or pieces of chopped chocolate into the supersaturated solution and they'll cool the liquid and shock the sugar into crystallization in one fell swoop. You end up with powdery grains of chocolate for a truffle coating (p.336) or sugar-coated nuts that you can use to garnish a sundae or just eat as a snack (p.377).

Banana and bacon cookies

I first tasted the combination of bacon and banana in a toasted sandwich at a Hard Rock Cafe in South Africa when I was a teenager. I was surprised how well they went together, and I think you will be too.

The dough can be frozen in individual portions and baked for surprise guests.

Makes approx. 20 cookies

40g	Smoked streaky bacon (approx. 5 slices)
220g	Plain flour
¼ tsp	Bicarbonate of soda
½ tsp	Baking powder
½ tsp	Salt
120g	Cold unsalted butter, cubed
260g	Unrefined caster sugar
2	Large eggs
60g	Dried bananas, roughly chopped

Pre-heat the oven to 190°C.

Place the bacon on a baking tray lined with baking parchment and place the tray in the oven for 10 minutes. Remove the tray and pat the bacon dry with pieces of kitchen paper. When cool enough to handle, cut the slices into small pieces.

Sift the flour, bicarbonate of soda, baking powder and salt into a bowl and set to one side.

Using a mixer fitted with the paddle attachment, cream the butter and sugar on medium speed until the mixture becomes light and fluffy (approximately 5 minutes).

Reduce the speed of the mixer to low and add the eggs, one at a time, and continue to mix until well incorporated.

Add the sifted flour to the creamed butter, sugar and egg mixture. Continue to mix for 3–5 minutes until the dry ingredients are thoroughly incorporated and a dough is formed. Add the bananas and bacon and continue to mix for 2 minutes.

Using an ice-cream scoop, portion the dough into balls (approximately 40g per ball). Place them on a parchment-lined baking tray roughly 10cm apart.

Place the tray in the oven for 8–10 minutes or until the cookies are golden brown and crispy at the edges. Remove the tray from the oven and allow the cookies to rest on the tray for a few minutes before placing on a cooling rack.

The cookies will keep for up to 5 days in an airtight tin.

Golden syrup cookies

This is a versatile recipe that can be used to make many different cookies. You can replace the syrup with an infusion of Earl Grey for the variation, right, or indeed any flavouring that captures your imagination.

The dough can be frozen in individual portions and baked for surprise guests.

Makes approx. 20 cookies

440g	Plain flour
5g	Bicarbonate of soda
5g	Baking powder
5g	Salt
230g	Cold unsalted butter, cubed
520g	Unrefined caster sugar
2	Large eggs
70g	Golden syrup (see tip, right)
15g	Vanilla bean paste (Specialist ingredients, p.395)

Pre-heat the oven to 190°C.

Sift the flour, bicarbonate of soda, baking powder and salt into a bowl, and set to one side.

Using a mixer fitted with the paddle attachment, cream the butter and sugar on medium speed until the mixture becomes light and fluffy (approximately 5 minutes). Reduce the speed of the mixer to low and add the eggs, one at a time. Add the golden syrup and the vanilla bean paste and continue to mix until well incorporated.

Add the flour mixture to the creamed butter, sugar and egg mixture. Continue to mix for 3–5 minutes until the dry ingredients are incorporated and a dough is formed.

Using an ice-cream scoop, portion the dough into balls (approximately 40g per ball). Place them on a parchment-lined baking tray roughly 10cm apart.

Place the tray in the oven for 8–10 minutes or until the cookies are golden brown. Remove the tray from the oven and allow the cookies to rest on the tray for a few minutes before placing on a cooling rack.

The cookies will keep for up to 5 days in an airtight tin.

Earl Grey cookies
Add the contents of two Earl Grey tea bags to the butter with the sugar.

Replace the golden syrup with 100g whole milk infused with four Earl Grey tea bags: place the milk in a saucepan, add the tea bags, bring to a simmer over a medium heat, then remove from the heat and allow to infuse for 5 minutes. Add to the creamed butter after the eggs have been incorporated.

How to weigh honey and golden syrup

Given their stickiness, weighing honey and golden syrup can be a problem, so here's a tip. Lightly grease a small bowl or a measuring spoon with groundnut or grapeseed oil before adding the honey or syrup to be measured. This will prevent them from sticking to the bowl or spoon, therefore making sure that the amount you add to the recipe is accurate.

Chocolate chip cookies

Freezing the chocolate chip mixture first ensures that the chips survive the baking process and are meltingly soft when the biscuits come out of the oven. Instead of the golden syrup chocolate chips I suggest here, you could replace them with chips made from any of the flavoured truffle ganaches on p.336.

The dough can be frozen in individual portions and baked for surprise guests.

Makes approx. 20 cookies

For the golden syrup chocolate chips

20g	Golden syrup (see tip, p.359)
140g	Whipping cream
125g	Dark chocolate, broken into pieces (minimum 60% cocoa solids)
	Pinch of salt

For the cookie dough

440g	Plain flour
½ tsp	Bicarbonate of soda
1 tsp	Baking powder
5g	Salt
½ tsp	Instant coffee powder
230g	Cold unsalted butter, cubed
520g	Unrefined caster sugar
2	Large eggs
15g	Vanilla bean paste (Specialist ingredients, p.395)

For the golden syrup chocolate chips, put the golden syrup and whipping cream into a saucepan and place over a medium heat. Bring to a simmer.

In the meantime, melt the chocolate in a bowl over a saucepan of simmering water (p.304).

When the cream is simmering, remove the pan from the heat, stir in the salt and add to the melted chocolate a third at a time, making sure that the cream is thoroughly incorporated after each addition. Allow to cool slightly.

Pour the chocolate mixture on to a parchment-lined baking tray (20 × 30cm), and allow to stand at room temperature for 1 hour, then place in the freezer for 4 hours or until frozen hard.

Remove from the freezer and allow to stand for 5 minutes at room temperature, then cut into 5mm cubes with a sharp knife. Keep in the freezer until ready to use.

Pre-heat the oven to 190°C.

To start the cookie dough, sift the flour, bicarbonate of soda, baking powder, salt and coffee powder into a bowl and set to one side.

Using a mixer fitted with the paddle attachment, cream the butter and sugar on medium speed until the mixture becomes light and fluffy (approximately 5 minutes).

Reduce the speed to low and add the eggs, one at a time, and continue to mix until well incorporated, then add the vanilla bean paste, followed by the flour mixture.

Continue to mix for 3–5 minutes until the dry ingredients are thoroughly incorporated and a dough is formed. Add the frozen chocolate chips. Mix for a further 30 seconds.

Using an ice-cream scoop, portion the dough into balls (approximately 40g per ball). Place them on a parchment-lined baking tray roughly 10cm apart.

Place the tray in the oven for 8–10 minutes or until the cookies are golden brown. Remove the tray from the oven and allow the biscuits to rest on the tray for a few minutes before placing on a cooling rack.

The cookies will keep for up to 5 days in an airtight tin.

Florentines

The traditional Italian Florentine is a crisp caramelized disc rich with dried fruit and nuts and covered with chocolate – truly a luxurious experience. The flavourings, however, aren't set in stone. If you don't have or don't like a particular fruit or nut, you can leave it out or replace it with more of one of the others.

Makes approx. 20 biscuits

90g	Crème fraiche
75g	Unrefined caster sugar
45g	Glucose syrup
10g	Runny honey (see tip, p.359)
80g	Mixed peel
10g	Pine nuts
25g	Dried cranberries
10g	Chopped hazelnuts
10g	Sliced almonds
25g	Plain flour
125g	Dark chocolate, chopped (minimum 60% cocoa solids)

Put the crème fraiche, caster sugar, glucose syrup and honey into a saucepan and place the pan over a medium heat until everything has melted.

Mix the peel, pine nuts, cranberries, hazelnuts and almonds in a bowl, add the flour and stir to combine.

Pour the contents of the saucepan into the bowl of nuts, fruit and peel and stir thoroughly. Place the mixture in the fridge and allow to cool for 1 hour.

Pre-heat the oven to 190°C.

Line a baking tray with baking parchment and pour in the Florentine mixture. Place the tray in the oven for 17–20 minutes or until the mixture turns golden brown.

Once baked, remove from the oven and use a pastry cutter to cut circles immediately. Allow the biscuits to cool completely on the tray before handling.

Melt the chocolate in a bowl over a saucepan of simmering water (p.304). Remove from the heat and dip half of each Florentine in the melted chocolate. Place on a cooling rack over a tray until the chocolate sets.

Keep in an airtight container between sheets of parchment for up to 3 days.

Chocolate biscuits

Although they use cocoa instead of chocolate, these biscuits are crisp, crumbly and have a lovely concentrated chocolate flavour. To make them even more indulgent, add the golden syrup chocolate chips on p.360 towards the end of mixing for a double choc chip biscuit.

The dough can be frozen in individual portions and baked for surprise guests.

Makes approx. 20 biscuits

135g	Plain flour
10g	Cocoa powder
½ tsp	Bicarbonate of soda
½ tsp	Salt
115g	Cold unsalted butter, cubed
130g	Unrefined caster sugar

Pre-heat the oven to 190°C.

Sift the flour, cocoa powder, bicarbonate of soda and salt together into a bowl, and set to one side.

Using a mixer fitted with the paddle attachment, cream the butter and sugar on medium speed until the mixture becomes light and fluffy (approximately 5 minutes).

Reduce the speed of the mixer to low, then add the flour mixture to the mixing bowl. Continue to mix until the dough comes together.

Using an ice-cream scoop, portion the dough into balls (approximately 40g per ball). Place them on a parchment-lined baking tray roughly 10cm apart.

Place the tray in the oven for 10 minutes.

Allow to cool on the tray for 2 minutes before placing the biscuits on a cooling rack to cool completely.

The biscuits will keep for up to 5 days in an airtight tin.

Caraway biscuits

These were inspired by Naples biscuits, an old version of sponge fingers that were often flavoured with rosewater or caraway. Although it's not much used in Britain these days, caraway has a long history – it's said to be the oldest cultivated spice plant in Europe – and has a distinctive, slight citrusy flavour with a bit of a kick.

The dough can be frozen in individual portions and baked for surprise guests.

Makes approx. 20 biscuits

125g	Plain flour
½ tsp	Baking powder
½ tsp	Salt
50g	Ground almonds
150g	Cold unsalted butter, cubed
100g	Unrefined caster sugar
	Seeds from 1 vanilla pod
10g	Caraway seeds, lightly toasted
40g	Egg yolks (approx. 2 large eggs)

Sift the flour, baking powder and salt into a bowl, and then stir in the ground almonds. Set to one side.

Using a mixer fitted with the paddle attachment, cream the butter and sugar on medium speed until the mixture becomes light and fluffy (approximately 5 minutes).

Reduce the mixer speed to low and add the flour mixture, the vanilla seeds and caraway seeds. Continue to mix gently until the mixture resembles fine breadcrumbs.

Add the egg yolks one at a time and mix until the liquid has been fully incorporated and a soft dough has formed. Mould the dough into a flat rectangle and wrap it in clingfilm. Place in the fridge to rest for at least 2 hours.

After 2 hours, place the dough between two pieces of baking parchment and roll into a rectangle approximately 5mm thick. Place in the freezer for at least 20 minutes.

Pre-heat the oven to 150°C.

Cut the parchment and dough to fit a baking tray measuring approximately 30 × 20cm, then remove the top layer of baking parchment.

Place the tray in the oven for 10 minutes, then turn the tray round and continue baking for a further 3–5 minutes or until the dough is lightly golden all over.

Slide the baked biscuit on to a chopping board and, using a pastry cutter, cut out the biscuits, or cut into rectangles (approximately 3 × 5cm), depending on what shape biscuits you prefer. Remove to a cooling rack to cool.

The biscuits will keep for up to 5 days in an airtight tin.

Madeleines with chocolate sauce or lemon curd

If you've only ever had commercial, pre-baked madeleines, then these will be a revelation. They're lovely dipped in lemon curd or chocolate sauce, or some lightly whipped cream mixed with a little sugar and vanilla. You'll need a 12-hole madeleine tray.

Makes 12 madeleines

80g	Ground almonds
200g	Melted brown butter, plus extra for brushing (see tip, p.204)
80g	Plain flour, plus extra for dusting the moulds
200g	Icing sugar
6	Large egg whites
1 tbsp	Runny honey (see tip, p.359)

To serve

Chocolate sauce or lemon curd (right)

Place the ground almonds in a food processor and grind them to a fine powder (approximately 30–45 seconds).

Lightly brush the indentations of a 12-hole madeleine tray with brown butter and sprinkle a little flour over the top. Shake off any excess flour.

Place the finely ground almonds, flour and icing sugar into the bowl of a mixer fitted with a paddle attachment. Mix for 1–2 minutes or until well combined.

Whisk the egg whites until just combined and add them to the bowl of the mixer. Mix for 3–4 minutes, then add the honey and mix for another minute. Finally, add the remaining brown butter and mix for an additional 3 minutes or until well combined. Scrape the bottom of the bowl with a spatula and mix for a further 2 minutes.

Using a spoon, pour the batter into the moulds, leaving a 2mm gap from the top edge all the way round. Place the filled tray in the fridge and allow to rest for 3 hours.

After 3 hours, pre-heat the oven to 190°C. Place the tray in the oven. Bake for approximately 14 minutes or until golden brown. Turn the madeleines over on to a cooling rack and allow to cool for 20 minutes before eating.

Chocolate sauce

500g	Water
20	Coffee beans
180g	Cocoa powder
¼ tsp	Salt
340g	Unrefined caster sugar
60g	Chocolate, chopped (minimum 70% cocoa solids)

Bring the water, coffee beans, cocoa powder and salt to a simmer in a small saucepan. Turn off the heat and cover.

Place the sugar in a stainless-steel saucepan over a medium heat to make a dry caramel (p.307). When the caramel is golden brown, reduce the heat and slowly pour in the water mixture, stirring continuously. The mixture should automatically boil from the heat of the sugar.

Then add the chopped chocolate to the caramel and mix well. Remove from the heat. Pass through a fine sieve, cover and cool before serving.

Lemon curd

4	Lemons
170g	Unsalted butter, cubed
220g	Unrefined caster sugar
5	Medium eggs, beaten
1	Medium egg yolk, beaten

Using a vegetable peeler, take off the zest from three of the lemons. Roll all the lemons on a work surface with the palm of your hand (to make them release more juice). Juice them and measure out 150g.

Put the butter and sugar into a saucepan with the lemon juice, zest and eggs and place over a medium heat. Stir continuously for 10–15 minutes (do not allow to simmer) until the butter has melted and the sugar has dissolved. Increase the heat to medium-high and whisk the mixture until it reaches 70°C, then remove from the heat.

Pass the mixture through a fine sieve into a bowl. Cover with clingfilm to avoid a skin forming. Place the bowl in the fridge to cool for 1 hour.

Shortbread biscuits

The secret to these biscuits is replacing some of the butter with olive oil. It gives a lighter, crisper texture and a different flavour. And there are many possible flavour variations, too (see below).

It's important that the flour is added to the fat before the liquids, to stop the gluten in the flour from developing too much and making the dough tough rather than crumbly.

Makes approx. 20 biscuits

175g	Plain flour
½ tsp	Baking powder
½ tsp	Salt
110g	Cold unsalted butter, cubed
100g	Unrefined caster sugar
40g	Egg yolks, beaten (approx. 2 large egg yolks)
35g	Olive oil
	White caster sugar, for dusting

Sift the flour, baking powder and salt into a bowl and set to one side.

Using a mixer fitted with the paddle attachment, cream the butter and sugar on medium speed until the mixture becomes light and fluffy, being careful not to over-mix (approximately 5 minutes).

Reduce the speed of the mixer to low and add the flour. Continue to mix gently until the mixture resembles fine breadcrumbs.

Combine the egg yolks and olive oil and add them gradually to the bowl while mixing on low speed. Continue mixing until all the liquid has been incorporated and a soft dough has formed.

Mould the dough into a flat rectangle and wrap it in clingfilm. Place in the fridge to rest for at least 2 hours.

After 2 hours, place the dough between two pieces of baking parchment and roll out into a rectangle of approximately 5mm in thickness. Cut the parchment and dough to fit a tray measuring 30 × 20cm. Place the tray in the freezer for at least 20 minutes.

Pre-heat the oven to 150°C.

Remove the top layer of baking parchment and place the tray in the oven for 15–20 minutes. Turn the tray round and continue baking for a further 3–5 minutes until the dough is lightly golden all over.

While still warm, using a palette knife, slide the baked biscuit on to a chopping board and, using a sharp knife, cut into rectangles (approximately 3 × 5cm). Sprinkle with the caster sugar and allow to cool.

The biscuits will keep for up to 5 days in an airtight tin.

Almond shortbread
Replace 85g of the plain flour with ground almonds.

Walnut shortbread
Add 50g chopped walnuts with the flour.

Hazelnut shortbread
Add 50g chopped hazelnuts with the flour.

Millionaire shortbread

As with many sweet dishes, this shortbread really benefits from the addition of a little salt. When served at the Fat Duck, it's topped with what look like nuggets of gold. In fact they're flakes of fleur de sel coated in edible gold powder.

Makes 15 bars

For the shortbread

Shortbread biscuits (p.367), but using 125g plain flour and 50g ground almonds instead of 175g flour

For the salted butter caramel

200g	Double cream
190g	White caster sugar
150g	Unsalted butter
1 tsp	Salt
185g	Liquid glucose
190g	Whole milk

For the chocolate

250g	Dark chocolate, chopped (minimum 60% cocoa solids)
10g	Unsalted butter

Make and bake the biscuits as described in the shortbread recipe on p.367. Do not sprinkle with sugar. Keep in an airtight tin until required.

For the salted butter caramel, warm the cream in a small saucepan over a low heat but do not boil.

Place the sugar, butter, salt, glucose and milk in a large stainless-steel saucepan over a medium-high heat, stirring until the butter has melted and the sugar has dissolved.

Swap the wooden spoon for a whisk at this stage and continue stirring regularly as the caramel begins to thicken and change colour, so that it doesn't catch on the bottom of the pan. Once the caramel has reached a temperature of 100°C, it is important to whisk without interruption for the remainder of the time until it reaches its final temperature.

As soon as the caramel reaches 153°C, remove from the heat and add the cream in three stages, being careful of all the steam that will be released. After the last addition, stir well, making sure the caramel has come together well. Pass the caramel through a fine sieve and pour on to a 30 × 20cm baking tray lined with baking paper.

At this point, allow the caramel to set for at least 4 hours before continuing.

Cut the set caramel into rectangles measuring 3 × 5cm and store in an airtight container in between sheets of baking paper in the fridge.

For the chocolate, break the chocolate into chunks and melt it in a bowl over a pan of simmering water (p.304). When the chocolate has melted, stir in the butter until it melts and has been fully incorporated.

To assemble, place the caramel rectangles on top of the shortbread biscuits and put them on to a cooling rack.

Drizzle the melted chocolate over the top, making sure to cover the entire surface. Allow to stand for a few minutes, then remove the bars from the rack and place them on a baking tray lined with parchment paper. Allow to set in the fridge for 30 minutes.

Cornbread muffins

These were originally developed to go with chilli con carne (p.156). Although a chilli is more usually accompanied by rice, corn chips or a baked potato, I think that a soft, light muffin is a better foil for the pepper heat.

You can replace the preserved jalapeños with 50g of grated Cheddar or other hard cheese.

Makes 12 muffins

120g	Plain flour, plus extra for dusting
120g	Cornmeal
20g	Baking powder
1 tsp	Salt
40g	Unrefined caster sugar
280g	Buttermilk
100g	Whole milk
2	Large eggs, lightly beaten
50g	Unsalted butter, melted and cooled, plus extra for greasing
3	Preserved jalapeño chillies, diced

Pre-heat the oven to 180°C.

Sift the flour, cornmeal, baking powder, salt and sugar into a bowl and make a well in the centre. Mix the buttermilk, milk, eggs and melted butter and pour into the well. Stir with a wooden spoon until the mixture comes together. Stir in the chillies.

Butter and flour a 12-hole muffin tin and fill the moulds three-quarters of the way up.

Bake the muffins in the oven for 20 minutes.

Remove from the oven, de-mould and allow to cool on a cooling rack.

Pork scratchings

A classic pub snack, but if you make it yourself it'll taste so much better than anything you'd get in a packet. And it's dead easy to do, so long as you make friends with your local butcher, because that'll be the best place to get hold of some pig skin.

To turn pig skin into scratchings, you need it to have just the right amount of moisture. If you drive off too little, the skin will be chewy and pliable. If you drive off too much, however, it won't puff up, as it's that little bit of moisture left in the skin turning to steam that creates the light crunchy texture of good crackling.

The crackling for the braised pork belly on p.164 is made similarly: the skin is removed from the belly, placed in the oven only during the last third of the meat's cooking time (any longer would dry it out too much), and then given a final blast in a high oven. Here, though, because the pieces of pork skin are smaller, water is added to the baking tray under the pig skin for the last 10–15 minutes of cooking. This creates steam which helps to puff up the skin, and because the heat is less dry and harsh, there's less risk of burning the skin.

Serves 4

1	Piece of pig skin
	Salt

Pre-heat the oven to 70°C.

Clean the skin of as much fat as possible by scraping with a knife so that just the translucent skin remains.

Slice the skin into bite-sized pieces with a very sharp knife. Sprinkle with salt and place on a cooling rack. Place the cooling rack in the oven over a roasting tray and allow to dry for 5 hours.

After 5 hours, remove the cooling rack from the oven and increase the temperature to 240°C. Fill the roasting tray a third of the way up with boiling water, place the cooling rack on top, and return the tray to the pre-heated oven.

Cook for 10–15 minutes or until the skin has puffed up and become crispy.

Flavoured popcorn

Once the kernels are puffed and well coated in sugar (which here acts as a kind of glue to make the flavouring stick to the corn), you can coat them in cinnamon, tandoori or curry flavourings, or any other flavouring you like the idea of.

Serves 4

50g   Groundnut or grapeseed oil
115g   White caster sugar
130g   Popcorn kernels
       Chosen spice mix (below)

Heat the oil and the sugar in a large saucepan over a medium-high heat until it reaches 150°C.

Add the popcorn and stir with a wooden spoon to coat the kernels with the sugar and oil. Cover the pan with a lid and the corn should begin to pop for approximately 2 minutes.

When the popping becomes less rapid, remove the pan from the heat and allow to stand until the popping has stopped completely.

Pour the popped corn into a bowl and immediately sprinkle the spice mix on top. Using salad servers, toss the corn to ensure the spice mix is evenly distributed.

Cinnamon flavouring

1 tbsp   Ground cinnamon
50g   White caster sugar

Curry flavouring

1 tbsp   Curry powder
1 tbsp   Turmeric powder

Tandoori flavouring

2 tbsp   Tandoori spice mix

Toffee popcorn

The air bubbles caused by the addition of bicarbonate of soda give the caramel a lovely light structure. (The same process is used to make honeycomb.) However, it's important not to add too much bicarb as it can affect the colour and flavour.

Serves 6

450g   Unrefined caster sugar
250g   Groundnut or grapeseed oil
1 tsp Salt
½ tsp Bicarbonate of soda
250g   Popcorn kernels

Put the sugar into a large saucepan and place over a medium-high heat. Do not touch the pan until all the sugar has begun to melt, at which point use a spatula to gently mix the melted and un-melted sugar together. With a pastry brush that has been dipped in water, brush the inside of the pan to prevent the sugar crystallizing.

When all the sugar has melted, add the oil and stir to combine. Mix in the salt and bicarbonate of soda.

When the caramel begins to bubble, add the popcorn and cover the pan with a lid. The popcorn kernels will begin to pop for approximately 2 minutes.

When the popping stops, remove the pan from the heat and pour the popcorn into a bowl. Allow to cool before serving.

Puffed spelt

This began life as an accompaniment for a risotto: I took the idea of puffed breakfast cereal and turned it into a toasted rice tuile for the garnish, alongside a cup of mushroom velouté. Even then I thought that the puffed grains would make a terrific snack.

You could use other grains, such as rice or wild rice, instead of spelt.

Serves 4

100g	Cooked and drained pearled spelt (see packet for cooking instructions)
300g	Groundnut or grapeseed oil
	Salt

Pre-heat the oven to 80°C.

Spread the cooked spelt in a single layer on a parchment-lined baking tray and allow to dry in the oven for 2 hours.

Heat the oil to 180°C and drop the dried spelt into the oil in small batches. After a couple of seconds the spelt will puff up and float to the surface. Remove the puffed spelt with a slotted spoon and drain on kitchen paper.

Season immediately with salt.

Crystallized nuts

Here the magic of crystallization (p.357) is used to create a sweet nutty snack with a wonderful texture, which can be eaten by itself or used as a garnish for ice-cream sundaes (p.330) and other puddings. You can also turn the nuts into a more savoury nibble simply by sprinkling with salt before serving. You could use other nuts as well, such as pecans, hazelnuts or macadamia.

Serves 4

200g   Pistachios
200g   White caster sugar

Pre-heat the oven to 170°C.

Place the nuts on a baking tray and toast in the oven for 12 minutes.

In the meantime, put 150g water and the sugar into a small saucepan. Place it over a medium-high heat and bring to the boil.

When the temperature of the liquid reaches 135°C, or the syrup is beginning to colour at the edge of the pan, add the pistachios and whisk until the syrup has completely crystallized and coated the nuts.

Pour the coated nuts on to a baking tray lined with baking parchment and allow to cool.

The nuts can be kept in an airtight container for up to 6 months.

Spiced nuts

You can use any spice mix you like in this recipe – five-spice powder (p.264), barbecue, Cajun, tandoori, rose and coriander salt, ras-el-hanout – though if it's a really spicy mix you might want to use less than the recipe suggests. The egg whites act as a glue for fixing the flavouring (just as the sugar does in the flavoured popcorn on p.373).

Serves 4

250g   Mixed nuts
10g   Egg white, beaten (less than 1 egg)
10g   Spice mix

Pre-heat the oven to 180°C.

Place the mixed nuts on a baking tray and roast them in the oven for 7–10 minutes until beginning to colour. Remove from the oven and allow to cool.

Once cool, place the nuts in a mixing bowl with the egg whites and the spice mix and mix together well.

Return the nuts to the tray and place in the oven for 5 minutes.

Allow to cool completely before serving. The nuts can be kept in an airtight container for up to 2 weeks.

Pimm's

Like strawberries and cream and rain showers, Pimm's is a classic feature of the Great British Summer. Here I've given the drink a bit of an update, infusing it with fruit and herbs for several hours to make it truly aromatic, and topping it with a cucumber foam to create a stimulating contrast of textures. Serving the Pimm's with crystal clear ice cubes containing cucumber and borage just adds to the sense of occasion – even if it is raining.

Serves 6–8

For the cucumber foam

500g   Cucumber juice (approx. 1 cucumber)
30g   Egg white (approx. 1 large egg)

For the Pimm's

750g   Pimm's No 1 cup (1 bottle)
100g   Lemon slices (approx. 2 lemons)
75g   Lime slices (approx. 2 limes)
150g   Orange slices (approx. 2 oranges)
200g   Apple slices (approx. 2 apples)
10g   Mint leaves
600g   Ginger beer
1.2kg   Lemon tonic water

To serve

Cucumber and borage flower ice cubes (below)

For the cucumber foam, strain the cucumber juice through a fine sieve into a tall container.

Add the egg white and, using a hand blender, blitz together until thoroughly mixed.

Pour the cucumber and egg whites into a cream whipper charged with two N_2O charges (p.356). Place in the fridge for at least 30 minutes before serving.

Pour the Pimm's into a large container, add the fruit slices and mint leaves, and place in the fridge to infuse for at least 6 hours. Strain into a bottle or jug and discard the fruit.

To make the drink, in a large bowl mix the infused Pimms with the ginger beer and tonic water and pour into large jugs with the cucumber and borage flower ice cubes. You could also add some fresh fruit.

As you pour individual glasses, top each one with a layer of cucumber foam.

Cucumber and borage flower ice cubes

The de-ionized water will ensure that the ice cubes are completely clear, so you can see whatever is frozen within them. Try making ice cubes with raspberries, blueberries, herbs or lemon pieces, too.

Borage flowers (or other edible flowers)
Cucumber skin, cut into small batons
De-ionized water (Specialist ingredients, p.394)

Place a flower and several batons of cucumber skin in each compartment of an ice-cube tray.

Pour in de-ionized water and place the tray in the freezer until frozen hard.

Negroni

The story goes that this cocktail was invented in Florence in the 1920s, when Count Camillo Negroni asked a bartender to make him an Americano (equal parts Campari and sweet vermouth topped with soda), but with gin in place of the soda.

I'm a big fan of Campari – its acidity and bitterness make it a excellent palate cleanser that really wakes the mouth up. And here I've added my own twist to the Count's invention – an orange and prosecco foam topping the glass.

Serves 6

For the orange and prosecco foam

300g	Orange juice
20g	Fructose (fruit sugar)
5g	Pectin powder
	Zest and juice of 2 oranges
80g	Egg whites (approx. 4 large eggs)
70g	Prosecco

For the Negroni

250g	Campari
250g	Dry white vermouth
250g	Gin
	Ice cubes
200g	Soda water

For the foam, place the 300g orange juice in a saucepan and place the pan over a medium heat. Bring to the boil.

In the meantime, mix the fructose and pectin together in a small bowl, then add to the orange juice in the pan. Whisk continuously while the liquid comes back to the boil. Remove from the heat and allow to cool completely.

When cold, add the orange zest and allow to infuse for 2 hours.

Strain the syrup and mix with the fresh orange juice, the egg whites and prosecco. Blitz the mixture with a hand blender for approximately 10 seconds, then pour into a cream whipper charged with two N_2O charges (p.356). Place the whipper in the fridge for 2 hours before serving.

To make the drink, mix the alcohols together in a big jug.

Fill six tumblers with ice cubes and divide the alcohol between the glasses. Top up each glass with approximately 30g of soda water.

Using the cream whipper, dispense a layer of foam on top of the drink.

Spiced gin and tonic

This recipe uses a hot infusion (p.24) to give this drink a new dimension. Adding the flavourings, and then infusing them in the gin along with lemon peel, brings a spiciness that enhances the juniper of the gin.

Serves 8

For the infused gin

500g	Gin
5g	Coriander seeds
5g	Fennel seeds
5g	Juniper berries
	Peel of 1 lemon (use a vegetable peeler)

To mix the drink

Ice cubes
Tonic water
Lemon peel (use a vegetable peeler)

Place the gin in a saucepan over a medium heat. Add the coriander seeds, fennel seeds and juniper berries, allow to come to the boil and remove the pan from the heat.

Allow to cool to room temperature for approximately 45 minutes.

Add the lemon peel, having rubbed it between two fingers to release the oils, and leave to infuse for 2 hours. Strain through a sieve and keep in the fridge until needed.

To make the drink, fill a tall glass with ice cubes.

Pour the gin into the bottom of the glass so it is a quarter full, then top up the rest of the glass with tonic water. Using a stirrer, mix the drink.

Twist a strip of the lemon peel between two fingers in order to release the essential oils. Rub the edge of the glass with the skin side of the lemon and then drop it in the drink before serving.

Cucumber gin and tonic

In contrast to my spiced gin and tonic, this version uses a cold infusion (p.24) to bring a fantastic cucumber zing to the drink that's perfect for a hot summer's day. (Using a cold infusion rather than a hot one helps to preserve the freshness of the raw vegetable. Heat would produce more of a stewed cucumber flavour.)

Serves 8

500g	Peeled cucumber
500g	Gin
	Cucumber ice cubes (p.379)
	Tonic water
	Lemon peel (use a vegetable peeler)

Place the cucumber and the gin in a tall container and, using a hand blender, blitz for approximately 10 seconds. Cover and place in the fridge to infuse for 16 hours.

Strain through a sieve and keep cold until needed.

To make the drink, fill a tall glass with ice cubes.

Pour gin into the bottom of the glass so it is a quarter full, then top up the rest of the glass with tonic water. Using a stirrer, mix the drink.

Twist a strip of the lemon peel between two fingers in order to release the essential oils. Rub the edge of the glass with the skin side of the lemon and then drop it in the drink before serving.

Whisky sour

Along with juleps, flips and slings, sours are one of the original families of cocktails and date back to at least the 1860s, when they appeared in Jerry Thomas's legendary *Bar-Tender's Guide*. Nowadays, these simple vintage cocktails (a really traditional whisky sour consists of three parts whisky, two parts lemon juice and one part gomme syrup) are often overlooked in favour of later, fancier concoctions, but there's much to recommend a whisky sour, with its complex, subtle whisky flavours and that hint of citric sourness.

Here once again I've added a foam for textural contrast, but this time it contains a little white truffle oil. Truffles have an almost paraffin-like note that works very well with a peaty, smoky and leathery malt like Laphroaig, though it's also good with a fruity Oban. Whatever whisky you choose, make sure it's a good-quality malt.

To make the lemon syrup, place the lemon slices and fructose in a container, cover tightly and place in a warm place for a couple of days until the fructose has turned into a syrup. Strain through a sieve and reserve the syrup, discarding the lemon slices.

Place 120g cold tap water along with the rest of the ingredients for the whisky base in a cocktail shaker, and shake for 30 seconds until well combined.

Place 120g cold tap water and the ingredients for the foam in a tall container and blitz using a hand blender for 30 seconds. Pour into a cream whipper charged with two N_2O charges (p.356). Place the whipper in the fridge for 30 minutes before serving.

Fill a tall glass with ice. Add the whisky base to fill three-quarters of the glass. Squirt a layer of the foam over the whisky and serve immediately.

Serves 4–6

For the lemon syrup

1	Lemon, sliced
20g	Fructose (fruit sugar)

For the whisky base

280g	Whisky, such as Oban or Laphroaig
	Lemon syrup (see above)
40g	Lemon juice
	Angostura bitters, 16 drops

For the foam

50g	Lemon juice
15g	Egg whites
	White truffle oil, 2 drops

To serve

Ice cubes

Hot chocolate

Rich, sweet and warming, hot chocolate has got to be the ultimate comfort drink, and I've added cream and real chocolate to make it about as comforting as you can get. Frothing the mixture with a hand blender gives it a lovely light, velvety texture.

Serve with pineapple, orange-blossom or rosewater marshmallows (p.345).

Serves 2

100g	Dark drinking chocolate
55g	Dark chocolate, broken into small pieces (minimum 60% cocoa solids)
60g	Whipping cream
	Pinch of salt

Put 200g cold tap water and the drinking chocolate into a saucepan and bring to the boil over a medium heat.

When boiling, add the dark chocolate, whipping cream and salt, and stir until the chocolate has melted.

Using a hand blender, aerate the chocolate before pouring into a big mug to serve.

Specialist kit

I'm not going to be exhaustive about this. If you're a keen cook you've probably got most of the basic kit, like a vegetable peeler, a sharpening steel, a few spatulas, some large kitchen spoons, slotted spoons and wooden spoons (some of which have a squared-off edge for scraping right into the corners of the pan), and a whisk with enough wires to really get some air into a mixture. I would make a case, though, for a solid set of pans and some good knives.

Pans that don't have a heavy base tend to warp and don't cook as efficiently, making it more difficult to control the temperature and easier to burn the food. A heavy-based pan gives you a much better chance of a successful outcome. Using a sharp, well-balanced knife is one of the pleasures of working in a kitchen. It performs tasks quickly and efficiently, and it won't damage the food. (A blunt knife bludgeons the food cells apart rather than cutting through them neatly.) It's safer, too, because it's much less likely to slip and cut you.

These, then, are the basics. But there are a few other pieces of kit that I think are almost as essential. Some of them will be familiar but probably not much used, others are modern technological innovations, and all of them will make a big difference to what you achieve in the kitchen.

Blow-torch
Essential for caramelizing the sugar and getting rid of the bubbles on the top of a crème brûlée or parfait, a blow-torch can also be used to flame alcohol, melt cheese and, of course, brown meat and fish. Buy a heavy-duty one from a DIY store rather than those dinky little things on sale in most kitchenware shops – they're too weak to do the job properly.

Cream whipper
Also known as a whipped cream dispenser or creamer, this is useful for aerating cream, but it has also proved to be an invaluable tool for creating foams (p.356). It works by injecting air into ingredients by means of an N_2O cartridge (or cream charger), or a CO_2 cartridge (or soda charger). There are other ways of getting bubbles into a liquid, such as a whisk or hand blender, but the cream whipper is less labour-intensive and produces a light, delicate structure. The dispenser and its cartridges are available in good cookware stores and online.

Digital probe
I know that many people think probes are too high-tech for the domestic kitchen, but they really take all the guesswork out of cooking items such as meat, fish and caramel. Many of the recipes in this book give a probe-temperature for when the food is ready, because that's the clearest and least subjective method of passing on precise cooking instructions.

Giving a temperature, rather than describing in words the exact moment at which a custard has thickened sufficiently, makes it much easier to explain exactly when to remove the pan from the heat. A digital probe is also the easiest way to find out what's going on inside a joint of meat without cutting it open. Probes are not particularly expensive or difficult to find these days, and they soon become indispensable.

Digital scales
The tiniest thing can spoil a dish. Too little seasoning, and the flavours appear flat and bland; too much liquid, and the texture's sloppy rather than firm. And so, while intuition, instinct, touch, taste and smell are all essential to good cooking, so too is precision, not just for baking but for every area of cuisine. A decent set of scales is, therefore, a must.

Mechanical clock-face scales are often inaccurate and unreliable (try weighing 45g of flour on one – it'll be different each time), particularly since you have to judge by eye where the needle is resting. Digital scales take the guesswork out of this, and a good set will be able to measure in 1g increments, which gives the cook a lot of control and can be useful for particularly complex recipes. They also have the practical advantage that you can recalibrate them to zero, which makes it easy to put a number of ingredients together, weighing each one as you go. Equally, it makes it easy to weigh liquid by putting a bowl on the scales, then returning the readout to zero before pouring in the liquid.

Digital timer

Timing may be one of the secrets of good cooking, but an awful lot of people still rely on an inaccurate wind-up egg timer for their kitchen tasks. Some ovens now come with a digital timer built into them, but if yours doesn't, it's worth buying one. It will time accurately, right down to the seconds, which is the kind of precision you often need in the kitchen.

Food mixer

A mixer is expensive and can take up a lot of counter space, but if you like making desserts, cakes and pastry, it's definitely worth buying one. It's not just a labour-saving device, cutting down on the elbow grease involved in creaming and combining, it also does the job better. Mixing by machine incorporates the ingredients much more thoroughly and evenly than mixing by hand. Besides, if you want to make dry ice ice-cream – and you will, because it has a smoothness like no ice-cream you've ever tasted before – you'll need a food mixer for the churning.

Hand blender

Even if you already have a liquidizer, a hand blender is a very useful tool to have in the kitchen for the quick blitzing of ingredients – to aerate soups, for example, or whip cream, or break up a set liquid to create a fluid gel. It's also essential for my special technique for improving the texture of ice-cream by giving it a blitz after it has been churned (p.277).

Ice-cream machine

Although it's technically possible to make ice-cream without one, the ice-cream recipes in this book are designed to be made either with dry ice (p.279) or with a machine. There are all sorts of ice-cream makers on the market, from the traditional bucket-style freezer that uses ice and salt, to sophisticated, expensive machines with an integral refrigeration unit. The recipes in this book employ the latter, but you can also use a machine that has a canister which can be pre-frozen in the freezer. These are moderately priced and freeze quickly, which is very important, because the faster it freezes the smoother the final ice-cream will be. Many ice-cream makers

churn at −5°C. However, a removeable canister will be placed in the freezer first, chilling it to −18°C. When it's returned to the machine, that colder temperature will kickstart the freezing and crystallizing process very efficiently.

Mandolin

There are a number of occasions when the cook needs to slice vegetables finely and consistently: thin discs of potato for a creamy gratin; aromatic vegetables sliced small so they give up lots of their flavour to a stock or soup; ribbons of fennel to garnish a risotto or for use in salads. Unless you've got the knife skills of an automaton, a mandolin or Japanese slicer is the best way to cut fine slices of the same depth, time after time. It's basically a frame with a sharp blade set into it, over which the vegetable is repeatedly slid in order to shave off slices. It's a very useful, practical piece of kit, but it is extremely sharp. Make sure you employ the safety guard when using it.

Muslin

Muslin is easy to get hold of in fabric shops as well as kitchen stores, and is extremely useful in the kitchen. It's great for lining a sieve for a seriously fine straining (wet the muslin first, which makes it better at trapping particles), and is a neat material for bagging ingredients that you want to use for flavouring and then discard, such as a bouquet garni (p.34) or the spices for the brine for the braised pork belly on p.164 and the juniper berries for the braised cabbage on p.250.

Oven thermometer

The precise regulation of temperature is as important as the precise weighing of ingredients. You might think that the thermostat on your oven means you've got this covered, but in fact thermostats are often inaccurate and inconsistent.

Since one of the main tasks in the kitchen is controlling the amount of heat applied to food, it's vital that the cook is in control of it. If you've gone to the trouble of accurately preparing a recipe, you don't want to close the oven door and just cross your fingers. And, if a recipe does go wrong, you need to be able to find out whether

the oven is the culprit. An oven thermometer is the best way to achieve these aims. It'll establish how accurately your oven performs (if it's way off you might want to ask the manufacturer to recalibrate it), and it'll show you that food is being cooked at the designated temperature. This gives the cook one less variable to worry about, and is particularly valuable when cooking meat slowly at very low temperatures, where the difference of a degree or two can affect the outcome.

Pressure cooker

The foundation of so many soups, sauces and risottos is a good stock, and a pressure cooker really maximizes the amount of flavour you can extract from a stock's ingredients. Because it's a sealed, pressurized container, it holds on to lots of the flavour that normally evaporates when you make stock in a stockpot. And it heats liquid to a temperature above 100°C, generating lots of reactions that produce new, complex flavours. A pressure cooker is the stock-maker's secret weapon. It might seem a big outlay for a piece of equipment to make stocks, but once you've tasted the results, you'll see it's worth it.

Refractometer

The natural sugar content of fruit can vary a lot, making it difficult to judge exactly how much you need to make a sorbet (pp.290–2), or a syrup for the passionfruit pastilles (p.342) or the arlette with pressed apple terrine (p.315). One way of eliminating guesswork is to use a refractometer, which measures the way light bends as it passes from one material to another. The more sugar crystals are present in a mixture, the more the light refracts. By putting a drop of liquid on its lens and looking through the eyepiece, you get a reading measured in degrees Brix that effectively tells you how much sugar is present. The higher the number, the higher the percentage of sugar crystals.

Once you've made a syrup to exactly the consistency you want, you can take a reading and use that number as the guideline the next time you make the same syrup. It's an inexpensive and relatively uncomplicated piece of equipment, and is available online and at good kitchen equipment suppliers.

Sieves

I suspect that in many domestic kitchens the sieve is used only for sifting flour. In a professional kitchen, however, sieves are in constant use, straining sauces and soups, caramels and custards. Picking up this habit can have a real impact on the food you serve at home. Straining is simple to do – for the recipes in this book a regular and a fine sieve will cover all your needs – but it produces a lovely silky texture and brings a refinement to a dish. Although any fine sieve will do the job, it's worth investing in a conical sieve (or chinois) because it holds a decent amount, making it easier to filter large quantities.

Sous-vide machine and water-bath

Up until recently the water-bath and sous-vide machine were mainly used in the science lab or for food storage. This has changed, and now restaurants are increasingly employing them to cook all sorts of dishes. The food is placed in a bag from which the air has been removed (sous-vide means 'under a vacuum'), which is a very clean and efficient vehicle for cooking, and placed in a water-bath, which cooks the food very evenly to exactly the temperature the cook chooses, with no danger of overcooking. The technology makes it easy for any cook to produce precisely and perfectly cooked food – and to do so consistently. The process and the technology are described in more detail on pp.191–5. As far as I'm concerned, sous-vide is one of the most exciting developments in the culinary world for years. It's going to revolutionize the domestic kitchen.

Specialist ingredients

The recipes in this book use some unusual ingredients. Until recently many of these would have been hard to find, but Asian and other ethnic supermarkets are cropping up all over the place, and the internet offers a way to source even the most obscure of foods.

Agar-agar flakes
Although lacking the melt-in-mouth texture of gelatine, agar-agar is a useful setting agent since it's heat-resistant and can therefore be used in warm dishes where gelatine isn't a viable option. It's also a practical vegetarian alternative to gelatine. Agar-agar is available in good supermarkets and health-food stores.

Bonito flakes (katsuobushi)
Katsuobushi is the Japanese name for a preparation of skipjack tuna also known as bonito. Parts of the fish are smoked, fermented and dried over a period of three to five months until they are light brown and look like blocks of wood. These are then shaved into little flakes. Bonito flakes give a smoky characteristic to the Japanese stock dashi, the foundation of miso soup, as well as the umami broth on p.183. Bags of bonito flakes are available from Asian supermarkets.

Brik pastry
Extremely thin and crispy once cooked, brik pastry is similar to filo pastry. Moroccan in origin, it can be found in ethnic stores and bigger supermarkets. I find it more delicate and less floury than standard filo.

Citric acid
Citric acid is what gives citrus fruits their tartness. It is also an anti-oxidant, meaning it prolongs the life of such things as elderflower cordial. It is available as a powder from pharmacies or online.

De-ionized water
De-ionized water is a form of purified water that has been processed to remove minerals such as sodium and calcium. This makes it a great liquid in which to braise pulses – the presence of calcium can prevent lentils from softening fully. The absence of solids means de-ionized water can also be used to make crystal-clear ice cubes that hold their temperature well and melt slowly. It's used in car batteries, so it's available in garages.

Dried konbu
Used extensively in Japanese cuisine for stock (dashi), sushi and sashimi, among other things, konbu is a type of seaweed that is especially rich in the savoury umami taste. It comes in dry sheets and can be bought in Asian stores and some mainstream supermarkets.

Dry ice
Dry ice – the solid form of carbon dioxide – is the stuff used to create mist effects on stage. It's extremely cold (–80°C), which makes it ideal for freezing an ice-cream mixture very quickly so that it's as smooth as possible. Too cold for the freezer, dry ice is best stored in a styrofoam box or whatever packaging it came in. It's available online, and safe so long as you remember that, due to its low temperature, it must be handled with protective gloves.

Freeze-dried raspberries
These are the desiccated raspberries found in breakfast cereals and muesli, available in health-food shops or online.

Glycerine
Glycerine – also known as glycerol – is a mildly sweet, colourless liquid that is hygroscopic: it attracts and holds on to water molecules. It is often used by the food industry to make foodstuffs such as gummy sweets moist. This is the role it plays in the edible wrappers on p.337, keeping them flexible and preventing them from drying out too much. It is available from pharmacies.

Matcha green tea powder
Matcha is a finely milled Japanese green tea often used not just for drinking but as a flavouring for noodles or green tea ice-cream. It's becoming increasingly popular and is available from Asian supermarkets and online.

Mirin
Similar to sake but less alcoholic, mirin is a Japanese type of rice wine. The condiment is used in sushi, teriyaki sauce and as a seasoning for grilled fish. It's available from bigger supermarkets and Asian stores.

Miso paste

Miso is a traditional Japanese seasoning made from fermented brown rice, barley or soya beans. It forms the base of miso soup and is rich in umami. It is available from bigger supermarkets and Asian stores.

Mushroom ketchup

Mushroom ketchup is great for boosting the flavours of stews, sauces, soups and vegetarian dishes. Long before the invention of tomato ketchup in America at the start of the nineteenth century, ketchup-type condiments were made with all sorts of other ingredients, including walnuts, lemons, anchovies and even oysters. Mushroom ketchup is available from bigger supermarkets.

Nori seaweed

Nori is a dried seaweed used to wrap sushi rolls, available from bigger supermarkets and Asian stores.

Panko

Panko is a type of very light breadcrumb used in Japanese cuisine as a crunchy coating for fried foods. It is available from Asian supermarkets and online.

Ras-el-hanout

A Moroccan spice mix typically made with cardamom, clove, cinnamon, ground chilli peppers, coriander, cumin, nutmeg, peppercorns, rose petals and turmeric. It's available in most good supermarkets.

Shaoxing wine

Shaoxing is a Chinese rice wine that is drunk as well as used in Chinese cuisine as a marinade or to add flavour to sauces. It is similar to dry sherry and, if you can't get hold of it, you can use Manzanilla instead. It is available from bigger supermarkets and Asian stores.

Smoking chips

You can smoke foods using all sorts of substances, such as tea leaves and essential oils, but wood chips are most commonly used. These are available from good kitchen shops, some garden centres and online, and there's often a choice of several kinds of wood – you might want to experiment with different types to see which you prefer.

Sodium citrate

Sodium citrate is the sodium salt of citric acid. It helps cheese to melt together well during cooking, which is why it is used by food companies to make cheese slices. But it's also perfect for ensuring that the cheese sauce for cauliflower macaroni cheese has a nice loose texture. It is available as a powder from pharmacies or online.

Soy sauce

Chinese soy sauce comes in light and dark forms. Light soy is thin, pale brown and salty, with a distinctive flavour. Dark soy is thicker, darker, richer, less salty and slightly sweeter than light soy. It's more often used for cooking than seasoning. Chinese soy sauce is made mainly from soy beans, but the Japanese version often includes wheat, which makes it light-coloured, sweet and aromatic, with an alcohol note from yeast. Make sure to use a good-quality version, which will have plenty of umami taste.

Soya lecithin

Lecithin is an emulsifier. The usual source is egg yolks, but soya lecithin is an egg-free alternative. It is available in powder form from health-food shops or online.

Szechuan peppercorns

Unrelated to black pepper or chilli pepper, Szechuan peppercorns are the dried outer fruit pods of a couple of trees in the citrus family. Used in Chinese food as a spice, the peppercorns have a unique lemony aroma and cause a tingly numbness on the tongue when eaten. They are available from Asian supermarkets or online.

Togarashi pepper flakes

These Japanese red chilli flakes are a spicy seasoning. Available from bigger supermarkets and Asian stores.

Vanilla bean paste

Less expensive than the pods, vanilla bean paste contains vanilla seeds and vanilla extract for a powerful vanilla flavour. It's available from bigger supermarkets or online.

Wonton wrappers

The thin egg pastry squares used to wrap Asian dumplings are available from Asian supermarkets or online.

Using this book

Modern recipes are often designed to be as brief as possible, in the mistaken belief that shorter means more accessible. This demands a lot of reading between the lines on the part of the cook, and can be singularly unhelpful if things don't go according to plan. I've tried to write my recipes with enough detail that they're easy to follow, but at the same time they should help you to understand the culinary processes behind a particular dish.

There are, however, a number of points relevant to all the recipes that I'd like to outline here – the first concern how to get the best out of the recipes, and these are followed by some specific technical considerations.

Sourcing

It should go without saying that good ingredients are at the heart of good food. It's not just a matter of taste and flavour, it's a question of how the ingredients behave during cooking. Cheap meat that has been artificially plumped up with water, for example, will stew in the pan rather than fry, so it won't gain the flavours you're looking for. If you want the food you produce to look like the pictures in this book, and taste similar to mine, you'll need to search out the best ingredients you can.

Tracking down top-notch produce takes a bit of effort. Most food has a particular season when it's at its best, so it's worth taking this into account. For some foods, such as caul fat or fish bones, you'll most likely need to make friends with the butcher and the fishmonger. In any case, finding reliable, conscientious local suppliers is probably the best way of making sure you've got access to ingredients that you can trust to do the job well.

Precision

Cooking is about having fun and being creative. It's about following your nose – sometimes quite literally – to see whether ingredients will work together. However, there's also a place for precision in the kitchen and, contrary to popular belief, precision is not the enemy of creativity, nor does it take the emotion out of cooking. It's always puzzled me that while most people accept that baking requires exact measurement, they consider precision unnecessary when cooking a starter or main course.

Good cooking often depends on a delicate interplay of ingredients, and the more the cook takes control, the more likely they are to achieve the result they're looking for. When I'm creating recipes I might start by chucking a few things together, but somewhere along the line I'll be experimenting with tiny increments of different ingredients, just to gain exactly the effect I want. The best way of giving you the chance to reproduce these recipes at home, it seems to me, is to specify precise weights, timings and temperatures. That's why weights are given only in metric and not in cups. While cups might seem like a convenient system that's appropriate for a book on home cooking, it can be quite inaccurate, particularly with irregular solids.

Reading the recipes

It might seem odd to include this advice, but you'd be amazed how many cooks just jump right in. Getting in the habit of reading through a recipe, and visualizing what's involved before you start, will make you a better and more efficient cook. Understanding the techniques and having ingredients and utensils ready from the outset gives you a much better chance of success with a recipe than shuttling from cookbook to cooker and back, juggling tools and tasks and liable to miss a step in the recipe or find, suddenly, that you don't have a key ingredient halfway through cooking.

Chopped weights

'200g carrots, peeled and finely sliced' is *not* the same as '200g peeled and finely sliced carrots'. The latter is a precise amount, calculated once you've got rid of the skin and tough outer layers. The former is an approximate quantity. If a recipe requires a specific amount of a vegetable, a chopped weight will be given. Otherwise, a whole weight or number of vegetables will be given. The same distinction is applied to garlic and herbs.

Weighing liquids

Have you ever tried to keep a measuring jug level while holding it up to your eye? It's easier and more accurate to weigh liquids on a scale rather than measure them by volume, not least because liquids have different densities, so a cup of oil won't weigh the same as a cup of water.

A decent pair of scales should have the capacity to recalibrate to zero, which makes the process simple: you put a jug on the scales, adjust the readout and then pour in the liquid. If your scales don't do this, you'll have to measure the jug, note the weight and take that into account as you add the water. It might sound like a hassle but inaccurate measurements can have a surprisingly big impact on a recipe, particularly when baking.

Small measurements
Amounts below 5g are weighed out with teaspoons, and should be flat, not heaped. Round measuring spoons with a deep bowl are more practical than ones with a shallower, oval-shaped bowl – you can run a finger over the top to flatten the contents.

Timing
Where an exact timing is crucial to the outcome of a dish, the precise time will be stipulated. Where more latitude is possible or necessary, a range is given with a qualification. For example: 'boil for 1 minute and 45 seconds exactly', as opposed to 'cook for 8–10 minutes until golden brown'.

Cooking oil
I use groundnut or grapeseed oil because they are light, odourless and have a high smoke point, so they can be used at reasonably high temperatures. Using olive oil for frying is less practical as it is expensive, it has quite a low smoke point, and most of its 'goodness' is destroyed by intense heat. In general, use it only for roasting, finishing soups and in suitable dressings.

Alcohol
'If you wouldn't drink it, don't cook with it' is a culinary cliché, but no less true for that. Treat alcohol as you would any other ingredient, and use the best quality you can find. Cooking with alcohol often involves reducing it, which intensifies whatever flavours are already present. Bad booze will become acrid and ruin a dish.

Seasoning and herbs
I use plain table salt rather than sea salt to season during cooking, as the smaller grains disperse more evenly. For finishing dishes, on the other hand, I use sea salt, particularly fleur de sel, smoked salt and other flavoured salts, as much for their texture as their flavour.

Herbs start deteriorating as soon as they're cut, and lose some of their flavour. Some of pepper's aromatics evaporate quickly after grinding. So, don't chop herbs or grind black pepper until just before you use them.

Over-fishing and sustainability
Keeping track of which fish are currently sustainable can be tricky, but unless we adopt a responsible attitude towards buying and eating them, we're going to run out of fish. This would be bad for our diet and health, and remove a great culinary pleasure. It would also be a disaster for the world's ecosystem and biodiversity. Anyone who loves food and cooking should have an interest in preventing this from happening.

The website www.goodfishguide.co.uk is an excellent guide to which fish are sustainable. Buying from places supplied by fisheries accredited by the independent charity the Marine Stewardship Council (MSC) is also good practice.

Index

403

Acknowledgements

Making things simple is a complicated business. In terms of time, organization and research, this book turned out to be more difficult and labour-intensive than any of my other books – except, of course, *The Fat Duck Cookbook*. So I'm hugely grateful to the following, who helped make *Heston Blumenthal at Home* happen:

My agent, Zoe Waldie, for setting up the project in the first place and enthusiastically supporting it through the long process of cooking and writing. At Bloomsbury, thanks must go to my long-suffering commissioning editor, Richard Atkinson. There were times, I know, when he was tearing his hair out in frustration at the chaotic and halting way in which this book proceeded, yet he never wavered in his faith that it would work out, and patiently coaxed and cajoled the text into shape. He was aided in this by the inspired efforts of Pascal Cariss, who took on the herculean task of putting the tangled mass of information in my head into some kind of order, and of Susan Fleming, whose extensive, clever and authoritative edit improved the book a thousandfold. Thanks should also go to Penny Edwards, Natalie Hunt and Xa Shaw Stewart, for the roles they played in turning my manuscript into a beautifully presented book. And to Rachel Calder of the Sayle Literary Agency and Bronwen Jones for reading and commenting on early drafts of the manuscript. I must also single out the contribution of Camilla Stoddart: her editorial skills and boundless enthusiasm helped make the book what it is.

Huw Morgan at Graphic Thought Facility and Angela Moore, Lesley Dilcock and Bruce Robinson did an amazing job of making the book look visually stunning. Huw in particular was brilliant at taking what was said in design meetings and somehow turning it into exactly what I'd imagined on the page. I really appreciate his dedication and perfectionism.

Co-ordinating the whole project has been a mammoth task, so at the Fat Duck I have to thank Deborah Chalcroft, Melissa Lyons and Claire Gibbs for keeping the juggernaut on the rails. I'd like to thank Val Clarke, Adam Bishop, Simon Wilder, Luke Bordewich and Vicki Bordewich for the sometimes thankless task of recipe testing – your comments have been invaluable. Preparing the recipes took over the lives of many of my staff and research chefs, who responded to the challenge with characteristic energy, imagination and attention to detail. Thanks are due to James Petrie, Stefan Cosser, Susie O'Leary, Mark Ebbels, Ben Godwin, Ed Cooke, Dale Bowie, Joanna Mair, Annie Evans, Kim Ohman, Sam Gordon and, especially, Otto Romer, who has been a linchpin of this project from the start, tirelessly cooking and revising the recipes to make them the best they could possibly be.

For the three magical J's in my life, Jack, Jessie
and Joy; Zanna, for her tireless energy and her light;
my mother, for being there always; and in memory
of the most incredible man I have ever met, my father.

First published in Great Britain 2011

Text copyright © 2011 Cape Press Ltd.
Written in cooperation with Pascal Cariss

Photography © 2011 Angela Moore
Illustration on page 14 © 2011 Annabel Milne

The moral right of the author has been asserted.

Bloomsbury Publishing Plc
50 Bedford Square, London WC1B 3DP
1385 Broadway, New York, NY 10018
Bloomsbury Publishing, London, New Delhi, New York and Sydney

A CIP catalogue record for this book is available
from the British Library.
UK ISBN 978 1 4088 0440 7
US ISBN 978 1 60819 701 9

20 19 18 17 16 15 14 13 12 11

Art direction and design: Graphic Thought Facility
Photography: Angela Moore
Styling: Lesley Dilcock

The publishers would like to thank the following for all their help
in the creation of this book: the staff at Waitrose, Maidenhead;
Staub, member of the Zwilling Group; Kenwood for electrical
appliances; John Lewis; David Mellor, Sloane Square; Sebastian
Bergne at buysebastianbergne.com; Juliette Raine, Westye Group
for the Sub-Zero fridge; Theo Fennell for silverware; Skandium;
Mike and Sasha Davies; Nick Webb; Sophie Smallhorn; Michael
Lisle-Taylor at Studio Grid; Jane Cumberbatch; Ellie Gill, make-up
artist; Jonathan Self, Studio Boardroom; Eleanor Harrison,
Pearson Lloyd; Holly Bruce; Ryan Stamatiades; Matthew Kneebone;
Eibhlín Doran; Bastien Conus; Richard Dawson, Housestyle.

Typeset in Monotype Sabon

Printed and bound in Italy by Graphicom

All papers used by Bloomsbury Publishing are natural, recyclable
products made from wood grown in well-managed forests.
The manufacturing processes conform to the environmental
regulations of the country of origin.

www.bloomsbury.com/hestonblumenthal